Modern Jewish History

Henry L. Feingold, *Series Editor*

John
Street

New York Jews and the Decline of Urban Ethnicity, 1950–1970

Eli Lederhendler

Syracuse University Press

Syracuse, New York 13244–5160

First edition 2001

01 02 03 04 05 06 6 5 4 3 2 1

The paper used in this publication meets the minimum requirements of American National Standard for Information Sciences—Permanence of Paper for Printed Library Materials, ANSI Z39.48–1984.∞™

Frontispiece: The Brooklyn Bridge. Photograph by Klaus Lehnartz, courtesy of Stapp Verlag.

Library of Congress Cataloging-in-Publication Data

Lederhendler, Eli.
New York Jews and the decline of urban ethnicity, 1950–1970 / Eli Lederhendler.
p. cm.—(Modern Jewish history)
Includes bibliographical references (p.) and index.
ISBN 0-8156-0711-3 (alk. paper)
1. Jews—New York (State)—New York—Intellectual life. 2. Jews—Cultural assimilation—New York (State)—New York. 3. Jews—New York (State)—New York—Identity. 4. Jews—New York (State)—New York—Politics and government—20th century. 5. New York (N.Y.)—Ethnic relations. I. Title. II. Series.
F128.9.J5 L43 2001
305.892'40747 21;aa05 12-13—dc00 00-068771

Manufactured in the United States of America

To my mother, Bluma, first native New Yorker in our family,
and to my children, Adina, Aryeh, Sivan, and Yoav,
the Israeli generation, who may yet find here a sort of legacy

Eli Lederhendler teaches Modern Jewish History at the Hebrew University of Jerusalem, where he holds the Stephen S. Wise Chair in American Jewish History and Institutions. He is the author of two previous books, *The Road to Modern Jewish Politics,* winner of the 1990 National Jewish Book Award, and *Jewish Responses to Modernity: New Voices in America and Eastern Europe.* He is also coeditor of the journal *Studies in Contemporary Jewry.*

Contents

Illustrations

Tables

Preface

This book had its genesis in a number of unrelated events, remarks, and impulses that finally convinced me to undertake a topic as dauntingly enormous as an account of New York Jewish life during two momentous decades of the post-World War II era.

In the most immediate sense, the idea for such a book was prompted when Haim Avni, one of my colleagues at the Institute of Contemporary Jewry of The Hebrew University, co-opted me some years ago onto a committee to plan an academic conference on the Six-Day War and its impact on Diaspora Jewish communities. In considering the American Jewish community in this context, I volunteered the opinion that in order to properly understand how and why American Jewry reacted to the Middle East war of 1967, one would have to look at the entire decade's trends and events as they affected Jewish life in the United States. Although such a wide-ranging effort was beyond the scope of a conference paper, it struck me that there was not a single study of that period to which one might refer for a comprehensive background discussion.

From there it was not a very big step to narrowing the focus from American Jewry at large to New York Jewry in particular—not because the two are at all equivalent, but because there was so much material related to New York that, had I set out to write about "American Jewry" at large, I would likely have ended up with a New York-based book masquerading as a survey of the whole American Jewish community. In order to avoid overgeneralizing the New York case, I determined to explicitly limit myself to what could be said about the Jews there in their own right.

"The locus of study is not the object of study," Clifford Geertz pointed out. One studies "*in* villages (tribes, towns, neighborhoods)," but what one seeks is something that can most readily be observed in that particular setting.[1] It became clear to me that a book about New York would allow me to focus on the nexus between Jews and the city: in particular, on the historic and unique encounter between Jews and this particular metropolis, and how the changes in the life of the city had changed the Jews.

There is much here that applies generally to cities, to Jews in cities, and indeed, to other ethnic groups as well. Conceptually it is very difficult to distinguish precisely between one urban experience and another, given the mobility of America's urban population. For all that, it did seem to me that New York Jewish-related issues might be profitably discussed as a "case" with distinguishing characteristics primarily because of the unprecedented size of the Jewish community in New York, relative to other urban Jewries and relative to other New York population groups. And while one cannot simply extrapolate the Jewish situation in large American cities or suburban communities from the New York situation, one can certainly draw relevant insights from the New York situation, given the way that New York's images and realities are constantly projected outward.

My aim, therefore, became to describe the premier urban Jewry in the world as far as possible from within, always recognizing that, given New York Jewry's size and influence in the Jewish world, and given New York's own national functions in the media, finance, politics, and the arts, the subject of New York's Jews could never be discussed in splendid isolation from general American political and social trends. What is implied here is that what happens in New York is never limited or unique to New York, and it would be a mistake to set about writing a book with such a premise in mind; but neither is what happens in New York quite the same as what happens elsewhere.

Rather than argue for or against New York Jewry's uniqueness, therefore, I determined simply to produce a credible portrait of the recent past as it would have appeared from a New York Jewish perspective. The time frame for this study changed from one decade to two when I determined that continuity of narrative demanded it. To cite just one among several considerations, Jewish movement out of New York to the suburbs began in earnest in the late fifties, indicating to me that my story ought to begin in 1950, rather than in 1960.

Another conceptual stimulus came from one of my students, Amos Morris-Reich, whose master's thesis challenged me to consider the paucity of "messianic" themes in the historiography of American Jewry. This apparent silence was suggestive of deliberate neglect, Amos claimed, given the ubiquity of messianic themes in the historiography of premodern and early modern European Jewry, to say nothing of their place in Zionist historiography. Was messianism, as a scholarly paradigm, reserved, then, for Zion-related subjects, and if so, was this not direct evidence of an ideological intrusion into depictions of the Jewish past? That challenge prodded me to elaborate some fresh ideas about utopian impulses (a word I still prefer to "messianic" in the American Jewish context.) In turn, this led me to reconsider the nexus between Jews and great cities in terms of cultural and political aspirations, rather than solely as a social-historical fact of life.

At about the same time, I was involved in co-teaching a course on New York Jewry in history and literature with another colleague and friend, Sidra Ezrahi. Our rewarding interdisciplinary engagement with the topic gave me the opportunity to delve into cultural and literary sources and helped me to further conceptualize the book.

Finally, once I had settled down to researching the topic, I realized that I had got hold of one of the few areas in American Jewish history in which a sizeable body of scholarly literature exists (Jewish religious denominations and the American response to the Holocaust being, perhaps, the only other two such areas that come readily to mind). This is no mean thing, for it is seldom that American Jewish historians can afford the "luxury," so readily available to our peers in other areas of scholarship, of intertextual dialogue. Most works in our field stand alone, resting on their own merits or demerits—the field itself being a relatively new one in the academy. With New York as a topic, however, I had the opportunity to sharpen my own ideas against the most fruitful and incisive findings and perspectives of my predecessors and colleagues. Promoting this sort of dialogue between books is, I believe, one of the most useful tasks that we have as scholars.

It will be apparent to the reader that one work which stands out as a counterfoil to mine is Deborah Dash Moore's *At Home In America: Second Generation New York Jews.*[2] Like her book, which deals with the interwar era, mine selects a twenty-year period in which to follow the trends in New York Jewish life. By choosing the twenty years that follow her period, I am consciously trying to raise issues about long-term continuity, comparing the "sequel" to its earlier stages.

Like Moore, again, I devote my study to one aspect of New York Jewry: the nature and context of Jewish ethnicity. Other aspects certainly abound: One need but compare Moore's book to Beth Wenger's *New York Jews and the Great Depression,* which deals with the same period but discusses extensively subjects that Moore did not broach; or, similarly, one might take Henry Feingold's book on American Jewry between 1920 and 1945 *(A Time for Searching: Entering the Mainstream*) to get an inkling of other possible agendas and methods.[3]

The topics relating to ethnicity that I have chosen do differ, however, from the model provided by Moore. This is due, in part, to her having written chiefly as a social historian, whereas my interests run toward cultural history. Her book hinged, primarily, upon her research on neighborhood-based communities and institutions. My own presentation deals far less with local communities because I have focused, instead, on issues of the city as such.[4]

These different emphases are probably due in part to the small generational gap between us: Moore's work was influenced by trends that were dominant in American historiography and social science from the sixties to the eighties—the stress on social history (as both subject and method), for example, but also the attention then being redirected toward the salience of race and ethnicity in American life, and the centrality imputed to neighborhood communities in both urban studies and urban policy. I, in contrast, have been more influenced by works published in the eighties and nineties in cultural studies generally, and American studies in particular, whose discourse is related to *Zeitgeist,* cultural construction and deconstruction, and the mutual influences and conflicts that abound in modern society.

From all this, however, it should be clear that it is the seriousness and well-founded character of Moore's research that prompt me to reexamine its conclusions in the first place. I offer my own reading of New York Jewry as part of what I trust will be an ongoing collegial exchange.

It is possible, too, that different formative experiences lie behind the different approaches we have taken. Moore comes from Chelsea on Manhattan's west side, not far from the Village. To her, the city was a genuinely exciting social and cultural patchwork, and her book about New York does seem to be informed by that perspective.[5]

I, by contrast, found my childhood surroundings rather prosaic. I grew up in the north-central part of the Bronx, a largely Jewish and Catholic neighborhood that was wedged between parks and elevated subway lines. There were quite a few Irish "bar-and-grills" and Hebrew National butcher shops advertising *"boser kosher"*; Italian barbershops, pizza parlors, and shoe repair shops; the requisite Chinese laundry and Chinese restaurant; two Catholic churches (each with its own parochial school); Jewish doctors, dentists, and teachers. There were also those neutral pillars of neighborhood culture: the public school, the public library, the playgrounds, the local Democratic club (located in somewhat sleazy backstairs quarters—I was paid on election day in 1965 to distribute "Beame for mayor" leaflets but I was put off by the ambience, and most discouragingly, Beame lost); and two long-since defunct movie theaters (at one of which I saw "In The Heat of the Night," with a political message that inspired and thrilled me: "They call me MIS-ter Tibbs."). I attended both public school and a secular Yiddish afternoon school *(folkshul*), and on Rosh Hashanah and Yom Kippur my family went to services at one of the three local Orthodox synagogues (which were the sole choice available). So, on the face of it, I was a product of an exotically ethnic web, suitably socialized to decently liberal ideas, and (pardon the oxymoron) traditionally secular.

Yet, it was not until I read the literature on urban ethnicity that I encountered the argument that neighborhood-based concentrations of ethnic groups were a primary basis for ethnic culture and "unconscious" ethnic consciousness. To me, ethnic Jewish culture and activities were distinct by design and deliberate choice from the everyday life of my public school, my neighborhood, and most of the people in it. As I grew older, I sought such culture and ethnic involvement mainly outside my immediate surroundings: in Manhattan (which had institutions of higher Jewish learning, the best political demonstrations, as well as the first Israeli clubs), and finally in Jerusalem.

That, perhaps, accounts for why I found the neighborhood-ethnicity argument less than compelling, though I felt that it was historically accurate. It was in the gap between the descriptions of Jewish neighborhoods of the past and my own experience that I saw the possibility that things had changed, made me want to look for the reasons why, and prompted me to read Jewish life in New York against the backdrop of the city as a whole.

This is not to imply that this book is merely self-referential. On the contrary: I was too young in the fifties and sixties to be fully aware of the events and issues that I detail in the discussion that follows. Most of what I am about to discuss here lies beyond the bounds of my direct memory, so only very rarely will I interject a comment as a former participant-observer. Rather, this book has given me the opportunity to revisit places and events that have acquired, over time, the feel of long familiarity, but which I approach with the semidetachment (and hopefully the advantages) of professional interest and the distance afforded by both time and place.

While this book is not devoid of controversial opinion or a political point of view, I believe that readers may be frustrated if they try to pigeonhole me politically. I will, undoubtedly, leave both Left and Right upset with me, and I even have some nice things to say about Hannah Arendt. One advantage in living outside the community I am describing is that I need not become identified personally with its internal feuds or step too lightly around its conflicts with other groups.

In this book, among other things, I take issue with widely held views about the nature of Holocaust consciousness in American Jewish culture, partly on the basis of my own experiences. Contrary to popular notions, I do believe that the Holocaust as an event had a significant impact on Jewish culture and concerns as early as the fifties and certainly by the beginning of the sixties. And, once again contrary to general assumptions, I do not share the idea that changes in the tenor of Holocaust consciousness at the end of the sixties are explained by the Six-Day War or the greater willingness of survivors to speak publicly (i.e., in English) about their experiences. Rather than focus on such internal Jewish factors, I believe that the paradigmatic change in this regard—from viewing the Holocaust as a potentially threatening precedent for human society at large, to viewing the Holocaust as proof of Jewish victimization and, therefore, as the moral basis for Jewish relationships with others—is related above all to the politicization of victimhood itself in late-sixties American society.

The reader who is au courant with the latest discussions on this subject will undoubtedly see a parallel here between my treatment of this issue and that of Peter Novick in his recent book, *The Holocaust and American Life*. The kind of intertextual dialogue to which I referred previously would certainly apply to the overlap and the differences of approach between Novick's book and my own, and I can only regret that I had completed work on my text quite some time before I came to read Novick's thought-provoking work.[6]

Similarly, I might add, two other recently published books also dovetail in specific areas with some of my discussion here: Kathryn Hellerstein's bilingual English-Yiddish collection, *Paper Bridges: Selected Poems of Kadya Molodowsky* (a poet whose work I discuss and quote from in chapter 3—although, interestingly, my selections are not included in Hellerstein's book); and Hasia Diner's new book on the postwar cultural construction of collective American Jewish memory, with reference to the New York's famous immigrant quarter, *Lower East Side Memories: A Jewish Place in America*.[7]

The issues that form the core of this book are well reflected in the public record. Indeed, it is the public face of New York Jewish life that interests me most. Accordingly, I have made use as much as possible of the written testimony of witnesses and participants who (unlike myself) really were involved at the time. For the sake of authenticity, most of those quoted here are New York Jews, although, naturally enough, there are occasions when I have turned to outside sources, too.

Circumstances of location and personal matters prevented me from spending the extensive time in the United States that developing a systematic and significant body of interview material would have required, which therefore constitutes a missed opportunity (a lacuna to be filled, it is to be hoped, by another author). Without benefit of formally organized oral data, I have, however, found corroboration for my thesis in a variety of conversations conducted over the past several years with other participant-informants.

It is my pleasure to have the chance to thank those, apart from those very important persons already mentioned, whose assistance over the past few years has been indispensable.

An initial travel grant from the Littauer Foundation, administered through the YIVO Institute for Jewish Research in New York, helped me to get started. A two-year research grant from the Israel Academy of Sciences and Humanities allowed me to gather much of my research material and paid for a part-time assistant. I would like to thank Vardit Ginzburg Sadeh, now pursuing her own doctorate in American history, for squinting for too many days at *New York Times* microfilms on my behalf. Amos Morris-Reich, whose role in helping me to clarify some of my ideas has already been noted, also lent me his assistance in double-checking footnotes and in helping to prepare the index.

My good friend Steven Zipperstein was the first reader of my draft chapters. As always, his comments were judicious, enlightening, and helpful.

Henry Feingold, who edits the series at Syracuse University Press in which I have the honor to participate, was my teacher in graduate school back in the mid-seventies. At a critical point, Henry encouraged me to continue my project, provided moral support, sent timely reminders, and above all showed patience and faith when I began to run afoul of contract deadlines. All those at Syracuse University Press who had a hand in the editing and production of the book have my thanks and appreciation for their professionalism and helpfulness.

This book is dedicated to two generations of my family, my mother and my children, for the reasons stated. But Lisa, my wife, who engaged much of my attention during these past several years, merits special mention. But for her, as she herself has put it, this book might well have been finished some time ago. As she knows very well, however, to have finished the book earlier would have been poor compensation indeed for all I have been lucky enough to discover with her.

New York
Jews
and the Decline of Urban Ethnicity, 1950–1970

1

Jews and the Great Urban Utopia

The Jews in New York are New Yorkish through and through. . . . Someone will someday write the history of Jewish New York [and will] certainly make note of the fact that there is a *New York-type Jewishness, a Jewish lifestyle that is New Yorkish.*

—Shmuel Margoshes,
"Nyu-yorkish," 1970
(translated from the Yiddish)

All your children love you, New York, but the Jews among them love you even more. Seventy national groups, races, and tongues are devoted to you heart and soul—for them, even your ordinary days are like the "great Sabbath" that comes once a year, as if they'd never known the taste of home until they found their way into your lap—and the Jews, all the more. For the love of the gentiles is modest in comparison, while the love of the Jews is out in the open, worn on their sleeves.

—Shimon Halkin,
'Ad mashber, 1945 (translated from the Hebrew)

In 1800, few if any great urban centers or capital cities in either Europe or America were associated with more than a token Jewish community. Cities with populations of some ten to fifteen thousand contained, at most, several hundred Jewish families.

The mass of Jews lived more typically in innumerable provincial hometowns. In terms of both geography and social function, they inhabited the space between the local grain, livestock, and forest-products economy and the wider regional or inter-regional markets. Jews were generally involved in agricultural processing (milling, brewing, distilling, and refining), or in metalwork, handicrafts, transport, trade, service occupations, management, and credit. Thus, their lives were less rustic than those of most of their non-Jewish counterparts, who were to an overwhelming extent tillers of the soil. Nonetheless, the towns they lived in were still characterized by modesty of scale and by insularity of cultural perspective: urban perhaps by comparison with the surrounding populace, but scarcely "citified."

In some major cities, such as Berlin, Vienna, and Warsaw, the number of Jewish residents was still legally restricted in the second half of the eighteenth century, making it difficult for them to establish large-scale, permanent communities there. Historically, of course, there had been major urban Jewries. In antiquity Alexandria and Rome, and in more recent memory, Constantinople, Amsterdam, and Prague, were home to comparatively large Jewries that set the tone for Jewish life in their respective countries. In the Moslem world, which contained a shrinking proportion of world Jewry after the seventeenth century, Jews were urban to a great extent. Within the memory of most Jews alive in the early 1800s, however, daily life was quite provincial.

All this would change dramatically over the course of the next century, when Jews in virtually all countries became not only *an* urban people, but arguably *the quintessential* urban people. In trying to account for this, one is inclined to look first at urbanization as a more general social phenomenon. Much of the story of Jewish urbanization can indeed be explained as follows: On the basis of the fact that the growth of cities at the expense of the countryside has been a universal and characteristic feature of modernity, it is wholly appropriate to suggest that Jews simply shared in what was a general trek to the city. Just as an agriculture-based economy and premodern transportation systems had offered myriad opportunities for townfolk to live and work in smaller local and district centers, so now did a developing industrial and trade economy and modern rail, shipping, and road transportation multiply opportunities in larger cities. Jews followed the crowd as cities took on primal importance, paralleling a decline of the old economic order.

But this only accounts for part of the story. Compared with other populations, Jews urbanized at an accelerated rate. Even in highly developed countries where the general rate of urbanization was quite rapid, Jews outdid their neighbors in this regard. Jews became, over time, almost exclusively urban, whereas only a proportion of their non-Jewish fellow citizens did so. In many cases, of course, Jews were not merely moving to the city, but emigrating to a new country, where they remained in the major port cities and other urban centers. Even among immigrants, however, they stood out. Some immigrants were former peasants seeking a new existence as independent farmers in their new land, while others went to work in mining and mill towns; but immigrant Jews included only a very small percentage of aspiring agriculturalists and virtually no miners. Relatively few Jews moved into the countryside (though there were some who did), and once again in contrast to immigrants from other ethnic groups, very few indeed ever returned to the old country.[1]

Jews did not just urbanize: they concentrated in the biggest metropolitan centers. In a comparatively short time, they came to represent the most thoroughly citified ethnic and religious element in virtually every society, leading one observer to call them "perfect urbanites." They fit into the city so well, he claimed, because of three significant attributes: First, they had never tended to idealize the pastoral village as essentially more secure, natural, or innately positive, so they did not hanker after it. Second, the trade, manufacturing, and service occupations they engaged in readily lent themselves to large-scale urbanization. And finally, they tended to "espouse the liberating possibilities of the city" rather than attempt to recreate an enclosed and protected "urban village" in the midst of the metropolis.[2]

London and Paris, which housed small Jewish communities in the eighteenth century, were preeminent in Anglo-Jewish and French-Jewish life, respectively, by the mid-nineteenth century.[3] Berlin, too, already loomed large in the constellation of major urban Jewries—though in absolute numbers these communities did not yet rival the vast Jewish hinterland of central and eastern Europe. By the turn of the century, Vienna, Budapest, and Warsaw became fabled Jewish metropolises, drawing ever greater numbers of inhabitants from the provinces, while London, Paris, and Berlin became important destinations for Jews migrating across the continent. By the First World War, there was a clear pattern of concentrated Jewish residence in the world's largest cities, a process continually fed by the huge outpouring from eastern Europe, which resumed after 1918.

Even in Russia, Poland, and the Ukraine, the trend toward the transplantation of large Jewish populations to the major cities had set in during the late nineteenth century (Odessa, Lodz, Warsaw), only to intensify after 1917 (expecially in Moscow, Kiev, and Petrograd/Leningrad—today St. Petersburg).

In this light, New York City may be considered the modern example par excellence of Jewish metropolitanization. By the eve of the First World War, when Warsaw, the world's second largest Jewish community, numbered some 300,000 Jewish inhabitants, New York City, in first place, had almost one and a half million.

Thus, in the early twentieth century the district or provincial town was displaced as the chief venue of Jewish life. Observers in the late nineteenth century took for granted the demise of small town Jewish life, disagreeing only on the consequences: Some lamented the passing of the old way of life, while others lampooned the pathologies of its disintegration. Some worked to enshrine its fading memory in poetry, prose, song, drama, and painting, while others were intent on sweeping the past as quickly as possible into the maelstrom of revolution. Some were formulating a defensively fervent religious conservatism fully capable of entrenching itself in the big city, while others projected onto an already abstract image of the old home a neoromantic, secular remystification.[4] Few national cultures experienced so rapid and so complete a rupture in terms of environmental change.

The urban metropolis was not merely a ubiquitous by-product of modernity that happened to drag Jews along with others into its orbit. It was, rather, a manifestly compelling magnet for a widely scattered Jewish population. It was, culturally and politically, the new Jewish home.

I suggest that the city (taken here, for the sake of argument, as a generic type) appeared to offer Jews a solution to their particular social dilemma and that this helps to explain the disproportion between Jewish and non-Jewish urbanization patterns. In the premodern hinterlands where they had lived for so long, Jews were marginalized culturally, socially, and economically. As nineteenth-century nationalist and class-grievance politics developed, Jews were targeted, in addition, for political marginalization. The effects of this process were felt by Jews most threateningly in the countries of central and eastern Europe, including the vast Russian empire—countries where the introduction of democratic government and egalitarian citizenship progressed only by fits and starts, if at all.

In contrast with small-town or provincial life, however, the truly great cities appeared to reinvent all previously known social arrangements, most notably in the West, which offered Jews civic equality. Implicit in the effort to find a new home under new terms of existence was a sweeping reformation of the Jews' social status.

The city was sustained by the harnessed agricultural surplus of the countryside, so that within the city all were food consumers, none were food producers. Here, therefore, Jews might shed one of the long-recognized marks of their social separateness. Again, whereas the small town or rural center had a designated place and a special day of the week set aside for market, offering a strictly limited social encounter that perpetuated and reinforced status differences, in the city every day was market day and every street, a market. The city's population defied fixed status arrangements because it was forever transient, forever undefined, and therefore almost anonymous: No one could expect to encounter and assign a place to each and every fellow citizen, the way that one might, in the normal course of things, encounter every townsman or townswoman at the village well, the river, the tavern, the market square, or the house of worship. Everything that small-town life offered was personalized and individual; their big-city counterparts, starting with the very streets and houses, were always more nondescript, even interchangeable.

In terms of human interaction, the city seemed designed to offer neutral ground. Herein lay its potential as a solution to "the Jewish question," for it offered new terms of social integration and participation. "My heart pounded with joy when I saw New York in the distance," wrote a Jewish immigrant, describing his idealistic hopes to the editor of the New York Yiddish socialist daily, the *Forverts*. "It was like coming out of the darkness when I left my town. I came to the Big City where I sensed the freedom and where I became a proletarian." Said another Jewish observer, "New York was the first city to announce it had room for everyone and the first city to prove the truth of its own announcement."[5]

Little wonder, then, that the imprint of this urban universal vision became what one student of the subject has called the "informing myth" of modern Jewish writing: "The marginal person emerges from the shtetl and seeks a place in the freer, more complex, and cosmopolitan life of the city . . . in which protagonist and [his/her] people might participate in the general enterprise of western culture."[6]

The metropolitan city—an engine of progress that depended on the synergy of all its human resources—would provide level ground to equalize relations between Jews and non-Jews.[7] Related, but more broadly defined, was the notion that the equalization and democratization of human relations in general was a realizable goal in an urban society. Even without the aid of Marxian determinism on this score, the sheer necessity of cooperative activity in a mass community appeared, like a historical compass, to point in the direction of a common humanist solution.

This was the essence of the new democracy that Jews came to champion in urban America, as Moses Rischin argued in his classic study of New York Jewry in the Progressive Era, *The Promised City.* Combining Jewish communal ideals and industrial-age doctrines of social responsibility, Jewish writers, labor leaders, educators, social reformers, and journalists helped to transform the older, more individualistic values of Jeffersonian bourgeois-agrarian democracy while combating Tammany-style machine politics.

Promoting their view of the city not merely as a great industrial and commercial hub powered by a politics of self-interest, but as the cradle of a new social order, was, following Rischin's argument, the Jews' major contribution to American culture, certainly to American political culture. This view was shared by the Chicago sociologist W. I. Thomas, who had observed just after World War I:

"Our interest in the organization of other immigrant communities is limited to the possible discovery of devices which may assist these groups until they are able to enjoy the benefits of American institutions. In the case of the Jewish group, we find spontaneous, intelligent, and highly organized experiments in democratic control which may assume the character of permanent contributions to the organization of the American state."[8]

It was utopian to attempt a solution to the "Jewish question," to imagine a thoroughly restructured existence, one that was beyond the ken of any who set forth on this journey. It may have been similarly utopian to stretch the foundations of American democracy to envision a mass community that could be at once heterogeneous, egalitarian, and self-regulating. Moreover, there was a utopian element in the very notion that a better world was within the grasp of human endeavor.

Articulating some of these elements in poetic form, Shimon Ginsburg, a newly arrived immigrant in early twentieth-century New York, wrote a Hebrew ode to his new city. At first both awestruck by the city's sheer scale and power as well as intimidated by the terrible inhumanity of this industrial Molokh-monster, the poet comes to sense in the fused animation of so much concentrated human endeavor an irresistible, transcendent force:

> The night train carries me across
> Williamsburg Bridge . . .
> Strands of small flickering lights,
> beckon and call to one another.
> In that instant, my soul, too,
> plunges into the night, seeking its
> sisters, the flames, kindled like itself, to
> light the night world . . .
> And all that night long a new song welled up
> within me.
> The burden of New York passed and became
> a hymn of faith.
> And on my return to the city in the
> morning, . . .
> I turn and behold yet another Og-giant
> bridge, stretched out frozen on its harpstring
> limbs . . .
> like the strings of God's own lyre,
> waiting in latent, confident expectancy,
> for that Unseen One to come and play
> the great song of the future.[9]

The harps the Jews once hung up in lamentation by the rivers of Babylon, destined not to be played again in bondage and exile, are reincarnated here in the form of the Brooklyn Bridge; but rather than a symbol of exile, loss of hope, and the cessation of creative human activity, the harpstrings by the waters of this great city are taut with expectancy, power, and divine benediction.[10]

However, the Jewish encounter with urban society was never as unidimensional as such anthems of progress and enlightenment might suggest. The flip side of the city's anonymity was the threat of social atomization, the reduction in significance of the individual human being, the slide from existential meaning to the merely statistical. At its best, metropolitan life offers a piquant ambiguity, drawing upon both individual personality and impersonal environment, upon the individual's sense of past and future as well as the city's insistent, repetitive present.

In this vein, we can quote from the work of another immigrant poet, Aaron Leyeles (pen name of Aaron Glanz-Leyeles), "By the Rivers of New York," taken from his collection, *Amerike un ikh (America and I,* 1963). Using the same Scripture-based motif almost forty years after Ginsburg's poem, the sense of Leyeles's poem is nevertheless entirely different—but not only because in the one we had a newcomer's inspired vision of the future with its untapped and unlimited potential, while here we have the weariness, indeed the melancholy, of an old poet who contrasts his aspirations of long ago and their scant fulfillment. More than that, there is in the later poem a gray tonality, a wry diffidence that comes from a writer long inured to urban realities.

"Recalling all and nothing at all," the sense of time here is not linked with movement and progress. In place of bridges and trains and their urgency, we have here a willow tree, motionless—and perhaps as out of place in the concrete landscape as the poet himself:

By the rivers of New York I sit me down,
recalling all and nothing at all,
and I weep not.
Near me a willow, frozen where it stands.
I reach toward the harp that is not there
and I am ashamed.
The willow speaks and I comprehend it:
"Haven't you strung enough songs
from the towers hereabout,
or crammed enough of them
between the cobblestones?
Now be still and just observe."
Now the branches seem to be faces,
gathering in silence
to inscribe each one a year,
each one a label: "dream—reality, dream—reality."
The faces scrutinize me,
take my measure with regret.
Grieve not, I encourage myself.
Indeed (I go on), the restlessness of my
soul now
quite matches the fullness and brightness of my
yearnings then. . . .
I weep not.[11]

But this self-criticism, this ironic, grudging acknowledgment of dreams tempered by truths, this reluctant self-affirmation, hardly begins to express the range of ambivalences that mass urban society aroused. It was not just that the individual and his or her dreams might be lost, superfluous amid the numberless towers and cobblestones. It was also that the vision of mass society as a vast constructive synergy, an open-ended culture of common achievement, was never as fully realized in reality as it was imagined. The social dynamics of big cities tended to heighten, rather than to erase, the Jews' conspicuousness. The big city, for all its modernity, revived the use of the term "ghetto." City elites were often well entrenched and actively resisted the efforts of newcomers to lower social barriers. Minorities had to fashion their own separate spheres if they were to make any headway at all, creating a new particularism as they progressed. Rather than being distributed randomly throughout the city and throughout the urban economy, they were concentrated in specific territory, both physical and socioeconomic.

In his 1920s study of Chicago's Jewish quarter, *The Ghetto,* Louis Wirth had argued that the phenomenon of ethnic segregation was temporary, but he also asserted that the self-insulation that he perceived in ghetto life was a misguided retreat in the face of uncomfortable but necessary social pressures. Successful assimilation to modern, urban social and economic forms would inevitably demonstrate that the "ghetto" was an anachronism.[12] Rischin's *Promised City* was a vigorous reply to Wirth, contending that the ghetto was no mere anomaly or cultural throwback, but that it allowed for the concentration and release of tremendous social and cultural energy that fed, not on the past, but on the metropolitan present: that it was, in fact, the crucible of a new urban democracy that reached out to embrace the city.

Beyond the clear ideological distinction between Wirth and Rischin (the former championing assimilation, the latter, pluralism), it bears asking whether Wirth's Chicago and Rischin's New York were quite comparable. The size and influence of New York and of its Jewish community made them sui generis. As Deborah Dash Moore has noted, only in New York could Jews believe that their city "*was* America"[13]—or, to spell out the point, only in New York could Jews so roundly ignore "Main Street, U.S.A." without at the same time reverting to an inner world of relevance only to themselves. In Chicago, Cleveland, or Kansas City, Jews were bound to be aware of "America" as a more compelling geographic and cultural reality, just as they were bound to be aware of New York as something other, the alternative home for Jews *in* America.[14]

H. Leyvik (pen name of Leyvik Halpern, the socialist Yiddish poet and essayist), who came to New York in 1913, gave voice in one of his early poems to this palpable sense of territoriality. The Jewish immigrant districts of New

York, as crowded as Calcutta and containing more Jews than any other community in the world, seemed to him to rise up toward:

> Fantastic gates, soaring columns,
> rising from all the dilapidated stands
> upward, to the far and empty New York sky.
> Gates—on all their cornices
> glowing, sparkling signs, inscribed:
> Here lives the Jewish People.[15]

This, too, is a kind of Jewish utopia: a vision of ingathering that calls less upon a myth of cosmopolitan participation than upon particularist Jewish yearnings for home, for collective security, for recognition and pride. Leyvik was describing not just a Jewish city *('ir vaeim biyisrael)*, but a world Jewish capital!

Jews had, in the past, commonly projected such longings upon a mythic landscape of the heart, which they called *Eretz Yisrael* (the Land of Israel)—which was, simultaneously, a real landscape, and therefore susceptible to being both metaphysical and concrete, beyond reach as well as within reach. In keeping with this distinction, Jewish tradition retained the dual designation, "earthly Jerusalem" and "heavenly Jerusalem" *(yerushalayim shel matah, yerushalayim shel ma'alah)*. When reformulated with reference to a great metropolis like New York, the desire for an ideal community may have been retained ("Here lives the Jewish People"), but the old dualism has been blurred: In New York, heaven and earth are always touching, owing to the vertical impulse that guides the eye (in Leyvik's gaze upward to the heavens, Leyeles's towers and cobbled pavement, or in Ginsburg's top-to-bottom perspective of heaven-bridge-city).[16]

In keeping with this blurring, there could also be no clear demarcation between the two utopian ideals (the cosmopolitan and the tribal). As Rischin had suggested, those aspects of life in New York that offered support for Jewish particularist dynamics and activities—neighborhood community, work, politics, an ethnic press—had also tended to promote an expansive, citywide perspective. The burden of the chapters that follow will be to explore the gaps that began to grow between the two utopias in the post-World War II period, to the detriment of both.

The History of New York Jewry

"Is the history of New York City Jewry local history?" asked historian Lloyd Gartner. The very question arises because—given the immense scale of the community—New York is "different in kind" from every other American Jewish community. It has been, as Gartner aptly put it, the "capital of American Jewry since the 1890s and of the Diaspora since 1945." Yet, as he correctly noted, "the city as a whole has had few Jewish historians."[17]

There is in fact no single work of scholarship that relates the entire history of the Jews of New York City, although separate studies abound on specific topics concerning the Jews, or including the Jews. The most important general studies, to date, cover successive periods in the growth of the community, from 1654 to the Second World War: Hyman B. Grinstein's *The Rise of the Jewish Community of New York, 1654–1860*; Moses Rischin's *The Promised City*; Irving Howe's *World of Our Fathers*; Beth Wenger's *New York Jews and the Great Depression*; and Deborah Dash Moore's *At Home in America*.[18] The period beginning in the 1950s has not yet been studied at length, save for the ethnography of small subgroups (such as the Hasidic communities of Brooklyn).

The fact that the important general histories are devoted mainly to the century from the 1840s to the 1940s, during which a population of several hundred reached an eventual apogee of some 2.25 million, more or less assures the reader of an optimistic saga. Their story, in other words, is one of forward progress, of energetic adjustment and effective expansion, of solidifying roots and multiplication of branches—an American success story. Their very titles are laden with positive verbal cues ("rise" and "promise") and cozy references ("home" and "father").

To recall that these earlier works have dealt with the more constructive and expansive periods in the history of New York Jewry is not to disparage them as either simplistic or naïvely optimistic. Howe's "world," as he knew very well, was one that belonged entirely to the past: to mothers and fathers but not to sons or granddaughters. It was written partly in response to the New Left's oedipal betrayal, in the 1960s and 1970s, of the Old Left, and it incorporates a passionate, if wistful, defense of the latter. Moore, for her part, grappled with some of the more difficult issues of ethnic acculturation. One of the superb, more specialized studies of our subject, Arthur A. Goren's *New York Jews and the Quest for Community,* chronicled the *failure* of an ambitious attempt, between 1908 and 1922, to forge a citywide Jewish communal authority.[19] Grinstein's work on the "rise" of New York Jewry up to 1860 was informed by a certain cultural pessimism: "The period ending in 1860," he wrote, "left the 40,000 Jews of New York City with dubious moorings to the Jewish community and its synagogues and institutional affiliates. . . . [T]he leadership seemed unqualified to resolve the dilemma of assimilation. . . . For the moment, the positive forces seem to have been weaker than the negative."[20]

Nevertheless, Grinstein's major point was to show that the Jewish community on the eve of the Civil War already contained the seeds of its considerable expansion after the 1870s. "This study . . . is still only a description of the foundations on which a later generation built a mighty community," he concludes.[21] Similarly, Howe may have been engaged in composing an elegy to a lost world, but he never cast into doubt the basic integrity of that world, which is portrayed as a utopia of the past. Moore, for her part, used the language of acculturation (as opposed to assimilation) to argue that second-generation New York Jews made their neighborhoods into a "home," possessed of a certain intimate verve and ethnic vitality amidst the urban world: "Middle-class Jewish ethnicity extended the ideal of a pluralist society as it rewove the web of urban community." She does not suggest, however, that embedded in this second-generation experience were fundamentally unstable elements that would prove much less viable for the next, the third generation.[22]

Thus, it is really only in Beth Wenger's recent study of New York Jews in the thirties that we find a different nuance. Wenger strives to explain how the Jews of New York, though statistically among the more fortunate of the city's residents, still experienced the Great Depression as a period of special anxiety. Though they quickly recovered their upward socioeconomic momentum after the Second World War, in an atmosphere far less marked by antisemitic discrimination, she argues that the patterns of postwar growth were rooted in lessons learned under duress.[23]

For the most part, then, the major histories of New York Jewry, on balance, preserve a record of achievement, despite obstacles—and rightly so. In a city where Jews came to make up between a quarter and a third of the total population, taking considerable part in its economic, political, and cultural life while maintaining an enviable infrastructure of ethnic, philanthropic, and religious institutions, it is difficult to evaluate the historical record without using superlatives. It is not my intention to revise this established historical picture altogether, but merely to add a restraining note. In this I second Wenger's point of view. By addressing the topic of New York Jewry at the height of the postwar urban crisis, I will be describing a downward curve in the community's historical trajectory, one that may have more lasting impact even than the Great Depression. This downturn is manifested first of all in simple numerical terms. New York Jewry has declined since 1960 by 50 per cent: it stood as of 1991 at just over one million, which included over a hundred thousand recently arrived immigrants from Israel and the former Soviet Union. Even were we to take the New York metropolitan area as a whole, we find a decline from 2.6 million to 2.1 million in the fifty years between 1936 and 1986. These trends were not anticipated by the experts. A demographic study commissioned by the New York Federation of Jewish Philanthropies in

1958 had predicted that the Jewish population of New York City would remain stable at just over 2.1 million, or rise slightly, over the next sixteen years. The study also predicted that the number of Jews in the larger metropolitan area (the five boroughs plus Nassau, Suffolk, and Westchester counties) would reach 2.7 million by 1975.[24]

The fact that those who examined the situation most closely did not anticipate the significant decline of the city's Jewish population is an indication of late-1950s perceptions of urban stability. A new accounting of the life of New York Jewry in the period since the 1950s must, therefore, deal with the themes of instability and decline that became more characteristic of the community as time went on. I regard the period since the 1950s as a time of testing for the ethnic and civic models that Jews in New York had evolved since the early twentieth century.

I will argue that numerical decline is but one among several interrelated problems, all of which may be summed up as a new, more pessimistic Jewish response to city life—a response that is more attuned to *limits* than to promise. In no small measure, disillusionment with the big city is a cultural phenomenon that Jews have shared with the rest of their neighbors. Daniel Boorstin, writing at the beginning of the 1970s, formulated the malaise this way: "As Americans felt more entangled with their cities, more obsessed by city problems, as they sought to cure the city's ills or to flee from them, they were bewildered over what (besides crime and pollution) they had lost, and they wondered where urban community could be rediscovered."[25]

For New York Jews, however, some of whom had harbored a clearer sense of what urban life was supposed to offer, the losses may have been more specific. Certainly their responses contained elements that were specific to them. This book is intended to explore those responses.

The Postwar Jewish Community in Its Heyday

In the mid-1950s Max Lerner, the respected columnist, summing up some of the social theory then current, stated that it was unlikely that suburban development outside America's large cities augured a major trend toward permanent and widening dispersal of the population. Rather, such growth would eventually lead to a larger form of urban life: an "industrial-residential complex" or "cluster city." So sure was he that America's very cultural fabric—its "civilization," as he put it—depended on its major cities, that he doubted even that, in the event of a nuclear war, dispersal of the population in outlying communities could save the nation: "The city grew out of the expansive energies of America and . . . if the city does not survive a suicidal war the civilization itself may perish. The destinies of the two are intertwined, and the best way to save both is by the kind of affirmation from which the cities originally drew their strength."[26]

Lerner's defense of the city as a way of life indelibly imprinted into the American psyche—for better, and not for worse—stands in stark contrast to Boorstin's assessment of urban malaise, that came some fifteen years later. Lerner's understanding of the matter was that it was not city folk who ran the risk of bewilderment at what the loss of their homes might mean, but all those other American souls, not counted among the urbanites, who would be lost even if their lives were spared.

We needn't quite go to this extreme to define the urban ideology of postwar New York Jewry. As we shall see presently, Jews were certainly part of the move to the suburbs. But we do need to take stock of how New York Jewry emerged from the Depression and the Second World War into a metropolitan existence that more nearly matched its aspirations than ever before. What was Jewish New York in the postwar period, and why was the city so indispensable a resource for this community?

The answer, in essence, lies in the way that New York afforded Jews the chance to fulfill both of the urban utopias alluded to earlier: the one being the quest for a cosmopolitan paradise, providing unhindered participation in the life of a world-city; the other being the effort to build a Jewish cultural center that might sustain the entire Jewish people. New York, more than than any other city in the world at that time, served as the Jewish Camelot, the setting for both of these ideals. Some combination of the cosmopolitan and the parochial existed in every Jewish community, but only in New York could both elements come *simultaneously* to such complete fruition. To do complete justice to what this represented in historical terms, we would have to go back and cover ground already intensively and richly described by others. For our purposes here, however, a short recapitulation should suffice.

God's Own Lyre: Jews and the Cosmopolitan City

Jewish cosmopolitanism in New York rested on several interrelated factors: the impact of numbers, the politics and economics of organized labor, and the rise of a Jewish "culture caste" that stood apart from the Jewish public at large but that articulated some of the latent ideas and aspirations embedded in the Jews' adjustment to city life.

The massive volume of Jewish settlement in New York was a phenomenon unique to that city and unique in Jewish history. The share of the total New York population represented by Jewish residents may have been (at its high point) just under one-third, but Jews nevertheless constituted the city's largest single "ethnic-religious element" from 1920 to 1960. They were most heavily in evidence in sections of Manhattan, the Bronx, and Brooklyn (and since the 1950s, in Queens); they were also a presence throughout the city, if we take into account not just the neighborhoods where they lived but also certain workday centers of commerce and manufacturing. In addition, this "presence" was tangibly felt in political clubs, universities, the public school system, the judiciary, the arts, and the media, entertainment, and publishing world.[27]

All this had further, intangible implications, such as the absorption of Yiddish words in New York slang, which tended to magnify the purely physical statistical realities.[28] Or to take another example: The ubiquitous presence of Jews (in certain parts of city life in particular) made it possible for Dan Wakefield, a young journalist in 1955, fresh out of Columbia University, to assume that his new female acquaintance, employed in the publishing field, was Jewish—"based on the fact that she had dark hair and was highly intelligent."[29] Despite the fact that the assumption proved to be wholly erroneous, it was not an unreasonable assumption for Wakefield to have made in New York, though it would not have occurred to him so readily in his native Indianapolis.

Numbers alone assured that Jews would have a major stake in city economic, political, and cultural affairs. As often occurs in such discussions, the question might be raised as to whether they were "present" in these various milieux as *Jews* or simply as residents, employers, employees, PTA members, students, art critics, theatergoers, and so forth. Although this may make for an interesting and delightfully insoluble debate, it is more or less beside the point here: For what, if not the unlimited opportunity to function in any given urban capacity, was the gift that the children of the immigrants sought from the cosmopolitan city?

The point, rather, is that their massive numbers—and hence their wide distribution—was one factor that allowed Jews to embrace a vision of the city as a whole, without at the same time losing a sense of themselves as a defined group. A perfect example is the closure of New York City public schools on the Jewish fall holidays—Rosh Hashanah and Yom Kippur—beginning in 1960. At that time Jewish pupils constituted 33 percent of the school enrollment, Jewish teachers accounted for 45 percent of the total, and Jews were a great majority among the school principals. Inevitably, though they were "present" in non-Jewish capacities, this ostensibly nonethnic civic presence and group recognition went hand in hand.[30]

Second in this list of factors that facilitated the emergence of a Jewish cosmopolitan vision of the city was the emergence in New York of a powerful group of labor unions dependent on Jewish membership (in the earlier decades of the twentieth century) and Jewish leadership and political support (which continued on into the post-Depression era). The advent of these unions, most famously in the garment trades, was certainly a direct consequence of our first factor—namely, the mass Jewish immigration, consisting mainly of the working-class poor; but the long-term influence of Jewish labor activism was above all qualitative, almost independent of the number of Jews personally involved.

This influence was felt in the prevalence among Jews of a particular kind of social vision. Jewish labor and its allied leftist political groups, their press organs, and their educational institutions historically supported cooperation with other ethnic working-class groups, believed in racial equality, mobilized its membership for progressive American political parties (in various periods the Socialist Party, the Labor Party, the Liberal Party, and the Democratic Party), and in general fought for a liberal social agenda and "good government" candidates. This posture persisted long past the time when Jews were a numerically prominent segment of organized labor. (In chapters 5 and 6 we will discuss the manner in which this civic and political posture began to come undone.)

By aiming to submerge ethnic origins within a class-oriented—and subsequently, civic or liberal-reform-oriented praxis—the Jewish labor movement embodied, for many Jews, the actual possibility of cosmopolitan fulfillment. Yet, retention of overt Jewish *affect* within a nonethnic sphere (labor politics) inevitably fed dissatisfaction on both counts, as the unions themselves became dominated by a non-Jewish rank-and-file, on the one hand, and on the other hand, as Jewish leftists found fewer reasons to anchor their politics in ethnic sympathies.

Pursuing the implications of Jewish unionism one step further, we can also say that the struggles won by organized labor on behalf of its membership provided the crucial economic boost that lifted many Jewish wage earners into the lower middle class, cushioned for many the blows of the Depression, and in turn enabled younger family members and children to pursue higher and professional educations. Economic buoyancy of this sort certainly played a role in enhancing Jews' ability to function as cultural consumers, patrons of the arts, and creative members of New York's intellectual community.

Thus we come to consider the widely touted cultural elite that has become known collectively as the "New York Jewish intellectuals," and the manner in which it tried to resolve the tensions between Americanization and ethnic consciousness. Here we are dealing, in the first place, with the distance that second-generation writer-intellectuals and artists were eager to put between themselves and their immigrant parents, perceiving this as a move up and out from the ghetto. This impulse propelled many in this group toward a modern, urban culture in the interwar period.[31]

The trend then continued beyond the forties into the postwar period;

only now, second-generation writers and critics found themselves as estranged from their middle-class, second-generation Jewish contemporaries as they were culturally removed from their European parents—perhaps even more so. The urban sophistication projected by the Manhattan-based Jewish culture elite drew substantially on this double alienation. Like the prophets of a jealous god, they abhorred cheap perversions of the true faith. Standing at the cutting edge of American political and aesthetic discourse, they saw much of what was stereotypically Jewish as woefully lacking in breadth or universal reach. Essentially, the critics were holding middle-class urban Jewry accountable for selling its birthright for a mess of pottage.

Consider, for example, the following acerbic description, a verbal skewering of the middle-class, second-generation Jewish lifestyle as observed along the Bronx boulevard that, at the time, symbolized comfortable affluence. It should be juxtaposed, perhaps, to Moore's far more ennobling characterization, quoted earlier ("Middle-class Jewish ethnicity extended the ideal of a pluralist society as it rewove the web of urban community"). Note the conscious pairing of southern American provincialism and the bourgeois Jewish home ground—two of the most prominent "regional" cultures in mid-century American letters:

> At the threshold of the Bronx . . . there immediately emerges a Jewish community as dense, traditional, and possessive as William Faulkner's Yoknapatawpha County, and through it flows a great middle-class river, the Grand Concourse. . . . The assumption has taken root in the Jewish West Bronx that all satisfactions of palate, of vanity, and of intellect are attainable. . . . To confirm their faith in themselves, and in America's promises, they become conspicuous consumers of silver foxes, simultaneously of learning, gift-shop monstrosities, liberal causes, and gargantuan pastries. A generous, expansive life! . . . In the neighborhoods where Jewry has for many years been able to take its existence for granted, and to live an undefensive middle-class life, I think it is the older, European generation that has better exploited its freedom. We have seen in this generation a blurring of fanaticism, an adaptability that is able to stand even the breaking away of its children. The latter, rigidly associating their [parental] homes with conservatism, parochialism, and repression, have been provincialized by their own revolt.[32]

The intellectuals' perception of the city's potential for creative excellence was not merely a figment of the imagination. It is generally recognized that New York from the 1940s to the mid-1960s went through a period of cultural primacy: a time of "intellectual ferment and artistic creation," as one observer has put it, "unsurpassed in the history of the modern city."[33] Nor were the New York Jewish intellectuals alone in their estrangement from their own family backyard. Their non-Jewish counterparts, drawn to New York from the Midwest and South, also tended to view the city as an ideal cultural environment, totally at variance with what they had left behind. "I came to the city and it changed my life. I was exalted by it, exulted in it." That is how Willie Morris begins his memoir, *New York Days*. "Is it surprising that in time I grew to deem myself more a New Yorker than a Mississippian? New York was my patron city, crux and apogee of our national experience, matrix and pinnacle for me then of all the human artifacts." Dan Wakefield, comparing his generation to that of the twenties, wrote that "exile was the place far enough from the censure of home and middle-class convention to feel free enough to create. Our own chosen place of exile from middle America was not Europe but New York, . . .like Paris in the twenties."[34]

The difference in the case of Jewish writer-intellectuals was that "the provinces" were right around the corner, not some place that could be left far behind. The Jewish equivalent of middle America was located in the same city that the elite wished to see as a reflection of their own cultural strivings. It was, therefore, in some sense more disturbing, even threatening, while at the same time it was less of a challenge for young Jews to leave home. In the descriptions written by observers and participants, we do find both points of view. On the one hand, Nathan Glazer noted that

> For the young Jewish radical or bohemian [in Greenwich Village], the break [with home] was much less sharp. He had come from the Bronx or Brooklyn . . . ; he went home now and then for the holidays or some family gathering. If he was a Communist, his father had been a Socialist (or vice versa), and . . . he could usually depend on a little financial help from anxious parents. The non-Jews in these circles were a million miles from home, the Jews but a subway ride away.[35]

On the other hand, there were those who felt that to achieve the distance of creative "exile," Jewish intellectuals and cosmopolitans had to push that much harder against "home and middle-class convention"—to commit treason, as Norman Podhoretz has put it. The Jewish provincials and antiprovincials were involved in a messy, rancorous, and almost incestuous relationship with the same city. "In choosing the road I chose, I was pronouncing a judgment upon [my family and friends]."[36]

The leading intellectual lights of New York Jewry (in a symposium of writers published in early 1944) had collectively pilloried the community as mediocre, smug, and insipid. Lionel Trilling had complained of American Jewry's cultural aridity. Clement Greenberg had harangued it for its "suffocatingly middle-class" posture: "No people on earth are more correct, more staid, more provincial, more commonplace. . . , none observe more strictly the letter of every code that is respectable." "What a pity," Alfred Kazin sneered, "that [the American Jew] should feel 'different'. . . , what a stupendous moral pity, historically, that the Fascist cutthroats should have their eyes on him, too, when he asks for so little—only to be safe, in all the Babbitt warrens." [37]

Consider, however, Norman Podhoretz's insightful reading between the lines of the sentiments just quoted: "Below the harsh words . . . lay an assumption obviously shared by most of [them]—that, by committing themselves to the Ideal in culture and politics, they were being more truly Jewish than the community which called itself Jewish." [38]

That is, these intellectuals thought of their Jewishness as a quality of intellect: a demanding, even austere, aesthetic and moral posture. It was, for them, a cerebral religion that had—ostensibly since Abraham had smashed his father's idols and Moses had made mincemeat of Pharaoh's magicians—respected only the authentic in human spiritual genius. They juxtaposed this pristine faith to the idolatry of material comfort, mediocrity, and mass culture.

If the god of this religion was the modern human being, the city was undoubtedly its temple. "The city," in this instance, was quite clearly modeled more on New York than on, say, Boston or Philadelphia and was defined by the more abstract of its qualities—its chameleon-like malleability, its modernism, and its pockets of resistance, such as Greenwich Village, to the dominant spirit of commercialism.

Moreover, this ideal city transcended the gritty and petty details of neighborhood, class, and smarmy ethnic chauvinism. Perceiving that Jewishness either mired one in such trivia or else provided the ideological means of escape from them, they opted for a nominally "Jewish" sensibility in matters of urban culture while jettisoning the need to anchor that sensibility in more substantive qualities.

Was this a "Jewish" cosmopolitanism (pardon the oxymoron)? Evidence for a self-consciously Jewish factor is basically circumstantial and only just barely admitted by those directly involved. Irving Howe, for example, asserted that the group of writers that he dubbed the "New York intellectuals" were consciously trying to "break clean" of their immigrant milieu. "If this severance from immigrant experiences and Jewish roots would later come to seem a little suspect, the point needs nevertheless to be reemphasized that . . . Jewishness as an idea or sentiment played only a minor, barely acknowledged role in their thought."

Only with the retrospective advantage of some thirty years did Howe come to believe that he and his friends were shaped willy-nilly by their families' immigrant status and by the fact that "in New York Jews still formed a genuine community reaching half-unseen into a dozen neighborhoods and a multitude of institutions, within the shadows of which we found protection of a kind."[39]

It bears noting that Howe's latter-day perception that his and his colleagues' Jewishness was more than just an accident of birth but was, rather, an operative and formative factor in their lives, confirms the thrust of the recent literature on Jewish ethnicity in America. That literature has tended strongly toward social-deterministic theories, emphasizing the potency of geographical and social-class networks in the construction of individual and group identity. I have, therefore, for the purposes of the argument presented in this book, collapsed these two quite different genres into one discussion: the general observations of memoirists and essayists and the more specialized research of social historians. Nevertheless, it ought to be pointed out that, whereas the research literature has taken on an unabashedly self-celebratory tone (especially of late), Howe and others tended to acknowledge frankly the fragile and elusive quality of their "subconscious" ethnic selves. It is as if, for Jewish social historians, the urban ethnic paradigm has become an article of faith, while, in contrast, the cosmopolitan writers were owning up to their own provincialism, "after all," and even then, still pleading extenuating circumstances.

Thus, Lionel Trilling (again in retrospect) happily asserted his own appreciative attitude toward Jewishness, in an obituary for his friend, critic Robert Warshow. Warshow, Trilling approvingly and sympathetically observed, had "acknowledged, and with pleasure, the effect that a Jewish rearing had had upon his temperament and mind, [yet] found that the impulses of his intellectual life were anything but Jewish, and that the chief objects of his intellectual life were anything but Jewish." Alfred Kazin, for another, had "learned long ago to accept the fact that I was Jewish without being a part of any meaningful Jewish life or culture." Or again, taking Sydney Hook: "We took ourselves for granted as Jews and were concerned with the Jewish question primarily as a political one"—meaning thereby that he had viewed it as a detail or by-product of the underlying problems of the economic and social system.[40]

Given this type of Jewish-cosmopolitan sensibility, literary scholar Emily Budick has recently argued that these intellectuals were in effect opting for a "racial," or involuntary Jewishness, a sort of perpetuated identity that was a fact of life but did not require conscious efforts of preservation—something, in fact, very much like blackness.

> In this way they are able to maintain an elusive difference that does and does not quite matter to them, in the same way that color may or may not matter to American blacks. . . . [I]t meant imagining the possibility that Jewish identity might be realized through a universalism that nonetheless did not totally eradicate the Jew's distinctive markings.[41]

We shall have occasion (in chapter 5) to reconsider the ways in which Jewish misunderstandings of American racialism constituted an obstacle in Jews' relations with African Americans. For now, however, it is important to explain just why some of these same cosmopolitan intellectuals set about reclaiming their Jewish identity, starting in the mid-1950s and continuing over the following decades.

Those intellectuals who had earlier viewed Jewishness, at its usable, stripped-down best, as a legacy of critical inquiry, an uncompromising dedication to the "Ideal," were taking up a position on the rim of the culture they were in the process of adopting. It suited them, then, to make of Jewishness not so much a culture to be valued in its own right as much as a perennial season ticket as cultural gadfly and social critic. Both Delmore Schwartz and Isaac Rosenfeld—among the writers participating in the 1944 symposium on Jewishness and the American writer—had made precisely this point: that the "asset" of Jewishness was that it helped them to feel doubly alienated from America.[42]

But in the fifties, "outsiders" the likes of Alfred Kazin, Sydney Hook, Meyer Schapiro, and Lionel Trilling (Trilling, who had had so much trouble obtaining a tenured post at Columbia) became insiders. Members of the Jewish culture elite found themselves welcomed in the world of American letters, the academy, and the arts. The cosmopolitan Jewish utopia was as close at that point to full realization as it had ever been. City culture, moreover, seemed to have become almost coterminous with American culture (recall Max Lerner's remarks), not at odds with it. The role of New York as "cultural capital" in those years made nonsense of claims to congenital alienation. The "house organ" of the New York group, *Partisan Review,* asserted in 1952 that "most writers no longer accept alienation as the artist's fate in America. . . . They now believe that their values, if they are to be realized at all, must be realized in America and in relation to the actuality of American life."[43]

Not coincidentally, many of those who had been on the anti-Stalinist radical Left in the thirties became in the fifties intellectual stalwarts of an anti-McCarthyist democratic liberalism, and positions further to the right: positions situated well within mainstream American politics.

A second avenue of explanation is based less on *security* than on a newfound *insecurity,* bringing in its wake a retreat from utopia. References to the terrible encounter with radical evil in the form of Nazism, on the one hand, and the juxtaposition of American democracy and Soviet totalitarianism, on the other, formed the backdrop for many personal and intellectual readjustments.

Norman Podhoretz, in retrospect, recalled how he began, during the course of a fellowship at Cambridge University the slow intellectual process of bridging his literary sensibilities (the "tragic sense of life") and "anti-utopian" political views that pointed away from "illusions regarding the perfectibility of man and the perfectibility of society." Living outside of his New York environment, he also at this time lifted the veil of universality from the Western literary tradition, seeing with new eyes the particularist assumptions in every culture, including the American one. Both the political and cultural utopias appeared less credible.[44]

Howe, an older veteran of the intellectual wars (and one who would retain greater fidelity to his earlier ideas), also recalled the postwar moment as one of significant realignment, even "severe crisis" in terms of his circle's inability to maintain a coherent self-definition. "Everything that had kept them going—the vision of socialism, the defense and exploration of literary modernism, the assault on the debasements of mass culture, their distinctive brand of socioliterary criticism—now came into question. . . . A sharp turn followed into uncertainty, fashion, and social accommodation." This intellectual anxiety and sense of displacement, however, occurred in a cultural moment that opened avenues of adjustment previously unavailable to them: "A benign philo-Semitism, the consequence of some shudders over the Holocaust, settled over the culture for a decade or two."[45]

There was, then, some link between Jewishness and the retreat from utopian radicalism—a link that resided in the dark spaces of recent events, but that was also predicated somehow on the virtual fulfillment of many older aspirations. Having successfully escaped the magnetic field of the urban immigrant and middle-class/middlebrow milieu, protected from death and tyranny by the circumstance of their Americanness, they were thrown off balance by a world that was less susceptible to coherent ideological definition than they had imagined. Backpedaling, they found new virtue in affirmations of the imperfect but livable American social order, which did, after all, afford them far more than it had before the war. The security to let go of marginality as a defense was self-fulfilling proof that diversity, criticism, intelligence—even Jewishness—could be domesticated as urban American virtues.

As insiders and coparticipants, however, more was required of them than the challenging but limited role of the critic, something in the nature of a positive contribution. The cosmopolitanism of postwar New York tossed together the *gravitas* of the Anglo-American literary canon, the frank authenticity of Harlem, the spontaneity and daring of the avant-garde, and the unreflecting self-confidence of American popular culture. A self-styled Jewish component that possessed some, at least, of these characteristics seemed to be required as well. Without a specific tradition to adhere to and to develop in the new American context, wrote Alfred Kazin, "there is no spiritual marriage at all between America and its newcomers, and the great epic of immigration simply becomes a picture of the lesser breeds attached to the white Protestant majority."[46]

Jewish intellectuals turned in the first instance not to the contemporary Jewish community, which (as we have seen) they believed to be barren, but rather back to what was conceived as its East European parent-culture. One of the key cultural events, in this regard, was the publication in 1952 (reissued in 1962 and 1967) of the now classic (if idealized) ethnography of Jewish life in eastern Europe, *Life Is With People,* produced by a team of researchers at Columbia University. Margaret Mead, the renowned anthropologist, wrote the foreword and back-jacket copy for the book, where she took pains to make explicit what the book itself left tacit: namely, the ostensible continuity between the shtetl and Jewish life in America. "The culture . . . lives on in the habits and memories of thousands of Jewish Americans, and through them is becoming part of the American tradition." Harold Lasswell, the noted sociologist, chimed in, too: "This is by all odds the most illuminating contribution that has been made to the understanding of the background of one of the most virile elements in American civilization."[47]

Norman Podhoretz, then the recently chosen editor of *Commentary,* noted in 1961 that "at least half" of the New York intellectuals had become "enthusiasts" of Martin Buber, the celebrated philosopher from Jerusalem, widely published in English in the postwar years, who effectively rendered Hasidic lore for modern, existentialist consumption.

"The whole of the New York literary world," Podhoretz continued, "was ringing with praise of the Yiddish storytellers, the Hasidim, Maimonides." Yiddish writer Judd Teller understood that "the bearded generations, . . .decimated by German genocide, are beyond making demands or causing embarrassment. Because they are remote and unreal, like the weightless, levitating figures of Chagall's canvases, one may vaguely relate to them without the risk of being mistaken for them."[48]

More recently, two scholars, David Roskies and Steven Zipperstein, have commented independently on this phenomenon. Roskies observed that American Jewish writers were apparently incapable of bridging the distance between Greenwich Village and the real world of Yiddish culture and letters that was available to them just around the block, choosing instead to rely on symbolic memory of a culture already destroyed. Zipperstein, for his part, has highlighted the desire of Jewish writers and critics in the fifties to recognize in the East European past a connection that could "deepen one's humanity, . . .a source of pedigree, . . .proof that Jews had in the past personified spirituality, wholeness, and communal cohesion, perhaps also widespread scholarly distinction."[49]

Here was a new spin on an older cosmopolitan theme. Formerly, the congruence between Jewishness and urbanness had rested on the proposition that it was as the generic "homo urbanus" that a Jew was being most "Jewish"—that is, most unsettled, and therefore most willing to readjust, to improvise, to treat the city as an open frontier. Jewishness as such, emptied of particular content, was incidental to other urban capacities.[50]

Quite appropriately, for example, Kazin's originally chosen autobiographical persona was the Brownsville-bred but compulsively outward-bound *Walker in the City.* Even more significantly, Kazin postulated that the predicament of the Brownsville boy—"alienation on native grounds"—was identical to the badge worn by the best of modern American fiction:

> To speak of it only as a struggle toward the modern emancipation—and it was that—does not even hint at the lean and shadowy tragic strain in our modern American writing, . . .from Dreiser to Faulkner, an often great depth of suffering. Nor does it tell us why our modern writers have had to discover and rediscover and chart the country in every generation. . . , but must still cry America! America! as if we had never known America. As perhaps we have not.[51]

He thereby projected himself into the vital core of American culture itself—for *Walker* encapsulates his own estrangement and his own passion to discover the America he had not known.

But now the reverse claim was being made: It was the *Jewish* part of the urban "everyman" that made the urban bearable as a life form—not because the Jew was the personification of restlessness, deracination, and outward journeys of discovery, but rather because the Jew's culture, as it was now being promoted (enter Buber, the Hasidim, and the shtetl) was an inner lens for seeing the possibilities for positive survival despite impossible odds. The prosaic world of everyday held the secret and sanctity of creation; meaning lay inside the apparently meaningless: What better metaphor was there for the atonal surface qualities of urbanism?

It was no coincidence that Jewishness was once again being repackaged as a form of mentality, as the ability to cut through cultural despair by using the power of radical imagination. This was, after all, the very ideal that had animated the cosmopolitan intellectuals before, but that seemed to elude them in the postwar period. It was now fortuitously rediscovered, not as a by-product of exile and alienation, but as a feature of the highly verbal, highly literate, Jewish tradition. In an essay on Sholem Aleichem and the world of eastern European Jewry, Kazin reveled in this Jewish (defined as *non-Christian*) existential point of view: "The word is not the beginning of things, the foundation of the world; it is a response to the overmastering reality—to the world and the everlasting creation, the eternal struggle and the inestimable privilege of being a Jew."[52]

Kazin's generic *Walker* (1951) became his *New York Jew* (1978). But it was far easier for him and most of his colleagues in the culture elite to don once again the mantle of the Jewish cultural spirit, defined in terms of their own angst, than it was for them to forge any connection to the Jewish community as it really existed. Daniel Bell suggested that, for those of the generation that followed his, Jewishness was best thought of as an aspect of the past, a memory to be carried along. "One cannot wholly escape it. . . . At its best, the parochial identification exists as a tie of memory through pity." Kazin himself, though he averred that an immigrant group could only truly encounter the hope of America out of "a specific tradition sharp enough to arouse the possibility of its fulfillment" in the New World, never really put his finger on just how the Jewish tradition of the past could reach fulfillment in America, other than through a realization of the self.[53]

In his study of the New York intellectuals, Terry Cooney concluded sardonically that "it gradually became apparent in the postwar period that, as an understanding of the place of ethnicity, the cosmopolitanism of the New York Intellectuals could remain viable only if a good many people rejected it."[54] That is, only where an actual particularist ethnic culture maintained itself could elite members of such groups continue to contend against the particular, seeking to project their own wider vision of a composite urban culture.

We turn, then, to consider postwar New York Jewry in its particularist, tribal mode.

"Here Lives the Jewish People": New York as Jewish Capital City

If there be irony in the fact that the universalist vision seemed after a while to wilt, to curve in upon itself, leading to a rediscovered Jewish particularism, it is perhaps understandable that this came at a time when New York Jewry's importance in American and world Jewry was just peaking. The issues involved here are (once again) numbers, politics, and culture.

Lewis Mumford, the great advocate of a livable urbanism, called the city "the point of maximum concentration for the power and culture of a community. . . . Here is where the issues of civilization are focused."[55] New York, as a Jewish metropolis, served an analogous function within the Jewish world. New York Jewry can hardly be seen, therefore, as a typical American Jewish community—no other urban Jewry has yet matched it—but ought rather to be regarded as a premier or hub community.

Sheer numerical weight is the key factor here. In the postwar years, Jewish population was still concentrated overwhelmingly in the Northeast and Middle Atlantic states, New York City itself accounting for almost 40 percent of the entire Jewish population of the United States. What affected Jews in New York had by definition a major impact on Jewish life in America (and beyond). Robert Warshow, for example, asserted in the late forties that "the life of New York can be said . . . to embody the common experience of American Jews."[56]

That this was an exaggeration becomes clear if we consider the distinctive profile of New York Jewry, when compared to other urban Jewish communities in America: New York's Jewish population has historically included a higher percentage of the foreign-born, a higher percentage of poor, of working class, and of lower-middle class Jews, and a higher percentage of Orthodox Jews. It is also the case that New York Jewry was notoriously diffuse and subdivided, when compared with smaller communities that often exhibited a more close-knit or more organized quality.

Nevertheless, despite these considerations, Warshow's intuitive remark should not be dismissed out of hand, especially given the time in which it was made. A good many Jews living in other communities and in other parts of the United States had originally lived in New York. They retained in many cases family ties and other connections to that city. They also retained (as pointed out by Deborah Dash Moore, in her above-noted comment) an image of New York as a real alternative to their own community. The New York influence was magnified through Jewish magazines and newspapers sent from there to subscribers around the country.

Finally, despite local variations, the urban experience of Jews in other major cities did parallel in significant ways the lives of Jews in New York: heavy residential concentration in particular neighborhoods; relatively rapid transition from blue collar to business, white collar, and professional occupations; and relatively high levels of educational attainment.[57] In short, the Jewish ambience of the great metropolis was sufficiently familiar to Jews elsewhere as to take on symbolic importance.

New York was unrivaled as the recognized headquarters for virtually every major national Jewish organization. The American Jewish Committee was here, as were the American Jewish Congress, the Anti-Defamation League, the Jewish Labor Committee, the United Jewish Appeal, the American headquarters of the World Zionist Organization, and the national offices of the three main synagogue denominations—the Union of Orthodox Jewish Congregations, the United Synagogue of America (Conservative), and the Union of American Hebrew Congregations (Reform)—to list but a few. Perusing the directory in the 1955 volume of the authoritative *American Jewish Year Book*, for instance, we see that twelve of the fourteen national Jewish organizations devoted to community and political relations were based in New York. So were twenty-two of the twenty-five national institutions and organizations in the cultural field; all fifteen agencies dealing with overseas aid; thirty-nine out of fifty in the sphere of religion and religious education; seventeen out of twenty-three in the area of social welfare; and each and every one of the fifty-six Zionist or pro-Israel organizations.[58]

The city was also the home campus of two Jewish degree-granting institutions of higher education: Yeshiva University (Orthodox) and the (Conservative) Jewish Theological Seminary of America. (Cincinnati's Hebrew Union College—the Reform seminary—also had a New York branch.)

The Jewish Theological Seminary maintained The Jewish Museum, one of the nation's foremost institutions of its kind. Growing from a collection established in 1904, it moved to Fifth Avenue along "museum mile" in 1947 (and will be referred to again later, in chapter 5). The Seminary's library housed the largest Judaica collection in the world at the time.

There were three other important such collections in New York: In addition to the Jewish Division at the New York Public Library's main branch at 42nd Street (then comprising over 125,000 volumes), two private Jewish research institutes with major libraries and archival holdings were based in the city after the Second World War—the Leo Baeck Institute, specializing in material related to the history of Jewish communities of German-speaking lands, and the YIVO Institute, specializing in Yiddish-language materials and the cultural heritage of eastern Europe.

This high concentration of flagship institutions, major cultural resources, service agencies, and national offices reflected not only the size and significance of New York Jewry. Even without the massive Jewish presence, New York might have accounted for the lion's share of major Jewish institutions and organizational networks because of the city's high-exposure national and international character, enhanced in the postwar world: headquarters of the United Nations, world center for communications, culture, and commerce.

In New York the Jewish elites found it easy to work with willing partners. Commenting on the postwar social order in New York, one perceptive observer noted:

> WASP and Jewish New Yorkers acted together—in the political and economic realms as well as in cultural affairs. . . . The doctrines associated with the postwar national and world orders—internationalism, liberalism, modernism—can be regarded as the ideology of this WASP-Jewish coalition. . . . In the name of those doctrines, the members of the WASP-Jewish coalition came to exercise a remarkable measure of influence in American political, economic, and cultural life.[59]

Thus, the combined factors of population size, financial means, and political efficacy worked together to make the city the logical choice as a central Jewish clearinghouse. Most of the organizations headquartered in New York had been there long before the postwar period—some of them as long ago as the beginning of the twentieth century. Their initial establishment then had attested to the unprecedented ease with which Jewish communal resources and leaders could be mobilized and centralized in New York. Thereafter, they could continue to count on being more effective there than anywhere else.

The "thick" layer of Jewish organizational activity was never synonymous with a comprehensively organized community, however. The rapid proliferation of groups, both at the grassroots and at the high-policy level, indicated a tendency within New York Jewry to achieve intense levels of communal activity only within highly defined subgroups or subcultures. And even then, the organized "cells" of communal or cultural activity never actually accounted for the majority of the Jewish population. Nathan Glazer only confirmed this widely recognized reality when he wrote that "Only a minority belongs to synagogues, is sent to Jewish schools, deals with Jewish welfare agencies, is interested in Jewish culture, speaks a traditional Jewish language, and can be distinguished by dress and custom as Jews." That New York Jewry was notorious for low synagogue membership is indicated by the fact that the community supported one congregation for every 7,350 Jewish inhabitants, or approximately one for every 1,800 families, a hypothetical ratio of members to synagogues far in excess of the actual membership of the average urban congregation.[60]

A study of a neighborhood in Queens that had become heavily Jewish in the postwar years—with about thirty thousand Jews in 1960—showed that the area had five synagogues at that time: theoretically, a ratio of one for every six thousand Jews. But the actual *combined* membership of these synagogues (three Orthodox, one Conservative, and one Reform) was only thirteen hundred (or 15 percent of local families).[61]

Historically, of course, New York's immigrant Jews were an immensely variegated lot. Drawn from all over Europe and from the Levant as well, they split along lines of religious preferences and antipathies, place of origin, generational and class differences, political outlook (radical/liberal/conservative, Zionist/non-Zionist), and language. Added to this pluralistic condition, the associational freedom taken virtually for granted in American society seemed only to magnify the already existing basis for fragmentation. Still today, as one observer has put it, "The very existence of a critical mass of Jews . . . makes it possible for a variety of Jewish groups to function, each totally independent of the others and not driven by the need that impels Jews . . . in smaller communities to seek out one another for mutual sustenance."[62]

It was this quality of intense but diversified activity, in a setting where many Jews took Jewishness quite for granted, that could be taken as reminiscent of Jewish life in Europe before its destruction. As long as New York remained a center of European Jewish culture, albeit altered in an immigrant mode, that connection had a basis in fact. Components of the imported European ambience included Yiddish language, religious Orthodoxy, and secular political movements such as Zionism and labor socialism. In the immediate postwar period, with the original cultural setting of Europe destroyed, its New York "shadow" assumed a significance in its own right, despite the fact that the population of Yiddish-speakers in the United States had peaked between 1920 and 1930.[63]

In 1940, U.S. census figures showed that over 924,000 foreign-born Americans claimed Yiddish as their mother tongue, as did almost 774,000 of their children (native-born Americans whose parents were foreign-born) and 53,000 of their grandchildren, making a total of 1.75 million. Of the foreign-born, over half lived in New York City. However, the trend of Yiddish-speaking among second-generation American Jews was already on a downward curve. As a consequence, the number of Yiddish speakers fell dramatically between 1940 and 1960 (declining nationally from 1.75 million to an estimated 965,000, half of whom lived in New York State).[64]

The arrival of Yiddish-speaking refugees and Holocaust survivors in the forties and early fifties provided a floor for the waning of Yiddish in postwar America. Some 137,450 Jewish immigrants arrived in the United States between 1940 and 1952, of whom 85,000 settled in New York City. They included ultra-Orthodox Jews (estimated as about 12,000) intent upon reconstructing their community life, including a thoroughly Yiddish-speaking ambience, in New York City, where they provided a counterweight against slippage in Yiddish-language use and especially Yiddish-language education.[65]

Thus, although New York's secular Yiddish-language afternoon schools *(folkshuln,* affiliated in four separate school networks, each with its own ideological orientation) experienced a rapid decline in the postwar years, the number of Orthodox all-day schools in which instruction took place in both Hebrew and Yiddish increased. By 1960 there were 47 such schools in New York City, almost double the number for all of New York *State* in 1952, serving the growing number of children born to the postwar Orthodox refugee immigration. There were 98 secular Yiddish schools in the United States in 1960, many in the Northeast; in contrast to the ultra-Orthodox sector, however, secular Yiddish education by that point was "actually related more to a web of sentiments and memories of the teachers and school board members than . . . to any viable culture into which children are or can be socialized," noted sociolinguist Joshua A. Fishman argued.[66]

The secular Yiddish dailies had declined in circulation, from just over 217,000 in the Middle Atlantic states in 1950 to about 160,000 in 1960 (actual readership is estimated at double the circulation figure), but this was still a significant audience. There were two major daily Yiddish newspapers: the liberal, pro-Zionist *Tog/Morgen zhurnal* and the veteran pro-labor *Forverts* (as well as a third, with a very small readership, the pro-communist *Fray-hayt*[67]). These were among the *only* Jewish daily newspapers anywhere in the world outside the State of Israel (one existed, as well, in Buenos Aires). In addition, until the 1960s, the bulk of the programming broadcast over New York's WEVD radio station ("the station that speaks your language") was in Yiddish.[68]

Of no less significance was the fact that postwar New York was the home of an accomplished and respected cadre of Yiddish writers, poets, and critics. A "short list" of the most eminent ones would include Sholem Asch (emigrated to Israel in 1955 and died in 1957), Aaron Glanz-Leyeles (d. 1966), Jacob Glatstein (or in Yiddish, Yankev Glatshteyn, d. 1971), Chaim Grade (d. 1982), H. Leyvik (d. 1962), Kadia Molodovsky (d. 1975), Shmuel Niger-Charney (d. 1955), Joseph Opatoshu (d. 1954), Isaac Bashevis Singer (d. 1991), I. I. Trunk (d. 1961), and Aaron Zeitlin (d. 1974). The older immigrants among them had done the bulk of their work before the fifties, but significant new work was being done by the younger ones and the more recent arrivals (such as Glatshteyn, Grade, Molodovsky, and Singer—see chapter 3).

Moreover, the Holocaust had magnified the significance of the New York Yiddish literary center, as had the murder by Stalin of the entire Yiddish literary elite of the Soviet Union in 1952. An average of about 75 books by American Yiddish authors were published each year from 1950 to 1960 in the fields of fiction, poetry, literary criticism, history/biography/memoir, children's literature, education/pedagogy, and politics. The world total was about 125.[69]

Symbolic of New York's role as a preeminent center of Yiddish intellectual life was the relocation of the YIVO Institute from Vilna (Vilnius, Lithuania) to Manhattan in 1940. Traumatic in itself and dictated by dire necessity, the move was providential as well. The American occupation of Germany after the war enabled YIVO to recover large portions of its German-confiscated library and archives. (The rest, having been secreted in Vilna during the Nazi occupation, would remain hidden, its fate unknown, until the collapse of the Soviet Union. It was ultimately recovered in 1995 after lengthy negotiations with the Lithuanian government and its archival authorities.)

With this core of unique materials to work with and the existing Yiddish cultural environment in New York to look to for support, the Institute was able to function once again as a kind of "ministry of Yiddish"—a cross between a national language academy, a refuge for survivor-intellectuals, a focus group for working out scholarly and cultural agendas, and a direct sponsor of academic programs in Yiddish language studies. Uriel Weinreich, son of YIVO's director, Max Weinreich, assumed the newly established chair in Yiddish Language, Literature, and Culture at Columbia University in 1952. The group around YIVO and Columbia was responsible, among other things, for the publication of the (to date) only authoritative Yiddish thesaurus (1950). It published an academic journal in Yiddish and a parallel one in English, and in 1954 it presented to the scholarly world, in English, a volume of studies in Yiddish linguistic, folkloristic, and literary research—the first such collection to be published since the Second World War anywhere in the world.[70]

In the fifties the world of Yiddish letters was still an insider culture, just beginning to be recognized by a non-Yiddish-reading American audience. Classic works by the European masters Sholem Aleichem and Isaac Leybush Peretz were available in English translation. Isaac Bashevis Singer, recently arrived in America, was being published in English in the fifties (*The Family Moskat*, 1950; *Gimpel the Fool*, 1954; *Satan in Goray*, 1958). When Dan Wakefield offered to write a review essay on Singer for *American Heritage*, however, he was informed that Singer was "too limited in appeal" to warrant such a piece. By contrast, Putnam, the firm that was publishing Sholem Asch in English, was interested in commissioning the foremost Yiddish critic, Shmuel Niger, to write a book that would introduce Asch's life and work to an English readership (an offer that Niger declined, out of a literary antipathy to Asch).[71]

It was certainly not on the reputation of Yiddish culture alone, however, that New York's importance as a Jewish cultural center rested. A recent study entitled, with conscious irony, *The "Other" New York Jewish Intellectuals*[72] showcased a collection of men and women—less generally recognized, less politically cohesive as a group, less scintillating, perhaps—but no less serious in their cultural undertakings than the celebrated *Partisan Review* and *Commentary* crowd. These modern religious philosophers, Zionist thinkers, writers, and other public intellectuals were not Jewish only by association, but avowedly Jewish in their preoccupations, though never "parochial" in their cultural or political worldview. For the most part, their careers were rooted in the interwar period. Quite a few, however, continued to play pivotal roles in Jewish intellectual and cultural discourse in New York in the postwar period, such as: Mordecai M. Kaplan, rabbi, teacher, religious critic and founder of the Reconstructionist movement (d. 1983); Marie Syrkin, the writer/editor and Zionist polemicist (d. 1988); Will Herberg, the former-Marxist-turned-conservative analyst of religion and its social significance, influential among the postwar generation of clergy (Jewish and Christian) and among readers at large (d. 1977); and Horace M. Kallen, theorist of ethnic pluralism and cultural democracy in America (d. 1974).

At The Jewish Theological Seminary, the postwar period saw the emergence of a civic-oriented, interreligious think tank: the Institute for Social and Religious Studies. Under the guidance of Seminary president Rabbi Louis Finkelstein, who believed that the "religions of democracy" had a moral obligation to influence public discourse, the Institute became one of New York's leading venues for airing such postwar issues as urban problems, interfaith dialogue, and interracial relations. In addition to Finkelstein and Kaplan, the Seminary was also the home of a recently arrived refugee scholar destined to play a particularly high-profile role in interfaith and interracial discourse and in the peace movement in the sixties, Abraham Joshua Heschel.

Succinctly stated, all of these activities—political, cultural, and civic—reflected an urban outlook that steered clear of theories of alienation, marginality, passivity, and loss. The city as Jewish capital—that is, a place where one might immerse oneself in group culture at various levels and still be "in" the city—was defined entirely differently from the city inhabited by the cosmopolitan culture elite. The affirmative qualities evoked were those of particularity, attachment, and involvement: abstract names for participatory patterns of behavior. This "behaviorist" Jewishness contrasts, then, with the Jewishness of mentality embraced by the subgroup of intellectuals discussed earlier. In the fifties, both types of Jewish urban culture were viable options in New York.

From Heyday to Turning Point: The End of the Fifties

As much as New York's central position in American Jewry depended on such factors as cultural excellence and rootedness in a mature particularism, the continuation of such preeminence was predicated upon communal stability. By the late 1950s, however, such stability was no longer assured. There were a variety of factors involved: political, cultural, and social.

As a political nerve center for American Jewry, New York was as yet unrivaled. But on the international level, the emergence of the State of Israel as a political actor in its own right was beginning to have its effect. The fifties brought a mass immigration to Israel that, by the mid-sixties, would put its population on a par with that of New York Jewry. More important, however, was the qualitative difference between the political weight of a sovereign country, on the one hand, and a loose community of a voluntary nature, on the other. The wartime leadership of American Jewry, so used to playing the role of a Jewish cabinet with global responsibilities (loosely organized, to be sure, and never able to achieve one common policy), was succeeded by younger organizational functionaries who no longer comprised a compelling leadership force. The New York-Israel axis was weighted heavily in Israel's favor. Moreover, Israel was bent on developing its own channels to Washington, not always bothering to use its New York intermediaries.

The Zionist organizations were most directly overshadowed by the State of Israel and its leaders, and therefore they were the ones most immediately affected. They had ceased to represent a cause awaiting fulfillment and demanding militancy; instead, they now appeared virtually redundant as exponents of an idea already realized, enjoying the widespread sympathy of the Jewish community at large and of American public opinion. With the exception of the women's Zionist group, Hadassah, which apparently drew on a different set of energies, Zionist groups' membership and influence plummeted.[73]

The Israeli impact went beyond the official Zionist community, however. The American Jewish Committee—traditionally known since 1906 for its independent voice, unwilling to join major Jewish coalitions, and wary of politicizing issues that it preferred to present as civic or humanitarian ones—retained some of its elitist posture but edged much closer to the prevailing pro-Zionist consensus. New York's traditionally non-Zionist Jewish health-and-welfare umbrella organization, the Federation of Jewish Philanthropies, would retain the clear distinction between the local agenda and the international one. Unlike its counterpart in virtually every other Jewish community in the country, it remained separate from the United Jewish Appeal, the major Jewish fund-raising apparatus that was closely associated with financial support of Israel. But this arrangement would last only until 1973. In a process that began in that year and was finally consummated in 1986, the New York Federation and UJA came under one roof.[74]

Yiddish culture in New York, as we have noted, retained qualitative significance. Sooner or later, however, the effects of a dwindling social base would be expressed (outside the relatively small and insulated ultra-Orthodox communities) in a devastating loss of cultural confidence and cultural product. By the mid-fifties, clear signs of this were in evidence. When Kate Simon wrote her guide book, *New York Places and Pleasures,* at the end of the decade, she already described the Second Avenue Jewish theater district as a thing of the past, a subject worthy of nostalgia (always the kiss of death):

> Twenty years ago and more, Second Avenue below 14th Street was the Via Veneto, the rue de la Paix, the Broadway and the Fifth Avenue of the Jewish intellectual and older Bohemian. . . . What is now the Phoenix Theatre, at the corner of 12th Street, was the Yiddish Art Theatre. . . . Farther down the street, one could see the Habimah Players, who acted in Hebrew, or the Vilna Troupe, a famous repertory theater whose avant-garde productions

> were carefully observed by the whole theater world. Other theaters featured gay, fleshy musicals or tear-jerkers. . . . The playwrights, poets, journalists and publishers lived and worked here too, and in the evening would gather at one of the local cafes for a glass of tea. . . . All the lovely, gaudy people are gone.[75]

Judd Teller, the Yiddish poet and journalist, put it just as starkly: "Second Avenue, heartland of Yiddish culture, was picked by time, bone by bone. . . . One year there were seven bright marquees on Second Avenue, then five, then none." The last holdout, the Cafe Royale, "the Sardi's of the Yiddish actors, the Algonquin of the Yiddish writers . . . passed away shortly after the death of Herman, its busboy-owner and money-lender. It was like the closing of the lid on a coffin. . . . Outside, the darkened slab, with its name in electric bulbs, hung like a flag over a razed fortress until new occupants reopened the place as a dry cleaning establishment."[76]

"Can we imagine," asks literary scholar Benjamin Harshav, "the tragedy of writers—H. Leyvik, Jacob Glatshteyn, A. Leyeles, others—who felt such a mission of beginning in their own lifetime and stood before the abyss of the end, losing first their readership, then their source, their people in Europe (along with their own parents), and finally the very language that they had made into such a fine instrument?"[77] Quoting from Glatshteyn's "A Few Lines," Harshav evoked the poet himself, appearing to hold his art like a handful of water in his palm: "A few trembling lines on the palm of my hand/I held them long/And let them flow through my fingers/Word by word."[78]

Or, if we turn to Leyvik's ode "To America," written in the poet's final years, we find a similar note of resignation:

> I am not trying to cast part of the blame on you, America.
> And may God in Heaven witness that you are not yet worthy
> To feel free of guilt . . .
> You see—you yourself should have come to my aid right now,
> To ease my task of finding proper words
> Expressing intimacy and fusion and farewell . . .
> Farewell?—the stronger the fusion, the closer I can see
> The moment of farewell.[79]

By far, however, the most important source of change in New York Jewish life at the end of the fifties lay in the nature of the city itself. The urban crisis that would form the backdrop for the following decade was already noticed in 1959. In that year, several reports were published that raised serious issues about the quality of life in the city. The New York Metropolitan Region Study, a nine-volume report, contained predictions of "loss of population, industry, trade, and jobs." *Newsweek* called New York a "Metropolis in a Mess." *The Nation* published an issue on "The Shame of New York," which began as follows: "New York is a sprawling, voracious monster of a city. It covers 315 square miles; it is crammed with some 8 million people. At least a million . . . live in packed squalor, six and ten to a room. . . . Symbolically, perhaps, there are in New York more rats than people—an estimated 9 million of them."[80]

New York's population had grown by a million from 1930 to 1950 (from 6.9 million to 7.9 million). But in the next twenty-year period, between 1950 and 1970, while about one million people migrated or immigrated to New York City, the population remained constant at just under eight million. Clearly, out-migration had balanced in-migration.[81]

The Jews of New York City, no less susceptible than other citizens to quality-of-life concerns—and possessing the affluence to consider other options, residential and occupational, outside the city—were on the verge of a long-term numerical slide at the end of the fifties, a trend that would accelerate over the coming decade as Jews moved both to the suburban areas around New York as well as to distant parts of the United States, mainly in the West and the South. In 1970, Jews still formed the largest European group (a third of the city's white population), with the Italians in second place. By 1980, Italians comprised the largest such group. As one observer put it, this was because, "alone among the older immigrant groups they tend to stay in the city."[82]

More will be said on this further in our discussion, but let us note, at this point, that there was a direct link between the perceived quality of urban life, the shrinkage of Jewish population in the city, and the quality of Jewish community life. The vision of an ingathered megacommunity ("here lives the Jewish people") was inevitably undermined by a reversal of the ingathering process. When this unraveling made itself felt, it tended to reveal fissures or inner contradictions, previously unnoticed, in the very fabric of Jewish urbanism.

Thus, the neighborhood-based society of mass ethnic concentration—what Moore referred to as a "home" and an "urban web"—had only *apparently* been a force for social stabilization, fostering secular ethnic institutions that were in harmony with a wider vision of city life. In reality, the neighborhood had been a circumstance more than a home, easily shed when no longer perceived as a source of security. The values that the second generation had cultivated in the urban landscape were far more focused upon family and the individual, and far less dependent on the intimacy of group life. "Jews as a group," observed sociologist Marshall Sklare, speaking of Jewish despair over urban disintegration, "carry within themselves the seeds of their own urban problem; the Jewish urban crisis, in large part, derives from the insufficient attachment Jews have felt for their own neighborhoods."[83]

By the same token, the rival vision of a cosmopolitan merger of Jewish and universal values, having laboriously worked its way back to its point of origin, was now in danger of losing that particularist mooring, too.

2

Past and Premonition

Mass Society and Its Discontents

> It was no good simply saying that the past was cancelled.
>
> —Arthur Miller,
> *Timebends: A Life*

> For Jewish adolescents in particular, the Nazis were not so long defeated, and Hitler was the most compelling of all bogeymen. . . . Rumors and images and random facts did seep into our consciousness. Photos of camp survivors, not yet stereotyped, floated through popular culture like stray bones, and lodged, once in a while, in our collective throat.
>
> —Todd Gitlin,
> *The Sixties*

> Like many people who had seen the world collapse once, Mr. Sammler entertained the possibility it might collapse twice. He did not agree with refugee friends that this doom was inevitable, but liberal beliefs did not seem capable of self-defense. You could see the suicidal impulses of civilization pushing strongly.
>
> —Saul Bellow,
> *Mr. Sammler's Planet*

The editors of *Fortune Magazine* devoted their February 1960 issue to New York City and included a feature story called "The Jewish *Élan.*" Noting that more Jews lived in New York than in the State of Israel, or in any other single country outside the United States and Russia, for that matter, its author asserted:

> As no other city is, New York is their home; here a Jew can be what he wants to be. Here he lives out of the shadow of his historic crisis. . . . And surely it can be said that Jewish élan has contributed mightily to the city's dramatic character—its excitement, its originality, its stridency, its unexpectedness.[1]

That élan and that sense of being at home were surely related to the two Jewish visions of urban life outlined in our discussion thus far: the cosmopolitan and the parochial. Indeed, as glib as the passage from *Fortune* may sound, it conveniently sums up what we have suggested earlier about the mystique of the city—and this one city, specifically—as a solution to the Jewish question. "Here a Jew can be what he wants to be. Here he lives out of the shadow of his historic crisis." What the Jew "wants to be" is defined here as liberation from the burdens of a negative history, a victim's history. What the Jew wants, in effect, is to be "normal," self-defining, and unbound by the past.

What does makes the assertion in *Fortune* sound so glib, however, is that by 1960, as we have seen, there were visible cracks in the earlier utopia—in both of its twin versions. As for the unspecified reference to the Jews' "historic crisis," this formulation, too, had an almost disingenuous quality, written as it was only fifteen years since the end of the Second World War and a mere seven since the death of Stalin.

While a straightforward assertion of American Jewry's well-being, *circa* 1960, might be taken at face value, the "shadow" of recent Jewish traumas cannot be so blithely dispensed with. Todd Gitlin's memoir of the sixties (quoted in the epigraph to this chapter) did not omit mentioning, for example, that his New York boyhood in the fifties had been influenced by "rumors and images" of recent nightmares.

The Shadow of the Past

Some 35,000 survivors of Auschwitz had gathered at the site of the former concentration camp on 26 January 1960 to mark the fifteenth anniversary of their liberation. Two months later a smaller contingent, some 750 Jewish survivors of Auschwitz living in New York, held their first official reunion in the Bronx, at the Concourse Plaza Hotel, where New York Senator Jacob Javits brought his constituents greetings from President Eisenhower.

In April that same year, 3,500 gathered under the auspices of the *Yidisher Kultur Kongres* (Jewish Culture Congress) to mark the anniversary of the 1943 Warsaw Ghetto uprising. Messages were presented from three Democratic presidential hopefuls: U.S. Senators John F. Kennedy, Hubert H. Humphrey, and Stuart Symington.

Meanwhile, New York governor Nelson Rockefeller and Warsaw Ghetto heroine Zivia Lubetkin Zuckerman addressed yet another group of 4,000 at a "Third Seder" sponsored by the National Committee for Labor Israel (the U.S. support group of Israel's labor federation, the *Histadrut*[2]). The speakers paid tribute to the "memories of the six million Jews exterminated during World War II." The governor and the mayor, Robert F. Wagner, Jr., joined together to declare 19 April "Warsaw Ghetto Day" in New York. The following month, CBS-TV aired a ninety-minute documentary on the ghetto revolt.[3]

Thus, the assumption that Jews in New York were no longer living under the impressions of the recent past—were not somehow still involved in processing that past—skated a bit too quickly over extremely complex issues of collective consciousness.

Arthur Miller (whose plays, "After the Fall" and "Incident at Vichy," made direct reference to the Holocaust), was traveling in 1960 in Germany with his future wife, Inge Morath—an Austrian Catholic, herself a former victim of the Nazi regime. This is how he registered the gravity of the "historic shadow" and its challenge to his mission as an artist:

> We drove on up a mountain and stood before a castle overlooking the Rhine. Majestic. It had all been run by the Ku Klux Klan, on the same level of argument. But Heine had stood here once. Maybe the past really had been severed and the avant-garde was right. Even so, I had to search out a continuity. One had to explain all this so that people could understand it and not do it again, but . . . no conventional realism could illuminate this murder-by-civilization.[4]

At about the same time, in the fall of 1960, Leonard Bernstein was also in Germany, conducting a Beethoven concert in Berlin. The night before the concert was the first night of Rosh Hashana (the Jewish New Year), and Bernstein found to his amazement that there were five synagogues in Berlin. "What are they all doing here?" he could not help but wonder, as he, his brother, and a friend went off to services. The episode prompted more than surprise, however. "I feel so damn guilty about being in Berlin, of *all* places, over Rosh Hashana," he said, and insisted on greeting his concert audience the next night with a Hebrew benediction, noting with heavy irony: "I honestly don't think it will do the Berliners any harm to hear a little Hebrew once in a while."

The concert was being filmed live for later broadcast on American television at Thanksgiving, which prompted Bernstein's friends to question the propriety of the Hebrew benediction (Thanksgiving not being a Jewish holiday); but Bernstein would brook no disagreement. Claiming that the blessing would do perfectly well for Thanksgiving, too, he said, "And anyway, it's that Hebrew in Berlin on Rosh Hashana that will really make this show for me."[5]

Taking Bernstein's words emblematically, we might say that the Jews' responses to their "historic crisis" were in fact the source of their "élan," their "stridency," their "originality," their utopianism—and even their quest for economic dignity that sometimes led to middle-class complacency. It was

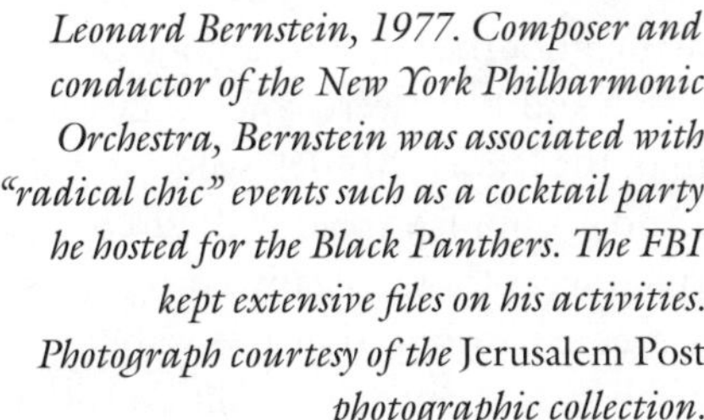

Leonard Bernstein, 1977. Composer and conductor of the New York Philharmonic Orchestra, Bernstein was associated with "radical chic" events such as a cocktail party he hosted for the Black Panthers. The FBI kept extensive files on his activities. Photograph courtesy of the Jerusalem Post *photographic collection.*

reading their present against their past that "made the show" for them. To strip them prematurely of their historic shadow was to miss the crucial point that their awareness of the past was still very much a factor in their lives, including their relationship to the city and its potentialities.

The past crept up on one for reasons that were not just related to its lingering shadows. The present had a way of redefining the relevance of the past, of forcing one to consider the similarities and the distinctions between "now" and "then." The decade that began in 1960 was to open one of the most troubled periods in America's history, and this was no less true of New York. The divisions in American society between poverty and affluence, racism and the movement for racial equality, war and peace, tore wide open in the sixties. The entire decade was punctuated by violence or the threat of violence: the fear of nuclear Armageddon, the sickeningly and frighteningly repetitive trauma of political assassination, a seemingly unending war in Southeast Asia, urban riots, and other dramatic, sometimes bloody, domestic confrontations. The fruits of the postwar era—peace and affluence—could hardly be enjoyed for long if they were not enjoyed by all Americans alike or if they failed to dispel some of the darkest nightmares of organized civil society. How could anyone who lived then feel that they stood "out of the shadow" of crisis, least of all in New York City, one of the country's most sensitive nerve centers?

For Jews and others in New York, the developing national debate over society's future was not theoretical. What was at stake was their way of life. Such issues bore particular resonance for the children or grandchildren of immigrant Jews who—as we have seen—had developed a vision of a dynamic, pluralistic, mass democracy in the first half of the century. The somewhat generalized threat to ideals of a modern mass polity involved them personally.

Within this overall vision, their sense of life in the city was linked with notions of the benefits of such a social order: steady generational upward progress, leading from immigrant tenements to opportunity and affluence.

Thus, when New York writer Norma Rosen, in a novella called *Green,* wished to evoke the personal shame of failure that might assail a Jewish family in a deteriorating upper Manhattan neighborhood, she had one character tell her sister: "You are back where Mama and Papa were when they came—in a slum. You fell down to the bottom of the ladder, Muriel, when you and Herbie weren't looking, it happened. And it's not fair to your children."[6]

Even more profoundly disturbing were those negative prognoses on the character of modern society that seemed to question the viability of mass democracy itself—the ideal that, again, was the bedrock political faith of first-generation urban Jews. The negative discourse on modern, urban, organized social systems that emerged in America in the fifties and sixties was not limited to New York, let alone to New York Jews. But it did touch their world in a dangerously intimate manner. When it drew upon images of totalitarian oppression, it quite readily evoked associations drawn from the trauma of the Holocaust.

The Dystopian Character of Mass Society

It was one of those "only in New York" things: In February 1960, Mayor Wagner honored the city's Sephardi (Hispanic Jewish) community by proclaiming 1960 "Solomon ibn Gabirol Year," marking the nine hundreth anniversary of the great medieval Spanish Jewish poet and philosopher.[7]

Nevertheless, the new decade opened rather inauspiciously for Jewish New Yorkers with a spate of swastika-daubings and vandalism against synagogues, including (for the very first time ever) Fifth Avenue's "cathedral" synagogue, Temple Emanu-El. It was even reported that students at Columbia University were noticed wearing swastika pins or armbands as a "fad." The frequency of such incidents had been rising throughout the previous year and thus seemed to imply a pattern. There was speculation (though subsequent investigation suggested otherwise) that one or more neo-Nazi groups were fomenting and coordinating hate crimes against Jews. Moreover, the outbreak was worrisomely consistent with a simultaneous wave of anti-Jewish incidents in other American cities as well as in Europe—London, Paris, Brussels, Stockholm, Oslo, Vienna, and Cologne, to cite only several of them.[8]

The situation prompted strong statements by the mayor and city council of New York, the police commissioner, and Governor Rockefeller. But the response to the outbreak in the city and around the country went beyond the routine. Not only did leading Protestant and Catholic clergy feel compelled to intervene, but so did President Eisenhower. In fact, the matter was the subject of a resolution adopted in March 1960 by the United Nations' Subcommission on Prevention of Discrimination and Protection of Minorities, meeting in New York in late January.[9]

Why were local incidents of vandalism (even if they were unaccountably widespread) treated as a national—even an international—issue? One might recall that 1960 was an important election year, for one thing, and that America as a society was becoming more sensitized to issues of bigotry, for another. Indeed, the increased awareness of social issues in general would play a significant role in the Democrats' political victory later that year and in the changes that took place in America in the years to come.

But there was more to it than election-year public relations. Although that particular wave of antisemitic incidents ebbed, allaying immediate fears of a resurgence of anti-Jewish currents in society at large, the outbreak was widely understood to be rooted in a far more endemic problem: the inadequacy of democratic values and communal norms in complex, modern social settings. In that sense, although the 1960 episode itself passed quickly from memory, it blended into a continuing discussion that had widespread ramifications for Jews as Americans and as urbanites.

We are dealing here with a climate of opinion that was deeply concerned with the ills of mass society as it had taken shape in metropolitan America by the end of the 1950s. America at the height of the cold war was supposed to stand for political values squarely at odds with antidemocratic impulses. Its people were meant to exemplify an independence of mind that would enable self-government to achieve beneficial goals. Thoughtful critics were convinced, however, that American society was deeply troubled, caught between a disaffected and defective citizenry, on the one hand, and an enormous governing apparatus, on the other, that wielded unprecedented power, but to less and less positive effect. "Man's problem of self-determination," Daniel Boorstin later recalled, "was more baffling than ever, for the very power of the most democratized nation on earth had led its citizens to feel inconsequential before the forces they had unleashed."[10]

It was in this context that sophisticated observers had come to understand the phenomenon of antisemitism as a problem inherently related to a wider malaise. Antisemitism was conceptualized as a hostile response to the uneven distribution of socioeconomic gains in society and, in addition, as the product of the moral anonymity of modern society itself. Insofar as it was a symptom, a pathological by-product of the formation of mass societies, antisemitism was not about the Jews at all, really. It was an irrational response mechanism—the social fallout, as it were, of vast human agglomerations in which the individual might literally "fall out" of the advancing line of social progress. This reasoning was reflected in the response by the American Jewish Committee to the swastika epidemic of 1960. John Slawson, executive vice-president of the group, ventured the opinion that "tensions in intergroup relations, particularly in our urban life," might afflict the new era of affluence.[11]

In the waning forties the Committee had sponsored a major study of anti-Jewish and anti-"Negro" bias among army veterans, the results of which were published as the book, *Dynamics of Prejudice.* It was now dusted off and republished under a new title, prefaced by several chapters reporting new data and updating the discussion. The study's authors, Morris Janowitz and Bruno Bettelheim, noted that "the trends of advanced industrialization are generally considered to imply social change in the direction of less prejudice because of . . . higher levels of education, growth of middle-income occupations and professions, and increased urbanization." Yet, they explained, "new societal pressures and disruptions" occur in advanced societies. Perhaps as many as 20 percent of the male population might still experience downward social and status mobility, giving rise to problems of prejudice.

It was in a mass society, they continued, that the individual lost a sense of autonomy, was more dependent on "external support," and was therefore easily led or misled. Thus, on the one hand, irrational hatred and the impulse toward violence were the response by society's marginal members to their marginality; on the other hand, the "masses" (by definition, not "marginal") could easily be manipulated in antidemocratic directions. Unless people living in large masses could master the art of autonomy, the future appeared bleak.[12]

(It is worth noting that Jewish authors and their sponsoring organizations were at this stage talking about the urban problem in terms of white middle-class disharmony and economic maladjustments. Inner-city black alienation and economic despair were not yet defined as the key issue of the urban crisis.)

The attempt to grapple with social anonymity, behavioral conformism, democratic values, and modern political morality was in fact something of an American preoccupation in the immediate postwar decades, and it seemed to draw the attention of an inordinate number of Jewish commentators—perhaps because they came from a culture that had a great deal invested in modern, large-scale, and ethnically diverse communities.

In a city like New York, whose social value had been formulated in terms of the human alchemy that only a giant metropolis might perform, the implications of social dysfunction, political disaffection, and the attendant threat against a workable democracy were of particular import. The incipient crisis of urban governability was the front line of America's struggle with the most fundamental issues of mass democracy, and Jews, the most urban of all Americans and the most closely identified with the nation's largest city, were directly in the line of fire.

An early expounder of these issues was Erich Fromm, whose seminal 1941 book, *Escape from Freedom,* would be republished in more than twenty editions over the course of two decades. Fromm argued that individuality and personality constituted the major psychosocial achievements of modernity—achievements that remained, however, elusive. "Freedom," he said, "though it has brought [modern man] independence and rationality, has made him isolated and, thereby, anxious and powerless."[13]

Fromm, a Jew who had come to New York as a refugee from Nazism, wrote the book as an attempt to account for the "flight from freedom" into totalitarianism, with particular reference to what he called the "psychology of Nazism." But Fromm warned his American readers against complacency: "There is no greater mistake and no graver danger than not to see that in our own society we are faced with the same phenomenon that is fertile soil for the rise of Fascism anywhere: the insignificance and powerlessness of the individual."[14] In essence, the argument was that personality and conscience were not merely character traits, but were also functions of the socioeconomic and political order.

Fromm's work was followed by those of other famous Jewish refugee intellectuals, such as *The Authoritarian Personality,* by Theodore Adorno and colleagues (1950), and *The Informed Heart: Autonomy in a Mass Age* by Bruno Bettelheim (1960), which continued to probe the nature of individual behavior in mass society.[15] Related to these works by refugee scholars were also such influential books by American social critics as David Riesman's *The Lonely Crowd* (1950), which examined American social character and the question of autonomy; William H. Whyte, Jr.'s *The Organization Man* (1956), which analyzed what he called the emerging "social ethic" of American "collectivism"; and C. Wright Mills's *The Power Elite* (1956), which focused critical attention on the immense new concentrations of power and authority.

Riesman, whose research team included Nathan Glazer, was also a friend of Erich Fromm's. *The Lonely Crowd,* which influenced an entire generation of social analysts,[16] contended that Americans—especially those who were younger or were involved in the newer professions—were becoming increasingly "other-directed," that is, dependent as never before on the approval and confirmation of their peers. The ascendant forms of social organization, culture, and socialization, he argued, were equipping Americans with the requisite "radar" to pick up the all-important cues of conformism. Not only was individuality thereby undermined, but people who were not "inner-directed" were rendered less capable of using their own moral compass. That this type of character was functional for a mass, corporate America, dependent on a highly mobile and interchangeable work force, was understood as the driving force behind these developments.

Thus, a considerable body of American social scientific, psychosocial, and political thought had crystallized around the idea that modern society generated particular dilemmas precisely because it was based on the manipulation and control of mass populations. Totalitarian systems—detestable forms of total social control in which the individual personality was entirely suppressed—were actually an extreme case along a continuum that began with less overtly malign phenomena. Mass politics, mass media, mass marketing, mass housing in "faceless" suburbs or mammoth high-rise urban projects, patterns of mass production and consumption were all related to social conformity, to mass consciousness, and also to protests (sometimes misdirected) against the impersonal power structure.

These phenomena were understood to be immediately relevant to postwar American society. Small wonder that one of the most widely revered figures in the fifties was a solitary adolescent Dutch Jewish girl who had perished in the Holocaust, but who had bequeathed to readers of her *Diary* a model of the individual's struggle for self.

Rereading the literature of the fifties and sixties on modern mass society and on racial and ethnic prejudice as presented by Jewish observers, one comes away with the clear impression that it was pervaded by an awareness of the Holocaust. Indeed, this must be considered a characteristic form of response to the Holocaust at that time. This form of response tended to focus on the Holocaust's universal implications for life in advanced, mass societies rather than on the identity of the Holocaust's victims.

Cultural historian Stephen Whitfield has noted that specific references to the Holocaust and its influence were relatively few, muted, or muffled among Jewish intellectuals in the fifties and sixties. But he also urges us to look more closely at what he terms "wayward and personal" reflections, such as this evocative passage from Norman Mailer's 1957 essay, "The White Negro," which recalled "the psychic havoc of the concentration camps and the atom bomb upon the unconscious mind of almost everyone alive in these years. . . . We have been forced to live with the suppressed knowledge that . . . we might still be doomed to die as a cipher in some vast statistical operation in which our teeth would be counted and our hair would be saved, but our death itself would be unknown, unhonored, and unremarked."[17]

This was no mere idiosyncratic perception. The link between the "psychic havoc" wrought by events of the recent past and the tendency to regard the unsettled present with foreboding is also present in the work of other New

York Jewish writers. By the end of the sixties, when he left New York to return to Chicago, Saul Bellow, for example, had created two characters, Herzog (1964) and Sammler (1969), to evoke the truncated, divided, threatening, and peculiarly anonymous quality of the new urban, American experience—an experience that no longer enticed one to venture far from the secure confines of one's inner world.

Indeed, hiding and surviving become explicitly linked: Herzog, the neurotic survivor of a destructive marriage, is subject to murderous impulses, scribbles random but profoundly disturbing insights about violence and the state of the world (firing these off in overwrought letters to friends and adversaries), and finds escape and respite deep in the countryside. Sammler is a survivor of the Holocaust living on Manhattan's Upper West Side whose inner world is his most compelling reality. His relations with family members, while intense, are also, somehow, detached, as is his relationship with the city around him. He has survived before by relying on himself, hiding in forests and cemeteries. And he has personally (and with great, yet disturbing, satisfaction) killed a German soldier. He is thus alive because of violence and alive past his time—a ghost—and that is the source of his detachment, which is his protection. "His life had nearly been taken. He had seen life taken. He had taken it himself. He knew it was one of the luxuries." He is "only an old Jew whom they had hacked at, shot at, but missed killing somehow."[18]

Yet Bellow tries to suggest that somehow Sammler's inner experience is not at all in conflict with the life afforded by a contemporary urban America.

An earlier Bellow character, Augie March, had proclaimed, "I am an American, Chicago-born"—a native-son assertion that depended to no small degree on the *Chicago* element. "I am an American, New York-born," would have lacked the same power of conviction. The second half of the statement would have *qualified* the first half, rather than supported it—New York never having been perceived by the rest of the nation as being definitively American. But in *Sammler* Bellow reclaimed the American label for New Yorkers, suggesting that America itself fully mirrored Sammler's (and New York's) frenetic disquiet:

> Inside [one's own world] was so roomy and took in so many people that if you were in the West Nineties, if you were in fact here, you *were* an American. And the charm, the ebullient glamour, the almost unbearable agitation that came from being able to describe oneself as a twentieth-century American was available to all. To everyone who had eyes to read the papers or watch the television, to everyone who shared the collective ecstasies of news, crisis, power.[19]

Both Herzog and Sammler are unmistakably marginal men, but their marginality no longer counts as a positive, assertive, chutzpah. Neither can be

Saul Bellow, noted author and Nobel laureate, who made his home in New York in the 1960s. His novel Mr. Sammler's Planet *incorporated notes he made while covering the 1967 Arab-Israeli War for New York's* Newsday. *Photograph courtesy of the* Jerusalem Post *photographic collection.*

described as possessing élan or creativity. What they possess, rather, is a moral barometer for judging the capacity for evil in all things and all people. That barometer works because, aware of their own capacity for violence *in extremis*, they are keenly sensitive to the social and cultural legitimation of violence. And they are scared out of their wits.

Obliquely similar considerations led Columbia University historian Richard Hofstadter to ponder the tangled and disturbing violent roots of American political culture. As a liberal historian, he was haunted by the evident recurrent pattern of extremism in American life. In 1969 (the year before his untimely death), he coedited and introduced a volume of documents dealing with violence in America from the seventeenth century to the 1960s. Hofstadter conjectured that the sixties would come, in retrospect, to take their place as one of those periodic spasms of violence that punctuate American history—"another peak period, rather more pronounced than many."[20]

"It requires no remarkable ingenuity," he had stated in his preface, "to see how some of the recent trends in American society, continued and magnified, could bring about the eclipse of liberal democratic politics." It was fitting, therefore, that Hofstadter—whom Alfred Kazin called "a secret conservative in a radical period . . . in some strange no-man's land between his Yiddish-speaking Polish father and his dead Lutheran mother"—should have been the one to plead at Columbia's 1968 commencement exercises (held off-campus that year because of the May student disorders) for "learning, civility, understanding."[21]

Cry the Beloved City

The discourse of threatening, destructive, atomizing processes was by no means universally adopted and it is perhaps no coincidence that New York Jews were among those who also raised a positive voice in defense of their way of life. Those who sought to alert postwar Americans to the counterutopian qualities of mass, urban concentrations confronted a forceful pro-urban polemic.

This point of view was perhaps best represented by New Yorker Jane Jacobs's now-classic book, *The Death and Life of American Cities.* Jacobs argued that misguided urban renewal programs were driving city life into further deterioration, but she insisted that the diversity, vitality, and essential civility of metropolitan cities could be saved.[22]

All the elements of Jacobs's point of view—antipathy to the prevailing schools of urban planning; preference for people-oriented values rather than abstract, aesthetic ideologies; opposition to the separation of work-space, pleasure-space, and living-space; and appreciation of the street's function as the prime locus of actual urban civilization—all this had already been anticipated in a remarkable little book by the two New York Jewish brothers, Percival and Paul Goodman: the one a prominent architect, the other a poet, novelist, playwright, social critic, and educator. Their book, *Communitas,* was first published in 1947 and reissued, in a revised edition, in 1960. The Goodmans' effort at rethinking the entire issue of urban living from the design *and* social points of view was what sociologist Herbert Gans called no less than an attempt to reintroduce "utopian thinking" to the subject.[23]

Other voices were also heard in praise of New York's form of civilization. Responding to the image of New York as a vast, dehumanized, unmappable realm, novelist Hortense Calischer, for example, remarked (in her book *The New Yorkers*): "Never think . . . that New York is a wilderness without connection; that is only the provincial view; even the sea gulls know better, and have their patrons, and their lanes."[24]

Making a similar argument, but from the sociological point of view, both Herbert Gans and Daniel Bell, both of whom were then at Columbia University, challenged the popular negative analysis of mass society and vigorously defended contemporary American urban life (even, for Gans, suburban life.) Not only was democracy alive and well, they asserted, but individual personality and autonomy were not lost.

Gans, while disagreeing with Jacobs's penchant for portraying New York's Greenwich Village as a model for viable neighborhood life, did agree that mass, heterogenous, high-density urban living was salvageable as a way of life and disagreed with those analysts (going back to Louis Wirth) who felt that pockets of intimacy and diversity were destined to be overwhelmed by the city's atomizing and uprooting effects on people.[25]

Bell, paraphrasing his opponents as he set about debunking their ideas, summarized: "In a world of lonely crowds seeking individual distinction, where values are constantly translated into economic calculabilities, where in extreme situations shame and conscience can no longer restrain the most dreadful excesses of terror, the theory of the mass society seems a forceful, realistic description of contemporary society."

As Bell read this formulation, however, it came down to an amalgam of stereotypical, elitist cultural attitudes, a diffuse sense of the "breakdown of values," and an array of propositions that had not actually been proven. He maintained, rather, that the social realities of urban life in America suggested an ongoing, healthy development of meaningful social existence, citing the vitality of voluntary social activity and intimate communication networks—labor union locals, neighborhood and community newspapers, and ethnic associations.[26]

Bell turned specifically to the subject of New York City in an essay, "The Three Faces of New York," published along with other articles on life in the city in the summer 1961 issue of *Dissent*. Bell laid out an analysis of major problems besetting the city as it began to alter its character. That analysis, however, was based on his own positive acknowledgment of New York City's unique urban heritage and it took a fairly upbeat (indeed, overly optimistic) view of the city's economic outlook. The newly emerging New York of the 1960s, Bell argued, was a city dominated by the influx of major corporate headquarters. The city had increased its office space by half again as much as it had possessed in 1947.

Bell was interested in capturing the essence of the synergy between the city's massive economic base and the special life of the city, while paying close attention to the role played by New York's Jews over the previous thirty-year period. He was too sophisticated not to point to the negative as well as the positive forces at work in bringing the city to the brink of uncertain change. His essay was by no means a dirge for a bygone era, but he did put his finger on what was about to be lost, and by whom, as history turned a corner.[27]

It was the Jewish entrepreneurial class, he claimed, that had spearheaded and that best personified the small-firm type of manufacturing that had made New York, originally a mercantile and shipping center, what it was in its second, post-nineteenth-century phase: the country's largest manufacturing city.

> In essence, New York is a bazaar in which speed, variety, and specialization are the hallmarks of the services it offers. . . . New York exists really because of its fantastic variety of *non-rationalized* enterprises and services, easy to break into because of low capital requirements, but in which survival de-

> pends upon ingenuity, "shmearing," cutting a corner, trimming a margin, finding some other way to make a fast buck in the swift race. This is what has given New York its particular beat and distinctive character.[28]

The growth of New York as a premier manufacturing city, a "bazaar" of small industries, coincided with the Jewish mass immigration. Its "archetypical novel" was Abraham Cahan's *The Rise of David Levinsky.* Its core epic was the progress of an entire class from "the sweatshops of the lower East Side to the lofts of Seventh Avenue." The pattern, not limited to the apparel industry alone, was repeated in the formidable "array of small-unit, single-plant firms" engaged in printing, plastics, electronics, and small-scale machine-work—enterprises that survived on a thin margin, maintaining little or no internal bureaucracy, and therefore also highly dependent on agents, banks, and other finance agencies. The dominant position of manufacturing and commercial financing, at one end, and the dependence of small manufacturers on a highly developed network of wholesalers and suppliers, at the other end, maintained this intensive economy at a dynamic pace.[29]

It was this economic underpinning, largely unseen by the casual eye, that fueled what Bell called the "visible portions" of the economic "iceberg": "the theaters, art galleries, museums, universities, publishing houses, restaurants, night clubs, *espresso* cafes, smart stores—all the activities that give the city its particularly glittering place as the metropolis of America."

The pervasiveness of the small-enterprise manufacturing model in New York, and commercial network that it supported, had produced "an extraordinary large middle class . . . probably the largest middle-class aggregate in any urban center of this country." This middle class, so heavily Jewish,[30] appeared to Bell to be quite "unlike the traditional, small-town, Protestant middle class." It was:

> sharp, shrewd, and like as not, cynical. And yet, because so many of these businessmen were Jewish, it was a middle class that hungered for culture and self-improvement. The chief contribution of the Jews to the City of New York . . . has been in their role as "consumers of culture." The large symphony orchestras, the theaters, trade-book publishing, the avant-garde magazines, the market for drawings and paintings—all have, as their principal audience and consumer, the Jewish middle class. And this was made possible largely by the entrepreneurial wealth of small-unit firms.[31]

Bell credited Nathan Glazer for this insight. But although Glazer recognized that the Jews' most important contribution to New York's cultural life was in their role as consumers of culture—"[N]either tourists, the working-class masses, nor the small Protestant elite could have filled or could fill today the audiences for chamber and contemporary music, modern dancing, and poetry reading"—he did not go so far as to make a *causal* or inherent connection between Jews and New York culture. As he put it, great cities are inevitably the places where new things are tried and cultural products marketed to mass audiences. And New York had been a cultural center even in the nineteenth century, before the arrival of the mass Jewish immigration. "Even if all the Jews had gone to Argentina or Canada, New York would still be New York, and Buenos Aires and Montreal would still only be pretty much what they are." [32] (This is a point of view with which I concur, and to which I will return in the concluding chapter.)

Bell read with some apprehension the signs that small-scale manufacturing was declining, as new, mass-production industries went far afield outside the city—indeed, outside the region—to find lower labor and transportation costs, and the corporate city replaced the entrepreneurial middle class with a new, white-collar "salariat." [33] What he did not say explicitly, but what was clearly implied by his analysis, was that the "Jewishness" of New York was also slated for obsolescence.

Yet, years later, positive assessments of life in the city continued to be expressed. For historian Deborah Dash Moore, who grew up in Manhattan's Chelsea district in the 1950s and 1960s, the texture of her memory of that place and time finds expression in such adjectives as "diverse, street-smart, and idealistic. . . , integrated, energetic, visionary, and filled with boundless promise." [34] Jazz critic Dan Morgenstern felt that "New York is like a living organism that constantly regenerates and reconstitutes itself." [35]

Using a similar metaphor, journalist Jim Sleeper noted that New York could be imagined as "a great human heart which draws into itself . . . immigrant bloodstreams and, after working its strange alchemy, pumps them back out again across America . . . bearing athletes, impresarios, engineers. The city has done this uncomplainingly for so much of the country for so long that one in eight Americans can trace family ties to Brooklyn alone." [36]

And Alfred Kazin, as ever a devotee of the city, also used the language of organic order, even finding it possible to graft a positive urban mystique onto a "machine"-image that normally evoked impersonal, technological modernity: "New York was the greatest living machine," he wrote, reminiscing about the view from the roof garden of the then-new Museum of Modern Art in 1947, "the great avenues [going] up and down in ruler-sharp order." [37]

But there were cross-currents and contradictions, as befits the inner conversation of close observers of any great city. Kazin himself, for example, could find the seamier undersides of New York life unbearably oppressive: The Upper West Side, he wrote, had always seemed to him "shadowed, overcrowded":

> [T]oo many colossal apartment houses into which the sun did not shine, too great a show of garbage pails in front of every door. . . . The West Side as a whole was ethnic territory, foreign, "Jew land," the cheaper side of town, and the last stand of all exiles, refugees, proscribed and displaced persons. . . . Nothing would release me from the burden of so much common experience; so many old European habits, hungers, complaints; so much Jewishness, blackness, clownishness, vulgarity, old age, amazement, ugliness, anxiety. . . . Nowhere else in New York could one see on the street, on the subway platform, in the rush hour, such public suffering.[38]

Irving Howe, writing in 1961, maintained that such ambivalence was nothing new, but actually a legacy of the past. In his retrospective memoir of New York in the thirties, he spoke of extreme political and social alienation as well as of the closest sort of filial intimacy. In the Jewish, Depression-era slums of the East Bronx, he wrote, "New York did not really exist for us as a city, a defined place we felt to be our own":

> Too many barriers intervened, too many kinds of anxiety. In the thirties New York was not merely the vital metropolis, brimming with politics and contention, . . .it was also brutal, ugly, frightening. . . , the embodiment of that alien world which every boy raised in a Jewish immigrant home had been taught, whether he realized it or not, to look upon with suspicion. It was "their" city. . . .
>
> [Yet] if someone had asked me in 1939 what I thought of New York, I would have been puzzled. . . . It was quite as if I had been asked what I thought about my family. . . . I no more imagined that I would ever live—or be able to live—anywhere but in New York than I could find myself a more fashionable set of parents. . . . The provinciality of New York in the thirties, which tended to regard a temporary meeting of ethnic cultures and social crises as if it were an unalterable fact of history, led us to suppose that only here, in New York, could one bear to live at all.[39]

No doubt, some of these ambiguities and inner contradictions can be traced to the built-in duality of life in the city, given the differences between Manhattan and the outer boroughs. One observer, for example, was able to contrast the neighborly involvement with people that he recalled from his youth in Coney Island, Brooklyn—"like a small town in a big city"—with the "twenty-story mausoleum" he currently lived in on Manhattan's Upper West Side. "It's pretty, but there are no stoops and, maybe, I know the names of five neighbors."[40] Yet, at the same time, the atrophy of the outer boroughs (certainly true for large parts of the Bronx and Brooklyn) meant that whatever economic and social vitality remained in the city was concentrated in Manhattan.

Similar issues were addressed by writer Leonard Kriegel, who revisited the Bronx neighborhood of his youth (as it happens, also my own neighborhood), and offered a similarly conflicted memoir. Although Kriegel found abundant signs of new life, the old neighborhood had certainly seen better days, and he confirmed that essentially the Bronx as a whole had remained a backwater, "the borough of the Great Denial": "The man or woman who lives in Manhattan is *the* New Yorker personified, one whose soul beds down in dreams with the souls of ancient Thebans and Cairenes, urban standard-bearers to the world. . . . But the Bronx shames even memory. . . . [A]t best, . . .a place to come from."[41]

Memory seemed composed of such bittersweet evocations where a past that "mattered" was contrasted with what can only be described as urban trauma. Writer Marshall Berman (who, in the eighties, coined the term "urbicide" to describe the devastation of New York's worst neighborhoods), looked back at the collective portrait of the city painted in 1961, in a memorable issue of *Dissent*:

> The experience of looking back to New York in the summer of 1961 is a little like Philip Larkin's poem about pictures of England in August 1914. The poet's refrain: "Never such innocence again." Those of us who lived through the 1960s and 1970s in New York often felt like soldiers in that Great War: under fire for years, assaulted from more directions than we could keep track of, pinned down in positions from which we couldn't seem to move. These were years when violence, and violent death, became everyday facets of city life. . . . [A]ll the tensions that have been seething throughout American society—tensions between races, classes, sexes, generations—have boiled over instantly on the sidewalks of New York.[42]

New York, Berman allowed, was still a "thrilling and beloved place," with a street life that made for positive as well as destructive experiences. But the power exerted by images of the past made it difficult for him or his peers to formulate what he called "a new social contract."[43] By the end of the sixties, it was very difficult to believe in urban utopias except as a relic of memory.

When Moses Rischin penned a new epilogue to his book, *The Promised City*, for its 1970 edition, he observed that "by the middle of the twentieth century . . . the Jews of the great migration had become welded to the great metropolis in their lives and in their descendants. . . . To the extent that this American baptismal still operates in their lives, they retain a vivid sense of the promise of a democratic community in a metropolis where few observers are inclined to be sanguine about such possibilities."[44]

Clearly the recasting of mass society as a dystopia constituted a breach in the earlier understanding—still upheld by a great many Jews—that the big city was the modern answer to the needs of society; that it was "home" in a particularly congenial and fulfilling sense; and that it was the great altar of modern, universal culture.

What further complicated the issue for some Jewish observers, and what endowed it in their eyes with a particularly Jewish cast, was the powerful association they made between the underlying questions of city life—diversity, anonymity, autonomy, governability, violence—and the ominous lessons drawn from the recent European past, where modern social ideals and regimes of mass democracy were first corrupted and then turned into agents of mass murder. Although much attention in this regard was directed toward the Soviet case in the fifties, in the sixties an increasing amount of attention was paid to the case of Nazi Germany. The contemporary urban experience and the shadow of the past were subtly interwoven in ways that affected both the image of the past and the reading of the present.

The Eichmann Case

Confusion between good and evil, the justification of violent means by their ostensibly positive ends, and the redefinition of individual responsibility in terms of collective moral accountability, were the essential dilemmas that would haunt the American sixties. They were the issues that underlay the polarized response to the United States's military involvement in Southeast Asia, just as they also informed the debate over racial equality, the prerogatives and limits of political protest and civil disobedience, and the legitimacy of a counterculture of personal freedom that challenged previous social norms.

As we shall see, these were precisely the issues that would come to the fore in the debate over the trial of Adolf Eichmann, which therefore constituted an important link between shadowed past and troubled present. The Eichmann debate in some ways seemed to radiate from Jewish New York, even though it in fact spanned countries and continents. It unfolded in the months and years following the 1961 trial of the infamous German war criminal in Jerusalem and focused mainly on Hannah Arendt's controversial reportage of the case. What makes the affair relevant to our particular discussion are a number of seemingly ancillary issues.

First, in her work both before and after the Eichmann affair, Arendt, one of New York's refugee luminaries, built upon and helped to further entrench the view that the issues related to the rise of totalitarian regimes were inseparable from the more general problems of modern mass society and bureaucratic government. She made it clear that she did not see the Eichmann trial as a "case closed."

Second, the extended discussion around the Eichmann trial brought the recent past into greater proximity to the present. Wounds that had barely begun to heal were once more exposed. In the sudden glare of public scrutiny, the contours of the Jewish community—as elusive a concept as that might be—were illuminated. Its public life was revealed to be a deeply contested arena. The intensity of that contest derived precisely from a passionate, shared engagement with the issues raised by Arendt.

Third, the controversy broached issues of personal political responsibility in terms that explicitly highlighted the Jewish role in large political systems and in the postwar world.

Originally published as a series of five articles in the *New Yorker* in February and March of 1962, Arendt's book, *Eichmann in Jerusalem: A Report on the Banality of Evil,* was much more than a trial report: It was a sharply polemical critique of the prosecution, the defense, the general atmosphere surrounding the trial, and certain issues that the judgment failed to clear up.

The prosecution's case, Arendt complained, was "built on what the Jews had suffered, not on what Eichmann had done"—to her, the key issue. Eichmann was convicted on four counts of "crimes against the Jewish people" as well as eight other criminal counts ("crimes against humanity"). Arendt would have preferred Eichmann to have been tried, not for "crimes against the Jewish people," but for "crimes against mankind committed on the body of the Jewish people."[45]

Arendt made this seemingly subtle distinction into a major point because she believed that the international political system had not yet come to grips with the outrage of state-sponsored genocide (something that is still true at the end of the 1990s). The comity of nations had simply failed to make it an ultimate crime against world civilization and had not taken the political steps necessary to prevent its recurrence. By portraying the Nazi genocide as a crime "merely" against one small group of humans, the Israeli court missed an opportunity to internationalize the implications of the case.[46]

Her fears and criticisms derived quite explicitly from her conviction that similar crimes might be committed again. As she put it, "[T]he frightening coincidence of the modern population explosion with the discovery of technical devices that, through automation, will make large sections of the population 'superfluous' even in terms of labor, and that through nuclear energy make it possible to deal with this twofold threat by use of instruments beside which Hitler's gassing installations look like an evil child's fumbling toys, should be enough to make us tremble."[47]

Although Arendt stirred intense debate, it was not primarily because of this last perception: namely, that modern, technological societies, under the control of depersonalized, powerful regimes, were a source of great potential danger to humanity. Dark visions of this nature were, as we have seen, common coin. Arendt merely added her voice to the chorus.

She evoked sharp criticism in part because she had bracketed Eichmann, a figure who stood in the popular mind for radical evil, together with the perception that "the essence of totalitarian government, and perhaps the nature of every bureaucracy, is to make functionaries and mere cogs . . . out of men, and thus to dehumanize them." Those who failed to read Arendt meticulously enough inferred (erroneously) that she held the "system" responsible rather than the individual.

But even this argument was not entirely new, given the climate of ideas at the time. Indeed, as we have seen, the degraded character of humanity under systems of regimentation had already been discussed for some twenty years. A year before the Eichmann trial, for example, Daniel Bell had described the Holocaust as "the bureaucratized murder of millions in concentration camps and death chambers." More to the point, Raul Hilberg, upon whose massive work *The Destruction of the European Jews* (1961) Arendt leaned so heavily, had made the bureaucratic nature of Germany's assault against the Jews the armature of his whole thesis, yet he found that this evoked no comment or protest. Saul Bellow, in *Sammler*, would later echo the refrain: "Man is a killer. Man has a moral nature. The anomaly can be resolved by . . . delusions of consciousness . . . maintained by organization, in states of mad perdition clinging to forms of business administration. Making it 'government work.' "[48]

The more controversial aspects of Arendt's book were those that entered, rather, into other particulars of the Eichmann trial and of the history of the Holocaust *per se*. Arendt, who was quite in agreement with both the verdict reached and with the death sentence that was imposed, went to some lengths to criticize the actual handling of the trial. This in itself aroused the ire of a great many people in Israeli and American Jewish life who took strong exception to her acerbic, judgmental style and her way of riding roughshod over significant historical and legal details. There ensued one of the great polemics in the postwar world of Jewish letters, much of it fought out in the pages of New York-based journals.

Even more than her legal-political critique of the trial, however, Arendt's treatment of Jewish victimhood in the Holocaust aroused the sharpest response. From our point of view, it is this aspect that merits a closer look because it will help to refine issues directly related to our consideration of New York Jewish life in the years that followed.

It may be added that the heat generated by the Arendt controversy, extending far beyond the survivor community and its own immediate periphery, testified to the fact that the Holocaust was never as far from the surface of public Jewish consciousness as has sometimes been alleged.[49] Once again, the notion that Jews had shed their historic shadow must be rejected.

The Controversy over Hannah Arendt's *Eichmann in Jerusalem*

In depicting the "Final Solution" as a crime against humanity (and racial antisemitism generally as an aspect of a wider moral and political collapse of European society), Hannah Arendt was actually in agreement with certain cosmopolitan Jewish values that, as we have seen, informed much of the discourse of the fifties. The Holocaust, in that sense, was a tragedy that indeed befell the Jews, but it was not their "own" story, not *their* defining experience in the possessive sense.

But Arendt, whose own connections to Jewish life were no longer as close as they once had been (see chapter 3), trespassed against what historian Richard Cohen has called the "code" of the community.[50] A basic idea the community code upheld was that Jews, though they were involved as individuals in the warp and woof of society, were neither politically defined as a group nor politically accountable. This was routinely asserted by cosmopolitans who denied the existence of a "Jewish vote" as well as by others (including "parochial" Zionists and Jewish liberals) who, for various reasons, preferred that ethnic Jewish interests be subsumed under the rubric of bipartisan good citizenship. It also undergirded the increasingly frequent assertions that Jews were "no longer an imperiled minority, but part of the American Establishment."[51] And, finally it was also part of the professional rhetoric on the problem of antisemitism which, as we have seen, tended to see Jew-hatred as a symptom and generally did not discuss it in terms that might require a collective Jewish response, independent of the state or of society at large.

Arendt, however, argued that Jews in Europe in the century prior to Nazism had been politically myopic and that they were as accountable as any other members of society for their own action or inaction. This was a thesis that she had developed earlier in her seminal work, *The Origins of Totalitarianism* (1951), the first part of which was devoted to an exposition of modern European antisemitism up to the late 1890s. In tying antisemitism integrally to the next two stages in her historical analysis—"imperialism" and "totalitarianism"—she sought to demonstrate the inherent (rather than the merely in-

Hannah Arendt, iconoclast on the New York intellectual scene. Her controversial book, Eichmann in Jerusalem, *became a focal point of heated controversy in the Jewish community. It would take thirty-eight years for a translated Hebrew edition to appear under an Israeli publisher's imprint. Courtesy of the* Jerusalem Post *photographic collection.*

strumental) function that Jew-hatred had played in the development of German National Socialism. "It is no mere accident," she had written in 1946, "that the catastrophic defeats of the peoples of Europe began with the catastrophe of the Jewish people."[52]

By hitching racial and political antisemitism to the forces unleashed by the rise and subsequent demise of the European nation-state, Arendt defined it not as an outgrowth of earlier religious hatreds, but as a modern political phenomenon. It was in this modern period that Jews had played a far more integrated and consequential economic and civic role than in previous historical periods. She thus stood the cosmopolitan argument on its head: Precisely because Jews were *participants* in the unfolding history of modern capitalism, modern culture, and modern politics, they were integrally part of the society that molded the patterns of their time and thus shared historical responsibility, despite the fact that they became victims. Jews did not have the luxury of standing outside their fate, as it were.

It was not, of course, that Jews could be held directly responsible for Nazism; rather, Arendt suggested that Jews were targeted by the Nazi assault for reasons that were "logical." She understood Nazism as a revolt against a society and a state-system that Jews had helped to build, that Jews had clearly and (she thought) blindly identified with, and that Jews had sought to maintain—even while remaining aloof from political life and from the "masses" of gentile society. Some Jews had amassed economic power, but had not been able (or not been ready, as Arendt would have it), to match wealth with political wisdom and political power. Civic responsibility implied that minorities, too, had choices and were social actors—subjects, not merely objects.

In *The Origins of Totalitarianism,* Arendt had impugned the notion that victims were, by definition, "excused" from being part of the political loop. They, too, were accountable. But she wielded the doctrine of personal accountability to much greater effect in *Eichmann in Jerusalem.* There the thesis of personal civic responsibility was turned mainly against Eichmann to support her analysis of Eichmann's real and personal guilt. It constituted the moral foundation of her refusal to entertain any version of the "hapless cog in the machinery" argument as a mitigation of Eichmann's personal culpability.[53]

Arendt's analysis held unstated implications, as well, for Jews who were not mere bystanders in their social surroundings, but essential participants—as, of course, Jews were in contemporary metropolitan America. Arendt drew no operative conclusions with reference to American Jews. She herself was not politically active and gave no sign that such action was even on her agenda.[54] But in the American discourse of the sixties, political passivity and activism became key issues. Jews, among others, were involved in this discourse and Jews, perhaps *more* than others, now possessed a historical reference point for their own relationship to the question.

It was possible, of course, for Jews to use the rhetoric of civic responsibility in mass society without reference to Germany and Eichmann. Sociologist Nathan Glazer, in a talk he gave in June 1961 on "City Problems and Jewish Responsibilities," used an argument that was in some ways similar to Arendt's. Noting that Jews were "troubled by some relatively minor irritants, but they have no major issue as a group" compared to other urban constituencies (Catholics and blacks), and contending that Jews and white Protestants shared both political contentment and economic advantage, he went on to argue: "[T]hey are, by the same token, left with a great measure of responsibility for dealing with those situations that upset and disrupt the society."[55]

Glazer's talk was, of course, pre-*Eichmann,* and it is moot to speculate on whether he would have thought of the connection with Arendt's civic ideology had he made the same speech several years afterward. At the very least, one can say that Glazer's "agreement" in principle with the notion of political responsibility helps us to place Arendt herself within an existing school of contemporary thought. But further applications of these ideas were also not long in finding expression.

Arendt's biographer, Elisabeth Young-Bruehl, noted that Arendt's work on Eichmann assumed "immediate political relevance" within two years of its publication. Even though Arendt herself was haunted more by John F. Kennedy's assassination, which, for her, echoed with ominous memories of Weimar Germany, many of her readers connected her message with other burning issues of the day.

Thus, "After . . . [President] Johnson had ordered American bombers to

Vietnam, antiwar activists of the New Left were looking to *Eichmann in Jerusalem* for support of their claim that a new form of fascism had taken hold in America."[56] Or, to put it as one young Jewish leftist did, in the wake of a vociferous open forum held to discuss Arendt's *Eichmann* book:[57] Hannah Arendt's view of political responsibility was "necessary in every modern state to prevent the reemergence of the totalitarian movement which ravaged Germany."[58]

Todd Gitlin, in his memoir of the period, affirmed that "We learned when we were children that massacres really happen and the private life is not enough; . . . [T]he Holocaust meant that nothing . . . could ever supplant the need for a public morality."[59]

And historian Henry Feingold would later comment that, upon consideration of the fears and energies that drove the protest movements of the sixties,

> one realizes that the protest against corporate processing, alienation, dehumanization, depersonalization and the dozens of additional catch words devised to describe the torment of our time, is summed up in the world of Auschwitz. . . . So runs the radical critique, and there is just enough truth in it to make it particularly attractive to Jewish youth. In their hands the meaning of the Holocaust naturally transcends its Jewish confines.[60]

Thus far, Arendt's political critique found a number of adherents. But as she developed her critical reading of Jewish behavior under the Nazi regime further, leading her to discuss the highly sensitive issue of compliance and collaboration with the Nazi regime on the part of Jewish ghetto councils, she clashed directly with much of the Jewish community, especially among those who had the closest personal connections with the slaughtered Jews of Europe.

It was not only survivors who took Arendt's report as a frontal assault, however. With few exceptions, Jewish commentators felt she had trespassed flagrantly and unforgivably: first by exposing sensitive family matters raised at the Eichmann trial to a wider, unknowledgeable audience, including non-Jews and antisemites; second by presuming to distinguish between "good" and "bad" Jewish martyrs; and third, by appearing to muddy the issue of exclusive German culpability.[61]

Even those inclined to be sympathetic to Arendt have pointed out that the tone of the book as well as its factual inaccuracies did Arendt a disservice. Young-Bruehl, for example, owned that "Arendt's book did lend itself to misinterpretation . . . its conclusions were shocking, it contained numerous small errors of fact, it was often ironic in style and imperious in tone, and some of its most controversial passages were peculiarly insensitive." Arendt's friend, political scientist Hans Morgenthau, later recalled: "In fact I told her time and again, 'You have raised monumental questions and have disposed of them in subordinate phrases. It just doesn't work. It's not that simple.' "[62]

So outrageous did Arendt's polemic appear that it hit Jewish New York like no other cultural controversy ever had before—or has since, for that matter. Irving Howe has referred to it as a "civil war" (though a heavily lopsided one). "Arendt's book provoked divisions that would never be entirely healed."[63]

"The Jewish community is up in arms," Morgenthau wrote, describing the bedlam at a meeting on the City College campus. "After ten minutes everybody was screaming, calling each other liar and threatening libel suits. It was a kind of collective psychoanalysis."[64]

Gideon Hausner, Eichmann's prosecutor, was flown in to New York to address a crowd of some thousand people in what was fast becoming a modern excommunication. Hausner pilloried Arendt for depicting Holocaust victims as passive: in his words, she had charged the victims with "cowardice and lack of will to resist." Popular writer Barbara Tuchman (in a subsequent review of Hausner's book on the trial, *Justice in Jerusalem*), apparently took seriously the notion that Arendt had been motivated by "a conscious desire to support Eichmann's defense." And Lionel Abel averred that Arendt's Eichmann "comes off much better . . . than do his victims."[65]

Even more than a decade after the Arendt controversy, German-born refugee immigrant Dan Morgenstern (a jazz historian and critic) would tell an interviewer, "I'm still very conscious of the whole horror [of the Holocaust]. It doesn't take much to set me off. Reading about the trial of a war criminal or hearing Hannah Arendt's name mentioned is provocation enough."[66]

◆ ◆ ◆

The Arendt controversy may be said to have represented the culmination of an entire phase in the postwar consideration of the Holocaust in America—that phase that, as we have seen, focused on those aspects of antisemitism and the Holocaust that could be universalized.

Arendt was interested in these themes because, as she saw it, the dismantling of civic virtue and individual political-moral responsibility in an age of mass politics and mass society threatened the very future of humankind. So far had she been from granting that Jews had some right to claim the Holocaust as their own narrative of victimhood and grief, that she went out of her way to eliminate from her writing any sensitivity to such a claim.

But in the years that followed, the universalized view of the Holocaust would give way to a particularized and personalized one, much more focused on the victim and on the survivor as innocent targets and as figures permitted to express collective rage. This would become true of Jews as Holocaust victim-survivors, as it would be true of other groups who would use the Jews' vocabulary in pursuit of their own claims as victims. In the prevailing political and social climate of the sixties, the entire concept of victimhood would be turned into a springboard for political action and hence, political legitimation.

New York Jewry in the early sixties was just beginning to relate in a different way to the "shadow" of its history. When Nathan Glazer had first written his popular survey, *American Judaism,* in 1957, he had ventured the opinion that "the murder of six million Jews by Hitler [has] had remarkably slight effects on the inner life of American Jewry." By the time, six years later, that he and Daniel Patrick Moynihan published their work on ethnicity in New York, *Beyond the Melting Pot,* Glazer called attention to the "events of the Nazi era" as a binding factor, performing an important cultural function for Jews of "widely disparate situations and beliefs."[67]

Jews would become increasingly prone in the sixties to believe that the catastrophic past could be understood as paradigmatic, rather than as a definitively closed episode, and that Jewish victimhood was not merely an artifact from the past or a warning signal for the entire human race. This notion came to undergird common Jewish opinions regarding the perils facing both Soviet Jews and the State of Israel in the latter part of the decade.

Acceptance of the posture of victimhood, with its attendant notion of constant endangerment, would also be extended to issues closer to home, bearing on the physical and even the spiritual security of American Jews—even in New York, their most secure urban domain.

"The Holocaust did not bring me a new theology but a new anthropology. I became a great pessimist," recalled Jewish historian Gerson D. Cohen. "I developed a terrible fear of the demons let loose. . . . [W]hen some of the riots occurred in New York City [in 1964—E.L.]—that burned out the retail businesses on 125th Street—I was deeply troubled by them and by the series of uprisings in cities throughout the United States where the Jewish retailers were literally driven away." The Jew-baiting that accompanied the 1968 teachers' strike in New York City (see chapter 6) propelled Cohen on a national speaking tour, lecturing on "The Sociology of Pogroms."[68]

Getting back to Glazer: Though he recognized the salient factor of Holocaust memory in the mental makeup of New York Jewry by the mid-sixties, he also pointed out that the Jewish community was not primarily "created or maintained" by that memory: "[T]hat would be too narrow a view of Jewish history and would ignore the group-making characteristics of American civilization." Rather, he argued, "the historical drama shaped a community intensely conscious of its Jewishness."[69]

While it is true that the stigmata of the recent past neither created nor maintained that community, we shall have to ask in the following chapters whether those other elements that had maintained the community were still as effective as they once had been. Was the community still generating a vital cultural, religious, and political life? Was it secure in its urban setting and confident of its future there? Or were negative associations—a blend of past shadows and counterutopian premonitions—taking their toll?

3

A Culture of Retrieval

> The more "Jewish" we became, the more we were open to the new horror: *the past did not exist unless you had lived it yourself.* There was no historical memory if you chose not to have one. The buoyant, the storm-laden, the tumultuously revolutionary sixties filled up the present. The pleasure principle mocked the "atavistic" Jewish demand for a sign from one's fellow men. [emphasis in the original]
>
> —Alfred Kazin,
> *New York Jew*

> Tomorrow is the anniversary of the death of my father and I am seeking a new law that prescribes for me what vows to make and no longer to make, what words to say and no longer say. . . . All things considered, I think that tomorrow I shall go to the synagogue after all. I will light the candles, I will say *Kaddish,* and it will be for me a further proof of my impotence.
>
> —Elie Wiesel,
> *Legends of Our Time*

Glazer's assessment of a strong Jewish consciousness was apt, though it was deliberately vague. The Jews of New York were, as he said, heterogeneous, displaying "widely disparate situations and beliefs"; and they were, indeed, paradoxically, "intensely conscious" of what they shared in common: their "Jewishness."

Consciousness, however, is not a verb: that is, it does not describe or prescribe an action. It refers to a state of mind, which cannot easily be defined, much less perpetuated, without its reification in social or cultural media. And Jewish-*ness* is a term that again refers to some quality of being, some form of mentality and awareness. But what did the possession of such a quality translate into, in terms of an active culture? That is the question to be addressed in this chapter.

The elusive, inchoate quality of "Jewishness" in New York is referred to by numerous other observers, who speak of the possibilities of being Jewish by osmosis in the city, but never quite define what underlay that impression. Hans Morgenthau (the political scientist), trying to pin it down, reflected that in general terms "[T]here is so much that is specifically Jewish here. You expect to run into Jews continuously: you always expect to be touched by the emanations of Jewish life. How else could it be in a city one of whose main ethnic characteristics is Jewishness?" Clearly, he was at a loss to define the "emanations" other than to cite their frequency.[1]

Journalist Midge Decter, originally from St. Paul, who had come to New York as a college student and settled in thereafter, working at such publications as *Harper's, Midstream,* and *Commentary,* was able to make the following comparison: "If I had been living in St. Paul with [my children], I would certainly have sent them to a Talmud Torah (Hebrew school). I would have had no choice. [But] living in New York meant living in a Jewish culture anyway." Her children had grown up believing that "everyone was Jewish. . . , that they were members of the majority culture."[2]

Of course, the counterpart of this taken-for-granted Jewishness was the ability to remain rather detached from it, while affirming it at some level, nonetheless. Marion Sanders, writer and editor at *Harper's,* noted that she had not been actively involved in Jewish affairs (after a brief period in the thirties). Despite the palpable ethnic presence of so many fellow Jews, "it is possible to be completely caught up in other currents of metropolitan life. . . . There is no all-inclusive 'Jewish community'—as there is in Cleveland, Baltimore, Cincinnati, or Detroit—which keeps in constant touch with its members."[3]

And author Grace Paley, whose life reflected the variegated culture of Greenwich Village, admitted that her children "did not get much Yiddishkeit (Yiddish culture). I feel bad about that, I didn't do what my parents did. But they understand that anti-Semitism means them"—which calls to mind a type of Jewishness that literary critic and scholar Robert Alter once described as "the shadow of a vestige of a specter."[4] And it calls to mind Emily Budick's perception that this Jewishness was "racial" insofar as it could be ignored, but was somehow not susceptible to change.

The "Jewish" personality of New York turns up even in the comments of visitors from abroad. "New York is a Jewish city," was the blatant way a writer for the British journal *New Society* chose to put it in 1966. "For an Englishman, New York is a strange and familiar place, and its Jewishness has a good deal to do with this. It is loud and bright and un-Anglo-Saxon (compare it with Boston, for example), it is the wrong part of home . . . Golders Green or the Whitechapel Road when you expected . . . Regent Street."[5]

If we recall *Fortune*'s reflections on the Jewishness of New York—"its excitement, its stridency, its unexpectedness"—we begin to see that certain conventions or clichés were observed when reaching for "Jewish" adjectives. (Were Chinatown or Harlem, one wonders, havens of comparative tranquility and monotony?)

The British visitor went on to cite those other easy-to-pick-out ethnic influences: foods and common slang expressions and cadences of speech. Nevertheless, he was perceptive enough to inquire whether Jewishness was really "nothing more than the consciousness of being a Jew?" The self-questioning by Jews themselves about the nature of their own identity was a "painful, moving scene—as if you had asked an Elizabethan playwright to define his debt to his culture, and he could only stutter. . . . Most of the people who have talked or written about Jewishness in America have either told the story of their lives or fallen into that . . . craving for generality . . . : Jews are socialists, Jews love their family, and the rest."[6]

In the same vein, the writer noted that although Leslie Fiedler, the critic, had described poet Allen Ginsberg as "Jewish in his deepest memories," the point appeared to be "as interesting as the fact that Dante was an Italian."[7]

Whether one identified with some vague Jewishness-at-large or participated more actively in the production or consumption of Jewish culture, New York seemed to make this possible.

The theater was one of the important places where Jewishness and Jewish-related topics were literally on display in New York—and thus available to both passive and active consumers, the involved and the detached alike. The first half of the 1960s was a conspicuously prolific period for both serious theater as well as light musicals that were engaged with Jews and their concerns. Such productions included included Paddy Chayefsky's *The Tenth Man* (1959–60)—a suburban, happy-end version of *The Dybbuk,* the dark Yiddish classic by S. Ansky about star-crossed lovers, mystic secrets, and possession; *Milk and Honey* (1961), starring Molly Picon, veteran comic performer of Yiddish stage and film; Harold Rome's *I Can Get It for You Wholesale* (1962), with Elliot Gould and Barbra Streisand; *Fidder on the Roof* (1964), the long-running, smash, hit musical based on Sholem Aleichem's Tevye stories, starring Zero Mostel in the original cast; Rolf Hochhuth's controversial play, *The Deputy,* about Pope Pius XII's sin of silence (1964), a shortened English version of which opened in New York the year after Hannah Arendt's *Eichmann* was published;[8] and two plays by Arthur Miller, both in 1964, *After the Fall* and *Incident at Vichy* (the former dealing only in passing with a Holocaust theme, the latter in a more sustained manner). Films such as *Exodus* (1960), *Judgment at Nuremberg* (1961), and the Czech production, *The Shop on Main Street* (1965), helped to complete the cultural *mise-en-scène.*

Of them all, *Fiddler* was undoubtedly the cultural artifact that resonated longest and most intimately with Jewish popular culture. Made subsequently into a movie as well, it became a virtual icon of Jewish culture in America. The song "Sunrise, Sunset" became the unofficial anthem of many bar/bat-mitzvah celebrations and American Jewish weddings. *Fiddler* was for Jewish culture in the United States what *Gone with the Wind* was for American culture at large. In its depiction of the shtetl as the home of a lost cultural integrity ("Tradition, Tradition"), the scene of historical dangers thankfully escaped, and the focus of sentimental longings ("I belong in Anatevka"), the play managed to evoke the themes that spoke most directly to a Jewish romance with the past.

As a "show," a vehicle for commercial entertainment, *Fiddler* should not, on the one hand, be made to bear an overload of retrospective social analysis. On the other hand, the very dimensions of its success lent it a significance far beyond its artistic value. Without actually being dramatically complex, the show nevertheless conveyed an assortment of messages, some of them contradictory, each pleasing to different people—and therein perhaps lay one secret of its success.

At one level, for example, *Fiddler* indulged in nostalgic homage to the past—quite in contrast to the Sholem Aleichem original, which had poked affectionate but trenchant fun at a society in the throes of disintegration. Obeisance toward the past was fast becoming the most important hallmark of postwar Jewish culture, and the relationship between the Yiddish original and the Broadway Tevye is a clear indication of what this implied: In New York, a culture that was losing its proximity to its Yiddish roots was also losing the possibility of using those roots for cultural innovation. It was, instead, thrown back on mimicry of the past.

At another level, piety toward the past was merely the show's cover story, while underneath it lay a different message entirely that addressed the American present. The new version of the story inserted elements that legitimized American Jewish life. Thus, whereas Sholem Aleichem had Tevye depart for the Holy Land, *Fiddler*'s Tevye embarks for America. This transfer made America's Jewish audiences Tevye's true heirs.

When read against an American Jewish background, the story seems to anticipate the present, and not simply because of the hero's ultimate destination. Tevye's naïve discovery of romantic love, for example, and likewise his coming to terms with his children's freedom to choose their own destiny, anachronistically "prefigure" and thus appear to legitimize the embrace of such modern ideas by American Jews. They, presumably like "Papa," had learned to temper tradition with love and forbearance, relinquishing patriarchal authority in favor of filial autonomy.

As for non-Jewish members of the audience, the American motif helped to make Tevye an American folk hero and claimed some of his aura for his Jewish descendants. Tevye the Dairyman recalled a literary tradition that, as one observer has noted, "bestows upon laborers—especially rural laborers—greater energy, vitality, and sexuality than it does to the pale, thin, beardless, repressed pencil pushers who inhabit the offices of the world. . . . [Such characters] are impulsive, strong, intuitive, passionate—capable of great anger and great tenderness."[9]

In telling "Papa's" story to the Americans, Jews linked themselves to this elemental, adrenal force—close kin to some American folk figures (Huck Finn?)—though in reality they had long since completed the transition from rustic to urban.

Thus, *Fiddler* was a parable of self-validation *at the expense of the past,* which is what made it counterhagiographical. American Jews could not help but see Tevye's story as an affirmation of their own transformation, compared to their immigrant parents and grandparents. The poor dairyman's wish to be "a rich man" had become the American Jew's reality. Here the show tended to subvert its own nostalgia for the past. The question that was being asked was, 'Am I, who am neither pious nor dirt-poor like my immigrant grandfather, at all linked to his tradition?' Tevye's wishful dreaming answered this question reassuringly in the affirmative.

By taking part in the spectacle of *Fiddler on the Roof,* by celebrating his precarious existence, a safe, affluent audience could reap comfort from the memory but also from the distance it had traveled. Tevye is a stoic figure, a hero perhaps, but also a victim: defeated not only by the village thugs, the local priest, and the authorities, but also by his own daughters. American Jews, by contrast, could consider themselves the heroes of Tevye's imagination. *Fiddler* pandered to its audience's ego, propping up its insecure sense of self.

The play was merely the kickoff for an even longer-running, continuous Jewish campaign of self-validation through retrieval of the past. In the fall of 1966 (and again from April to July 1967), the Jewish Museum mounted New York's first major exhibit dealing with Jewish immigrant life on the city's Lower East Side. Symbolically, it picked up where *Fiddler* had left off. The exhibit catalogue included Irving Howe's essay, "The Lower East Side, Symbol and Fact" (which anticipated his later book on the subject, *World of Our Fathers*). In the essay, Howe articulated a theory of direct cultural continuity that linked New York Jewry with its shtetl background:

> If our contemporary existence winds back into the Lower East Side, . . .then the experience of the Lower East Side winds back into the world of the Russian and Polish Jews, *finding there its premise of survival. . . . [T]he Lower East Side was a fulfillment of energies from the immediate Jewish past: it was Kamenetz Podolsk revived, Berdichev released.* . . . By making the Lower East Side into a replica of the proletarian quarters of Warsaw and Lodz, the Jews might renew their strength, their culture, their morale. . . . The Jews came to America . . . *to complete their collective experience* [my emphasis—EL].[10]

The projection backward into the world of Berdichev—as imagined through the exhibit—was, thus, in turn, a projection *forward* to New York. Warsaw and Lodz become New York *in utero*. The collective existence of Jewry in the New World is at once justified and enlarged by that of the Old World. It is not mere continuation, but "completion," a coming to fruition.

"For two centuries," Howe explained, the East European Jewish world had been "accumulating insoluble problems. It could cope with them neither within its own limits nor through a strategy of dispersion into the surrounding cultures." Coming to New York, the Jews could "begin to realize their Old World selves, so long frustrated and misshapen."[11]

If *Fiddler* had offered a showbiz version of these ideas, the museum exhibit and Howe's interpretive remarks stripped away the tinsel but left the set, the characters, and the audience arranged in exactly the same configuration. Retrieving the past became the best available mode for defining a culture of the present, perhaps because of the insubstantial quality of Jewishness in the present. As one observer put it, "the present is unimaginably impoverished without the intrusion of the past."[12]

Howe himself articulated this need to compensate for an impoverished present: "There has, I suppose it must be said, been progress since our fathers and grandfathers streamed through Ellis Island to settle into those wretched tenements on Hester and Rivington Streets . . . but it is also hard not to feel that the price of progress, whatever that may be, has come very high."[13]

This sense of cultural diminution was hardly assuaged by the prospect of "alienated Jews and radical Catholics coming together on a Sabbath eve" (as Morris Dickstein, with deliberate, though appreciative, irony put it) to hear Allen Ginsberg recite his "heretical kaddish for a Communist Jewish mother"—a scene that took place on the Lower East Side, at the editorial offices of the *Catholic Worker*. Neither would it have been of great comfort to know that tough Brooklyn kids like Leon Wieseltier were finding "exhilaration" in the provocative release from old burdens provided by Leonard Cohen's lyrics: "When young the Christians told me/how we pinned Jesus/like a lovely butterfly against the wood." These were marginal agonies and ecstasies.[14]

To cherish what had been lost and to retrieve some of it, even while acknowledging its irretrievability, became the cultural credo of the Jewish community. The contrast between this posture and the general urgings of American culture in the sixties—with its emphasis on the "torch being passed" to a new generation, on kicking over the traces of the Eisenhower years, on the abstract and the sensual, on the experimental in both outer and inner space, on the *new*—could scarcely be greater (as indicated by Kazin, quoted in this chapter's first epigraph). Self-validation in the American idiom turned toward the future, while self-validation in the Jewish idiom turned toward the past. The utopian possibilities of an urban Jewish culture were finally relinquished—one is tempted to say forfeited. Possibly for this reason, those who tried to define the quality of Jewishness in New York were hard-pressed to identify it with anything that was actually present.

The lost or relinquished utopia was reduced to a specific time and place, and there it has remained forever fixed: the immigrant East Side. Howe, whose sense of loss ("the price of progress") was stirred by the East Side retrospective, succeeded finally in calling the utopia by its proper name: "Tightly knit and momentarily coherent within its own perimeter, the Lower East Side nevertheless represented an experiment in collective rootlessness, a brief transcendence over nationhood by a people that had not been able to become a nation. It was a provincial world with universalist values."[15]

That this was Howe's own preferred utopian synthesis is evident from his own pilgrimage through reincarnated forms of "provincial worlds with universalist values"—from his streetcorner Trotskyite youth in the Jewish East Bronx, to the dining-hall alcoves of precociously political Jewish students at City College, to *Partisan Review* and *Dissent*. But though he saw these later forms as faithful to the original in spirit, they were also failed, truncated, or illusory echoes of the real thing, which was now given its due.

"A provincial world with universalist values" was a fairly good encapsulation of Moses Rischin's argument in *The Promised City*. Rischin, however, had sought to root his account in the political culture of American Progressivism and in the emergence of New York as a new kind of city in the early twentieth century. His historical rationale was not primarily dependent on a sense of loss *in the present*, but on a recapitulation of the past in its own setting. As such, his portrayal was not of something briefly incandescent, but rather of an enduring contribution. Moreover, he made it clear that there was as much discontinuity as continuity in the relationship between the culture of the East Side and the culture of eastern Europe that preceded it. His study, nonetheless, became part of the major rehabilitation effort that was directed at the once cast-off immigrant past.

Yiddish and the Culture of Retrieval

The effect of this 'past-ism' was perhaps felt most strongly in the transformation that befell the world of Yiddish letters. The caesura of the Second World War endowed that world with a new quality that it had never aspired to possess: that of being an echo, a shard, of a murdered culture. Yiddish writers and poets in the postwar period readapted their calling accordingly. But it is noteworthy that those who read these works in English translation—as they became increasingly available in the 1960s and afterward—took it almost for granted that even prewar works, or postwar writing set in the prewar world, were primarily documents of *preservation* rather than inventive creations in their own right. The use, in other words, of Yiddish literature for American Jewish readers, lay in its 'pastness' rather than any other artistic quality.

Literary scholar Anita Norich, in her masterful study of I. J. Singer (elder brother of Isaac Bashevis), who died in New York in 1944 at age fifty, has made this point very convincingly. Norich contrasted the reception of I. J. Singer's work by Yiddish literary critics in the thirties with the reception it received in the sixties by American critics. While the earlier Yiddish critics had seen the older Singer brother as bracingly innovative and sophisticated, adhering to a modernist ethos bent on exploring themes that went beyond Jewish confines, "themes at once more universal and more psychologically interesting," the later commentators belittled his modernism, his ability to convey psychological depth in his characters, and instead "herald[ed] . . . the mirror Singer had held up to Eastern European Jewry in the years before its destruction." As Norich goes on to observe, "Yiddish texts were museum pieces, archaeological finds even at their moment of creation."[16]

The Holocaust was not entirely responsible for this metamorphosis, but it made it virtually inevitable that Yiddish literature—especially in English translation—would come to function commemoratively.

The artists themselves were forced to contend with the disjunction between the *intended past,* embodied in the life and work of Yiddish writers, and the newly minted *commemorative past.* The problem is dealt with specifically in a poem of Glatshteyn's from just after the war, entitled, "My Children's-Children's Past" *("Mayn kinds-kinds fargangenhayt")*:

> In the now, I lived as a heder-boy should live,
> With Gemore-melodies, with a sun saved up for me,
> In an invented palace of Jewish grief.
> Oh, my palace glowed brighter than a thousand-and-one nights:
> Great-grandfathers had invented the fires of my Destructions. . . .
> In middle age it fell upon me to see face to face
> My childish once-upon-a-time, my palace of Jewish grief,
> Is no longer a legend. . . .[17]

The displacement of consciousness is a dual one here. In the first place, Glatshteyn was renouncing the historical and cultural optimism that had once led him to distance himself from the "invented griefs" of Jewish folk culture and to adopt a personal, modernist, "introspectivist" poetic mode. After the Holocaust, that former abandonment of his childhood's mythic world of Destruction and Exile appears to have been overhasty and naïve. Because actual destruction had occurred in his own lifetime, his childhood's familiarity with Jewish martyrdom and exile had come home to roost:

> How could I have thought that the Jewish past
> Is a historical graveyard?
> How could I have talked myself into the belief
> That Jewish children are brought up
> In the luxury of invented grief?

But beyond this first displacement of his art and his consciousness, Glatshteyn understood (and feared) that in time, the destruction visited upon his own generation would come to figure in the minds of those yet unborn as a symbol, a cultural construct, a catastrophe of "once-upon-a-time"—as powerful to them, but also as ethereal and as removed from their own time-bound memory as the ritualized tales of destruction ("Assyria, Babylon, Greece") had once been to him. Indeed, he himself, his art, even his very language, will then have become artifacts of history, fulfilling a commemorative function alone: "The deaths of my own time will reach me fast/ God, I am becoming my children's-children's past." [18]

Glatshteyn's choice, as an artist, was to engage the Jewish past more explicitly, albeit still in a very personal vein.

Ruth Wisse has reminded us of the contrast between this turn toward the past and the earlier regnant mood in Yiddish literary circles. American Yiddish letters, she noted, had once borne a future-oriented message: "*Forward* and *Future (Forverts* and *Tsukunft*) were the names of the leading American Yiddish daily and monthly, founded at the turn of the century." But by the late thirties, certainly by mid-century, not only Glatshteyn, but also the entire galaxy of immigrant Yiddish writers and poets turned to historical subjects (including Sholem Asch, Joseph Opatoshu, H. Leyvick, A. Leyeles, and others.)[19]

David Roskies, citing Glatshteyn's, Isaac Bashevis Singer's, and Chaim Grade's postwar works, concurs: "Once the surviving Yiddish writers had committed to memory their memorial poems for the countless dead, it was time, for the last time, to revisit the study house, shtibl [chapel] and synagogue of yore, not as symbolic settings for the crisis of faith and for youthful acts of rebellion, but as real places at the very center of Jewish particularism and Jewish genius." [20]

Revisit, yes; but these modern writers were unlikely to reformulate the tradition in a present-continuous mode. It is fairer to say that this is not what they attempted, since that was a task beyond the cunning of literature. They could but *represent* the past as a compelling locus of meaning.

The impotence implied is conveyed in the quotation from Wiesel in the epigraph to this chapter: to turn back to the synagogue "after all," with the sense of its already having been lost. They had found a fallback position, nothing more. In this, they resembled the New York intellectuals of the Old Left, whose fallback politics of American democratic liberalism provided a postwar shelter in the wake of the shattering of their own radical visions. Even more to the point, when such postethnic, secular intellectuals lamented the loss of Jewish ethnicity and turned back to the East Side and its riches, they were engaging in the same sort of forlorn exercise as the Yiddish writers.

Not surprisingly, then, Howe celebrated Glatshteyn for having transcended "the esthetic restriction of his early poems, which were marked by such *luxury motifs* as the difficulty of sustaining a personal self in the modern city [my emphasis—EL]." Howe thanked the poet "for the pleasure and solace [he provided in helping his readers] to endure in a terrible time." It should be noted, too, that Howe was being consistent here with views he expressed at that time regarding African American writers: The proper aim of literature by the oppressed, he argued in a critique of Ralph Ellison, was to engage the reader in the trauma of oppression, not to soar 'above all that' in a realm of pure aesthetics. Perhaps unintentionally, he reserved 'all that' for white, non-Yiddish-writing Americans. As Emily Budick details in her analysis of how the exchange was played out, this was a position that Ellison found invidious. He, therefore, called Howe to task for taking such a position while himself presuming to speak—dishonestly—not as a Jew, but as an 'American,' hence as a supposed spokesman for American (white) culture. Ellison threw this back in Howe's face by himself claiming an American birthright, prior to Howe's spurious second-generation claim, by defending his right to write as an American, not merely as an oppressed black person.[21]

Most Yiddish writers failed to make Ellison's claim. Within their craft—in a language whose cultural orbit was growing steadily narrower—Yiddish writers had discovered the means of retrieval by reversing their own literary strategies of prewar years—to go back to their culture's mythic roots; but this was still only retrieval, not recovery.

One possible escape hatch was indicated by I. Bashevis Singer: to make the transition to a different kind of mission. "To be a Yiddish writer in America is to be like a ghost," he told *Harper's* in 1965. The interview took up the question of how a Yiddish writer might make a literary career in the picked-dry, "ghostly" world of Yiddish letters. Writing in Yiddish, Bashevis said, was its own reward, undertaken without hope for wider recognition or adequate remuneration. "I hope one day to find a Yiddish publisher who will not ask for an advance from me," he quipped. It was as a writer being published in English that he conceived of a career, and he pointed out that things began to look up in 1960 when his first English publisher, Noonday, merged with Farrar, Straus and Giroux. Meanwhile, "my original [Yiddish] manuscripts are slowly turning to dust."[22]

Bashevis, however, had not only refocused his attention on having his work translated, thereby having his cake and eating it too; he had also broken out of the assumptions of Yiddish literature much more thoroughly than had his other contemporaries, as David Roskies has argued. He maintains that *Satan in Goray,* Bashevis's first translated novel, was "antihistorical. . . , collapsing history and psychology," thereby denying a secular salvation through art: "So much, then, for the novel, a genre that expressed dynamism, change, and confrontation with the future."[23]

Bashevis did not just despair of the power of the Jewish God and the gentiles' enlightened culture, as did Glatshteyn, who could then turn his face resolutely back to the world of his fathers. Bashevis evinced a radical despair of humanity as such: despair of the individual wrestling without much hope or choice with his or her demons; but even more, a despair of humanity in groups, humanity in its guise as seeker for a moral order. The retrieval of the past, therefore, is cut off as an option: Neither politics nor a simple return to the past is an adequate answer. There is only a coming-to-terms with a harsh human reality that is limited, never fully comprehended at the surface level of rationality and articulated emotions.

In yet another interview, Bashevis dripped heavy irony as he once again denied history any specificity, denied religion its consoling power, and argued against human happiness:

> I think it's nice that people do go back to religion because, with all my many doubts, I'm a believer. . . . [B]ut at the same time I don't flatter the Almighty. I say He has created a murderous world. . . . To me the Holocaust began from the moment man was created. . . . [T]he whole history of humanity is one big holocaust, with some short interruptions. . . . Even before the Hitler destruction I had the feeling that human life is one big slaughter. That was my feeling. Not just as a Jew. As a human being. . . . I see us all as miserable human beings who did not ask to be born. We fight for things, we are fooled, we are disappointed. . . . To me, individuality is the very essence of art. . . . I deal not with what unites people but with what separates them and makes everyone unhappy and misunderstood in his or her own way.[24]

This renunciation of the moral-political collective project of human history ("what unites people") and its correlate, the literary restoration of the

Isaac Bashevis Singer, 1978. Singer, the first Yiddish writer to win the Nobel Prize for Literature, was one of the preeminent figures among New York's Yiddish literati in the postwar period. Photograph by Éditions Stock. Courtesy of the Jerusalem Post *photographic collection.*

Jewish people, through a retrieval of its past, earned him widespread criticism in the small, overheated Yiddish world. In the words of one of his characters:

> There was no end to the complaints against me. I was too pessimistic, too superstitious, too skeptical of humanity's progress, not devoted enough to socialism, Zionism, Americanism, the struggle against anti-Semitism, the activities of the Yiddishists, the problems of women's rights. Some critics complained that a Jewish state had sprung up before my eyes while I busied myself with the cobwebs of folklore. They accused me of dragging the reader back to the dark Middle Ages.[25]

There was in Bashevis, of course, a deep-seated revulsion against suffering, injustice, and moral depravity. He was, as another observer has put it, horrified by anarchy. But, like his older brother whom he admired and imitated, he had no resolutions to offer. He was wary of would-be redeemers who, in fact, would "[open] the gates to a world of chaos, not redemption."[26]

His portrayal of his father's rabbinical court *(In My Father's Court)* as a laboratory of life is therefore more convincing than is his attempt to assert that it could serve as a paradigm for a just moral order. Such justice, Bashevis admitted, was available as a human option only insofar as it could be based on the depoliticization of society and on the renunciation of power: "The Beth Din [rabbi's court] could exist only among a people with a deep faith and humility, and it reached its apex among the Jews when they were completely bereft of worldly power and influence."[27] (In this he was really the polar opposite of Hannah Arendt, with her validation of politics as the highest human vocation and her demand for an internationalization of the rule of law as a function of government.)

His "pastness" is therefore of a different sort than that encountered elsewhere in postwar Yiddish literature. He may evoke a more authentic world, but he denies the image of its ghost any real, immanent power. There is no catharsis of rage against history, God, and the world. He could not hold out to readers the kind of "pleasure and solace" that Howe discovered in Glatshteyn, even in Glatshteyn's most painful moments of self-laceration. Rather, there is in Bashevis the sense that retrieval is just not available on a retrospective or vicarious basis—that is, not by the literary imagination alone. There is only whatever there has always been: the finite possibilities of life in the here and now.

When Bashevis tried to explain to a general audience the significance of the ultra-Orthodox Jews seen going about their business in New York, he spoke of their historically sanctified, intent inwardness: "This [form of] segregation is as old as Jewish exile itself." But self-segregation was not merely a strategy of survival: it was also a safeguard against falling prey to the ever-present moral pitfalls of human nature. "Any effort to mitigate this or that rigor leads promptly to licentiousness and assimilation," so that greater and greater vigilance is required. It is a life conducted under duress, both from within the Jewish world and from the gentile world at large.[28]

Bashevis could appreciate this response because his own life as a Yiddish writer was a kind of self-segregation, an act of willed discipline in the face of formidable odds. He was, of course, not an actual proponent of ultra-Orthodoxy, but he fancied that the ultra-Orthodox, in their unreconstructed view of the world as a dangerous place, came closer to his own view of things than those Jews who were still capable of utopian beliefs. He was, in that sense, choosing a postmodern sensibility, and his "pastness" was therefore of a kind more in tune with the moodiness of the sixties.

In reaching beyond the commemorative function of his art, he alienated some readers and fellow writers—as portrayed so cleverly by Cynthia Ozick in her memorable send-up of these family squabbles[29]—but he opened up an avenue of discourse that he thought more universal.

Bashevis had in fact caught the tenor of the long-festering postwar disillusionment with the city and with modern society (described in chapter 2), which is what placed him close to the mainstream of American culture in his day and helps to explain his popularity. In his writing he often evoked a pre-urban environment (the small Jewish town, "peopled," as all pre-urban places are, with demons, sprites, and the spirits of the dead), but not as an icon of simpler virtues. His shtetl is not an antidote to the modern condition; rather, it is a surreal *anticity* whose myth, like that of its modern, urban counterpart, is textured with the demonic, the capricious, the uncontrolled.

Here was his protest against what he called, in his 1978 Nobel Lecture, "the abyss of cruelty and injustice," and here he recast Yiddish retrieval, not as an exercise in collective memory, but as the voice or modus of postmodern pain. "In a *figurative* way," he concluded the Nobel Lecture, "Yiddish is the wise and humble language of us all, the idiom of frightened and hopeful humanity" [my emphasis—EL].[30]

Having thus confessed that he had a moral purpose all along, Bashevis could assert moral purpose on behalf of his medium. But he gave the game away by honestly noting that he referred only *figuratively* to Yiddish as a universal language of humanity, just as it was only *figuratively* his chief medium. In actual fact, by consciously placing Yiddish behind the oriental screen of translation, he discreetly hid its particularism and sought to use it for a purpose far more ambitious than commemoration.

◆ ◆ ◆

With so much to keep Yiddish writers engaged with the disheartening themes of history and of life in general, with human frailty, and with the pitfalls of literary ideologies, it is tempting to generalize that the Yiddish literary scene as a whole was preoccupied by these issues, but that would be an overstatement. Bashevis was not the only one in the world of Yiddish letters who attempted to move beyond the discourse of retrieval to address the here and now. Among such other voices was that of Kadia Molodovsky, a poet who spoke in mellower, calmer tones and was not preoccupied, as was Bashevis, by danger, delinquency, and demons. She therefore represents another type of "escape hatch" out of the powerful hold of remembrance.

Like the Singer brothers, she had immigrated to New York from Warsaw in the mid-1930s. Having spent the years 1950–52 in Israel, she then returned to the city as a recognized figure on the Yiddish literary scene. In the sixties she revived a small literary journal, *Svive* (pronounced "SVEEveh"—*Milieu*), that she had previously launched in the forties. Molodovsky wrote short stories, children's stories, and especially poetry. She also anthologized one of the early Yiddish volumes of Holocaust poetry.[31]

To a large extent, her own poetry revolved around affirmative, first-person meditations on the blessings of life. Unlike the sophisticated, unconventional, and highly inventive language of Glatshteyn's free verse, for example, Molodovsky used a simplified, transparent vocabulary as well as rhyme to produce verse that was accessible, graceful in its very simplicity, and sentimental. There is relatively little about "retrieval" themes, and a great deal of the present and future tenses, spinning out a central thread that might be called the sanctification of life.

Her volume of verse, *Light of the Thornbush (Likht fun dornboym)*, published in 1965, is indicative of her life-affirming point of view. The book's title and the accompanying epigraph refer programmatically to the burning bush ("and the bush was not consumed")—a metaphor laden with connotations of sacredness, suffering, rebirth, and immortality. But in her opening poem she declared her intention to bend the bush symbol in a direction that seeks survival in aesthetics, not in holy fire: "A Rose Blossoms upon My Thornbush" *("Oyf mayn dorn blit a royz,"* written in 1954). Here she asked how it was that beauty, life, and new art could thrive so unexpectedly, and she suggested that the blessing resided in the power of affirmation itself.[32]

Her poem of 1960, "A Prisoner" *("A gefangene")* reiterated the theme of art as renewal:

> I solemly swore to my angel that I would sing.
> Now I am trapped by my own words. . . .
> I had my heart convinced that I was dead and gone.
> But here I am, . . .
> A voice inside me answers—yes, oh yes . . . [33]

She produced a similar effect of tentative celebration by juxtaposing the harsh textures of the city with the little miracles of the world, as in "Daybreak" *("Fartog,"* 1964):

> Daybreak, an outburst of bird-cries.
> Even in stony New York,
> on a dusty, soot-covered, little branch
> I can hear God's orchestra playing.
> A dewdrop, straight from the Creation,
> bejewels a rusty wire. . . .
> For now there is composure in the blue sky.
> Before long the day will flood with mad disorder,
> drowning "And it was good" with raucous sound.[34]

But the most explicit of these poems of renewal is a personal anthem, written in 1963: "Kindle Your Light" *("Tsind on dayn likht")*. It is worth quoting at length because it conveys a great deal of what animated some members of the Yiddish literary community, small as it may have been by the sixties:

Perhaps I'm the last of my generation.
That is no concern of mine.
'tis not I who sets time's limits.
I have my day, my single chance, on loan.
. . .
I have been told, in any case,
no one is superfluous.
Your day, your single chance—
don't squander it.
It's your today, your yesterday, your forever.
No matter where your place is set,
kindle your light and step up to your lectern.[35]
Your flicker is one of a circle of lights,
lit, by whom and where you cannot know.
But once it flares, be you the bearer of its
brightness, as you bear its scorching, too.
. . .
A generation of chaos, that watched the heavens fall
and saw the sun suck darkness in;
that saw them desecrate Mount Sinai
with the abomination of their slaughter-houses
—at that very altar, yes,
all bent and wracked and crippled,
kindle your light.
And on that quaking earth, set up your lectern . . .
and guard your flame.[36]

Yiddish, Urbanism, and the Ultra-Orthodox

A paradox exists in the relationship between urbanism and Yiddish cultural continuity. Sociolinguist Joshua Fishman argued that immigrant Jews from the end of the last century to the 1930s placed little positive cultural value on Yiddish, favoring instead the advantages held out by English, precisely because they were being resocialized in a modern, urban, highly mobile American environment where all traditional relationships and cultural forms were uprooted or displaced. This contrasted quite sharply with those social environments in America that afforded real possibilities for bilingual stability: compact regions such as the Southwest, with populations that had lived in or colonized the area prior to the formation of the United States and the ascendancy of English, and rural environments (such as Pennsylvania Dutch country) that protected linguistic insulation. Neither of these conditions obtained in the case of Jewish immigrants in New York.

In addition, Jews did not, by and large, commit themselves ideologically to a program of ethnic language maintenance. In the big city, despite the highly concentrated pattern of immigrant residence, English possessed a high priority over Yiddish because of both material reward and symbolic preference. Yiddish had little prestige and no functional value in "becoming American." Young immigrant children and American-born children of Jewish immigrants arrived at public school with at least the basics of spoken English *from their own homes and wider family and social environment,* where the new language was quickly fostered. It is in this context that the decline of Yiddish up to the postwar period is best understood.[37]

Fishman reported that over the course of the decade from 1960 to 1970 the number of Yiddish speakers (that is, those for whom Yiddish counted as their mother tongue) declined further on a nationwide basis from approximately one million to somewhat over 650,000 (or just over 10 percent of the total American Jewish population). The number of Yiddish newspapers and journals dropped again, as did their circulation, and the publication figures for Yiddish books similarly declined. The number of Yiddish radio programs as well as the hours of Yiddish broadcasting fell, and only about fifty Yiddish-language afternoon schools (with a secular-cultural orientation) still functioned in the United States, with about three thousand pupils.[38]

The large urban environment, nevertheless (and herein lies the paradox), began in the 1960s to provide support for those aspects of Yiddish culture that managed to remain stable. As the suburban dispersal of younger families increased, the urban setting remained comparatively more "Yiddish-friendly." That is, large cities were more typically the home of the remaining, older, Yiddish-speaking populations. On another front, Yiddish language was becoming part of the academic study of Jewish culture at the university level (pioneered at such institutions as the City University of New York and Columbia University).[39] In 1968, for example, Columbia, in cooperation with the YIVO Institute, inaugurated an intensive annual summer program in Yiddish language and culture.

What is more, as Fishman maintained, the urban-based culture of complexity, mobility, and materialism that had in the past motivated Jewish immigrants and their children to favor a massive linguistic transfer to English, was now, in a period of affluence and overtly successful acculturation, the basis for a symbolic shift. In some quarters, especially among younger people, a positive reassessment of nonmaterial, "simpler," folk-ethnic values—Yiddish language and culture included—took place.[40] Yiddish as urban counterculture had become creditable in sixties terms!

Thus, despite the massive decline in Yiddish language *use,* the older, negative stigmas associated with Yiddish in the prewar period, when the language was often seen as a mere relic, a symbol of cultural backwardness, were being shed, allowing Yiddish and its literature to be appreciated and valued as part of "classical" Jewish culture, even among those who no longer spoke the language. This, as we saw in chapter 1, was a point of view that was also readily adopted by members of the New York Jewish intellectual elite.

The symbolic revaluation that Fishman spoke of was predicated in yet another way on the urban environment. He argued that the rehabilitation of Yiddish was not merely a function of third-generational hankering after immigrant folkways, but was dependent upon the influence of the city and Jewish culture upon each other. "This kind of positive turnabout could have occurred only where Jewish awareness was affected . . . by the influence of Jews and Jewishness on their surroundings."[41]

That is to say, a place like New York City, with its oft-cited "Jewish" aura, was conducive in a concrete way to the reevaluation and symbolic rehabilitation of Jewish ethnic culture, including Yiddish. The city as a cultural and social landscape was partly created by the ubiquitous presence of Jews and their activities, while the presence of other groups, just as ubiquitous, served as boundary markers. In such an environment, Jews seeking their cultural roots received positive feedback. Jewish "emanations" were more salient because they could bounce against a great variety of past and present associations of places, faces, sights, tastes, and sounds.

This is a different matter than the notion of passive, generic Jewishness. Rather, the implication here is that cultural actions and behaviors, once initiated, could achieve a high resonance in the city. This was more than mere nostalgia or the substituting of a bygone utopia for hopes never fulfilled. We are dealing here with contemporary forces that made the city an enhanced environment for cultural self-expression.

◆ ◆ ◆

The cross-hatching effect or counterpoint between Jewish cultural "product" and urban environment was also a significant element in the postwar growth of the ultra-Orthodox Jewish community in New York and the latter's impact on the texture of Jewish life in the city.

The ultra-Orthodox presence in such Brooklyn neighborhoods as Borough Park (or "Boro Park"), Crown Heights, and Williamsburg became more pronounced as nucleus groups that came before the Second World War were significantly augmented by the postwar refugee immigration. These were neighborhoods in demographic flux and the Jewish residential clustering clearly influenced the local ambience. Jews, who constituted 42 percent of the total white population in Crown Heights in 1940, had increased proportionally to 52 percent in 1957 (even though, in absolute figures, there were 5,500 fewer Jews in the neighborhood in 1957, compared to 1940). In other words, while some Jews and some other white residents moved out, a particular Jewish constituency solidified its presence.

Similarly, in Williamsburg the number of Jewish residents declined appreciably from 1940 to 1957 by some 16,000; despite this, they remained fairly close to their prewar share of the local white population (35 percent in 1940 and just under 32 percent in 1957). Once again, the departure of Jewish residents was selective, and proportional stability was the effect of ultra-Orthodox entrenchment. In Borough Park, a middle-class enclave that soon began to absorb Jewish residents from other ultra-Orthodox neighborhoods, the number of Jewish residents actually increased slightly from 1940 to 1957 (by some 2,000), and their proportional share of the white population went up more steeply, from 49.5 percent to just under 56 percent.[42]

Williamsburg, which became home in the postwar years to Hasidim of the Satmar, Klausenburger, and Novominsker *rebbes*, showed clear evidence of the displacement of earlier residents. Thus, a "tourist" to the neighborhood at the end of the fifties could still see the sign indicating that the building next door to the Satmar school on Bedford Avenue had once been home to the Williamsburg Boys Club. The Satmar institutions in the immediate vicinity of the group's headquarters included four *mikvehs* (ritual bathhouses), a matzah bakery, and a cluster of schools—all of which contrasted dramatically with the only abandoned, ruined, and roofless hulk on the block: a church.[43]

The interrelationship between ultra-Orthodox (in Hebrew, *haredi*) life and urban concentration is a characteristic and surprising development of the postwar period—surprising, in light of the extremely modern nature of the big city and the antimodernist culture of *haredi* groups. Israeli sociologist Menachem Friedman, a keen observer of *haredi* development, explains that self-segregating subcommunities like the ultra-Orthodox found it possible to reconstitute themselves as urban ghetto enclaves, thereby combining large numbers (necessary for the support of a completely self-contained infrastructure) with ecological isolation. The modern, metropolitan environment thus assumed an importance to *haredi* life that it had never before possessed. Indeed, cities had once been viewed in traditionalist circles as hotbeds of iniquity—in the same measure as antitraditionalist Jewish writers had seen the city as liberating.[44]

The overriding importance of this physical clustering was poignantly evoked in the memory of one Holocaust survivor, as reported to sociologist William Helmreich. The man, who lived in Yonkers, was in effect cut off from his brother and the rest of the Satmar enclave in Williamsburg. One of the local Hasidim, upon being introduced to the visitor from beyond the city line,

Crown Heights, Brooklyn, 1969. Satmar children in the "Torah Veyir'ah Yeshiva" schoolbus. Photograph by Klaus Lehnartz. Courtesy of Stapp Verlag.

asked, " 'Where does he live?' 'Yonkers' . . . He didn't say anything except: 'Shloime, do something with this Goy.' "[45]

The protection of ghetto "turf" becomes a matter of supreme significance in the city setting because of the constant threat of encroachment. Thus, the Satmar group in Williamsburg blocked a major public housing project for their neighborhood at the end of the fifties on the dual grounds that the character of their community would be disturbed by such an intrusion, and that Hasidic families would not benefit from the planned housing, because they would not live where elevators and other mechanical equipment would be run on the Sabbath.[46] The point of the episode is not only that a *haredi* community proved determined to defend its turf, but that this group of newcomers had established itself in the city so well—within less than two decades—that it was politically effective in opposing the city administration over a thirteen-million-dollar project.

The paradoxical nexus between city life and haredism goes even deeper, however. Friedman argues, for example, that the variety of the urban population tends to put a premium on the ability of very disparate groups to *function* side by side, while *living* separately. Thus, the "constantly deepening alienation affecting urban social relations" benefits groups like the *haredim* who can fit into specific occupational niches without being implicated in social networks outside their own community.

Perhaps the most important of these occupational niches, economically speaking, is a specialized component of international trade—the diamond trade—that by its nature is based in metropolitan centers of international import and export.[47] Another such urban-based niche is real estate. In both cases, a *haredi* entrepreneurial class emerged in the postwar period that was able, for many years, to underwrite the lifestyle of their community.

Moreover, haredism is a form of pietistic elitism, consciously formulated

Lee Avenue, Crown Heights, Brooklyn, 1969. A religious bookshop, the "Yerushalayim Sforim Store" over Herman Lax's Fabrics. Photograph by Klaus Lehnartz. Courtesy of Stapp Verlag.

to set a "heroic" Judaism apart from ordinary Jews—even those who may be nominally Orthodox, but who do not adhere to separatist standards. In other words, the viability and, indeed, the very point of ultra-Orthodoxy is predicated upon having another Jewry to be *separated from.* A city with a mass of Jewish residents is an ideal environment in that sense.

Ultra-Orthodox Jews are dependent on a large, non-*haredi* Jewish community financially, as well. The wider Jewish community helps to support the ultras both by direct contributions to yeshivas[48] and by employing *haredi* men to provide specific religious services (the production of Torah scrolls, *mezuzot,* and phylacteries, the supervision of kosher food production, or operation of burial societies)—functions that have become a virtual monopolistic preserve of the ultra-Orthodox, even though the market of "consumers" includes all types of Jews. *(Haredi* women are more typically employed within their own communities.)[49]

Given the context of contrast and diversity, the world of the urban ultra-Orthodox Jew is fraught with gradations and distinctions: between Jew and Jew, between Jew and non-Jew, between the old world and the new. The very complexity of this mental grid is a function of living in a multidimensional and variegated environment. The substantial growth and institutionalization of ultra-Orthodox Judaism in New York not only added to the complexity of the Jewish community; it actually derived its strength from that complexity, defining itself in resistance to the life of those with whom it shared the city.

Journalist Yossi Klein Halevi, who grew up in Borough Park, knew that his moderately Orthodox schoolmates were mocked by their ultra-Orthodox peers for wearing "mini" skullcaps (so-called "Pepsi-Cola bottle caps"), rather than the large, black ones favored among the pietists. And while Halevi's family had a television in their living room and a portrait of Theodor Herzl, the Zionist founding father, on the kitchen wall, ultra-Orthodox groups steered clear of both television and Zionism.[50]

Similarly, the boyhood of journalist Ari Goldman, who moved from Hartford to New York as a young child, was an intricate negotiation between Orthodox lifestyles. His education in the early sixties was a veritable pilgrim's progress from one type of Orthodox institution to another. He experienced it as a conflict between the outside culture and the one revered by his teachers. Beginning at a modern-style, coeducational Orthodox day school where Judaic and secular studies coexisted easily and where Zionism and modern Hebrew were culturally dominant, he was then transferred to a yeshiva on the Lower East Side. "There were no girls in sight, Zionism was regarded with suspicion and Yiddish was preferred over Hebrew."

A subsequent transfer brought him to a school in Crown Heights, in the heartland of postwar right-wing Orthodoxy, an environment where "not only were there no girls," but the Judaic curriculum focused exclusively on mastery of the Talmud, while the secular part of the curriculum (science, math, English)—demoted from the equal status it enjoyed in other Hebrew day schools—was relegated to the waning hours of the day, between three and seven o'clock. There, Goldman, who had developed a youthful obsession with reading newspapers, was taken aside and warned not to "fill [his] head with the filth of the marketplace."[51]

Schools such as those Goldman attended were a growing phenomenon in the fifties and sixties. By 1964, New York City had 28 Yiddish-speaking Hasidic day schools and 50 non-Hasidic, Yiddish-speaking, Orthodox day schools—both elementary and high schools. In addition, there were 52 Hebrew-speaking Orthodox day schools, including 11 high schools. Orthodox day schools accounted for 29 percent of all Jewish school enrollments in the Greater New York area by 1964.[52]

Of equal significance was the expansion of the *kollel*—the yeshiva world's "graduate division"—higher talmudic institutes for young married men in their late teens or twenties, a stage during which entry to the world of making a living may be put off for up to five years, sometimes longer. This "moratorium," as Friedman points out, was increasingly considered de rigueur in *haredi* society. As a yeshiva education became a virtual norm for all boys in the community (in contrast to prewar eastern Europe, where a more select group was involved), the grooming of outstanding religious teachers and leaders had to take place at a higher level. This was analogous to the heightened premium placed on graduate university degrees in many professions, once undergraduate degrees became popular and easier to obtain.

Both the "moratorium" itself, which placed an economic burden on the families involved, and the institutional development of the *kollel* were dependent on a supportive economic environment—which, again, as Friedman argues, brings us back to the nexus with the big city.[53]

This constant contrapuntal engagement of one culture with another turned New York into much more than a mere "location" for Jewishness. We have seen, for instance, how Bashevis, the post-traditional writer, expressed a certain kinship—from a distance, to be sure—with his ultra-Orthodox fellow New Yorkers. His literary "retrieval" of language, myth, and mystique from the world of Polish Jewry took place in an environment where he and his readers could see a *religious* culture of retrieval just over Brooklyn Bridge or in Manhattan's diamond district. His deliberate exoticism, in that sense, had a local point of reference.

Similarly, Gabriel Preil, the late Hebrew poet, was able to consider Old World Orthodoxy—so strange yet at the same time so very much part of the background of Hebrew and Yiddish culture—an occasional inspiration or consolation:

> Tomorrow I will slip away
> to orchard skies of Torah.
> Maybe there in Williamsburg,
> where a pacified, brute summer reigns,
> they cork rich wines of ancient prayer.
> And it may be
> the mirror of my room
> will no longer show
> the desert face
> of a Job-like Jew.[54]

In this context, but in a lighter vein, it is also worth recalling the last lines of Joseph Heller's novel, *Good as Gold,* where Heller chose to signal his protagonist's growing sense of inner reconciliation by describing the meeting of opposing worlds in a Brooklyn schoolyard:

> The school was a religious one, a *yeshiva*. Some of the teenagers had sidelocks, and some of the sidelocks were blond. Gold smiled. God was right—a stiff-necked, contrary people. *Moisheh Kapoyer* [i.e., topsy-turvy], here it was winter and they were playing baseball. . . . [A] stubborn dispute was in progress. . . . As Gold watched, the catcher, a muscular, redheaded youth

> with freckles and sidelocks and a face as Irish or Scottish or Polish as any Gold had ever laid eyes upon, moved wrathfully toward the pitcher with words Gold for a minute had trouble believing. "*Varf*! [Throw!]," shouted the catcher "*Varf* it, already! *Varf* the fucking ball!"[55]

The consolation, here, lies in the reconciliation of apparent opposites (sidelocks and profanity, Jew and non-Jew, Yiddish and English, religion and playgrounds, baseball in winter), rather than in Preil's mental gravitation toward the "orchard skies of Torah" or Bashevis's recognition of ultra-Orthodoxy as a viable strategy of self-segregation. That distinction is a function of Heller's perspective and the novel's point of view. But looking once again at the point that is relevant to our discussion, we can see how some forms of expression (the prose or poetry of modern, secularized, urban Jewish writers) can achieve their purpose partly by bouncing themselves off *other* forms of Jewish self-expression. That is one important effect of the cross-hatched, multidimensional nature of Jewish life in the city—any city, perhaps, but surely magnified in New York.

By these criteria, Jewish "culture" in New York existed, first of all, as a matrix or venue within which cultural "product" might be generated as well as received. Language, literature, and religion were central, both as tangible "product" and as media. To depict Jewish culture as lacking defined qualities (an amorphous or unconscious "Jewishness") was, therefore, only accurate insofar as it recognized that Jewish culture is open-ended; it was less accurate when it failed to connect culture with particular content or particular media. This may have suited quite well many Jews whose awareness of the specifics of the cultural matrix in New York was hazy.

Similarly, to see Jewish culture only as a past that might possibly be retrieved in memory was to miss the point that culture depended on constant regeneration of the matrix. Retrieval, in its apotheosis of the past, could not substitute adequately for a creative orientation to the present. It was, in that sense, a betrayal of the present.

Beyond Retrieval: A Jewish Historian in Postwar New York

At the end of the Second World War, Hannah Arendt went to work as executive secretary of Jewish Cultural Reconstruction, an organization chaired by Columbia University historian Salo W. Baron, dedicated to taking stock of, salvaging, and redistributing whatever Jewish cultural resources might be recovered from under the rubble of Europe.[56] On the face of it, this was a project in cultural retrieval par excellence, and who was better suited to supervise this effort than a historian?

Baron, born in Austrian Galicia in 1895, was a man of extraordinary erudition. In addition to his thorough training in Jewish texts, he held three doctorates from Vienna in history, political science, and law. He had come to New York in 1926 to teach at Stephen Wise's Jewish Institute of Religion,[57] and in 1929 he accepted an appointment as the first incumbent of a newly endowed chair in Jewish history at Columbia University (a position he occupied until his retirement from teaching in 1963; he died in 1989).

Baron is perhaps best known for his three-volume history of the Jews, *A Social and Religious History of the Jews* (1937) and its vastly expanded second edition, the eighteen-volume work of the same title (1952–1983). Because, prior to the sixties, academics in Judaic studies typically took up positions in sectarian Jewish institutions or else were situated in departments of religion, oriental studies, or philosophy, Baron's position as a senior Jewish scholar in the history department of a premier American academic institution was unique. Baron did much to pave the way for the wider acceptance of Jewish studies at American universities.[58]

But it was more than his advantageous position and his monumental scholarly oeuvre that accounted for his role in postwar Jewish culture. Baron actively promoted intellectual work as leader of an organization called the Conference on Jewish Relations (later the Conference on Jewish Social Studies), editor of its journal, *Jewish Social Studies,* president of the American Jewish Historical Society (1953–1955), and as a widely published commentator and lecturer. A man whose lifework was devoted to examining and explaining the past, he was nevertheless an advocate of a future-oriented approach to Jewish culture. In this, he articulated an intellectual position that leaned on retrieval, but went far beyond salvage and nostalgia—those twin impulses that were driven by cultural despair.

Salvage and nostalgia derived from and responded to a sense of profound loss. The culture of retrieval posited that authenticity resided only in the past and that the past was irrevocably lost. This loss was evident in the case of European Jewry and its culture, extinguished in the Holocaust. To an extent that is perhaps unappreciated, the latent cultural effects of the Holocaust on American Jewry could be read in the grip of "pastness" on postwar Jewish culture. But a similar sense of loss was also being expressed through the nostalgic evocation of the immigrant world of the Lower East Side, and by extension, through the products of that world in its various forms—including the second-generation intellectual culture of the left.

The richness of the past might be depicted in retrospect, it could be mourned, it could even be caricatured; but—the cultural retrievalists seemed to say—the culture produced in other times and other places could not be replicated or developed further. The loss, then, was double: not just the loss of

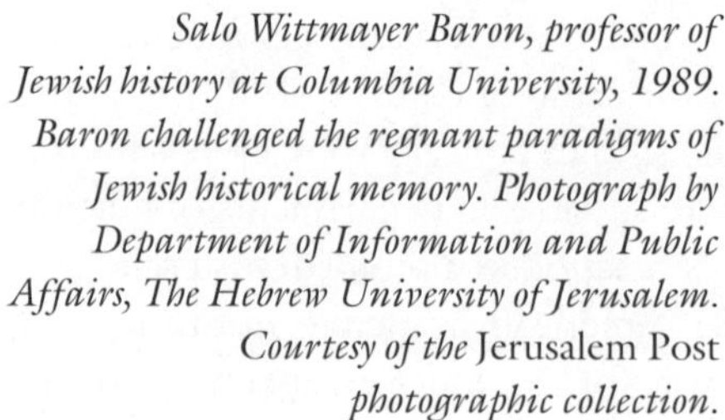

Salo Wittmayer Baron, professor of Jewish history at Columbia University, 1989. Baron challenged the regnant paradigms of Jewish historical memory. Photograph by Department of Information and Public Affairs, The Hebrew University of Jerusalem. Courtesy of the Jerusalem Post *photographic collection.*

particular cultural media or artifacts, but the loss of the very power of cultural creativity—of cultural confidence itself. In that sense, a culture geared solely to retrieval was barren. Moreover, for those who sensed that the receding past might not even be accessible, it appeared to be the end of the line. As Kazin put it (in *New York Jew*), "The past did not exist unless you had lived it yourself. There was no historical memory if you chose not to have one."

Baron, the historian, with his keen appreciation of what had been achieved by major Jewish communities of past eras, took issue with pessimistic readings of postwar Jewish life in America and thus challenged the underlying thesis of the retrievalists. In addresses and essays in the fifties and early sixties, Baron spoke directly to the issue of Jewish cultural creativity and noted that major Jewish communities of the past were typified by mediocrity or paucity of cultural output during the early, formative centuries of their development. By analogy, he argued, it was far too early to condemn American Jewry to the dustbin of Jewish cultural vitality. "Perhaps now, with the large majority of American Jews having been born and educated in this country, we may look forward to some genuine cultural achievements bearing a preeminently American coloring."[59]

In arguing for the enduring value of the cultures produced by major communities of Jews in the past, each in its own right, and in maintaining that the continuity of Jewish life was not broken, even after the Holocaust, Baron had to challenge the overwhelming force of the role of catastrophe in Jewish history. That was the underlying motive, it has been suggested, for Baron's massive reworking of his *Social and Religious History of the Jews.*[60]

Although his biographer, Robert Liberles, has cogently argued that a second edition of the great work was already being contemplated before the war, and thus it cannot be entirely read as a postwar response, it was only *after* the war that the plan for the revised work took definite shape. Baron's original plans for revision were altered, both in scope and in content, so that the new, multivolume edition became a highly detailed, almost encyclopedic study of medieval Jewish life—a period known stereotypically for its precariousness, and thus a prime challenge for a historian who was out to scale down the prominence in Jewish history of loss and suffering. Liberles agrees that "the main thrust of the intended revision was to unlock hidden and undiscovered doors of Jewish history that had remained covered by thick veils of the orientation toward suffering." It was also in the cause of limiting the catastrophic mentality, Liberles points out, that Baron considered the study of American Jewish history an opportunity to examine Jewish life under benign conditions.[61] Clearly, Baron understood the need to disengage culture from the cult of loss, if cultural confidence were to be restored.

The Shifting Cultural Paradigm

Deborah Dash Moore has argued persuasively that the common New York Jewish culture of the interwar period had emerged from, and was inherent to, the ethnic neighborhood experience. It was, therefore, a culture that was intimately engaged with the present-tense milieu of Jewish families, still tied by personal memory to their parents' immigrant odyssey, but resolutely oriented toward an American future. As the title of her work—*At Home in America*—clearly suggests, New York Jews from the twenties to the forties were both anchored "at home" in their own particular, postimmigration neighborhood ambience as well as lodged comfortably in an America that was their new "home."

The language spoken in the neighborhood (English), as well as the neighborhood's leading institutions—from the public school to the synagogue-center to the Democratic club—were all mediating instruments for the ethnic American Jewishness that emerged. The second-generation's Jewishness was thus "homogenized": a new, composite blend. Having relinquished the specificities of Galician, Lithuanian, and Polish Yiddish and having smoothed over the rough edges of parental Orthodoxy or blue-collar status, the resulting "New York Jew" could also move comfortably from neighborhood to neighborhood. This new, blended ethnic Jewishness was no longer a direct carry-over of immigrant, Old World culture, but something new: a particularistic group culture filtered by American urban and middle-class values, experiences, and behaviors.

When New York Jews looked around in the sixties and spoke of the "given" or environmental Jewishness of the city, it is likely that they were recalling a cultural mode that had existed in earlier decades, but that cultural mode was no longer supported by the new social realities. By the sixties, with suburbanization well under way, the neighborhood life that had defined New York Jewish ethnicity was showing signs of brittleness and decay.

A sure sign of this change was the conscious rehabilitation of the Lower East Side as a cradle of folk vitality and folk heritage. A now-faded Jewishness-of-venue was traded in for a more rewarding, idealized memory of "the old neighborhood" par excellence and, by extension, of the European home that had preceded it. The collective yesterday became an ethnic museum when the collective tomorrow came into question. The culture of retrieval was an overt response to disappointment in the present.

The best possibilities for a new cultural paradigm lay beyond the strategy of retrieval, but this required dislodging and replacing the amorphous Jewishness-by-default of the second generation's experience—something that began to occur by the late 1960s, as we will see in chapter 6. A generic Jewishness that was evaporating to the point of triviality and vagueness could be reconceived, not as an aggregate of neighborhood-bred regularities, but rather as a dense mesh of disparate Jewish cultural forms that jostled and intersected within New York Jewry as a whole. As a culture of specificity, not homogenization, it could be more inward-turning.

The small, intense, and highly contrasting worlds of the Brooklyn ultra-Orthodox communities and the remaining Yiddish literati; the public display of Jewish memory in Manhattan's museums and theaters; the emergence of an academic discourse of Jewish writing and research; the widely acknowledged sovereignty of the past—so strong and so tyrannical that some cultural activists went to some lengths to point to the inherent sterility of dependence on the past alone—all of this formed the potential basis of a different sort of New York Jewish culture.

Archaeological rather than topical or venue-dependent, it would have to be found below the surface of such easy-to-spot (and just as easy to discount) ethnic markers as slang words borrowed from Yiddish and certain cadences of speech; the ubiquity of kosher delis and the urban, non-WASP brashness that comic Lenny Bruce, not very originally, alleged to be "Jewish"; and the unflattering but popularly accepted male and female stereotypes that peopled (in all their vulgarity) the lexicon of New York Jewish humor.

But such a hypothetical renewal of culture had inherent problems. Although it could potentially rest on such affirmative aspects as Molodovsky's poetry, Baron's intellectual resistance to the catastrophic mentality, or the burgeoning school systems of the ultra-Orthodox, the culture of revival was overwhelmed by the more dominant strains of loss, relapsed hopes, and uncertainty. In that sense, the new Jewish cultural paradigm was not simply a reflection of the inner group experience; it was also a reflection of how the life of the city as a whole determined the modes of Jewish response.

In chapter 2 we saw that, in the face of postwar realities, a critique of mass society emerged that undermined older models of urban utopias. The city and all that it represented—including technology, mass democracy, and a social levelling (always more imagined than real)—no longer seemed to offer actual hope for an effective humanist solution. The urban crisis, full-blown by the mid-sixties, would merely confirm and deepen these profound anxieties. It was in the context of this relapse of hope for life in the city that the idyllic combination of particularistic community with universal or American values was consigned to the Lower East Side: to the past.

Turning to the past for memories of a viable culture was an essentially weak enterprise, however, and that may be why the cultural product of "retrieval" appeared so threadbare. The reasons for this must be sought in the very concept of "Jewish culture," which sometimes also went under the name "Jewishness."

Moore's study of interwar New York Jews not only argued that their ethnic culture was elaborated mainly in the densely Jewish neighborhoods, but also asserted that this neighborly Jewishness was essentially secular. That is unobjectionable, because the concept of Jewish "culture" was in fact formulated to define a postreligious Jewish identity, a mode of "Jewishness" that could survive the loss or the absence of faith and ritual observance. One could actively promote or partake of Jewish literature, theater, music, folkways, political activity, and historical consciousness without subscribing to a religious discipline. Jews could imagine Jewishness as a "culture" only after distinguishing between Judaism as a sacred way of life and Jewishness as the creative distillation of a particular, historical, folk experience. Thus, secularization and "culture" are conceptually linked.

Hannah Arendt had observed as much when, in 1947, she was asked to offer some thoughts on "Jewish Culture in This Time and Place." "Culture," she said, "made its appearance rather recently and grew out of the . . . dissolution of traditional values. . . . [S]ecularization transformed religious concepts . . . in such a way that they received new meaning and new relevance independent of faith. This transformation marked the beginning of culture as we know it—that is, from then on religion became an important part of culture, but it no longer dominated all spiritual achievements."[62]

But the notion of Jewish culture apart from religion presupposed a secular-ethnic community, which in turn was highly dependent on an immigrant language and its cultural media, and on an intimate communal lifestyle. It was similarly supported by specialized groups of cultural "producers," the likes of the "New York Intellectuals" or the New York Yiddish writers. These milieus did in fact flourish in the interwar period but were all on the wane in the postwar years. How, then, could a Jewish culture, as a sphere of experience in its own right, be retrieved in living form—not just in reminiscence—if its very basis was being removed? The "culture of retrieval" had, therefore, an inherently limited shelf life.

While the ultra-Orthodox subcommunity might appear to offer an example of retrieval that was not merely nostalgic but actual, and while this living example of "native" Jewish culture did serve the wider Jewish community as a reference point of sorts, the *haredi* ideology of self-segregation and deliberate exoticism meant that the majority of Jews could not draw upon it for applicable models.

Yet, as the culture of "Jewishness" appeared to lose its rationale, religion (albeit not in its ultra-Orthodox form) loomed larger as a component of postwar Jewish life. Judaism, rather than Jewishness, became relevant as an important issue once again. As Arendt had perceptively put it, "secularization is not the ending of religion."[63] As a postsecular phenomenon, this religion was not "retrieved" from the past. Rather, it would become relevant mainly as a response to the new setting of Jewish life in the sixties: a post-utopian urban community.

4

What's to Become of Man, Then?

> "But," I asked, "what's to become of man, then? Without God and without a future life? Why, in that case, everything is allowed. You can do anything you like!"
>
> —Fyodor Dostoyevsky,
> *The Brothers Karamazov*

> We are that group who, having stampeded into general culture, now find it a higher wisdom to reclaim our stake in our traditional faith. . . . We obviously do not believe as much as our grandfathers did, but we have discovered painfully that we believe far more than our society does.
>
> —Eugene Borowitz (1968)

It is generally accepted that the synagogue in America experienced a revival in the 1950s, closely paralleling the resurgent activity in America's churches. Further, it is argued, this took place in an atmosphere particularly congenial to organized religion—including economic prosperity, a conservative political ascendancy, and regular public endorsements (from the White House on down) of a pro-religious posture.[1]

The revival of Jewish interest in the synagogue took two interrelated forms: the establishment of many new congregations and an increase in synagogue membership among American-born Jews. In explaining these trends, analysts both at the time and since have offered a theory of postwar Jewish acculturation to American middle-class norms, while at the same time questioning the religious depth of this renewed synagogue Judaism. Many also cite the rapid growth of the number of younger Jewish families after the war, part of the "baby boom," which fed demand for American-style, family-oriented congregations. Finally, observers stress the significance of the large-scale postwar Jewish resettlement in suburban areas. Few Jews had lived in these areas previously, and newly settled Jewish suburbanites seeking to create some form of community frequently found an outlet for such energies in the construction of synagogues, which in this new setting became their representative institution.[2]

The thesis that a popular religious emphasis in American culture held sway in the years of the Eisenhower administrations has been reiterated by many authors in many forms, perhaps most memorably in the now-classic book, *Protestant-Catholic-Jew,* written by Will Herberg, the former-Marxist-turned-Jewish-theologian.[3]

Just as notable, however, is the recognition that the religious resurgence of the fifties was followed by a decade in which churches and synagogues languished, popular culture ceased to trumpet the virtues of religion, liberal Protestant theologians argued over the proposition that "God is dead," and organized religion as such was on the defensive.

Columbia University chaplain John Krumm wrote in 1963 that "Whatever religious concerns are felt by college students today are felt within an atmosphere of a fairly profound disillusionment with society as a whole and with religious institutions in particular." One of his Jewish counterparts, Rabbi Norman Frimer (regional director of campus services through the B'nai B'rith Hillel Foundations in Brooklyn), was moved to observe in 1966: "Enough sociological data are available to convince us that we are in the midst of a serious religious crisis. Except for the scattered oases of commitment, Judaism is by and large not a vital faith which addresses the daily lives of our people." A few years later, Rabbi Alfred Jospe, representing the (Reform) Union of American Hebrew Congregations, noted that "a strikingly large number of young people . . . reject any relationship to organized religion," although they were to be found in the forefront of movements for moral and social improvement.[4]

Then again, the suspicion that secularization might not be a one-way street and that American religious history shows persistent cyclical patterns of renewal and decline is a view that has become more widely accepted since the end of the sixties.[5] That view found further support in such disparate phenomena of the 1970s and 1980s as the increasing visibility and political mobilization of the Christian Right; the gravitation of a significant number of Americans to Islam and Eastern religions, or to "new" religious cults and sects; and the evident interest (evident to any shopper in large, commercial bookstores) in the eclectic, quasi-mystical religiosity that is dubbed "new age spirituality."

Moreover, a more nuanced theoretical literature in the sociology of religion has questioned inherited intellectual constructs, such as the once-preferred secularization model, which had construed religion solely as a vestigial aspect of premodern social relations. Instead, religion is now widely discussed as more than simply prayer, God, sanctuary, and congregation: It is construed more broadly as a perennial (perhaps inherent) aspect of human society—that aspect that provides coherent meaning to social relations and confers a sense of belonging to those who share in that system of meaning.[6] This is a construction that tends to rob the terms "secular" and "secularization" of much of their relevance. (Admittedly, it also makes religion harder to define.)

A religionist consensus has, thus, begun to emerge from the recent historical and sociological literature.

Yet, when it comes to analyzing the American Jewish case, one is struck by the lack of common understanding. There is, specifically, little consensus on the probable causes of the Jewish drift away from synagogues and observance from the sixties on, following so closely on the heels of a putative religious revival and in seeming contrast to broader trends in American culture.

The debate is in fact related to the way in which the religious revival of the fifties has been portrayed. Clearly, if the fifties revival rested more on a social and cultural trend toward greater Americanization rather than on an intensification of belief, observance, and piety, there may be more continuity than decline in subsequent trends toward secularization, intermarriage, and assimilation. But by the same token, however, if the religiosity of the 1950s was largely ethnocommunal and institutional in nature, it is quite conceivable that a more serious religious response began to take place only after the synagogue Judaism of the fifties became the object of internal Jewish self-criticism.

The intent of this chapter is to explore how some of these trends and themes were played out in New York City, where some of the conditions of Jewish life were similar to those elsewhere in America, while others were unique. The lack of a coherent analysis of the foundations of Jewish religious life in the city before World War II makes it necessary to review the prewar period before assessing those changes that set in after the war.

We will, in addition, try to extend the discussion of religion, moving beyond the somewhat frustrating issue of defining "revival" and "decline" to examine what it is that religion meant for Jewish culture in an environment that, as we have seen so far, was characterized by a growing degree of social and cultural instability.

Religion and the Jews Before World War II

The designation of Judaism as a "faith" was always a conventional usage in American parlance. Among American Jews themselves, especially in the nineteenth century, there was, indeed, a distinct preference for the religious self-designation, with its specifically and intentionally non-national connotation. Competing definitions (including "race," in its turn-of-the-century usage, as well as "national type") found relatively few adherents, although they were current.

However, in the first third of the twentieth century, massive Jewish immigration and dense urban concentration made an alternative definition of Jewish identity a plausible, even a persuasive option. Discerning observers recognized a widespread religious apathy among Jews that, nevertheless, did not negate their social distinctness: their concentration in certain neighborhoods and certain economic niches and their pronounced tendency to marry only amongst themselves. It was this perception that helped give rise to a colloquial distinction between "Judaism"—the religion—and "Jewishness"—the state of being Jewish.

Sociologist Nathan Glazer captured the meaning of these new terms of reference by describing the typical urban Jewish neighborhoods, such as those in New York, as "strongholds of Jewish irreligion and of Jewishness":

> It was in these almost totally Jewish areas, paradoxically, that Jews could live live almost completely unaffected by Jewish religion . . . that the proportion of synagogue members was always lowest . . . [and] that any special [political] movement in Jewish life . . . could be reasonably sure of finding a few adherents. . . . And it was in these areas, too, that one could live a completely Jewish life from a sociological point of view. . . . [O]ne could have only Jewish friends, eat Jewish foods, follow Jewish mores and culture patterns, and yet have little consciousness of being a Jew.[7]

This reality led early twentieth-century and interwar Jewish educators and communal theorists (Mordecai Kaplan being among the most prominent examples) to despair of the power of religion alone, as traditionally understood, to hold the Jewish community together—especially its younger generation. Instead, they sought a brake against assimilation that would include religion per se under a more appealing, more broadly conceived, more "modern" form of ethnocultural heritage community. That could mean Zionism, conceived as a bulwark of group pride, or the new synagogue-centers that developed social, cultural, and athletic programs as they strove to become magnet institutions in heavily Jewish neighborhoods.[8] Even with these innovations however, the effort was a frustrating one, as Kaplan complained: "What a Sisyphus affair, this trying to keep Judaism alive in this country."[9]

In contrast, anecdotal impressions still abound about the time when "everyone" in New York was Orthodox—meaning *not* that Jews were necessarily more observant, but that the Reform and Conservative movements made relatively shallow inroads in immigrant and even second-generation neighborhoods; and that, for a while at least, "the public platform was ruled by the secularists, [but] the physical environment . . . was dominated by the Orthodox. . . . Jewish neighborhoods were considerably darker on Friday than on weekday evenings."[10]

The typical New York synagogue for a long time was an Orthodox one, even if it *was* poorly attended;[11] Orthodox marriage (and divorce) ceremonies were the normative practice even among the most secularized Jews; the consumption of kosher meat and poultry remained widespread in the ostensibly secular community; sexual mores remained fairly puritan; and folk customs and popular superstitions were known and perpetuated.

How are we to understand such conflicting claims? Our confused picture of immigrant and second-generation Judaism is due to two factors: First, New York Jewry has defied categorization and comprehensive study because of its sheer size and diversity. Second, and perhaps more vexing, we have only the vaguest notion of the religious beliefs or experience of the immigrants before they left Europe or after they arrived in America. Irving Howe picturesquely suggested that, "God could easily be neglected in New York, it was probably not His favorite city, yet He was not at all forgotten. While only a minority continued to follow the rituals with literal exactness, the aura of faith . . . remained strong in the nostrils of the immigrants."[12]

Historian Arthur Hertzberg reminds us that even as staunch a secularist as Abe Cahan, editor of the socialist Yiddish daily, the *Forverts,* acknowledged that the majority of the early immigrants in the 1880s were Sabbath observers and lived in homes that were kept kosher. Yet, as Hertzberg also points out, "tens of thousands of these conventionally pious workers and petty bourgeois from Eastern Europe did work on the Sabbath, [though] they did so reluctantly, and with pain." And sociologist Charles Liebman concurs, adding that "some East European immigrants, forced by economic circumstances to work on the Sabbath, attended religious services in the early morning and then went to work."[13]

Idealized notions and generalizations abound concerning the "traditional" East European Jewish environment in which the immigrants had been socialized as children, although we now know very well that traditional Jewish society had been in a long process of breakup for at least half a century prior to the First World War—a process that was considerably accelerated by the mass migration itself. About one in every three East European Jews left home from the 1870s to the 1920s, with inevitably negative ramifications for social and cultural integrity. Thus, even though eastern Europe was a bastion of religious conservatism in the Jewish world at the turn of the twentieth century (and would remain so until the Holocaust), it was also the site of a major cultural and social upheaval that disrupted the fabric of traditionalism. Even if religion constituted a defining characteristic of that society—perhaps *the* defining characteristic—we would still have to take into account that both religious authority and the integrative role of the religious lifestyle and worldview were considerably challenged in each successive generation from the 1870s on.

More is involved, however, than the inroads of religious skepticism. Processes of religious development that had begun in eastern Europe in the latter half of the nineteenth century were, in effect, interrupted by the mass migration. For the immigrants themselves, those processes were simply cut off. In their own lives, Judaism had to be constructed anew, drawing in some ways upon traditional values and practices, but no longer rooted in the familiar milieu of home.

They had come from a social ambience in which a new pattern of Orthodoxy had begun to emerge: Religious roles and institutions that had not traditionally been set apart from the everyday lives of most Jews (such as the rabbinate and the yeshiva) were increasingly specialized, turning them into something closer to an elite religious establishment (a "church") with its own strict code. Inevitably, this left the rest of Jewish society in the role of a "lay" community, less coherent or less rigorous in terms of the demands of piety. Paradoxically, one might say, the new Orthodoxy promoted the development of a new "secularism."[14]

A modern type of yeshiva had developed in nineteenth-century Lithuania, imbued with a mission to create islands of pure devotion to sacred study—far beyond the prevailing norm and in conscious distinction to the "secular pursuits" of other Jewish youth.[15] Similarly, we can also cite the innovative consciousness-raising "orders" of young men, called the "Musar" movement, that had been inspired by Rabbi Israel Salanter and his disciples;[16] the development of a militant Orthodox press; and finally, the appearance of Orthodox social-political organizations—all of which took place in Poland, Lithuania, and Russia from the 1860s to the First World War: precisely the period of mass migration to the West.[17]

The conscious insulation of religion from modern incursions (by redefining its elite institutions as a separate, protected sphere) had also begun to make itself felt in the compartmentalization of Jewish education in eastern Europe. More and more Jewish young people of primary-school age or above received general schooling under state auspices, while the traditional primary school *(kheyder)* underwent few if any changes. In fact, as Steven Zipperstein has pointed out, the *kheyder* even found defenders among post-traditionalists who valued its unreconstructed traditionalism and felt that it was now a valued "part" of Jewish life that ought to be "preserved," as a sphere immune to modern tampering.[18]

Thus, East European Jewish immigrants to America represented a generation for whom religious life was being recast as a separate sphere, though they themselves would continue that recasting in their own characteristic fashion. *Kheyders,* for instance, found few defenders in New York and, as the traditional school and traditional teachers languished, they took a very distant last place in the scheme of Jewish families' educational priorities for their children. As for Orthodox politics, the religious Zionist Mizrachi movement was transplanted to America, but there (like other Jewish political movements) it was shunted into cultural and fundraising work, without a significant communal political role to play. The rabbinate, as we said, was only just beginning to be professionalized in eastern Europe. It would take decades of life in New York (and arguably, this can be said to some extent to be true even today) to sort out who was and was not a recognized Jewish religious authority, what constituted satisfactory training for rabbis, and what was the proper division of roles between rabbis and other functionaries.[19]

Put simply, the forms of role differentiation that had begun to take root in East European Judaism before and during the mass migration period had resulted in a rudimentary privatization of religion for those who were not institutionally involved in the new Orthodox establishment. In the absence of rigorous studies on the subject, we can only assume that the immigrants, to the extent that they were affected by broad trends in their native Jewish home-communities, were also affected by this privatization of religion. Having resettled in an alien environment where religious life was seriously disrupted, privatization continued apace in the virtual absence of any coherent reinstitutionalization—with the sole exception of the nascent "American Orthodoxy" of the interwar period.[20]

That is to say, there were indeed Jewish religious institutions and religious functionaries; but in the intimate chaos of immigrant life, religion was much more a collective experience that was nevertheless "private," insofar as it was unsupervised and subject to individual sensibility. As Howe points out:

> Ordinary immigrants went to *shul* at least several times a year, especially on Rosh Hashonah and Yom Kippur, . . .the Day of Atonement, having so sacred a resonance that they felt that to go then was to confirm one's identity as a Jew. In their homes they observed the rituals of *kashruth,* assuming as a matter of course that major ceremonials, *bar mitzvah* to marriage, would take place under the aegis of the *shul.* Were they believers. . . ? Perhaps not entirely, probably less so as the years went by, and certainly not with the rigor of their fathers. Were they disbelievers? By no means, and surely not with the fanaticism of the more extreme radicals.[21]

Judaism continued, then, to provide religious meaning. Leaving aside those Jews who became committed to secular ideologies, the *religious* culture of East European Jews could vary from defensive, stringent Orthodoxy to a diffuse, unreflective, and noninstitutional worldview that incorporated some elements of faith and practice but mixed them almost indiscriminately with conflicting values and mores.[22] Leftist Jews of an older generation could also be God-fearing; Jews who prayed weekly (or even daily) were sometimes among those who worked on the Sabbath; and Jewish sensibilites could be offended by the public breach of religious proprieties even when, privately, such proprieties were no longer adhered to.[23]

While the foregoing description is impressionistic, it is by no means merely speculative. Recognition that the nature of immigrant Jewish religiosity in the first few decades of the twentieth century was diffuse, selective, and institutionally "nonspecialized" (not wholly defined by or relegated to clergy or clerically dominated institutions) enables one to explain some of the most widely observed phenomena in New York Jewry before the Second World War.

Thus, for example, once we accept the thesis of an undermined but partially still operative religious culture, it is possible to account for the paradox of the universally touted "value of learning" in immigrant and second-generation New York Jewry. On the one hand, it is widely and almost automatically asserted that it was the privileged place of learning in traditional Jewish culture that predisposed Jewish, as compared with many non-Jewish immigrant families to proportionally overutilize public educational facilities in the city, from grade school through night school and college. This notion quite clearly assumes the ongoing relevance if not vitality of a religious tradition.

On the other hand, religious education as such—the actual point or "value" of the traditional Jewish veneration of learning—was drastically neglected by these same families. As a result, only about one-quarter of the Jewish school-age population in New York in the mass-immigration era was exposed to any formal Jewish religious training; only 20 percent were enrolled in Jewish schools in 1929; and it took a very long time for professionalization to be adopted in the field of Jewish schooling in order to place it on a more equal pedagogic footing with public education. In fact, it was well known that more affluent members and leaders in Orthodox congregations might continue to demonstrate their support of traditional learning by donating money to traditional religious schools but would also refrain from sending their own sons to study there.[24] Religio-cultural values, even when selectively transposed from their original context and meaning, have to come out of *some* accepted code—hence the presence of a set of values that is "alive" in some sense is presupposed. But at the same time, the selectivity involved in choosing one "value" (learning) over others equally embedded in the original culture (for example, Sabbath observance) and the reassigning of that value to a new and alien objective (secular and professional education) point toward an open-ended reinterpretation of the value code. Both the code and its breach, subversion, or reinterpretation are required as explanations for this situation.

Similarly, the strict interdiction of intermarriage—a documented fact of Jewish life in New York right up to the 1950s[25]—must be squared somehow with the indisputable weakening of religious authority. In the absence of any real sanctions exercised by religious leaders, endogamy (marriage within the group) can persuasively be related to the continued functioning of a family-based collective culture, a culture in which the freeing of the individual from traditional norms and taboos had not in fact fully taken place. The secular ethnicity of Jews in second-settlement areas, attested to in memoir literature and described by both Glazer and Moore, is in that sense overdrawn. Nevertheless, it must be recognized that immigrant-generation and second-generation Jews in New York had created an amorphous religious culture with built-in contradictions. Sociologist Thomas Luckmann has expressed the nature of such contradictions with particular insight:

> While "everybody" is still socialized into the "official" [religious] model, . . .the changing "objective" circumstances in the everyday lives of the members of the society will suffice to produce a marked degree of incongruence between the "official" model and the *effectively* prevalent individual systems of priorities. . . . In the following generations the discrepancy between the "official" model and effective individual priorities may become increasingly apparent. . . . In simple language, what the fathers preach but do not practice will be internalized by the sons as a system of rhetoric rather than as a system of "ultimate" significance. At the extreme point of such a development . . . everybody is still socialized into the "official" model of religion, but the model is not taken at face value by anybody.[26]

Postwar Judaism: The Religious "Revival"

This is the background, then, of our examination of religion in postwar New York Jewry. It is clear that we are dealing not only with a wide diversity of style and substance, but also with conceptual problems of a particularly difficult order. In addition, our pool of hard data is also very limited. Studies of American religion in the fifties and sixties rarely included large enough samples of Jews to be reliable. In other cases, although Jews were included in studies of special populations (such as college students), respondents were not always classified by religious affiliation.[27]

Still, some of these data can be suggestive. A 1957 study of college students in New York State found, for example, that—in contrast to Protestant and Catholic students, most of whom reported very positive feelings on the subject—less than half of the Jewish students in the survey felt that their childhood religious training and religious experience had been "constructive and positive," while an equal proportion felt that it had been merely "incidental"; and almost 7 percent of the Jews called their religious upbringing and education "negative and frustrating," as compared to only some 2 to 4 percent for the Protestants and Catholics.[28]

In studies conducted by Andrew Greeley in 1952 and 1965, we find that although Protestants and Catholics in America had not changed their stated belief in God, among Jews the affirmation of such belief had declined by 21 percent over that period. Nevertheless, Jews (represented in the study by just 128 respondents) showed the most rapid rise in "church membership"—the emphasis here being on *membership*: Jewish weekly attendance at services was actually reported to have diminished, although their *annual* attendance rate (i.e., once a year) had risen.[29] The keynote among Jews returning to synagogue was, therefore, affiliation rather than active participation—a pattern that was noted by observers at the time and since.

Apart from a miniscule survey (in 1940) of twenty families, no broadly conceived studies of religious practices among New York Jews were carried out from the forties to the seventies.[30] We do have, however, the results of a survey undertaken in 1981 by sociologists Paul Ritterband and Steven M. Cohen for the New York Jewish Federation.[31] The 1981 study, while documenting the state of affairs in the Jewish community about a decade or two after our period of interest, is nevertheless illuminating for a number of reasons.

First, it sheds some light on the *outcome* of trends (or at least the interim results of trends) that set in during the fifties and sixties. Second, since the survey asked questions not only about the respondents themselves, but about their parents' households as well, it helps us to look retrospectively at certain long-term developments that date from the interwar period and the first decades after World War II.

For example, the study confirms that outmarriages (marriages contracted between a Jewish and a non-Jewish-born partner) remained low in New York—under 4 percent—until 1950, but then began to rise moderately. (Outmarriage is often taken as a proxy for other indicators of religious assimilation and/or a thinning-out of ethnic bonds.) Among New York Jewish men, the rate of outmarriage increased to 6 percent in the fifties, 9 percent in the sixties, and 14 percent in the seventies. New York Jewish women married non-Jewish-born spouses at a rate of only 3 percent in the fifties, this rate then increasing in the sixties—8 percent—and on into the seventies—12 percent. Taking into account spouses converted to Judaism, Cohen concluded that by the end of the seventies, "among recently married New York-area Jews, about one in nine married a non-converting non-Jew."[32]

These rates, reflecting changing social and religio-cultural patterns in New York Jewish life, were still considerably below the national rate of Jewish outmarriage. In a major demographic study of the national Jewish population in 1970, Jewish males in the United States were found to have married out at a rate of 13 percent from 1960 to 1964 (compared to just 9 percent in New York).[33]

Of more direct consequence for our current discussion, the 1981 New York study compared variations in ritual observance among Jews in New York and among their parents, measuring the results across age—and generational groups.[34] The results do not differ markedly from the pattern outlined hypothetically by Luckmann (whose comment on religious change between generations we quoted above): namely, that religious forms do persist, but their meaning does not remain the same, nor do they necessarily reflect a link to everyday life.

Cohen noted that "large numbers of American Jews have indeed abandoned many traditional practices . . . [but] almost all later generation Jews sustain some sorts of participation in some sorts of holiday celebration."[35]

For example, third-generation American Jews born from 1932 to 1946 (i.e., who were born to American-born parents and who came of age from the end of the forties through the mid-sixties—our particular period of interest) scored lower than their parents on a scale of ritual observance: Among the respondents themselves, only 25 percent adhered to a "high" or "moderate" level of observance, as compared to 47 percent of their parents. Similarly, among the respondents, 58 percent said they adhered to a "low" level of observance, as compared to only 38 percent of their parents.[36]

The information thus gleaned indirectly about the parents' generation (the interwar generation) confirms our earlier suggestion that, despite the secularism that appeared to characterize their lifestyle, major proportions of the American-born, New York Jewish community in the twenties and thirties had retained substantial, if inconsistent, adherence to at least some ritual observances during the time when their children were growing up. Only 12 percent of the parental homes had been completely nonobservant in the interwar period.[37]

(We might note here, as well, that the small 1940 study of twenty New York Jewish families—not an actual "sample" in any rigorous sense, but effectively chosen to reflect "average," secularized, second-generation households with school-age children—had shown that three families out of twenty observed some laws of kashrut; nine out of the twenty women lit Sabbath candles; none of the adults attended synagogue regularly, though all but six families had members who attended at least once a year; and Passover rituals were observed minimally. In sum, most Jewish rituals were ignored, but exceptions were made for *kaddish* and *yizkor* [commemoration of deceased family members], Sabbath candle-lighting, the High Holidays, bar-mitzvah, and Passover; half of the children in these homes were exposed to some type of formal Jewish training.)[38]

While we can clearly account for these patterns in light of our previous discussion—patterns that show a diffuse, privatized religiosity among interwar, American-born Jews and an erosion of religiosity among their third-generation children—this is not the case for those respondents whose own parents were immigrants. Among these second-generation Jews surveyed in 1981, we discover that religion was more important in their lives. Whereas only *one-quarter* of the *third-generation* respondents, whatever their ages, claimed to maintain a high to moderate level of observance, not only was the proportion of second-generation ritual observers *higher,* but that proportion also grew *as the age of the respondents grew younger.*

That is, among American-born, New York Jews born from 1917 to 1931 to parents who were foreign-born immigrants, over a third (36 percent) claimed in 1981 to be moderately to highly observant. That figure rises to 39 percent for those born from 1932 to 1946; and rises once again to 45 percent among those who were born from 1947 to 1963. (This last group consists very heavily of children of Holocaust refugees and survivors.)[39]

It is for these particular Jews—children of later immigrants who came of age between the outbreak of World War II and the time of the survey (1981)—that we can speak not just of greater retention of religious observance, but also of a "religious revival." Although this is readily understandable in the case of very pious Orthodox Jews among the Holocaust-survivor groups, the pattern even fits those whose parents arrived in the United States before the Second World War, who were thus not part of the postwar refugee influx.

Not surprisingly, the New York data also show that more second-generation Jews than their third-generation peers labeled themselves Orthodox and Conservative, rather than Reform or "other."[40]

These results may appear puzzling in light of the "Americanization" thesis so often advanced to explain the postwar religiosity of American Jews. Stated simply, the notion (as argued by Herberg and others) has been that as immigrant cultures faded among children of second-generation ethnics, reflecting a concomitant readjustment to American, middle-class (Protestant), churchgoing mores, third-generation family members expressed their ethnicity through denominational affiliation (Protestant-Catholic-Jew) rather than through language or other cultural media. Hence, as the third generation after the mass immigration came into its own after the Second World War, so too did religious institutions go through a major growth spurt at that time.

Yet, in New York this was not the case. It seems clear that a tendency toward religious affiliation and especially religious practice was more pronounced among second—rather than third-generation Jews. It was *less* Americanization (or, to put it positively, closer ties to immigrant culture) that promoted Jewish religiosity through the sixties and seventies.

Just why the children of immigrants should have affected the tenor of

Jewish religious life in the city and its suburbs as late as the 1960s and beyond, at a time when third-generation (and even fourth-generation) Jews were becoming increasingly dominant elsewhere in American Jewish life, is something that is most plausibly related to the "New York factor." New York was home to a much greater concentration of recent Jewish immigrants and their children than were other American communities. The immigrant and second-generation presence was therefore more strongly felt (although the most recent groups of immigrants were smaller by far than the older waves had been).[41]

The social environment that was thereby created differed with respect to the experience of Jews in the rest of the country. That would help to explain why, for example, outmarriage continued to grow less slowly in New York's Jewish community than it did nationwide.

A Reinstitutionalized Religiosity

But this special condition—the higher profile of recent immigrants and their children—does not suffice to explain why second-generation New York Jews differed from their interwar predecessors. After all, interwar New York Jewry had been similarly dominated by immigrant and second-generation families, but their culture had been both more "ethnic" and less institutionally "religious" than was the case after the fifties. Why, then, did the postwar Jewish community in New York appear, by comparison, so much more "religious"?

First, as we observed in chapter 3, the Yiddish-based, East European cultural ambience of the interwar period had, by the sixties, become the object of nostalgia, despite the continued presence of more recent immigrants. The secular ethnicity of the second-generation of the 1920s and 1930s—a present-tense culture that was dependent on its neighborhood home ground, on Yiddish newspapers, theaters, and schools, and on a Jewish labor movement—was being replaced by a past-tense culture that, without the requisite institutions and media, could not be sustained except in memory.

Second, we need to take account of the ways in which New York Jewry was influenced by the development of Judaism in the suburbs as well as in other parts of the country. That is to say, despite its size and concentration, New York Jewry was not only a projector of influence beyond its orbit; it was also, in turn, affected by trends elsewhere.

As we noted earlier, East European Orthodoxy in the late nineteenth century had been in the initial stages of an institutional development that emphasized the "apartness" or "official" nature of religious culture—a development that had been cut off by the mass migration. Between the wars, the emergence of new Conservative and Reform congregations (chiefly outside New York) and the growth of a new, American Orthodoxy marked the reembedding of Judaism as a religious form of identity in specialized religious institutions.

These processes reached their peak, however, only after the Second World War. By the time the religious "revival" of the fifties had taken root and become institutionalized throughout much of American Jewry, the synagogue, the congregational school, and the professional clergy—rather than the Jewish home or neighborhood—had emerged as the official, undisputed (and sometimes exclusive) arbiters of Jewish group expression. The older diffuse but normative religious style, in which ethnic culture in the big city had freely mixed with inherited but privatized forms of observance, had been replaced by a new social form of religion that offered a focus for community life and an alternative to a less and less sustainable immigrant/second-generational ethnicity. "Jewishness," Glazer commented, was "everywhere in retreat," while Judaism "showed a remarkable, if ambiguous, strength."[42]

In 1961–62, enrollment in Jewish schools in the New York metropolitan area reached an all-time high of 144,000 (or about 35 percent) out of a total Jewish school-age population (ages 5–14) of 410,000. The fastest increases in such enrollment took place in the suburbs: Nassau and Suffolk Counties, followed by Westchester. In the city itself, elementary school enrollment in Jewish schools stood at only 79,000 (out of a pool of 314,000: i.e., about 25 percent, which was still 9 percent higher than it had been a decade before).[43]

Significantly, almost all the schools in question were under congregational or denominational auspices: Less than 3 percent of the total Jewish school enrollment in the city was under secular-Yiddishist auspices and an additional 4.4 percent was under "institutional," unaffiliated, or private auspices. In terms of the religious denominational distribution, the massive postwar Orthodox commitment to day-school education and other intensive schools gave them a disproportionate 60 percent of all Jewish religious school enrollment in the city (only 12 percent in the suburbs), followed by the Conservative group (21 percent of the enrollment in the five boroughs, 39 percent in the suburbs) and lastly by the Reform (11 percent in the city, but 45 percent in the suburbs).[44]

Thus, although in the city itself religious educational enrollment (along with synagogue membership) remained underproportional to the Jewish population, the keynote trend of that period was in fact indicated by the suburban pattern, which tended to express the mode of Judaism being adopted by younger, second—and third-generation families. It was liberal in its religious orientation and heavily dominated by the synagogue congregations. This, in turn, would undercut the legitimacy of the older New York ethno-Judaism that had relied less heavily on religious institutions.[45]

It was not only secular-traditional ethnicity that seemed to give way in the face of a reembedded religious establishment. Those who have studied the Orthodox Jewish community—especially its most traditionalist right wing—have noted a parallel development. In the Orthodox neighborhoods of New York Judaism moved in the postwar decades away from a diffuse, "mimetic" communal religious paradigm and toward a stricter formal adherence to law (as opposed to custom), systematic study of written text (as opposed to osmotic absorption of oral tradition), and the superior authority of schools and master teachers over home and parents.

"The shift of authority to texts and their enshrinement as the sole source of authenticity have had far reaching effects," noted one well-placed student of the subject.

> A religiosity rooted in texts is a religiosity transmitted in schools, which was hardly the case in the old and deeply settled [pre-Holocaust] communities of the past. . . . [T]he shift from [all-embracing] culture to [sectarian] enclave that occurred in the wake of migration means precisely the shrinkage of the religious agency of home and street and the sharp contraction of their role in cultural transmission.[46]

Another keen observer put it this way:

> When it comes to matters of *halacha* (religious law) or ritual, parents can guide their children primarily on the basis of their own strongly ethnic *minhagim* (customs). Their children, on the other hand, can more frequently refer to a precise knowledge of *halachic* texts and historical precedents. When conflicts arise . . . between parental guidance and youthful wisdom, the vocabulary of the conflict invariably reflects the battle between knowledge based on tradition and knowledge based on formal education. To the extent that the father is traditionally supposed to represent reverence for religious knowledge . . . he is fighting a losing battle with his children, whose religious education he has subsidized. . . . [A] shift seems to have taken place in the very nature of legitimacy, in Weberian terms, from the traditional to the legal-rational.[47]

Thus, a heightened support of specialized religious institutions for both worship and religious training was a feature of New York Jewish life across the denominational spectrum from Reform to ultra-Orthodox.

As for the clergy, Rabbi Irving Greenberg (a progressive Orthodox rabbi and something of an intellectual guru who came to prominence in New York Jewry beginning in the mid-sixties) noted in 1966 that all three major Jewish denominations were being taken over by a new, better-educated rabbinic leadership, the earmark of which was a greater commitment to denominational ideology. Greenberg, himself a representative of more critical thinking, thought that, "It may well be that the new leaderships will be more communicative [to their laity] and that we will see the end of gastronomic and sentimental Judaisms[48] and all their ilk. . . . This is all to the good. Surely the current nostalgia which is the cement of the American Jewish community will hardly stand a generation or two more of [bleaching-out]." Greenberg foresaw (accurately) that a more committed clergy might, nevertheless, have certain deleterious effects on the Jewish community as a whole, namely, "an increased partisanship" and polarization, rather than unification, among the denominations.[49]

These developments finally brought to a close the period of immigrant and second-generation Judaism—a form of religion that, as we saw, persisted through the interwar years and that compensated for the lack of thorough institutionalization of religion by diffusing certain religious behaviors throughout Jewish society.

Ironically, as Luckmann argues, it is precisely the successful institutionalization of religion as a separate sphere of life, in which an established professional clergy emerges to take religious responsibility away from the "laity" (with its notoriously lax and unreflective standards), that initiates a new cycle of privatization of religion.[50]

Patterns in postwar Judaism that are otherwise inexplicable become comprehensible in this light. Thus, we find a more "religious" attention to certain "part-time" rituals, such as refraining from work on the High Holidays (which suggests a "higher" level of observance) side by side with the abandonment of many more rigorous religious behaviors (such as Sabbath observance).[51] So, too, we find a higher profile for the rabbinate, the synagogue, and the synagogue school. Yet we also find the first significantly rising levels of outmarriage since the onset of mass Jewish immigration.

Eugene Borowitz, who taught at the New York school of Hebrew Union College in the sixties, put it this way: "Thus the paradox emerges. If the American Jew were truly religious, he would create a living American Jewish community, but though he organizes his community along religious lines, his life shows little religious belief and practice." His ironic conclusion: "[S]ecular Judaism, which could not dominate American Judaism under its own name, now may do so under the auspices of the synagogue."[52]

But no less an ideological secularist than veteran Yiddish educator Saul Goodman sought to co-opt the religious label for his own constituency—a fact that, in itself, testifies to the ceding of legitimacy to "religious" Judaism. Citing John Dewey's distinction between the noun, "religion" ("dogmas, institutions, precepts, practices"), and the adjective, "religious" ("any activity pursued in behalf of an ideal and against obstacles . . . because of conviction of its general and enduring values"), Goodman wrote:

> When a Jew bets his life on the survival of his people; when he makes an effort to inculcate his own child with Jewish values, or when he is deeply involved in Jewish cultural or spiritual activities—all of these experiences are then religious in character. Jewish secularism in America at the present time is then, in the Deweyan sense, *religious secularism* [*sic*], for this Jewishness obligates one to foster Jewish values and ideals—the values that are reflected in Jewish literature, in Jewish history, and in all emanations of the Jewish ethos."[53]

Perhaps we could ask for no more eloquent religious statement (though its Jewish roots, beyond its allusion to the shadow of destruction, are unclear) than the one that another secular-culturalist, Alfred Kazin, offered in a *Partisan Review* symposium on "Religion and the Intellectuals":

> In our time of annihilation, of the many deaths, of increasing terror against the very spirit of life itself, I have come slowly and painfully, but with increasing sureness, to accept the idea of gratitude as the wellspring of existence. It disposes of man's insincere pride, for we cannot be grateful to ourselves for life, and invokes the Godhead that is real because it is present in the intermediacy of our situation. Gratitude that we are here, that we are still here, and have a man's work to do. Gratitude to that which is always *given* us, in a world where nothing can be taken for granted, except death, and the fact that we did not make that world itself. To invoke the source, in gratitude that we are *here*, is to confront with our whole being a human situation not less difficult than we had thought it, but one that is newly astonishing, and alive with our own joy.[54]

When secular-culturalists need to avail themselves of the religious label, yet the institutions of religion are seen to be serving ethnocultural, secular ends, little further enlightenment will be gained from seeking to establish an "objective" measure of religious "revival" or "decline." In seeking to establish the actual place of religion in the lives of New York Jews, we will need, then, to go further afield in search of an interpretation.

Jews and the Problematic Secular Sphere

As we have seen (following Luckmann), there are two sides to the institutionalization of religion as a sphere unto itself. The first involves the emergence of a more independent religious "zone," presided over by a more assertive, exclusivist, more professionalized clergy.

The second, inherently parallel side, however, is the increasing independence of all other spheres of life—the family, school, work, the political regime—which are no longer perceived as "religious" in terms of their function or their basis of legitimacy. The institutional autonomy of religion also presupposes the institutional autonomy of what is no longer "religion"—for if "religion" were to pervade all aspects of life, there could be no separate zone specially reserved for religious observance.[55]

Postwar Jews were actively involved in promoting a specialized religious sphere and, in tandem, they were no less actively involved in promoting a separate, secular sphere. We recall that interwar, second-generation Jews gave the impression of having become thoroughly secularized, but in fact most of them retained group behaviors that tied individuals very closely to a collective, family-based, tradition-conscious lifestyle. The *postwar* experience of Jewish secularism, by contrast, could accommodate more visible "organized religion," but it was nonetheless more far-reaching in its secularism.

It is in this light that the data on increasing outmarriage among Jews in the sixties help us to understand how a revitalized religious sphere could coexist with a more intense secularization. When religion becomes less relevant in the choice of mate and outmarriage occurs, this does not necessarily indicate that a Jewish spouse in a mixed marriage is detached from Judaism. We know that in many cases it does not.[56] Rather, we may infer that, for that person, the *family* as an institution is no longer regarded as pertaining by its very nature to the religious sphere.

Outmarriage thus reflects and, in turn, reinforces the secularization of society, even when "religion" as such is held up as a value for the individual. The family, like other secularized social structures, no longer depends on religion to provide its structure of meaning. It depends more on its own value system—its "own," indicating boundaries between proper spheres—love, companionship, and so forth.[57]

This proposition gains added credence when we consider that Cohen's 1981 study had drawn the not unreasonable but—as it turned out—erroneous conclusion that the Jewish rate of nonconversionary outmarriage, like the generational decline in religious practice, had leveled off in the seventies (at around 11 percent for both sexes) and would probably remain stable. A major study of New York Jewry undertaken a decade later found that religious observance had indeed stabilized at levels noted in 1981, but that Jewish outmarriage in New York had taken another spiral jump, reaching 24–25 per cent among first marriages occurring after 1975.[58]

The secularization of the Jewish family as a social institution was, perhaps, still muted in the fifties and sixties (especially in New York), its effects becoming apparent only in the seventies and eighties. But when it came to the public spheres of work, school, community, and politics, there was no qualification or hesitation.

The delineation of social spheres buffered from religious dictates, subject only to the open market of private, individual preference and to rational criteria of performance, is something that we can easily recognize as a characteristic goal of American Jewish civic ideology. But whereas their religionist enterprise—promoting their faith as one of America's three quasi-official religions—placed Jews in a comfortable, uncontroversial position vis-à-vis Americans of other faiths, their secularizing enterprise pitted them against advocates of a Christian-influenced public sphere—and conspicuously so. In this confrontation Jews were evidently prepared to take a stand, despite the negative consequences.

That approach grew directly out of their pursuit of unfettered social mobility, still somewhat thwarted in interwar American society by widespread real or latent assumptions about Christian values as the legitimate and representative culture of the United States. The defense by Jews of religious freedom implied (for most Jews and for most of the twentieth century): public respect for religion as a private, individual concern; and public neutrality on religion in matters related to the marketplace, the election booth, and patriotism.[59]

The Jewish consensus was represented by a statement published in 1957 by the Joint Advisory Committee of the Synagogue Council of America and the National [Jewish] Community Relations Advisory Council, which was based on the following principle:

> Religious liberty is an indispensable aspect of democratic freedom; indeed it is the very foundation of American democracy. As a nation of people attached to different religious faiths, or to none, we owe our survival and our unity to the universal acceptance of the uniquely American concept that the relationship between man and God is not and may not be subject to government control or regulation.[60]

The support by Jews of an autonomous public sphere is related, of course, to what we have noted in chapter 1 about Jewish ideals of urban cosmopolitanism. It is this that led New York Jews, in the interwar period, to make common cause both on the local level with Mayor La Guardia—a fighter for meritocracy in the civil service—and on the national level with the Roosevelt New Deal. In the postwar period, the same heavy Jewish investment in the consolidation of a secular public sphere took its primary expression in the struggle to insulate public schooling from official endorsements or expressions of religion. This was the case for several reasons:

On the one hand, discrimination against Jews in the workplace, in higher education, and in housing quickly dissipated in the early fifties, thus allowing Jews to sense that much of their program had been achieved. On the other hand, the salience of the religion issue in postwar American culture virtually assured a renewed debate over the propriety of "church-state" separation. While religionist issues were sometimes introduced in political life (such as the introduction in 1954 of the phrase "under God" in the pledge of allegiance), it was in the area of public education that emotions and constitutional issues clashed most often and most bitterly.

The public school was also an arena especially close to Jewish hearts. Jews had not only a vested interest in the schools in terms of the education of their children—public education being the preferred type of schooling in all but the most sectarian branches of the Jewish community—but Jews were also heavily represented professionally in public education, especially in New York City.

The overwhelming Jewish consensus was to favor a strict "wall of separation" (although other options, such as "equal time" for both Christianity and Judaism, were entertained in some Jewish organizational circles, beginning in the sixties).[61] The active promotion of the separationist position was arguably the most important domestic Jewish policy priority of the fifties and sixties.[62]

This posture resonated throughout the American Jewish community, but New York was a hub of Jewish activity in this regard. The city was home to the major national Jewish organizations that pursued legal and legislative initiatives in the Jewish interest. The American Jewish Congress and the New York Board of Rabbis were prominently involved, in partnership with other Jewish defense agencies.

In 1952 the Board of Rabbis joined the American Civil Liberties Union, B'nai B'rith, the American Jewish Committee, and the American Jewish Congress in a suit that ranged them against the Protestant Council and the New York Archdiocese of the Catholic Church over the issue of "released time"—a system provided for by New York State law under which pupils in the public schools might be released one afternoon a week to receive religion classes conducted by a "duly constituted religious body" outside the public school.

Opposing the law, the Jewish organizations argued that the system bordered on an establishment of religion, that it placed the public school authorities in the position of enforcing attendance at religion classes (pupils "released" from school but choosing not to attend religion classes were penalized for being truant), and that it invidiously divided the "released" from the "unreleased" pupils in more subtle ways.[63]

More generally, the decision by the New York State Board of Regents to develop a "program on moral and spiritual values" for use in the public schools aroused grave concern in the Jewish organizational leadership. Representatives of the Board of Rabbis met for over two years with representatives of the Catholic Archdiocese, at the behest of the city's superintendent of schools, yet failed to reach a compromise.[64]

With these issues unresolved, the Board of Rabbis continued to issue statements, such as its declaration in early 1960 that "sectarian religious practices have no place in the public schools," and urged that "any doctrinal material or teachings" be eliminated from school programs (including "symbols, ceremonies, and representations identified with specific religions"). The proper place for such observances was in the synagogue, church, or home.[65]

In addition, the case that prompted the U.S. Supreme Court to rule against prayer in the public schools originated in a contested New York statute. A prayer approved in the fifties by the Board of Regents for recitation in public schools was struck down as unconstitutional in May 1962. That same year, citing a decision by a federal district court in Philadelphia, the American Jewish Congress protested the "widespread" practice of daily Bible readings in New York City schools. In June 1963, The U.S. Supreme Court ruled against Bible reading as religious devotion in public schools.[66]

Underlying the Jewish consensus in vigilantly opposing the use of the public sphere for religious purposes was not only a minority religion's sensitivity to the privileged position of the majority faith, and the consequent wish to eliminate such privilege from a "neutral" arena like the schools. In light of what we discussed in chapter 2, postwar Jews were also sensitive to the ways in which antisemitism might be related to deeply embedded aspects of culture, identity formation, and social structure—and this, in turn, was colored by the shadow cast by the Holocaust.

Given that frame of reference, the creation of a virginally secular public sphere—especially in such a crucial area as the education of children—was meant (to use a phrase of Luckmann's) to "remove from the primary institutions [of society] much of the (potentially intolerant) human pathos that proved to be fateful all too often in human history . . . [such removal being] an essential component in freeing social arrangements from primitive emotions."[67]

Thus, Jewish organizations reacted swiftly and resolutely when a Christian "backlash" occurred following the Supreme Court's ban on prayer and Bible reading in public schools. The Catholic journal *America* editorialized, "What will have been accomplished if our Jewish friends win all the legal immunities they seek, but thereby paint themselves into a corner of social and cultural alienation?" and warned that Jews might "[reap] a harvest of fear and distrust." To this the American Jewish Committee retorted that, "This seems to us a very strange piece of advice to offer in the name of pluralism," and vowed to continue to uphold the Jewish consensus on First Amendment separation of church and state.[68]

The Jewish position was an exposed one, and not only in relationship to antiliberal points of view. The liberal Protestant interdenominational biweekly, *Christianity and Crisis,* editorialized in 1964 that "we cannot assume that the best policy for the nation is to establish inhibitions on religious expression in the context of public life." Public opinion polls indicated 70 percent of the American people disapproved of the recent Supreme Court decisions.[69]

However, Jewish demands for strict church-state separationism were firm because they reflected something basic about Jewish goals in postwar society. Those goals were shaped not so much by postwar realities, as by the recent past. There was to be no going back to the marginalization of Jews by other Americans that existed before World War II.

Indeed, one might say that the dual quest for an egalitarian religionism (symbolic parity with Protestants and Catholics) and a nonsectarian, egalitarian, public secularism was a belated battle that truly belonged to the interwar period. In the twenties and thirties, Jews had waged that dual battle but with only limited success and with hobbled self-confidence. Their position was hardly relieved by the trauma of the Second World War: In the early forties, domestic antisemitism reached unprecedented intensity in America, on the one hand, while, on the other, Jews exhibited political hesitancy in pressing home their attempts to stir the conscience of the nation, of Congress, and of the Roosevelt administration in the matter of rescuing Jewish refugees. The account book with American society remained open, and it was important to lay to rest any doubt of the Jews' equal place in American society.

Ironically, their demand for a thoroughly secularized public sphere exposed the Jews' most marginal side; nevertheless, this proved to be a safe bet. The social price that Jews were called upon to pay for taking the stand that they did was not, in the end, a high one. The Supreme Court's position was upheld when efforts to enshrine Christian or generally religious declarations in constitutional amendments failed to gain majority support.[70]

◆ ◆ ◆

Engaged in winning a Depression-era battle in the fifties and sixties—and doing so with greater resources, more self-assurance, and much more success than before—those in the forefront of Jewish public activity may have only dimly perceived, if at all, that American society already faced a different order of concerns. Integrationist goals were won fairly easily; but once the sectarian barriers were cleared away, once one was in fact admitted without qualification to the public square, one faced the question of "integrated into what?"

In chapter 2 we noted the emergence of a discourse that critiqued modern, mass society from the point of view of the embattled individual. Here we will need to note the religious critique that emerged as well, for the intellectual discourse of the fifties and sixties included the recognition that modern, rationally functioning, *secular,* mass society had created a new set of social problems. Secularism and religionism, each pursued for its value in different spheres, might have appeared to be an ideal modern solution in the fifties; but by the next decade, such a division epitomized the problem of an overly segmented social system in which "ultimate" or existential meaning was unavailable.

New York writer Norma Rosen, in a novella that closed out the fifties, (*Green*), conveyed the view that the modern, liberal, postwar synagogue—the very instrument of Jewish integration in a society that recognized religion as a private affair—was something worthy only of suburban (hence debased) culture: enslaved to rampant materialism, the rabbi woefully lacking in moral sensitivity. But the novella itself is supremely religious in its questing after the sense of life's transcendent significance: "How could we begin to weigh everything? And how could we begin to speak of how we should live?"[71]

In a remarkable book that helped to set the countercultural agenda for that time, *Growing Up Absurd* (sections of which were serialized in *Commentary* in early 1960), Paul Goodman raised a number of interrelated problems that, he argued, contributed toward a depersonalized, "absurd" existence devoid of real significance. Goodman, one of the better-known "dissident" Jewish writers in New York, focused in particular on the problems of urban youth, but what concerned him generally was the problem that came to be called "alienation."

Goodman saw alienation as a byproduct of the division of social spheres into separate functional areas that lacked any integrative or overall humanistic values. Put simply, in modern society nothing was sacred or intrinsically valued. The segmented structures and arbitrary techniques of a bureaucratized society and economy were unrelated to issues of paramount personal importance, such as "worth," "justification," "vocation," and "honor." The tasks that society programmed for young people to undertake did not appear to be "real" or "serious" in themselves. Life as such was liable to be perceived as meaningless.

Goodman himself was aware that the problem he was outlining was, fundamentally, a religious one:

> [O]ur society weakens the growing youth's conviction that there is a Creation of the Six Days, a real world rather than a system of social rules that in-

> deed are often arbitrary. . . . [C]ity life turns into Urbanism; the use of our machines is submerged in the Industrial System. . . . But the worst effect of losing the created world is that a young man no longer knows that he is a creature, and so are his friends creatures. . . . He feels that the social roles are *entirely* learned and artificial. . . . If a person asks "How am I justified? What is the meaning of my life?" he will surely find no rational answer. . . . If the *question* arises, as an important question, something is wrong.[72]

This argument is certainly reminiscent of what we encountered in critiques of the "organization man" or the "lonely crowd." In the present context, we must also consider, however, how closely Goodman's argument is related to that of Luckmann's sociology of religion and in particular Luckmann's analysis of secularization. Luckmann, too, had argued that although the segmentation of society (including the emergence of a separate religious sphere) appeared to free the individual, "Autonomy of the primary institutions, 'subjective' autonomy [of the self] and *anomie* are dialectically related."[73]

Goodman's response to the problem of anomie or alienation was an early example of a new genre of radical social thought that would emerge in the course of the sixties. Here we are concerned to indicate the indirect but parallel connection between the radical critique of mass society and the emerging religious critique of secular society.

In assessing the Jewish religious climate in postwar New York, therefore, we need to take stock not only of indices of religious behavior—which are very ambiguous, as we have seen—but also of the renewed ideological discourse.

The New York Religious Intelligentsia

Given the prominent involvement of Jews and Jewish organizations in the postwar secular enterprise, it was not surprising to find that the most perceptive Jewish religious thinkers would find the "dehumanization" of modern society not only disturbing, but also of immediate concern to the cause of Judaism.

A number of remarkable religious intellectuals—Eugene Borowitz, Arthur Cohen, Will Herberg, Abraham Joshua Heschel, Mordecai Kaplan, and Joseph B. Soloveitchik, among others—were active in postwar New York. With its unique combination of a mass Jewish community that was unusually self-sufficient (unusual in terms of other American Jewish communities), containing the central religious and educational institutions of American Jewry, and commanding a frontline position in the emerging social and political debate, New York was a natural place for them to make their presence felt. Their contribution to the tenor of religious life became especially important in the sixties, when the nexus, as they saw it, between the crisis of Judaism and the crisis of modern humanity, became more explicit. The challenge, as Heschel put it, was "how to remain human amid the skyscrapers."[74]

This renewed religious discourse, it should be stressed, was more prescriptive than descriptive, as might be expected in programmatic argumentation. The orientation toward a Judaism *as yet unrealized* had several ramifications: It prevented the new Jewish religious-ideological discourse from retreating into a pastness-fixation or a retrievalist position. At the same time, it seemed to lack firm anchorage in the actual, prosaic practice of Judaism (which, as we have seen, was in an ambiguous state). But, by the same token, it did not suffer the liability of being trapped by conventional religion and it therefore proved to be an attractive religious alternative to those who, in the wake of the sixties, grew disenchanted with organized religion, secular politics, or secular ethnicity.

Although it would be difficult to talk of them as comprising a group in the strict sense of the word, the postwar New York religious intellectuals did articulate one common thesis: that Judaism ought to shift from being a mode of American integrationism to being a mode of symbolic distinctiveness. Herein lay the difference between their program and prewar Jewish discourse.

The anti-integrationist perspective did not seek to cut Judaism or the Jews off from non-Jewish society or to stymie interreligious dialogue; rather, it insisted that dialogue and involvement take place without undermining specific religious content. Heschel put it thus: "[T]he purpose of interreligious cooperation . . . is neither to flatter nor to refute one another, but to help one another, to share insight and learning, . . .in trying to bring about a resurrection of sensitivity, a revival of conscience."[75]

It was Arthur Cohen who challenged the sacred cow of religious integrationism most bluntly when he tore down "the myth of the Judeo-Christian Tradition,"[76] but this perspective was shared by all of the others, too. In staking out a postwar religious position, they found themselves moving beyond the accepted agenda of New York Jewry's organizations and institutions, beyond the quest to bring to completion the integrationist tasks of the interwar period, and therefore, beyond the secular-religious divide. (Typically, some of the religious intellectuals targeted the New York Federation of Jewish Philanthropies—the Jewish community's integrationist institution par excellence—for particular criticism.)[77]

The common, anti-integrationist viewpoint was the result of three converging lines of reasoning, which may be encapsulated as follows:

1. The "church" of American Judaism (synagogue, religious school, rabbinate) that had adopted as its credo a blend of patriotism and religious parity

Abraham Joshua Heschel, 1959. The theologian and one of the leading Jewish activists in the cause of civil rights, sitting in his office at the Jewish Theological Seminary. Photograph by John H. Popper. Courtesy of the Ratner Center for the Study of Conservative Judaism, Jewish Theological Seminary.

for all Americans was spiritually barren. In its American integrationist posture, it failed in its proper, religious function: to challenge the self-satisfaction of the average synagogue-goer and to adequately address primal human needs. Kaplan, still the intellectual gadfly despite his advanced years, found the Jewishness of American Jews "only skin deep . . . social rather than spiritual . . . the product of Jewish association."[78] True religious consciousness, rather, ought to depend less upon institutions and more upon individual commitment, sensitivity to the religious dimension, knowledge of the tradition, and the willingness to use that knowledge and that sensitivity to challenge the status quo.

2. Uncomfortable with middle-class, Americanized, and clergy-professionalized Judaism, they continued to perceive Jews as forming a moral community (i.e., a community with at least tacitly shared, distinctive symbols and values), rather than a "church" with designated pastors. "The Torah," wrote Soloveitchik, "whether in terms of study or practice, is the possession of the entire Jewish community. . . . The thrust of Halakhah is democratic from beginning to end."[79] Despite the apparently moribund state of their religious values and institutions, Jews (in this view) actually lived according to a religious commitment that was *mythic* (nonrational and collective) in the axiomatic character of its acceptance and transmission, and primarily *ethical* in its substance—ethics being related to a worldview grounded in ego-transcending, a priori principles. Borowitz, for example, concurred: "[M]en who know, not in a detached or technical way, but in a very intimate and personal way, that [social ethics] are not just individual caprice but are funda-

mental to the universe itself—such men are already religious."[80] The problem in this regard was that Judaism's inherent religious potential was being underutilized by the Jews themselves.

3. The Jews' religious/mythic/ethical commitment grew out of their special awareness of the utter collapse of alternative, relativistic ethical systems in the mid–twentieth century. That awareness was clearly based on their consciousness of the Holocaust, the persistence of race hatred, the cheapening of human life in a nuclear age, and the ubiquity of violence. Will Herberg, Arthur Cohen, and Eugene Borowitz all wrote along these lines, and I cite here key passages from each one in turn:

> Never in all recorded history has the collapse of the hopes of a civilization taken place so suddenly, almost in the sight of one generation. . . . Our fathers were concerned with fashioning the good life; for us today, the all-absorbing problem is life itself, bare survival.[81]

> It is, however, the irony of Jewish destiny and an adumbration of its divinity that where Jews have forgotten all—all belief, all conviction, all practice—they remember the outrage of history. One might surmise that it is this outrage—perhaps more than all else—which drove them to forgetfulness, which accelerates their passage from belief to unbelief. To deny is to forget—yet in the end, what impels denial cannot be forgotten.[82]

> Despite the relativism that we had learned in the thirties from the anthropologists and the psychologists, it was clear that the Nazis were unambiguously evil. . . . Their barbarities so violated our deepest sense of what is good that if God did not act against the Nazis, He did not exist—He was dead. But . . . [if] God is dead, . . .the Holocaust was a . . . direct reflection of the reality in the universe. As it is empty of meaning or quality, . . .man is free to do what he wishes. The death of God turned out to mean the death of moral value—and most Jews would not accept that. . . . And for some Jews this recognition has proceeded to the point where they acknowledge that their moral commitments do not ultimately arise from self or society. . . . Thus their . . . sense of human values lead[s] to a religious consciousness.[83]

Or, as Heschel put it more poetically: "Prophecy ceased; the prophets [however] endure and can only be ignored at the risk of our own despair."[84]

Clearly, this sensitivity and the agenda of moral reconstruction against the "outrage of history" shared some points in common with secular social and political ideologies. The point that the religious intellectuals were making, however, was that political approaches were insufficient. That is to say, the appeal to religious values depended on (and was in itself) a critique of the failure of secular society—American society, in particular—to maintain the Enlightenment vision of humanity. The religious intelligentsia questioned the very ability of "political man" to escape the relativity of means and ends. Herberg, the disappointed Marxist, emphatically derided the elevation of political principles to the status of moral absolutes: *"Idolatry is the absolutization of the relative."*[85]

Thus, although Judaism might be in crisis, Jewish responsiveness to *humanity's* crisis would offer a positive sign to the postsecular Jew that Judaism still had something worthwhile to offer. What it offered, in religious terms, was nothing less than a restoration of the cosmos—an order of meaning.[86]

That "something" varied, of course, among the different members of the New York Jewish religious intelligentsia. As a group (using that term loosely) that represented nonconventional thinking, their ideological range never conformed strictly to denominational concerns. Soloveitchik, the Orthodox halachist, was no less an ethicist than was Borowitz or Heschel. Thus, Soloveitchik: "Neither ritual decisions nor political leadership constitutes the main task of halakhic man. Far from it. The actualization of the ideals of justice and righteousness is the pillar of fire which halakhic man follows, . . . the perfection of the world under the dominion of righteousness and lovingkindness."[87]

Kaplan, perhaps, stands out in this group as somewhat different. Although he (along with the others) considered American Judaism as it emerged in the fifties to be lacking in religious spirit, he continued to view this as a long-term effect of the integration of the Jews into Western society.[88] Consequently, he seems to have been less cognizant of the new religious possibilities inherent in the social crisis of the sixties. He continued to preach a "naturalistic," "religiohumanist" faith in the individual's capacity to search for his or her own sacred ideals and "maturity."[89] This was a faith that presupposed the individual's psychic security within supportive social institutions (the family, the community, the nation). But these were precisely those institutions that could not effectively support "ultimate meaning" in a society whose basic problem was social alienation.[90]

The Descent of Man

The ascendancy of a renewed religious discourse on Judaism appeared to coincide with the institutional expansion of synagogues and synagogue-related institutions, though in fact the two phenomena were quite distinct.

The great bulk of the Jewish community in the postwar decades perceived that its minority faith, reinstitutionalized as a "church," posed no obstacle to full civic participation—provided only that the public sphere was more carefully insulated from Christian dominance. This Judaism of the foot soldiers was tailored to the rapid implementation of an integrationist policy.

The intellectuals' Judaism, in contrast, was conceived as a point of reference from which the civic order and the culture it produced might be criticized. For the most part, they perceived that the character of civic life was itself the major postwar religious problem. The spiritual uneasiness that hovers over almost the entire corpus of their writing is directly related to the question of the moral fitness of Western civilization in the wake of the Holocaust. Only by testifying to the absolute sacredness of human life, they concurred, could Man be restored to a life of meaning, and only thus could an absent God be recovered.

The Judaism-as-ethics thesis was championed in the first four decades of the twentieth century by such rabbis as Stephen Wise, for whom liberalism, Judaism, and American social ideals were virtually interchangeable (which made Judaism itself an integration enhancer). The postwar religious intellectuals, however, though no less insistent on the religious relevance of social issues, preferred to make the case for Jewish religious authenticity on the basis of the *disparity* between Judaism and American values—indeed, between Judaism and Western culture generally—given the regnant culture of moral relativism. Their Judaism was depicted as a hedge against overidentification with Western, American culture, even while advocating an activist social agenda.[91]

This argument in behalf of a different religious approach to Judaism—the position of "being elsewhere"[92]—was uncannily reminiscent of the outsider-as-critic posture favored between the world wars by the Jewish secular literary intelligentsia, whose influence faded considerably after the fifties. But there was no neat or simple transference of a continuous Jewish argument from one intellectual caste to another. As we saw in chapter 1, the secular-leftist literary intellectuals had based their outsider-insider argument on the fact that modern Jewish social thought was universalist in its highest strivings, despite (or more often, by virtue of) the social marginalization of the Jews themselves. The postwar religious intellectuals turned that argument on its head, finding that the path to the universal led them back to the most particularist parts of the Jewish heritage, even (or especially) at a time when the Jewish social-historical experience could no longer be viewed as marginal. It was a postintegrationist argument.

The shift of intellectual authority from a social-artistic to a religious point of view did not take place in a social vacuum. Despite the conceptual gulf that divided the religious intellectuals from the Jewish community as embodied in its religious institutions, a symbiosis did exist between them: Without the institutional resurgence of the fifties it is doubtful that religious critics would have had either the motivation, the audience, or the platform for their preaching. By the same token, without the weightiness and moral authority of the ideological discussion, the Judaism of the postwar synagogue had little spiritual sustenance to offer.

The fact that the secular literary intellectuals, after their interwar efflorescence, seemed to lose the rigor and independence of their moral argument and that, as a result, their moral discourse resurfaced in new form in the rhetoric of the religious intelligentsia, finds fitting (if ironic) corroboration in the career of Cynthia Ozick, who emerged in the late sixties and early seventies both as an important literary figure and a proponent of religious intellectual discourse. Ozick's career rehearses the transition from secular humanism to religious humanism. Along with Bellow (who returned to Chicago by the end of the sixties) and Isaac Bashevis Singer (whose art was in any case perceived as non-American), Ozick was among the serious American Jewish writers to surface in postwar New York who combined a religious-humanist commitment with their literary craft.

That a secular-humanist writer from the Bronx would come, at the end of the sixties, to adopt religious rhetoric as the only authentically Jewish voice open to her reveals much about the new cultural hegemony of the religious intelligentsia. Had Ozick begun to write in the thirties, it is doubtful whether she would have channeled her moral discourse into a mythic, religious terminology, as the secular-socialist (or anti-Stalinist) humanist rhetoric was then readily available and accepted as common coin. Coming to the subject as she did, however, as a younger, postwar writer, she adopted and championed moralism in art as "liturgy," positing further that the liturgical-moral function of art fulfilled basic Jewish cultural requirements.

Ozick's oft-quoted programmatic essay on the tasks of a Jewish writer and the potential for building a Jewish literary tradition in the American idiom neatly symbolizes the paradigmatic shift between the ethos of Jewishness as a secular ethnicity and that of Judaism as a religion. Originally entitled, "Toward a New Yiddish" (which she delivered as a lecture in Israel in the summer of 1970), the piece was subsequently published under the name, "Toward Yavneh." The substitution of *Yavneh* for *Yiddish* signaled a preference for an elitist rabbinic-theological discourse (Yavneh having been the site where first-century Palestinian rabbis, led by Yohanan Ben-Zakkai, laid the groundwork for the Talmud and for exilic Judaism generally), in contrast to the plebeian folk language of the immigrant generation, a language whose literary history was distinctly secular.

Ozick's essay claimed for the Jews a need "to passionately wallow in the human reality." This, she insisted, was a religious impulse. The non-Jewish, nonreligious option was to elevate to primacy the aesthetics of art, the form and the text:

Cynthia Ozick, author, 1974. Ozick spoke out for the importance of discovering a Jewish cultural agenda. Photograph courtesy of the Jerusalem Post *photographic collection.*

> The Jewish community in America is obviously undistinguished, so far, in its religious achievements; but the astounding fact is that *we define ourselves as a religious community* [emphasis in the original]. . . . The sociological explanations for our willingness to think of ourselves as a religious community, though most of us profess to be agnostics at least, are multiple, commonplace, accurate, well-known—but irrelevant. Our synagogues are empty; this too is irrelevant, because nowadays they are only cathedrals, and we have always done without cathedrals. But our conversations have become liturgical.[93]

Ozick defined "liturgy" as transcending aesthetics, which is "a private flattery." Liturgy, as she argued the point, is "in command of the reciprocal moral imagination rather than of the isolated lyrical imagination." Whereas poetry, she contended, "moves the heart, but to no end other than being moved," liturgy "means not to have only a private voice [but also] a choral voice, a communal voice, the echo of the voice of the Lord of History."

To her, the contrast to such "liturgy" lay in the "neo-pagan" categories of her day: "lifestyle" (morally relative, interchangeable, and optional); the "idolatry" or "sacrament" of pure text, removed from a historically engaged point of view and a historical community; and "moral anaesthesia"—for which she also gave her Russian-born father's pithy Yiddish definition: *"Amerikaner-geboren"*: American-born.[94]

Taking this jaundiced view of American *non-Jewish* culture (in which she included, as well, such Jewish figures as Allen Ginsberg), Ozick thus took up once again the burden of marginality ("perfectly at home and yet perfectly insecure, perfectly acculturated and yet perfectly marginal")[95]—only in her case she championed the particular as a virtue: "From being envious apes we can become masters of our own civilization—and let those who want to call this 're-ghettoization' . . . look to their destiny. . . . If we blow into the narrow end of the *shofar*, we will be heard far. But if we choose to be Mankind rather than Jewish and blow into the wider part, we will not be heard at all; for us, America will have been in vain."[96]

Ozick's quest for cultural meaning, taking off from a spiritual, particularistic point of departure, was hardly an isolated eccentricity. Bashevis Singer and Elie Wiesel were similarly embarked on such a trajectory. Unlike Ozick, they were immigrant writers and had come to their religious ideologies through non-American conduits: Bashevis, from a Warsaw rabbi's *beys din* to a postmodern spirituality, and Wiesel from the Hasidic world of Sighet to a crisis of faith in the wake of the Holocaust.[97] Likewise, their literary roots were non-American: Bashevis having traversed the artistic landscape via the European modernism that he had encountered in Poland, and Wiesel having cut his teeth on the postwar French avant-garde.

Nevertheless, in a way very much like Ozick, they were primarily concerned with reaching a universal, moral, mythic voice by invoking a universe derived explicitly from the Jewish experience at its most particular. Bashevis had an entire folkloristic pantheon to fall back on, whereas Wiesel used the world of Auschwitz, Buchenwald, and the entire unreality of the Holocaust as an allegorical dimension of space and time.

Whereas Bashevis, as we have seen, was given to disingenuous disclaimers of any didactic role—posing as a simple teller of tales—while simultaneously grappling with the problem of moral chaos, Wiesel unabashedly assumed the religious-didactic role: a survivor-prophet (not unlike his friend Heschel, the refugee-prophet-theologian). Famous for the passage in his first novel, *Night*, in which the hanging of a Jewish child in Auschwitz was seen as figuring the murder of God's image ("Where is God now? . . . I heard a voice within me answer . . . : Where is He? Here He is—He is hanging here on this gallows"), he soon returned to the prewar religious tradition for inspiration and material.[98]

Wiesel continued to retool himself as a religious guide to a lost generation. In one of many interviews, Wiesel donned a quasi-rabbinic mantle in responding to a question about the young American Jews who flocked to his lectures and read his books: "They come to me not to find an answer, but to ask a question. . . . I myself am still searching, but what is encouraging . . . is that all these young people are searching too."[99] He delivered a very popular lecture series on his favorite Hasidic masters on the Upper East Side, at New York's 92nd Street YM-YWHA, a high-profile cultural mecca. He nurtured his prophetic-didactic role, becoming an important activist for Soviet Jewry and for human rights generally as well as a vocal protester against genocide

Elie Wiesel, 1973. A well-known writer, Holocaust survivor, and spokesman for human rights, in the sixties Wiesel came to New York, where his literary career began to flourish. Photograph courtesy of the Jerusalem Post *photographic collection.*

(from Cambodia to Bosnia). Eventually the Nobel Peace Prize and the chairmanship of the President's Holocaust Commission made him a national and an international figure. Clearly, the heart of Wiesel's enterprise has been more religious than literary (indeed, in recent years, the critics of his literary oeuvre have not been kind). It has been quipped, but only half-jokingly, that he is the closest thing to a pope (a figurehead with uncommon consensual spiritual authority) that American Jews possess.

◆ ◆ ◆

Taken together, the New York religious intellectuals and the writers who joined them adopted a brooding, pessimistic, Jewish voice—a post-Holocaust, nuclear-age voice. Their lectures, essays, journals, books, and personal example made available to a wide readership a noninstitutional, sophisticated religious discourse that filled needs unaddressed by conventional religious leaders.

It is therefore inadequate, when reassessing the religious climate, to ask the quantified questions of "how much Judaism?" Jewish religion in postwar New York was both reinstitutionalized—seen to fulfill "churchlike" functions; and once again diffused—seen to provide a vocabulary of moral suasion, a posture to take up vis-à-vis American cultural and political issues, and an existential justification for life in troubled times.

Theological pessimism was the intellectual vogue, perhaps because it held out the only viable source for a renewed spirituality (though of course one can read this renewal of search as a form of optimism). In any event, the trend articulated an inward, postintegrationist, Judaism. Cultural pessimism was, as we saw in chapters 2 and 3, widespread. It had led to a cul-de-sac of nostalgia for what had been lost.

In its turn, political pessimism would emerge by the late sixties—and it is to this and to related issues that we turn in the next chapters. We will see that some of the themes that emerged in Jewish culture and religion, involving a retreat from universalist perspectives and the repossession of a particularist vernacular, were well suited to the social and political climate that took shape in New York in sixties. It may in fact be suggested that Jews were culturally primed for a political retreat from urban ideals and that, in turn, their inward-turning tendencies were reinforced still further by the political climate.

5

Why Can't They Be Like Us?

Race, Class, and Civic Culture

> Lesser asks Willie to grant him good will. "I know how you feel, I put myself in your place." In cold and haughty anger the black replies, . . ."Black ain't white and never can be. It is once and for all only black. It ain't universal if that's what you're hintin up to. What I feel you feel different."
>
> —Bernard Malamud,
> *The Tenants*

> No one was white before he/she came to America. It took generations and a vast amount of coercion before this became a white country. . . . Jews came here from countries where they were not white, and they came here in part *because* they were not white. . . . Everyone who got here, and paid the price of the ticket, the price was to become "white."
>
> —James Baldwin

> Ethnicity and race dominate the city, more than ever seemed possible in 1963. That was, after all, before the first summer riots. The civil rights revolution had not yet broken out of the South.
>
> —Nathan Glazer and Daniel Patrick Moynihan,
> *Beyond the Melting Pot* (1970)

Taking It Personally

As a preteen during the years of struggle for equal voting rights for African Americans and desegregation in the South, I took it for granted that in places like Mississippi and Alabama, the core problem that faced black people was the irrational, implacable hatred of white people toward them. In New York, by contrast (still according to my early layman's impressions), it was poverty, not hate, that was the problem. Not only could one not point to a principled, politically sanctioned segregation between people of different backgrounds—you would never see *our* governor on television barring the entrance of a college to black students—but also, as far as I could pick up from people of my parents' generation (relatives, friends, teachers), there was an active desire to put things right.

I don't recall ever wondering, however, whether black children my age saw a difference between southern white racist supremacy and northern white, supposedly nonracist, economic advantage.

I also don't recall whether or not I consciously saw Miss Thompson, the seventh-grade typing teacher, as a model of black integration through white-collar mobility (though in retrospect, I probably did think something of the sort, even if I could not articulate it). I do remember, though, that she was our only black teacher and that she was young, tall, slim, and pretty (all points in her favor). Her middle-class, Standard English diction sounded more naturally "American" than the slight roll of Irish *r*s in the speech of my ninth-grade algebra teacher.

The black children bussed up from "Harlem" (our word for any black neighborhood) to my junior high school in the Bronx were being transported far from home, I knew, because the economically depressed neighborhoods where they lived undermined their chances of obtaining a decent education and a chance for self-advancement. In 1961, when the program of "permissive zoning" was first initiated for some junior high schools, 4,000 out of an eligible 15,000 families opted to have their children transferred out of their local school districts to "unsegregated" schools. In 1965, black groups organized a school boycott to protest the slow progress in school integration—and 45 percent of city pupils stayed home.[1]

Just why basic services like public schools should have been inadequate in those children's own home environment, or why de facto residential segregation by color was a way of life in New York—why, indeed, did all those black kids live so far away, nowhere near my street?—were questions that would have taxed my limited powers of analysis and my limited awareness of racial thinking at that age. As it was, it only barely registered on me at the time that my own mixed Jewish-Catholic, middle- and lower-middle-class neighborhood constituted a pocket of relative privilege, at least in quality-of-life terms.

Yet register it did, because the question of black-white integration and the abyss of disparity between black and white parts of the city were among the first social and political facts of life that one learned in New York in the early sixties, even if one were white, and even at the tender age of eleven, twelve, or thirteen.

And still, I think that I (and many others) lived in a kind of conditioned ignorance where black-white relations in our city were concerned. It is perhaps not very unusual to read the following comment by an African American New York woman included in a 1964 study of black attitudes: "Well, I found a lot of white people who are not Jewish who think no matter how much education we get we still have a place. Jews mention nothing about color—not even to their children."[2] Certainly nothing explicit was ever mentioned to me.

It is true that a dawning awareness of the city's increasing diversity had taken hold in Jewish community circles; but the experts misread the scope of the demographic changes that would soon place Jewish New Yorkers in a new situation—one in which Jews would no longer be the dominant element among mostly white ethnics, but would be sharing the city in a new way.[3] Blithe unawareness of others' situations would not last under those new conditions.

But to have imagined, as I think I and many others did, that jobs and education were all it would take to resolve racial issues—that progress toward that goal was certain and that its realization could be entrusted to a color-blind, benign, liberal civic order—was probably naïve. It was definitely a white person's perspective. And it was an effect of (white) liberal attitudes floating freely in my environment, easy to imbibe and believe in, but preserving a blind spot where some of the tougher issues of race were concerned.

A wide-ranging study of black-Jewish relations in New York conducted by professional pollster Louis Harris in mid-1969 reported that two-thirds of the Jews living in Manhattan, the Bronx, and Queens personally favored an integrated society (though only 43 percent of Jews in Brooklyn did so). City-wide, fully 81 percent of those Jews who were unaffiliated with any of the three major Jewish denominational groups similarly supported that goal in principle. (The corresponding figure among Orthodox Jews was only 40 percent, which helps to explain the distinct profile of Brooklynites in this study.) But when asked whether the demands of black people in the city were justified—demands that black New Yorkers, as a group, were entitled to a greater and fairer share of the life of the city—only 38 percent of Manhattan, Bronx, and Queens Jews were prepared to agree. Similarly, Jews consistently underestimated the degree to which black New Yorkers felt they were subject to discrimination in such areas as housing, skilled employment, entry into labor unions, wage levels, and treatment at the hands of police.[4]

Although for the most part Jews were persuaded that it was right to support the black struggle against social and economic discrimination, they often did so out of an integrationist strategy that left them unable to entertain notions of enduring group distinctiveness. Historian Henry Feingold posits that Jews had typically internalized the American libertarian ethic that assured the individual's progress without interference, and linked that ethic to their own identity. In his words, they "cast their lot" with the "American experiment."[5]

Among the first to point out the pitfalls of this sort of integrationism and its ramifications for Jewish-black relations was the noted rabbi and writer-scholar, Arthur Hertzberg. Jews who were driven to ignore group distinctions, he argued, did a disservice not only to themselves (so clearly in need of retaining some sense of their own particularism), but to blacks, too, who were interested in integration but not at the price of their own identity. The point was echoed several years later by Zionist historian Ben Halpern.[6]

That sort of integrationism ultimately meant a desire to become immersed in the dominant culture—white America—and Jews could hardly accomplish this without it having some bearing on Jewish-black relations. "How could it be otherwise?" asked another leading New York Jewish communal figure, Albert Chernin of the National (Jewish) Community Relations Council. Jews ran the risk, he suggested, of taking on "white attitudes" in matters of race, including "the illusory image of white superiority." This, he warned, was "one of the unhappy consequences of acculturation."[7]

James Baldwin, the African American writer, complained of being told too often by Jews, "We suffered, too, but we came through, and so will you. In time." And he felt it necessary to remind Jews that the comparison was repugnant, under the circumstances:

> One does not wish . . . to be told by an American Jew that his suffering is as great as the American Negro's suffering. It isn't, and one knows that it isn't from the very tone in which he assures you that it is. . . . One may become reconciled to the ruin of one's own life, but to become reconciled to the ruin of one's children's lives is not reconciliation. It is the sickness unto death. And one knows that such counselors are not present on these shores by following this advice. They arrived here out of the same effort the American Negro is making: They wanted to live, and not tomorrow, but today. Now since the Jew is living here, like all the other white men living here, he wants the Negro to wait. And the Jew sometimes—often—does this in the name of his Jewishness, which is a terrible mistake.[8]

If a Jew "values his color and uses it," Baldwin went on to suggest, his Jewishness "has no relevance."[9] In playing the white man, he loses his claim to innocence:

> Jews in Harlem are small tradesmen, rent collectors, real estate agents, and pawnbrokers; they operate in accordance with the American business tradition of exploiting Negroes, and they are therefore identified with oppression and are hated for it. . . . The Negro, facing a Jew, hates, at bottom, not his Jewishness but the color of his skin. It is not the Jewish tradition by which he has been betrayed but the tradition of his native land.[10]

There may have been some substance to the idea that animosity toward Jews stemmed, at least in part, from actual friction in daily life in the ghetto.

Just as likely, however, was the proposition that it was not the individual Jewish shopkeeper or property owner who was perceived as acting like "whitey," but rather the Jewish community at large, which had invested so much energy and actually succeeded in joining the great white American majority. The local ghetto merchant or landowner was probably just a stand-in for a much larger projected Jewish image.

In any case, it was Baldwin, again, who resigned in protest (in February 1967) from the black journal, *The Liberator,* when that publication ran a series of articles on Jews and blacks that categorically accused Jews—as such—of exploiting black people in the city. Antisemitism, Baldwin declared, was "barbaric."[11]

The Melting Pot Boils Over

Nathan Glazer and Daniel Patrick Moynihan first published their now-classic study, *Beyond the Melting Pot,* in 1963, arguing that the melting "did not happen." New Yorkers of different background shared a common identity of place rather superficially. The realities of race and ethnicity ran deeper than expected. In their everyday lives, New Yorkers insisted on turning urban spaces, political fiefdoms, and occupational niches into turf aggressively claimed or tenaciously defended—often with explicit racial or ethnic connotations.[12]

Intergroup relations (meaning, essentially, racial rather than class or even interreligious relations) were the great looming domestic issue of postwar America. Yet, even as racial and group rhetoric heated up, some Americans—including many urban Jews—still preferred to think in terms that were raceblind. To think in such terms while being caught up in a verbal and political storm of interracial tension was sure to cause frustration, promote feelings of political inadequacy, and ultimately bring into question many earlier assumptions about the life of the city.

It may be stated, in brief, that the city as a concept, a pattern of life that ran along known, set paths that permitted collective endeavor to occur, was itself undermined when it became difficult to continue to see the city as an all-embracing framework.

"As a new group arrived in the city, it would stake out a neighborhood, welcome its kinfolk, and settle in for the long pull," the Harris survey of 1969 explained. "The city's history is replete with accommodations being made among the various ethnic strains to allow each to find its own center of gravity." However, this modus vivendi "requires minorities to stick together and find ways of accommodating each other. Otherwise, the city would fall apart."[13]

Writer and social critic David Bazelon had a similar understanding of what was at stake for city inhabitants in trying to keep the ways of the city within known bounds of social interaction. A younger groupie of the New York intellectuals, Bazelon had come to New York from Chicago at age twenty in 1943. He knew that ethnic coloration was part of the warp and woof of New York ("To the kid from Chicago, New York was an astoundingly bright new world, filled with Jews of marvelous variety: like a supermarket kind of candy store, with versions of heritage, row-upon-row, freely to be chosen from"), and he willingly took on some of this coloration himself.[14] Ethnic diversity did not undermine the life of the city: Precisely because it was filled with so many "somebody else's," the city taught an elaborate technique of social mapping, which made it all work:

> The regional or small-property view concentrates on the fantasy of self-centered Individualism, supported by some real or imagined organic culture—always local. The urban view, almost by definition, must be that of a people who live under the god of organization. . . . The urbaner . . . is a born psychologist and quickly becomes a sociologist as well, certainly as a status analyst. He is always looking out for himself, parry and thrust, but never overrates his capacity. Quixote dies in a city: if he wants to fight an organization, the urbaner joins with others to create an organization. . . . The urbaner spends all of his time knowing that he is surrounded by people, even when the doors are closed or his eyes are shut. And most of his time he is actively engaged with others, which includes thinking their thoughts—often in order to determine his own. . . . He needs always to know what they are doing, what they can do.[15]

To "know what they are doing, what they can do," implies a capacity for empathy: a sense of the "other" as a counterpart to the self, whose life and thoughts are comprehendible and predictable. This sort of understanding and ability to empathize was not based on sameness, either in ethnic or class terms, but on shared assumptions about civic participation.

We can cite here, too, social philosopher Horace Kallen's very similar use of the term "like-mindedness" (the capacity to think along converging lines) when contrasting the defining attributes of the public sphere in urban relations with the limited life of small, ascriptive groups: "The common city life, which depends upon like-mindedness, is not inward, corporate, and inevitable, but external, inarticulate, and incidental. . . , not the expression of a homogeneity of heritage, mentality, and interest."[16] The "common life" of the city was "incidental" in that one lived prepared to encounter strangers at every turn; but it was not haphazard, because such encounters could be relied upon to fall within known parameters.

But what if the disparities between peoples' lives were so wide that one could not really make an empathic leap of imagination and "think their thoughts"? What if imagining the inner world of the other were beyond reach? What would an "urbaner" do when no longer able to fathom the reality of the stranger? Increasingly from the end of the fifties and on into the sixties, life in New York entailed this sort of estrangement when it dawned on people, both white and black, that the crisis of the city boiled down to the incapacity for empathy between strangers.

It is not to be inferred, of course, that intergroup conflict (Bazelon's "parry and thrust") and jostling for position were necessarily new. Nor can it be plausibly claimed that Jews in the sixties felt greater hostility from others than had been true in the past, during the interwar period, for example.[17] Many social scientists tended to argue that nothing was going on other than the normal strains caused by the "succession" of one group by another, a standard feature of life in diverse cities like New York. Nor was it literally always the case that New Yorkers knew whatever there was to know about the other. Writer Paul Goodman pointedly remarked that "In the Empire City, the facades of the rich neighborhood were more anonymous than those of the poor. The poker face of Park Ave. told little, and threatened much. Here no Irish pennants hung out the windows to reveal that they still wore old-fashioned red drawers. . . . This orderly reticence was a symbol of stronger class agreement than the poor have, and it was a protection."[18]

But in the case of white and black New Yorkers, the terms in which differences were apprehended (or misapprehended) seemed altered. The experience of social tension was not new, but new rules were being written for intergroup conflict that raised the political costs of social empathy and raised the moral value of victimhood—and these were new elements.

In the conflation of ideas about mass society, mass politics, and the city that had emerged in the postwar years Jews, as we saw in chapter 2, were closely attuned to the issue of antisemitism. However, the professional literature on the subject of intergroup relations tended to emphasize a clinical, diagnostic approach by seeking the sources of hatred in universal behavior patterns, rather than voicing a response in the name of the Jewish group. The various studies and programs looked into the maladjustment of the offender but did not ponder the subjective experience of the victim, since the victim was ostensibly not the issue. Indeed, it was important to demonstrate that bigots targeted multiple victims, thus foregrounding a single pathology of bigotry in which the victims' identity was all but irrelevant: in fact, all victims of prejudice were, by definition, in the same boat (again, reinforcing the notion of civic empathy). Society itself was held up as the ultimate victim.[19]

Moreover, as an astute student of the subject has pointed out, this approach incorporated a studied apolitical point of view that afforded its advocates immunity from charges of radicalism. "The politics of anticommunism [in the forties and fifties], together with the principles of social psychology, encouraged intergroup-relations professionals to define their objectives in moral and psychological terms . . . [and thus] they failed to appreciate that intergroup relations might require a redistribution of power among members of various racial, religious, and ethnic groups."[20]

This "prejudice" approach, based on the notion of a pathology of prejudice in the offender, put the onus squarely upon those persons so ill-equipped for life in mass society that they were unable or unwilling to treat those who were different as individuals like themselves, but only as representatives of the hated "other kind" of people. This did not absolve society from treating the disease, but it did supposedly absolve the victims themselves from "taking it personally."

The solutions lay in greater economic justice, in social engineering toward desegregation by government, universities, hospitals, schools, and service agencies generally; in the removal of the stigmas related to occupational status (thus supposedly taking the sting out of "downward" occupational shifts); and most important, in the training of the next generation toward more constructive outlets for social and psychological tensions.[21] These were clearly matters for the state and other major social agencies, not to be dealt with at the level of the aggrieved parties themselves.

Because the "perpetrators" were not conceived of as a "group" or as representatives of a wide section of society, let alone a symptom of norms that were widely institutionalized in society, victimhood lacked reality except as a by-product of misplaced socioeconomic grievance. Victimhood conferred no status because the victim's own personhood and activity were never involved in the actual factors that might have led the hater to hate. It also lacked political merit, whether as a basis for demands for compensation, as a platform for group mobilization, or as a moral claim of priority over other groups.

It is well to recall that such ideas were propagated in the media and the arts, and not just in intellectual forums. Both *Gentlemen's Agreement* (the antibigotry novel by Laura Hobson, subsequently the film, starring Gregory Peck) and Arthur Miller's play, *Focus,* put across the message that an anti-semite would hate anyone presumed—even falsely—to be Jewish, since "Jew" was "merely a label," a projection of the bigot's hatred, not an actual, concrete, identifiably "other" human being.[22]

This reliance on socioeconomic and individual-projective explanations of racism was, perhaps, difficult to sustain in the long run. As more than one observer has pointed out, it was becoming implausible to argue that highly successful Jews and poverty-stricken African Americans were "in the same boat."[23] Yet, the evasion of a group-defined politics was not easily unlearned.

Jews often persisted in subscribing to color-blind or group-blind approaches to civic affairs even when such visions of life in the city dimmed. There are several ramifications of this persistent political behavior, to which we will return presently. For now, we may simply observe that many Jews, having succeeded under the banner of civic "likemindedness," much preferred to believe that the differences between urban dwellers were all of the same type and, hence, susceptible to negotiated competition, division of turf, or palliative solutions.

In a way, denial that other peoples' experience—black peoples' experience, for example—might not reliably point to the truth of these established civic verities was a liberal impulse: color and minority status were to be ignored in the interests of promoting "likemindedness." To have admitted otherwise would be to lose all hope in the city as a venue for a good life. But this also tended to give rise to complaints that cropped up in Jewish and black discourse when things did not turn out quite as expected. "Why can't they be like we were?" came the Jewish complaint; or, to say this in other words: Why is the ground for "likemindedness" less and less in evidence?[24]

The black retort—as reflected in the statements by Baldwin quoted earlier in the chapter as well as in the following one—was that empathy, to be true, depended upon recognition of how very different black realities were: "Very few Americans, and this includes very few Jews, have the courage to recognize that the America of which they dream and boast is not the America in which the Negro lives. It is a country which the Negro has never seen."[25]

Roy Innis, the national director of CORE (Congress of Racial Equality) (and a member of the board of the New York Urban Coalition), similarly pointed out: "The American way is the white way, and that's very good for whites. It has nothing to do with black people. Black people are not just another ethnic group like the Italians, Jews, or Irish. . . . I refuse to mix black-white problems with the class problem. . . . Our problem is unique."[26]

That an emphasis on race and group came to take precedence in the discourse of the sixties over class status and individual achievement was a disturbing development to some Americans, and to Jews in particular, who were loath to think that, in the long run, they were being judged by who they were, rather than by universal criteria of success. Historian Ben Halpern, a keen observer of the American Jewish scene, once pointed out: "Jews did not fail to fight discrimination . . . in the name of liberalism, . . .[but] their own highly successful social and economic adjustment was not won by storming the breastworks of entrenched illiberalism." Rather, "They skirted these barriers—that is, they avoided the issue and went on ahead."[27] Distinction and respect were rewards that might be shared collectively if status and prestige accrued to an increasing number of the group's members in the civic spheres of culture, business, the arts, politics, and the professions.

The same, however, could not be maintained about black people who sought to follow the same route. "Achievement by many individuals is supposed to dissolve collective denigration—and yet it has not," concludes one recent student of the subject.[28]

Jews, by and large, remained wedded nonetheless to the liberal, individualist approach that had worked for them. Thus, in the sixties, Jews emerged affluent but bewildered into a confrontational era in which the rhetoric of group, which they thought they had left behind in the thirties and forties, returned to haunt them.

Thus, the following anecdote (related in a study of New York mayoral politics) is very revealing. In the 1965 New York mayoralty campaign, Abraham Beame won the Democratic nomination in a four-way primary race—the first Jew ever to be selected as the party's nominee for the mayor's office. Opinion polls taken two months before election day showed Beame running well ahead of his Republican-Liberal opponent, John V. Lindsay, among the city's Jewish electorate. In October, however, while campaigning in Harlem (a Democratic bastion), Beame was introduced by local political heavyweight, Congressman Adam Clayton Powell, Jr.:

"It's time we proved we can elect a Jew in New York as mayor," Powell said, using the frank language of ethnic distinction. "If I don't get these Jews, these Catholics into office, how can I ever expect to be President of the United States?"[29] Powell's appeal to group pride and to bloc voting by "kind" boomeranged for Beame among middle-class, liberal Jewish voters. Beame lost the mayoralty, even though Mario Procaccino, running with Beame as candidate for city comptroller, was elected, as was Frank O'Connor, who ran with Beame for the post of City Council president. Beame had to wait eight more years for a comeback.[30]

The reluctance of Jews to relate in ethnoracial terms to matters that they considered to be civic or economic in nature was a bone of contention in black-Jewish encounters from the end of the fifties on. In 1959, for example, the New York branch of the NAACP (National Association for the Advancement of Colored People) undertook to pressure Harlem liquor wholesalers—most of them Jewish—to give black liquor salesmen a greater share of their business. The campaign failed to win results through negotiation, black salesmen complained that they were being shut out on racial grounds, and pressure was increased by the use of pickets. L. Joseph Overton, president of the New York NAACP, said at the time, "I was hopeful that we could find some compromise because of the closeness that had existed between Jews and the Negro community. Most of the white businessmen in Harlem are Jewish, and

I thought that they should understand from the long business relationship the nature of this problem."[31]

Clearly, Overton had expected Jews to be able to read their group experience (i.e., Jews' experience of discrimination) into their business relations with black entrepreneurs and customers. His frustration stemmed from the dissonance between this group-collectivist approach to economic uplift and the approach, still embraced by many Jews in the city, that would look only at individuals—not whole groups—as civic partners.

In 1962 (in a small incident now long forgotten), a Jewish businessman, Sol Singer, decided to open a restaurant in the heart of Harlem. His establishment was picketed for weeks by local residents who (according to wire service reports) "occasionally" resorted to anti-Jewish epithets. Prominent black figures, including labor leader A. Philip Randolph and baseball hero Jackie Robinson, tried to defuse the situation and condemned the anti-Jewish name calling, but to little avail. The protesters had defined the issue as one of boosting black economic interests. Singer had, in the end, no choice but to sell out to black businessmen.[32]

In 1961, in a more significant case, a black employee at a union shop in New York's garment industry, supported by Herbert Hill (the Orthodox-Jewish-educated labor secretary of the NAACP), filed a complaint against both the employer and Cutters' Local 10 of David Dubinsky's garment-trades union, the ILGWU, on the grounds of alleged racial discrimination. (The "ILG" was a pillar of New York labor that regarded itself—with some justification—as a paragon of progressive social responsibility.) The New York State Commission for Human Rights found in favor of the plaintiff, Ernest Holmes, the following year, despite the union's defense of its antidiscrimination record.[33]

But the affair was not over yet. Harlem congressman Adam Clayton Powell, Jr. conducted an investigation into the union's practices before a subcommittee of the House of Representatives Committee on Education and Labor. With the Hill-Dubinsky confrontation and the Powell Commission in the background, a vituperative, hysterical polemic burst out in print between Paul Jacobs (the professional union organizer, veteran *tummler* [troublemaker], former Trotsykist, and survivor of the bloody internecine wars of the inbred American Left on both coasts) and his former boss, Dubinsky. Jacobs accused Dubinsky of egregious paternalism, Jewish ethnocentrism, and toadying to the employers.[34]

The affair rang alarm bells precisely because of the race-conscious rancor that invaded the debate. The foremost Jewish union was stranded like a beached whale when its New Deal-era rhetoric of class-based, ethnically diverse solidarity came up against the urban reality of the early sixties.

New York Garment District, 1969. Photograph by Klaus Lehnartz. Courtesy of Stapp Verlag.

Elements of both the black and the Jewish communities had also clashed over tensions involving urban renewal projects. In the early postwar years an urban-planning juggernaut spearheaded by Robert Moses (the omnipotent parks, highways, and housing czar) in cooperation with large banking, insurance, and real-estate interests had sparked off a twenty-year struggle over neighborhood rehabilitation and construction. Some Jewish civic groups, along with others, were implicated in this war over the "relocation" of tenement-dwellers to "stabilize" and expand middle-class, white neighborhoods, while in fact removing old housing stock from use and forcing slum dwellers to move to overcrowded, bulging ghettos.[35]

In the fifties, the rhetoric in this battle was that of urban improvement, development, and slum clearing. By the next decade, the issues of slum tenements, public housing projects, neighborhood integrity and residential segregation—and the related questions of school integration, street crime, and public-supported welfare programs—had come out from behind the mask of urban renewal and were quite explicitly debated along race- and ethnic-conscious lines.

In 1969, a "task force" of intellectuals was charged by the American Jewish Committee with the challenge of drawing up projections for "group life in America" for the coming decade. The group, led by Seymour Martin Lipset, rendered its report in 1972, which included a limited, qualified endorsement of the notion of group interests, insofar as this did not harm the "primacy of the individual" in a free society. It backed a plan that would require greater taxation to redistribute wealth and services for the greater benefit of the inner cities.[36]

The rhetoric of group may have had a liberating effect in terms of pride, self-affirmation and self-assertiveness; but it inevitably also reverberated with grimmer echoes. Jews associated an overemphasis on race, group, and "kind" with the not-yet-buried memory of being marked out, excluded: in the extreme case, with having their relatives disappear in concentration camps. There was a distinction between admitting, on the one hand, that America was racially, ethnically, and religiously diverse but accommodating to everyone, and entertaining the view, on the other hand, that America was irrevocably divided as a society—so divided that individual advancement hinged on intergroup struggle. That distinction would sow contention within New York Jewry because it cut right across many of the "givens" of American Jewish life.

Thus the editors of the *American Jewish Year Book* wrestled for years with the seemingly trivial issue of what to call their yearly report on domestic American social relations. The practice until 1964 had been to call it a report on "Civil Rights"—indicating a preoccupation with the legal side of racial struggle. In 1965, "Civil Rights and Intergroup Tensions" replaced the older formula, indicating an uncomfortable awareness that a good deal of social tension was no longer a "civil rights" issue and could not be considered solely as majority-minority relations. By 1967, the title omitted all reference to civil rights and became simply, "Intergroup Relations and Tensions." In turn (by 1976) this would give way to "Politics and Intergroup Relations."

As one observer later described the prevailing atmosphere: "New York City itself became a verbal and at times a literal battleground between Blacks and Jews. . . . In many cases, ethnicity seemed to have taken over from ideology; in fact, ethnicity had become the dominant ideology." A later assessment of how city politics had developed since the sixties summed it up as follows: "The roles of [white] ethnic politics and of splits between reformers and party 'bosses' have become less prominent, and electoral politics . . . became increasingly a matter of positions on race relations."[37]

Issues like "identity," previously subordinated to the goals of integration, were brought to the fore. New York Jewish intellectuals of the older generation were either perplexed, like Lionel Trilling, to find themselves accused of being too assimilationist, or moved, like Irving Howe, to reconnect with the culture of Yiddish.[38]

Civic issues, once a promising arena of common engagement, could come to appear unbearably overwhelming and divisive: "Too much, we say, it is all too much," Alfred Kazin would complain. The "weight of guilt we all bear in the city" was intolerable. "[T]here is so much humanity packed up in these streets, so much friction, so much hatred. . . . Why should *we* have to confront all the injustice of our time just because we live in a big city?"[39]

Elsewhere Kazin would comment: "New York was [once] remarkably open. But now . . . I feel cheated by my old girlfriend, New York. . . . I've lost a lot of my romanticism about New York."[40] Perhaps that accounts for why Kazin went back to the past to recover the city that he had known in the forties and fifties—then, as a pioneer colonizer "on native ground" and seen in retrospect as a "New York Jew."

Years later, New York writer Phillip Lopate would reflect on the sense of decline and disappointment that beset those who remembered life in New York's halcyon days. "Bohemia's passing," Lopate offered, "needs to be seen in the larger context of the decline of the urban public realm."[41]

More disturbing, however, was Bernard Malamud's 1971 novel, *The Tenants,* in which common endeavor and common urban landscape fail to bring together Jew and black except in mutual bloodshed. Harry Lesser, a faltering writer clinging to his statutory tenant's rights in a derelict, rent-controlled building, and Willie Spearmint, part-time squatter and would-be creator of the great black novel, find themselves cheek by jowl in downtown Manhattan. There they hold out together against the hapless (Jewish) landlord. The entire city and the black-Jewish encounter are here reduced to microcosm.

The city (the "house") and culture form Harry Lesser's world. Just as he refuses to be bought off and abandon his home for a better neighborhood, he refuses to let go of his languishing novel. "Home," he believes, "is where my book is," though he "fear[s] for the house and what was worse sometimes feared the house."

Rivals in art, sex, and survival, Harry and Willie (like Jews and blacks generally) are similar enough for an encounter to be credible, but the combination of their proximity and their opposing experiences undermine a tentative collegiality. Ultimately they negate each other, cannibalizing each other's art and demolishing each other's personhood before finally turning on one another. In so doing, they violate the city's potential as a home for culture according to Lesser's own pithy logic: "Home is where, if you get there, you won't be murdered; if you are it isn't home." Levenspiel, the landlord, has the final word: "Mercy, the both of you, for Christ's sake. . . . Hab rachmones, I beg you."[42]

Perhaps nothing symbolized better the intertwining of black-Jewish miscommunication and the "decline of the public realm" than the incident of "Harlem on My Mind," the ambitious exhibit mounted at the Metropolitan Museum of Art in 1969 (by Allon Schoener, himself Jewish, who had also designed the Lower East Side exhibit at the Jewish Museum in 1967). The exhibit drew the largest crowds (and the greatest number of black visitors) in the Met's history. But the well-intentioned exhibit foundered on what appeared, in retrospect, to have been avoidable errors.

While some black leaders (Congressman Powell, for instance) praised the exhibit, the museum was picketed by other blacks who charged that the exhibit was a travesty. One (white) journalist wrote that Schoener's "show [was] naively patronizing. . . , rather like going slumming for pleasure," and that the images presented tended toward the flashy, the entertaining, and the deviant on the one hand, or the mutely defiant, on the other.[43]

Yet, the most incendiary aspect of the exhibit—the aspect that made the mayor apply the epithet "racist"—was the exhibit catalog, in whose introduction there appeared what had originated as a term paper by a sixteen-year old black high school student. The paper, which was based on the young woman's reading of Glazer and Moynihan's *Beyond the Melting Pot,* included paraphrases of points drawn from the book (admittedly not very felicitously drawn, but Schoener, as catalog editor, had advised the student to use her own words and forget about quoting directly from the book).

The student had written, "Behind every hurdle that the Afro-American has to jump stands the Jew who has already cleared it." That is an unsubtle way of summing up the dynamics of ethnic succession and the reinforcement of ethnic interests in the city, which was the thesis of the Glazer and Moynihan study; but the point was tactlessly put, implying that Jews per se were keeping black people behind hurdles. And where Glazer and Moynihan had suggested, inter alia, that "perhaps . . . a bit" of antisemitism among black people might derive from a "subconscious" desire to identify with the Christian American majority, the museum catalog text read: "Thus, our contempt for the Jew makes us feel more completely American in sharing a national prejudice."[44]

◆ ◆ ◆

When the life of culture became "impossible" (which was Saul Bellow's description of New York in its intellectual decline and lack of "equilibrium")[45] and when the burdens of injustice and social decay seemed to swing out of control, making city life a galling confrontation, characteristically it was culture's rival, religion, that seemed to be a legitimate—perhaps the only hopeful—avenue of discourse, as we saw in the previous chapter. For the moral avant-garde in religion (in a way like the avant-garde in the arts), addressed itself precisely to the sort of disequilibrium of which Bellow complained.

Religion, tuned to a moralistic key by New York's religious intellectuals, was a way to address the themes of social angst and political chaos—the "inescapable discrepancy between religious ideals and the facts of persistent barbarism." Heschel had put it this way: "God Himself is not at home in the universe where His will is defied, where His kingship is denied."[46] Because amorality, international lawlessness, and social injustice were prima facie evidence that God had no dominion, only by preaching against the hegemonic power of the inhumane could religious thinkers conceive of a path that might lead back toward God.

Despite the moral-humanistic imperatives embedded in the language of the religious intellectuals, however, religion helped to complete the loop that led back toward particularism and thus must be considered as part of the resurgence of group consciousness. There was an inherent difference between religion as moral protest in the sixties and socialism as moral protest in the thirties. The radical, secular culture of the Depression generation had deliberately and necessarily sought the common voice. It had drawn its empathic power from the experiences of Jews in the shared, urban setting: Jews as immigrant proletarians whose poverty and generally dismal human predicament were identical with that of millions of others (one thinks of Clifford Odets's play *Awake and Sing,* for example).

While the "common voice" and the clear impact of the shared urban setting were still discernible in the new religious discourse, the accent (in contrast to both the interwar, Old Left culture and the even older Reform Jewish social activism) was on regaining a specific Jewish voice in which to cry out in the moral wilderness.[47] It was within the discourse of religion-as-moral-compass that the Holocaust became a ready reference point as an example of radical evil. Jews were to be mobilized to restore humanity to godliness because, as Bellow's Mr. Sammler put it, "from personal experience, from the grave, if I may say so," the Jews "knew something about" the end of the world, and had a stake in preventing it.[48]

The relevance of post-Holocaust consciousness in this context is twofold. First, if the city (as a hopeful, humanist construct) represented rational mastery over nature, then, by contrast, the anxiety of insecurity, unpredictability, and looming violence that accompanied the postwar decline of the divided city implied a loss of control and engendered a greater sense of vulnerability and potential victimhood. Was it mere coincidence that this mood was accompanied by a new Jewish public discourse that assigned new prominence to the Holocaust—a metasymbol of vulnerability, uncertainty, and victimization?

Second, since the fifties, as we saw in chapter 2, Jews had succeeded in introducing the Holocaust into American discourse. What was seen previously (even by some Jews) mainly as a terrible warning for the civilized world that totalitarian power was all-corrupting and all-destructive, became, in the group-defined idiom of the sixties, a specifically Jewish tragedy. From the Eichmann trial to Elie Wiesel's books, through a spate of new scholarly and popular writing that reacted against the German-focused writings of Hilberg and Arendt, the spotlight began to shift from the perpetrators to the victims. Jews who had not been anywhere near Auschwitz were, nevertheless, able to "know" what it felt like to be a survivor and to bear the burden of ineffable grief. But to imagine that they could retain "copyright" to that discourse was akin to trying to stuff the genie back in the bottle.

Thus, it was precisely here, at their most sensitive spot, that Jews quickly found themselves on contested ground. The Jews' "own" words ("ghetto" was just the beginning) were appropriated when no other English-language vocabulary could adequately convey the new forms of modern, anonymous suffering. We find black writer Ralph Ellison, for instance, in Harlem in 1964, saying, "one wanders dazed in a ghetto maze, a 'displaced person' of American democracy."[49]

A decade later, historian Henry Feingold would observe: "The image of the gassed, open-mouthed mounds of corpses seen in the newsreels at the close of the war traumatized not only Jews, but all suppressed minorities and, particularly, American Blacks who talk incessantly about the imminence of genocide."[50]

Meanwhile, the Jews' self-identification with the victim's history was challenged as a case of bad faith, as in this passage from James Baldwin's memorable essay of 1967:

> The Jew does not realize that the credential he offers, the fact that he has been despised and slaughtered, does not increase the Negro's understanding. It increases the Negro's rage. . . . The Jewish travail occurred across the sea and America rescued him from the house of bondage. But America *is* the house of bondage for the Negro, and no country can rescue him. What happens to the Negro here happens to him *because* he is an American.[51]

And, perhaps more jarring still, because more explicit, was the statement made the following year by Julius Lester, who (in an argument that has since been repeated many times) attempted to explain why African Americans, by definition, could not be antisemitic because racism presupposed a position of power. (Lester was then a radical black radio personality; his role in the black-Jewish encounter in 1968 will be discussed in the next chapter; subsequently he became a convert to Judaism): "In Germany, the Jews were the minority surrounded by a majority which carried out heinous crimes against them. In America it is we who are the Jews. It is we who are surrounded by a hostile majority. . . . There is no need for black people to wear yellow Stars of David on their sleeves; that Star of David is all over us. And the greatest irony of all is that it is the Jews who are in the position of being Germans."[52]

Lester believed that by using the Jews' own vocabulary, by reaching for a metaphor most likely to viscerally convey to Jewish listeners the outrage that blacks felt in white America, he might find a way back toward mutual empathy and likemindedness. Such attempts misfired, however. Not only was the final sentence in Lester's analogy too chilling (and, had he meant it literally, patently false); but the larger analogy through which Lester sought to shock complacent Jews out of their identification with white America also fell short of eliciting positive empathy. This was because, rather than equate Jewish and black victimhood, the comparison of Jews with Germans "robbed" Jews of what was legitimately theirs ("yellow Stars of David") and reassigned Jewishness to blacks. Such a rhetorical ploy might still, perhaps, have been accepted in some Jewish circles, but it was increasingly resented in most others.

Black Power advocate Stokely Carmichael—the Bronx High School of Science alumnus chosen the previous year to head SNCC (Student Nonviolent Coordinating Committee)—was not reaching for empathy when he said, in May 1967: "To ask a Negro to register with the Democratic Party is like asking a Jew to join the Nazi Party" (an understandable, if somewhat hyperbolic sentiment, perhaps, with regard to southern Dixiecrats, but hardly apt to win friends among northern Democrats—who included most of the country's Jews). Roy Innis, similarly arguing against the value of black-white political alliances, remarked that, once such alliances broke down, the potential loss of black votes for white liberals would not much affect black people. "[W]hat has this vote done for us as a people?" he asked rhetorically. "Who has gained from these noble coalitions of blacks and liberal whites, blacks and trade unionists, blacks and Marxists? It is not black people."[53]

The line in the sand was drawn, not between Jews and blacks, per se, but between two opposing camps (each containing *both* Jews *and* blacks). One camp still promoted the belief that the basic empathy required for an ongoing social contract in the city depended upon the capacity to see "others" as simply that—other *people* like oneself, whose needs and problems were not essentially different from one's own. This camp looked toward a politics of citywide reform in the spirit of the "War on Poverty," rather than toward a politics of race and group.

The second position, again held by both Jews and blacks, though for different reasons, argued that an underlying empathy of this sort was no longer possible. Black supporters of this position tended to argue that, since African Americans had always been excluded from the circle of the urban "like-minded" by whites wielding power, any call for the solution of issues dividing poor blacks from affluent whites without first addressing issues of power and race was suspect and hypocritical, and probably aimed at further exploitation of black people.

Those Jews, meanwhile, who similarly denied the existence of a common base of empathy between Jews and blacks were prompt to cite abusive rhetoric, street violence, antisemitism among black people, and what they considered to be anticivic demagoguery.

Among both blacks and Jews, the role of victim was put forward as justification. Both blacks and Jews claimed to be victims, not simply "others." Blacks succeeded in raising the political and moral premium attached to victimhood in American discourse—a discourse that traditionally favored the underdog but even more typically rewarded the winner and often blamed the victim. But they also succeeded, as a by-product, in prompting others, including some Jews, to seek to adopt a similar strategy. "We're all forced to confront the question of what is a Jew," explained one New Yorker: "To me the status of the Jews as outsiders and as persecuted outsiders is at the core of what Judaism and Jewishness is all about.[54]

Another, in a similar vein, recalled that in the troubled sixties, "We all referred to the sense of Jews as victims, Jews as underdogs, in the sixties, and at least for me, of blacks as victims and . . . underdogs. And I think that I felt very deeply the bond with blacks. . . . It was very frustrating that blacks who I was politically educated to feel allied with through victimization and underdogism were becoming vehemently anti-semitic."[55]

But the victim's role had built-in defects in the real world of intergroup relations. Rather than forging mutual bonds, it prompted a "one-downmanship"—a competition over who had had it worse—that was always less than constructive, and at times grotesque. African Americans who decided to "take it personally"—that is, to insist that racism in America was not impersonal to them—were not really in a position to counsel Jews that hostility toward them on the part of black people was impersonal, or that it was not meant to offend them as Jews per se. ("All I'm saying is an economic fact," explains Malamud's Willie as he calls Levenspiel a "fartn Jew slumlord"; but Harry Lesser counters, "I'm telling you a personal one," as he makes it clear that as a Jew he finds the words offensive.)[56] By the same token, it ill became Jews who cried "antisemite" at every turn to then counsel black people to hew to the path so well trodden by white immigrant groups in New York—as if the racial hierarchy embedded in American society did not mean them.

With these issues in mind, we should turn back now to the 1969 Harris study of black-Jewish relations. The study (which elicited responses from Puerto Ricans, white Catholics, and white Protestants, in addition to blacks and Jews) concluded that Jews and blacks were widely separated in *what they understood about the other group* and in *how they felt the other group perceived them*. Moreover, only a small minority of each group actually had personal dealings, at any level, with members of the other group.[57] At the same time, they remained, in some other senses, closer to each other than to non-Jewish white groups. In other words, the grounds for empathy still appeared in some parts of the evidence, but seemed threatened with extinction in other parts.

Most New York Jews (69 percent) felt in 1969 that relations between Jews and blacks were far worse than they had been before; only 5 percent believed that things had improved. By contrast, only 39 percent of black respondents felt relations had worsened; 19 percent felt there had been an improvement; 34 percent thought there had been no change.[58] But probing the reasons for this split between black and Jewish perceptions, the Harris study found the following: The large segment of black people who felt there had been no change spoke of the maintenance of an already bad status quo; and many among those who said they saw an improvement cited opinions such as these:

> "The situation is clearer and better now [that] the black man is finally waking up and the Jews have to take notice."
>
> "Things are better now because they are out in the open for all to see."
>
> "Blacks are more vocal now on how they feel about being used in the world by Jewish merchants."

In short, as the report indicated, "beneficial results" in relations with Jews were imputed to a "new aggressiveness."[59]

Meanwhile, among Jews, there was a pronounced tendency to believe that blacks thought ill of them. Typically, however, black opinion of Jews was not as bad as Jews believed it to be, and more positive than Jews hoped for. (In fact, it was among the Puerto Ricans that the worst opinions about Jews could be found.)[60]

Large majorities of blacks (between 70 and 80 percent) claimed to have no preference as between Jews and other whites in capacities such as employer or supervisor, coworker, retail store manager, landlord, fellow union member, neighbor, and welfare worker; but when they did cite such a preference, it was usually (not always) in favor of Jews.[61]

These findings, while indicating some grounds for the belief that Jews were not being specifically targeted by black animosity, nevertheless represented a deterioration in black-Jewish relations when compared with data from a 1964 ADL (Anti-Defamation League of B'nai B'rith) study (which seemed to demonstrate the weakness of black antisemitism and the strength of positive black opinion about Jews). In the five years that had elapsed since that earlier study, the proportion of black respondents in New York who viewed Jews and other whites alike had gone up, and concurrently the Jews' positive image had been tarnished: that is, Jews were "as bad as" other whites.[62]

The Harris study (1969) found that blacks expressed deep feelings of alienation in the city (70 percent among those earning under three thousand dollars were deeply alienated, and overall an average of 57 percent of black New Yorkers felt that way). Jews, by contrast, were far less alienated. They reported positive feelings about their rootedness in the city and their sense of acceptance in the city landscape. They felt they were represented in city government, getting ahead on their jobs, and receiving good will and respect from other people.

But these positive assessments changed to negative ones when the questions turned to quality-of-life issues: safety on the streets, the tax burden on the individual citizen, the prospects for one's children's education, and the relative "decency" of the atmosphere in the city with regard to raising children. Most important, Jews were far more apt than non-Jewish whites to complain that "racial tension" was partly to blame for such quality-of-life problems.[63]

It should be noted, however, that this opinion was not universally shared. In this regard, consider the following observation by *Midstream* editor Shlomo Katz:

> The city has changed. . . . We grew away from each other but it is not because of the changing ethnic situation. I can say with a clear conscience that [I am] antiracist. . . . Yet somehow, I feel "out." If I had a place to hang my hat; if I could drop in some evening on *haimische menschen* [my kind of folks] who "know" what I "know," my attitude might be different. . . . The nearest thing [to such a hangout] is Zabar's [a popular food store]—thank you very much![64]

Blacks and Jews (the Harris study reported) were virtually on the same wavelength in agreeing that *Jews* still faced discrimination in New York, and black people stated feelings of empathy with Jews in that regard. Blacks' perception of *antiblack* discrimination, however, was much higher than the level of antiblack discrimination that Jews and white Protestants were willing to recognize.[65] And when it came to the key questions of evaluating black intentions, blacks and Jews were most sharply divided, even more so than blacks and whites generally: "Blacks showed themselves far more committed to integration than Jews believed," the Harris study argued, adding, "The Jewish group in New York City has developed some serious misapprehensions about the motives and intent of the black community. There appeared to be a disproportionate number of Jews willing to believe that blacks would resort to violence to 'tear down white society.' "[66]

How was it possible for Jews who, as individuals, were not prone to think in racial terms—who were even known to "ignore" race to a large extent when it came to ordinary life situations—to harbor strongly race-oriented ideas when it came to their understanding of black people in the aggregate? And by the same token, how was it possible that the same African American community whose individual members evinced a certain regard and appreciation for

Jewish individuals in a variety of capacities, also showed tendencies that eroded trust and empathy between the two groups?

This paradox may not be as great as it appears, for Americans in general, in the postwar years, have made exactly this sort of distinction between civility at the individual level and hostility at the group level. American political parties, for example, have been unable to forge effective coalitions between poor whites and poor blacks, reflecting a hostility that transcends class and perpetuates a politics of polarization.[67] And yet, the paradox was bound to augment the sense of miscommunication and, eventually, to spill over from attitudes to behavior.

In order to fully appreciate the extent to which this was the case, let us look at two key areas: Jewish participation in "white flight" and in public affairs.

Suburbanization and "White Flight"

In the decades that followed 1950, the population of New York City remained fairly stable in total size, but changed dramatically in composition. The steady and large-scale influx of Puerto Rican and black inhabitants (which was followed by a further influx of immigrants from the Caribbean, Latin America, and Asia) was more than offset by a steady outflow of white residents, mainly from the middle class.

Non-Hispanic whites began leaving the city in significant numbers (almost half a million) during the 1940s, but this trend accelerated in the fifties, when net out-migration of this group reached 1.24 million. About three-quarters of this outflow was absorbed by those suburbs closest to New York City. Nassau and Suffolk Counties (Long Island) alone gained more than a million residents in that decade. When northern New Jersey is included, the suburbs of New York grew in the fifties by 1.25 million. From 1960 to 1970, another million left the city, and while only 40 percent of the out-migrants resettled in the immediate environs, the suburban population (including northern New Jersey) grew by 763,000.[68]

The process by which more affluent and longer-resident groups moved steadily from the central parts of the city toward its periphery, and then beyond, into the suburbs, was not necessarily causally related to racial issues. Employment and other economic and class-status issues were involved, as well. In 1939, Manhattan had boasted the highest per capita income in the New York metropolitan area (63 percent above the metro area average). By 1956 it had dropped to only 14 percent above the average, while in Nassau County (26 percent below the average in 1939), per capita income had risen to 25 percent above. Similarly, Westchester had gone from 7 percent below to 24 percent above the regional average. Meanwhile, both retail employment and retail sales (especially department stores) went steadily downward in the city and, at the same time, showed long-term increases just beyond the city limits as well as farther out into suburban areas. Manufacturing jobs were no longer expanding in Manhattan after World War II: from 1954 to 1956, 90 percent of new plants in the New York area were being built outside New York City.[69]

Though economics and status considerations would explain much of this movement, nevertheless, it was the exit of so many middle-class white residents during precisely those decades that witnessed a paucity of in-migrating whites and an accelerating in-migration of non-whites, mostly from lower economic strata, that prompted the colloquial expression, "white flight."

Whether causally related to racial dynamics or not, the effects of these trends were clearly relevant to racial relations and urban life. Residential patterns in and outside the city did not simply perpetuate class and status distinctions, but ethnic and racial distinctions as well (group clustering in separate areas). At the beginning of the 1950s, blacks moving into white areas were generally middle-class people entering high-status white neighborhoods, but by 1960, mixed neighborhoods had very few high-status white residents.[70] In 1940 only 7.5 percent of African Americans in Brooklyn lived in areas where they constituted over 80 percent of the population. Between 1940 and 1950, however, Brooklyn's black population almost doubled, but five times as many black people lived in segregated communities in 1950 as had been the case a decade earlier.[71]

Although it has been argued that segregation by social class and ethnic or racial group was natural or at least inevitable (richer Jews segregated themselves residentially from poor Jews, richer blacks from poorer, Italians from Irish, and hence white-black segregation was no different in kind than these other patterns), it was more commonly thought otherwise. "The growth of the suburbs," one observer noted, "was more than simply a measure of the failure of the big city as a place to live. It was also a dangerous example of the continuation of racial segregation and racial antipathy in America."[72] Weighing in on the conservative side, Irving Kristol voiced his apprehension over the social consequences (for whites) entailed in their wholesale abandonment of America's cities.[73]

In all of this, Jews were participants as well as partial exceptions to the common pattern. The Jewish population of the city continued to grow in the 1950s (due to both in-migration and natural increase), whereas the rest of the white, non-Hispanic population was already declining. By the end of the 1950s, however, Jewish population trends began to follow non-Jewish trends. Jewish population in the city declined rather steeply from 1957 to 1970, showing a loss of almost 900,000, or about 42 percent. Some (though clearly not all) of this decline may be accounted for by a shift from the city to the three suburban counties of Westchester, Nassau, and Suffolk, where Jewish population rose during those years from 465,000 to 770,000 (see table 5.1).[74]

After 1970, the decline of the Jewish population began to slow down (partly due to an influx of Jews from the Soviet Union); the rest of the white population, in contrast, continued to diminish rapidly. In all, the size of the Jewish population by 1991 was 51.5 percent of its size forty years earlier; the non-Hispanic white population, in comparison, ended the same forty-year period with only 46 percent of what it had started with.

It was suggested in the 1950s and 1960s that Jews were among those white New Yorkers who were "particularly susceptible" to suburbanization and especially prone to leave changing neighborhoods.[75] Jews, for one thing, tended to be renters, not homeowners, and thus less prepared to "fight" for their houses; Jews, moreover, "reacted to blacks moving into their neighborhoods much less violently than did other white communities . . . [and simply] moved out."[76] We may recall, too, that sociologist Marshall Sklare criticized Jews for their lack of rootedness in their urban neighborhoods, arguing that their rapid disappearance from former ethnic strongholds was tantamount to being the cause of their own urban crisis.[77]

The participation of Jews from the city in "white flight," by all accounts, was significant and the Jewish presence in the suburbs burgeoned. But the figures in table 5.1 suggest that the impact of suburbanization on the Jewish community in the city was not as great as it was on the white population in general. It would appear, too, that Jews did not lead the way into the suburbs, but rather followed other city residents after a lag of almost a decade. Data from the 1958 New York Jewish Population Study tend to confirm this pattern, showing that Jews increased their share of the total city population and of the white population from 1940 through 1957, from 25.6 to 31 percent.[78]

Comparing these citywide figures to those in several key neighborhoods, as reported in the 1958 study, we still find similar results. In neighborhoods like Brownsville (Brooklyn), where the Jewish population fell significantly after 1950, the Jewish share of the white population fell more slowly (see table 5.2). In areas where the decline of Jewish population was slow or where Jewish population was stable, Jews actually increased their share of the white population (see tables 5.3 and 5.4).

Among the consequences of late Jewish suburbanization was the relatively greater exposure of city Jews to racially mixed residential situations. This would accord with findings from 1967 that reported that of all ethnic groups living in cities outside the South, Jews showed the highest proportion (21

Table 5.1
Non-Hispanic White and Jewish Population
of New York City, 1950–1991 (millions)

Year	*Non-Hispanic White*	*Jewish*
1950	6.87[a]	2.00[a,b]
1957	6.03[a]	2.14[b]
1970	5.24[a]	1.23[c]
1981	3.70[d]	1.14[d]
1991	3.16[d]	1.03[d]

Sources:
[a]Data compiled from Rosenwaike, *Population History of New York City*, 131–39, 155, 198–99.
[b]Data from Horowitz and Kaplan, *The Jewish Population of the New York Area, 1900–1975*, 15–17.
[c]Data from Massarik, "Basic Characteristics of the Greater New York Jewish Population," *American Jewish Year Book* (1976); 239.
[d]Data from Bethamie Horowitz, *The 1991 New York Jewish Population Study*, xiii-xiv, 10–11.

Table 5.2
Non-Hispanic White and Jewish Population
of East Flatbush-Brownsville (Brooklyn), 1940–1959

Year	*Total Pop. (000s)*	*White Pop. (000s)*	*Jewish Pop. (000s)*	*Jews as % of Total*	*Jews as % of Whites*
1940	202.8	189.7	145.2	71.5	76.5
1950	185.1	161.0	125.7	67.9	78.1
1957	172.6	134.0	95.6	55.4	71.4

Source:
Horowitz and Kaplan, *The Jewish Population of the New York Area, 1900–1975*, 239.

percent) living in census tracts where 5 percent or more of the inhabitants were black.[79]

Finally, among Jews—as compared to white non-Jews—the main wave of redistribution to the suburbs was largely spent by 1970, after which the pattern continued more moderately, and was somewhat blunted by in-migration.

We can try to corroborate the implications from tables 5.1, 5.2, 5.3, and 5.4 by looking at how the Jews in and outside the city stood in proportional relationship *to each other*, and to non-Hispanic whites in general. The data arranged in table 5.5 show that in the eight-county New York area (the five

Table 5.3
Non-Hispanic White and Jewish Population of Tremont (Bronx), 1940–1957

Year	*Total Pop. (000s)*	*White Pop. (000s)*	*Jewish Pop. (000s)*	*Jews as % of Total*	*Jews as % of Whites*
1940	161.0	160.5	48.8	30.3	30.4
1950	150.8	149.5	46.3	30.7	31.0
1957	131.5	126.9	42.5	32.3	33.5

Source:
Horowitz and Kaplan, *The Jewish Population of the New York Area, 1900–1975,* 185.

Table 5.4
Non-Hispanic White and Jewish Population of Park West (Upper West Side, Manhattan, W. 74th to W. 106th), 1940–1957

Year	*Total Pop. (000s)*	*White Pop. (000s)*	*Jewish Pop. (000s)*	*Jews as % of Total*	*Jews as % of Whites*
1940	242.9	234.0	63.1	26.0	27.0
1950	263.7	253.2	74.9	28.4	29.6
1957	245.9	226.0	70.9	28.8	31.4

Source:
Horowitz and Kaplan, *The Jewish Population of the New York Area, 1900–1975,* 149.

boroughs of the city, plus Westchester, Nassau, and Suffolk), Jews remained more heavily concentrated in the city than in the suburbs. While the overall Jewish population in the metropolitan area has been decreasing, between six and seven out of ten New York area Jews have remained city residents rather than suburbanites since the end of the sixties. From 1950 to 1960, the share of the overall non-Hispanic white population that lived in the city had shrunk by almost 28 percent; by 1970, another 32 percent drop left those in the city a minority (under 40 percent) of all whites living in the metropolitan area. Thus, in the twenty years from 1950 to 1970, the non-Hispanic white population of the metropolitan area went from being 78 percent urban to only 38 percent urban. At that point, the Jews, at their lowest urban ebb (61.5 percent), were still mostly concentrated in the city, at a rate over one-and-a-half times that of whites in general.[80]

Some of the reasons for the relatively delayed Jewish suburbanization in

Table 5.5
Percent of City Dwellers Among Metro-Area Jewish and Non-Hispanic White New Yorkers, 1950–1991

Year	*Group*	*% living in the boroughs*	*% change in ten years*
1950	NHW	78.2	—
1950	Jews	n.a.	n.a.
1960	NHW	56.5	-28
1957	Jews	81.5	n.a.
1970	NHW	38.4	-32
1971	Jews	61.5	-25
1981	NHW	55.2	+44
1981	Jews	67.9	+10
1991	NHW	52.8	-5
1991	Jews	72.4	+6

Sources:
Compiled from Rosenwaike, *Population History of New York City;* Massarik, "Basic Characteristics of the Greater New York Jewish Population"; Horowitz and Kaplan, *The Jewish Population of the New York Area*; and Horowitz, *The 1991 New York Jewish Population Study.*

the fifties may be traceable to the high concentration of "Jewish" jobs in Manhattan and in the city generally, rather than to any subjective "affinity" for the city (bearing in mind that most people continued to live within short commuting distance from their place of employment). We find, for example, that in 1956, Manhattan still accounted for 58.3 percent of the New York region's employees engaged in wholesale trades. Breaking down that category into "lines" of trade, we find figures show only a very small decline in Manhattan's very firm hold on dry goods and apparel wholesale employees (a category that also includes the fur trade and the diamond trade): from 97 percent of all such jobs in the metropolitan area in 1947, to 94 percent in 1956.[81] Industrial employment in apparel production, similarly, declined slightly in New York City between 1947 and 1956, but not by very much (from 84 percent of the region's employment in that field to just under 81 percent); and industrial positions also declined slightly in printing and publishing.[82] In the professions, though job opportunities were spread throughout the metropolitan region, professional workers' residences in the fifties were strongly concentrated in Manhattan.[83]

Looking at it yet another way—by income—we find that in 1949, the median incomes of those who worked in sales, the professions, and management in the New York area—all key job sectors for Jews—ranged between $2,500 and $4,000. Persons with incomes represented by that median range (bearing in mind that many of such persons would have earned up to twice the median income) tended most typically to reside outside Manhattan but within the city, and those with incomes from $7,000 to $10,000 tended to move out toward the "inner ring" of contiguous suburbs. Figures for the 1950s show that 60 percent of New York's Jews earned annual incomes of between $3,000 and $7,500—thus placing them squarely in the upper range of income-earners among city residents.[84]

Just as the solidity of the job market in the city for New York Jews up through the 1950s would go a long way toward explaining their delayed suburbanization pattern, the same line of reasoning would also illuminate the relative stabilization of the New York Jewish population after the mid-1970s. Once the city began to recover from its fiscal crisis of those years, certain developing economic sectors in which Jewish New Yorkers were prominently represented began to grow. These sectors included financial and corporate services; communications, media, and advertising; education and research; and health and social services.[85]

In terms of other, less tangible ramifications of Jewish "urbanism," relative to other non-Hispanic whites throughout the postwar decades, one must entertain two interrelated hypotheses:

1. The *relatively high urban profile* among the New York area's Jews would tend to involve Jews more personally and directly in any events or developments taking place in New York City, even if these did not happen to involve them as Jews, per se. This might be expected to apply both to urban affairs taken broadly and to mutual frictions that built up between groups in the city.

2. The *delay in Jewish suburbanization* may have tended to expose them, more than other non-Hispanic whites, to the atmosphere of crisis that developed in the city during the sixties. This matter of timing would seem to apply, for example, to questions of neighborhood "succession." The higher the share of the white population accounted for by Jews—and that share went up as other white residents left the city earlier—the more we can expect to find Jews present in city neighborhoods undergoing changes in racial composition. Jews, once they did begin to participate in the so-called white flight, did so at a stage when the process was already well advanced, and this might explain, for instance, why they left fairly precipitously. (Recall that the Jewish population of the city dropped by a massive 42 percent in just twelve years.)

Both of these propositions have a direct bearing on the discussion that follows, in which we will take up the ramifications of civic and political culture as they relate to New York Jews in the critical years of the urban crisis.

Public Affairs and Civic Consciousness

A useful way of understanding the approach of many Jews to civic issues is through the concept of "civility," as expounded by sociologist Edward Shils. Civility, Shils argued, defines a common ground, separate from the state but related to the upholding of the public peace, within which individuals and groups may safely compete. From this point of view it may be proposed that modern Diaspora Jews, because of their minority status, have made civility one of the values—if not the absolute value—enshrined in their political culture.

"Civility," Shils wrote,

> restrains the exercise of power by the powerful and restrains obstruction and violence by those who do not have power but wish to have it. . . . Civil society postulates and accentuates the pluralism of autonomous spheres and . . . accepts the diversity of interests and ideals which will arise in any numerous society. It allows diversity of the objectives pursued by individuals and institutions—but not by all and any means whatsoever. . . . Civil society provides for the individual pursuit of gain, just as it provides for the criticism of the existing social and political order. . . . Civility is a mode of political action . . . which postulates that antagonists are also members of the same society.[86]

In short, as a value system, it incorporates a dualism that is directly related to the internal contradiction of liberal societies, which depend on legitimate authority but must at the same time protect the individual from an encroaching authority. By locating the "civil" consensus outside the organs of state power, society is empowered to step in to preserve the balance between these two contradictory needs.

This sense of the term "civility" is generically related to what we have discussed previously as "likemindedness" or the vision of the city as a meeting place where many particular groups and individuals can, despite their diversity, undertake to create some collective form of civilization. Insofar as this enhances a minority's ability to survive and even to thrive, it also serves its own collective interest. Members of such a group might therefore choose to support a political position that enhances *both* autonomy *and* a vision of the whole society liberal enough to include them.

The kinship between this conceptualization of "civility" and much that is contained in American Jewish political culture is very close. As an explanatory device, it has an advantage over narrower theories that relate only to Jews' relative "liberalism," their affinity for the "American dream," or their support for civil liberties and universal, meritocratic criteria in the academy and the labor market. The concept of civility certainly illuminates the liberal side of Jewish politics (limiting the power of the powerful, enhancing diversity, safeguarding the individual but appealing to the individual's vested interest in the common welfare, and criticizing the social order when it no longer helps to maintain that equilibrium). But the value of civility is also related to the defense of the legitimacy and the authority of law, which is a posture adopted by many Jews, both liberal and neoconservative.

But even this wide-ranging values- and interest-based explanation may not go far enough as an explanation of Jewish political behavior and public consciousness. Edward C. Banfield and James Q. Wilson, political scientists who studied voting behavior and political culture as these compared across different urban ethnic and religious groups in the early sixties, advanced a theory that Jews—like high-status Protestant whites—eschewed a politics of group self-interest and promoted, instead, what appeared to be the greater public good.[87] In a subsequent study, they continued to argue that higher-income WASPS and Jews tended to vote against their pocketbooks—voting, for example, to approve such measures as municipal hospitals for which they would be taxed but from which they were unlikely to derive direct benefit. Lower-class and middle-class Americans, in contrast, tended to vote according to utilitarian interests.

Accordingly, they hypothesized, either those in the upper brackets were simply behaving irrationally (a possibility that they rejected), or such voters were engaging in a calculation of social goals that went beyond narrowly conceived self-interest. That is, those whose pocketbooks stretched farther also took a wider view of the "public interest" and of their own stake in that interest, and voted accordingly.

Undoubtedly, this calculus must also entail the value that those in the highest social strata (those who have the most to lose) place on the maintenance of civil peace. The study, however, did not enter into this aspect, and focused instead on factors of "culture." After comparing what it called the "public-regardingness" (or "civility," in Shils's terms) of various groups, the study suggested that, "[M]ost upper-income voters belong, if not by inheritance then by adoption, to an ethnic group (especially the Anglo-Saxon and the Jewish) that is relatively public-regarding" by virtue of "ethnic attributes" or "culture."[88]

It has, in fact, become a staple of both academic and popular conceptions of Jewish civic behavior that Jews are prone to vote "against their pocketbook," although it is less often that we read a good explanation of what they are voting "for" when acting in this manner. It has generally been argued that such behavior is rooted in Jewish culture—ostensibly "public-regarding" insofar as, for centuries, Jews were conditioned to provide for their community's needs. Reinforced in this respect by the preaching of certain religious values, they also routinely invested large resources in charitable welfare (though whether realities of minority life reinforced religious precepts or vice versa is hard to say). Philanthropic liberalism, it is generally agreed, has become an ethnic marker of the Jews within American society.[89]

In their important study of the Jews of "Lakeville" (a Chicago suburb) in the late 1950s, Marshall Sklare and Joseph Greenblum found that Jews ideologically supported principles of "social justice," believing that it was "essential" for Jews to support humanitarian causes. Although 67 percent of Jews in the study supported that consensus, only 39 percent felt the same way about giving to Jewish causes.[90]

Not everyone agrees, however, that Jewish altruism in America is rooted in age-old Jewish traditions of public-spirited social conscience. Historian Naomi Cohen, for example, argued that, in America, "[the quest for] respect from non-Jews made philanthropy a creative and vibrant force within the Jewish community." Jews' efforts to build hospitals were never matched by their financial outlays for Jewish education (a field in which the rewards were purely internal). Philanthropy, she suggested, has often functioned for Jews as "a surrogate for religion," rather than a product of religion.[91] Historian Arthur Hertzberg has similarly pointed out that the development of modern Jewish charitable agencies was linked to deracination and religious fragmentation. Jews "who have been able to agree on nothing else" have created an effective philanthropic infrastructure, he argued, but not as an outgrowth of an organized Jewish community or shared culture.[92]

The point, in any case, is that at least some of the culture of Jewish philanthropy was "made in the USA" and it was made with self-regarding considerations in mind. Certainly it was an adaptive behavior that helped to integrate Jews into American society through mobilizing Jewish resources. It is noteworthy, then, that the Banfield and Wilson study of voting patterns observed similar tendencies among both Jews and WASPs. The authors believed that Jewish ethnic values were the explanation for such parallel points of view, apparently overlooking the possibility that Jewish aspirations to acculturate to a positive reference group were (at least partly) at work.

Interpreting the matter somewhat differently—because I believe that more is involved here, given that American Jewish political behavior does not simply echo that of upper-class WASPS—I do agree that Judaic culture or Jewish ethnicity per se (understood as a rooted tradition brought over from Europe) has little to do with American Jewish civic behavior. If culture and history are at all responsible for American Jews' civic attitudes, that culture and that history are to be found in the American city in the early twentieth century—not in the nineteenth-century shtetl (where communal charitable institutions, from the almshouse to the schoolhouse, were chronically underfunded, but clubbing together in well-endowed "prestige" associations—burial societies are the famous example—was an established practice); nor even, despite the poetic appeal of the idea, in the Books of the Prophets, which, after all, highlight the *failures* of social conscience among the Israelites.

If, in short, Jews have been predisposed to take a "public-regarding" civic position, this may have as much to do with the situation in which they found themselves and the commitment they made to the urban experience once they had resettled in the metropolis, as with their religio-cultural background. Their commitment to metropolitan social welfare, as noted in chapter 1, had in turn a great deal to do with their need to dislodge older, vested interests and to insure a level playing field.

A somewhat parallel point can be derived from a remark made by Ed Koch, the former mayor of New York (1978–89) and a canny reader of the political map, to the effect that non-Jewish candidates with liberal WASP credentials do especially well with Jewish voters—which is, on its face, a selfless, public-spirited form of political behavior. Behind that posture, Koch suggested, lay a particular sort of self-serving, elitist point of view. Jews, Koch said, had ethnic aspirations in politics much as did everyone else, but they were "peculiar" about whom they would vote for. "They love to vote for someone whom they consider to be an FDR, a WASP with power and money whom they think loves them. And they'll vote for an FDR in preference to a Jew."[93]

Although this may not always hold true, it is a pattern that fits often enough. Franklin Roosevelt was, indeed, a Jewish political hero—even Jewish socialists voted for him.[94] Jews were also "madly for Adlai" Stevenson ("cool and patrician") in the fifties. In 1960, John F. Kennedy, with his elite East Coast entourage, was more the "FDR" (despite his ethnic and Catholic background) than his uncharismatic opponent, Richard Nixon. Jews considered Kennedy, of the two candidates, to be more favorably disposed toward them and a greater proportion of Jews voted for him than did Irish Catholics. In New York, Jewish precincts gave JFK a crucial plurality of 800,000 votes, enabling him to capture the state by a slim margin of 384,000 votes. (Having squeaked past Nixon to a cliffhanger victory, Kennedy told David Ben-Gurion in 1961: "You know, I was elected by the Jews of New York.")[95]

That Jews like to vote for the "classier," elite candidate, as Koch would have it, especially one with predilections that are perceived as pro-Jewish, does not support theories about Jewish avoidance of ethnic self-interest considerations. On the contrary, it points to a type of political behavior that, while appearing to be selflessly public-spirited, also enables Jews to position themselves advantageously close to a high-status group.

Arthur Hertzberg observed something in a similar vein on a matter that, in the context of this chapter, is crucial. Hertzberg, who was himself actively supportive of pro-civil rights activities, remarked at a symposium on race relations in 1964 that "Certainly one by-product of official Jewish support for the Negro cause has been to create among Jews involved in the struggle a greater sense of identity and camaraderie with important segments of Christian religious and civic circles . . . and Jews are not unaware of how very much more 'American' they are therefore becoming."[96]

Ethnicity, civic ideology, and the politics of status also intersected in the ostensibly nonpolitical realm of the arts, as we learn from the case of the Jewish Museum. One could say that the Jewish Museum, ostensibly an assertion of ethnic presence and particularism, nevertheless functioned in a "public-regarding" way. It constituted one way of asserting that culture in the city was not yet "impossible." In the sixties, it was one of New York's most influential and avant-garde "showplace[s] for contemporary art," as cultural historian Richard Cohen reminds us, at a time when the Whitney, the Guggenheim, and the Museum of Modern Art were considered to be lagging behind in this regard.[97]

We may easily relate the Jewish Museum's aesthetic rationale to the question of Jewish social aspirations. Thus, the Museum Committee's report of 1957 to its board of overseers stated: "Gradually, the function of a Jewish Museum is evolving in our minds: to so present the particular as to strip it of parochialism." Or, again, in 1962, the Museum's goals were said to include helping Jews "to relate to the current society by representing the contribution of contemporary Judaica to the social scene . . . [and] to contribute to the aesthetic life of the general community." The incoming director, Sam Hunter, wrote in the *New York Times* in 1965 that the Museum's "advanced art program" was consonant with "the efforts of the official Jewish community . . . to seek full intellectual participation in Western culture."[98]

In sum, we must add yet a third hypothesis to the two already entertained about Jews and the city during this period. To repeat, the first is that the Jews' relatively high urban profile (New York Jews having remained more urban than suburban) tended to make Jews as a group highly aware of and engaged by city affairs, perhaps more so than some others. Second, given their late or slow entry into the suburbanization trend, followed by a precipitous decline of the Jewish population in just twelve years, it is possible that Jews, as a group, felt more exposed to the urban crisis in its dramatic, sometimes violent, first decades.

Third, we now can entertain the thesis that Jews in New York perceived public affairs not only as an area that involved them directly, given their numerical presence; not only as a "problem" with ramifications for civility and the deterioration of the quality of life in the city; but also as an arena of crucial importance to their elevation into the social, cultural, and political elite of American society. It is only when we take all three of these suppositions into account that we can reach a synthetic understanding of Jewish civic culture and political behavior in New York, because there were three outcomes by the end of the sixties and the early seventies that bear upon our case.

The first is that Jews, while losing substantial numbers to suburbanization, also split into two camps. They were separated, as we discussed earlier, by their diametrically opposed beliefs about the possibility of empathy between groups in the city. This split corresponded to a large extent with social-status lines: The wealthier and the more highly educated—those most likely to view themselves as members of the cultural and political elite—tended to support policies of social reform, the redress of minority grievances through public initiatives, and in general, those aspects of civility that maximize the protection of diversity. The less well-off, less highly educated, and more religiously traditional—those less apt to view "public-regardingness" as a badge of caste—tended to support a platform of "law and order," middle-class interests and values, and those stabilizing aspects of civility that depend upon set rules for the conduct of public life.

The second outcome lies in the *effect* of that split. Paradoxically, a divided Jewish political constituency, within the framework of an ethnically and racially defined politics, raised the electoral value of Jewish votes, since both liberal and conservative candidates were impelled to compete for them. Liberals had to recruit Jews to augment black and Hispanic votes, in order to counter the prevailing conservative leanings of the rest of the white vote and produce a majority. Conservatives, in their turn, had to seek among Jews (because it was difficult to find them among blacks and Hispanics) those voters willing to disengage from the liberal camp in order to augment a shrinking white, middle-class constituency.

The split was apparent in 1966, when most white ethnics, including a substantial if comparatively smaller section of the Jewish community, rejected the civilian review board proposed by the new Republican-Liberal mayor, John V. Lindsay, to supervise police procedures. (About 50 percent of the Jewish voters opposed the review board, compared to 83 percent among Irish and Italian voters.)[99]

The same split was evident in the 1969 elections, when about half the Jewish voters in New York favored a conservative Democrat, Comptroller Mario Procaccino, over Lindsay, who ran this time as an Independent. Lindsay won the election with roughly the same proportion of the Jewish vote as he had gained in 1965 (in both cases, 42–44 percent. But the Jewish vote for Procaccino was also substantial: 44 percent according to one estimate, 49 percent according to another, as compared with the Democrat's share of only 35 percent in the city at large. Moreover, a small number of Jews (about 12 percent) voted for the still more conservative Republican candidate, John Marchi.[100] By the next mayoral election Jewish voters favored Democratic Party regular Abe Beame overwhelmingly for the party's nomination for mayor and gave very few votes to liberal Hispanic candidate Herman Badillo. "The 1973 race," it has been noted, was "the point at which Jews shifted their political alliances to be more in line with other 'white ethnics' and to withdraw support from candidates seen as favoring minority causes."[101]

The third, not unrelated outcome, is that we find more Jews contending for top city offices by the end of the sixties and, beginning in 1973, an effective replacement of the older, Catholic-dominated (Irish and Italian) higher echelon of the Democratic Party with a cadre of Jews, not all of whom were veteran party stalwarts.

This was already true by the time of the 1969 municipal elections, when Abe Beame ran (unsuccessfully) for Comptroller on the Procaccino slate; Sanford Garelik, a highly decorated senior police officer without any background in party politics, won the City Council presidency as John Lindsay's running mate; Abe Stark, a Democratic Party regular, retained the Brooklyn borough presidency that he had already occupied for eight years; Robert Abrams, a reform Democrat, became Bronx borough president; and Sidney Leviss won that office in Queens. (It is perhaps noteworthy, in this regard, that in the Democratic primaries that preceded the 1969 election, Herman Badillo, the liberal Puerto Rican Congressman, headed a slate with two Jewish running mates from the party's reform wing. Norman Mailer, the writer, also ran as a maverick mayoral candidate in the same primary election, campaigning to make New York City the "fifty-first state.") In the decade that followed, both Beame (in 1973) and then, in 1977, Koch, the liberal Congressman who remade himself into a populist champion of the middle class, won elections as the first Jewish mayors of New York.[102]

Close involvement by Jews in city affairs, the evident split pattern among Jewish voters (emulating the values of reformist WASPs like Lindsay, on the one hand, and conservative white ethnics on the other), and the ability to clear a place for Jews at the top, added up to a composite civic posture that was very "self-regarding" in effect—even when "public-regarding" in substance. Jews who gave Lindsay (the "FDR candidate") crucial support, reaped the benefit of that support when the Lindsay victory helped to topple some of the key (mainly Catholic) contenders in the local Democratic organization. Lindsay's Jewish *opponents* then also reaped a benefit when a Democratic regime—now more dependent upon Jewish candidates—subsequently returned to office.

Clearly, Jewish officeholders did not emerge as a bloc or even as "representatives" of their ethnic group, but rather as individual members of political

Abraham Beame, 1974. Beame taking the oath of office as mayor of New York City, as outgoing Mayor John V. Lindsay looks on (seated, front row, at the right edge of the photo). Beame, a Democratic Party stalwart, was the first Jew to hold the mayoralty of New York. Photograph courtesy of the Jerusalem Post *photographic collection.*

camps, organizations, and ad hoc alliances. Nevertheless, the rising prominence of successful Jewish politicians in the sixties and the seventies reflected, in part, the polarized politics of race, group, and class that developed over the course of that period. Without that polarization, the particular importance of Jewish "swing votes" and the split within the Jewish community—itself a consequence of the politicization of race and group—would hardly have had the same significance. And without that polarization, Jews might have remained more in the political background.

◆ ◆ ◆

In light of how intergroup relations had developed in New York in the sixties, Glazer and Moynihan found it necessary, in the second edition of *Beyond the Melting Pot* (1970), to revise some of the statements they had made in 1963. They had originally predicted that religion would continue to be a determining factor in shaping New York's social fabric. After 1969 they had to admit that, "it hardly seems as though religion defines the present, or the future, major fissures in New York life. Race has exploded to swallow up all other distinctions."[103]

Likewise, they owned up to having misunderstood the nature of race and ethnicity when it came to African Americans, as well as having overgeneralized the integrative patterns that had worked in the past in New York City. They had posited that in New York, "the larger American experience of the Negro, based on slavery and repression in the South, would be overcome, as the Negroes joined the rest of society, in conflict and accommodation, as an ethnic group." Instead, they had to admit, "For the first time in New York City's history. . . , racial conflict became determinative for the city's politics."[104]

The forces arrayed against likeminded, urban civility were formidable. To move toward acknowledgment of black difference within American society, one had also to concede that the city—New York City, in particular—was no longer functioning as it had done in the past vis-à-vis other groups. To recognize that without also accusing some other group either of changing the rules to suit themselves or of creating the obstacles that prevented civility from functioning, proved to be increasingly difficult for large sections of New York's black, Jewish, and other communities.

At the same time, to persist in demands that the city live up to its own best ideals of openness and equity—and thus make the city worthy of those who kept faith with it, rather than escape to the suburbs—required a transcendence of group that, paradoxically, only the most privileged were ready to perform. Often enough, they were willing to do so because it was precisely in their transcendence of group that they asserted for themselves the prerogatives of leadership. They called upon other groups, not nearly so privileged, to make a sacrifice of their own self-interest, which in turn was guaranteed to arouse strenuous objections. We will discuss the ramifications of these problems in the next chapter, as we consider the case of the 1968 New York teachers' strike and events that occurred within the Jewish community.

We will do so, however, not simply as episodes unto themselves but within the context of the culture of confrontation that was the hallmark of the sixties.

6

Fragment and Confront

The Politics of Division

> Quite obviously, the mounting disorder of the nation's largest city is unique in the sense that its scope cannot be duplicated elsewhere. . . . New York represents the fullest expression—for good or ill—of our urban culture. It is the macrocosm of every city's problems and aspirations.
>
> —Richard Whalen,
> *A City Destroying Itself*

> When institutions fail, there is disorder. . . . [This] does not resemble the disorder of war, revolution, epidemic. . . . Rather, the failure of institutions brings on a discontent and sense of grievance that leads to large-scale moralizing . . . [as well as the] intensification of political activity. Political parties are usually pushed out of the picture and are in part replaced by direct political action. . . , and there is quite evidently a deep crisis in public authority. . . . A nation that is in need of stability is also in need of change. It . . . needs law and *dis*order.
>
> —Theodore J. Lowi,
> *The Politics of Disorder*

East New York, Brooklyn, in July 1966 was the site of such a breakdown of civic culture and such volatile interracial hostility that keeping the peace took the unconventional combination of a city official, a troubleshooting rabbi, and the "persuasion" wielded by underworld muscle. Two of the central figures in this drama, Rabbi Samuel Schrage and Frank Arricale, director of Mayor Lindsay's Youth Board, subsequently told their side of what soon became a well publicized scandal.

Rabbi Schrage had been instrumental in persuading Arricale to approach crime boss Albert Gallo in a last-ditch effort to forestall a major race riot. Throughout the previous months, efforts to defuse the explosive situation by social workers, clergy, civil rights activists, and black nationalist figures in the neighborhood had been of no avail. The in-migration of black residents had been met by roving gangs of white teenagers proclaiming their unwillingness to share the neighborhood. After an eleven-year-old black boy was killed by a sniper, Italian and black youths armed with guns and firebombs began to converge on East New York from other parts of the city.

Schrage, a yeshiva school principal, then newly appointed to an executive position with the Youth Board, convinced his boss, Arricale, that Gallo was the only one with enough clout to overawe the Italian street gangs, and that the Gallo family and their associates were likely to know (or could find out) the identities of the snipers. They arranged a meeting with Gallo, who agreed to help (after his father told him, "Do it"). Gallo did in fact succeed in corralling and cowing the white toughs and thus prevented wholesale bloodshed from breaking out—although the city was not pleased when the story came out in the press.[1]

This was, however, only one occasion on which Rabbi Schrage was prompted to go outside official channels to deal with the deteriorating situation in Brooklyn. Two years before the spring of 1966, during a mounting crime wave in Bedford-Stuyvesant and the adjoining heavily Jewish Orthodox neighborhood of Crown Heights, students and teachers outside the Lubavitch day school where Schrage was the principal were physically assaulted by a group of black youths. The *New York Times* reported that some fifty black teenagers were involved in the incident, and that fifteen students and two rabbis were injured. A few weeks later, in another incident that provoked highly charged reactions, a rabbi's wife was sexually assaulted.

Schrage called a meeting of some 500 local Hasidim and then organized a neighborhood radio-car patrol group, which he styled "The Maccabees of the Community." Pressure from other ethnic and racial communities in the area against what appeared to be Jewish vigilantism quickly led to the inclusion of non-Jews in the crime patrols. When the New York City Human Rights Commission investigated the situation in June 1964, it found that the patrols were staffed by about 140 Jews and 60 gentiles (20 were black). Under a new nonsectarian name, the "Crown Heights Community Patrols," Schrage's squad of radio-cars won the approval of local church ministers, and on 22 June, thirty-five civic and religious groups formed an interracial and nonsectarian "Council of Crown Heights" to sponsor crime prevention and improve community relations in the area.[2]

By the following spring, black residents of Bedford-Stuyvesant had organized their own crime watch organization—foot patrols with "big dogs" as well as car patrols, said to be "modelled on the Maccabees . . . and cooperating with police." A similar group formed in March 1966, in the Bushwick section of Brooklyn, headed by a Lutheran minister; once again, it was described as being "modelled on the Maccabees of Crown Heights."[3]

Ostensibly lending support to law enforcement, private and even community-supported auxiliary "police" supplied added proof that the civil order was destabilized. Less than one month after the Crown Heights Patrols were set up, it became apparent that citizens' groups working against street crime were not an effective counterweight to the mounting head of violence in the city. In July 1964 there was serious rioting both in Harlem and in Bedford-Stuyvesant following the shooting of a fifteen-year-old black youth by police. Many local stores were looted and burned—a great many them, almost inevitably, owned by Jewish merchants.[4] The summer riots in New York in 1964 were a prelude (and a moderate one, at that) to the two hundred violent outbreaks that would take place across America over the following four years, including the famous riots in Watts (Los Angeles), Newark (New Jersey), and the conflagration in Detroit. (The official report to the president on violence in America actually spoke of "the Detroit holocaust" [sic].)[5]

In light of the positive role that neighborhoods were reputed to have played in fostering Jewish ethnic consciousness in the 1920s and 1930s, it is worth pointing out that the mid- to late-1960s cast the neighborhood in a different light: no longer a nurturing environment or a launching pad toward wider civic participation, it now denoted a retreat behind boundaries.

A phenomenon like the Maccabees is comprehensible against the background of a city that was losing a coherent sense of civic identity. The impulse to localize, privatize, or circumvent public services was a response that was not typical of most Jews; but as we shall see, it came to be accepted in late-sixties New York by both white-ethnic and black communities and by policymakers alike.

The Theory and Practice of Community Revitalization

Lack of public safety was but one manifestation of the larger crisis of governability, or what sociologist Theodore Lowi (quoted in the epigraphs to the chapter) might call the "failure of institutions" to address critical social problems. More than a quarter of New York's families were surviving on incomes of less than $4,000 in 1960, at a time when the U.S. Bureau of Labor Statistics said that a family of four in New York required twice that amount for a "moderate" standard of living. (A budget of $9,075 provided "one egg every two days and six cans of beer every two weeks. The Community Council of Greater New York calculated that an income of $4,000 for a family of four in New York in 1960 would provide $.96 per person per day for food.) New York City Health Commissioner Edmund O'Rourke reported that in Harlem, "the death rate is four to ten times higher than in Forest Hills [Queens]." New York State Commissioner of Housing James Gaynor stated that "In 1947 when I first encountered the housing field in New York City, we deplored the existence of some four hundred thousand substandard dwellings. In 1959, when I returned, I find the old score still standing . . . in spite of all the urban renewal and slum clearance."[6]

Housing was in shorter supply in New York than in any of the twelve next-largest U.S. cities. More dwellings had been subdivided into smaller units—often the first step toward creating a tenement slum—than the reverse (smaller units combined to make larger ones). The number of substandard dwellings occupied by whites had gone down by about a third from 1950 to 1959, leaving only about 5.4 percent of whites in dilapidated housing. The percentage of blacks living in substandard housing was 23 percent—albeit down from 33.8 percent, but still about four times higher than among whites. These data and similar figures on overcrowding led one observer to conclude that "Housing abandoned by the white middle classes in their move to the suburbs has not been reallocated equally to Negroes and whites. . . . Racial segregation, as well as poverty, has limited the housing gains of Negroes in metropolitan areas."[7]

The critical test of urban government in New York in the sixties was not primarily in the area of housing, however, but in municipal services. Decent housing for the urban poor, although recognized since the end of World War II (and indeed since the turn of the century) as a public responsibility, was nevertheless not a public service in the proper sense. No city ever offered to actually standardize its dwellings in terms of size, quality, and value. A city, after all, is not a commune. Diverse populations mixed together will almost surely find themselves living in diverse physical conditions depending on income levels, personal preference, and so on. Liberal urban housing policies were intended to remove the factor of unfair discrimination from among the variables—not to create a standard housing service.

But basic municipal services (public transit, public health, sanitation, police and fire protection)—are by their nature intended to offer city residents a fairly uniform standard of service. In that sense, these municipal services are constitutive of what cities *do* for the sake of the public's collective welfare, and that in turn illustrates what cities *are* as political communities. Remove such common public services, and the city as such would give way to myriad private enclaves and corporations.

Although most areas of public service were sorely tested and found lacking in the sixties in New York, it was the public school system that emerged as the key symbol of institutional failure. This was perhaps inevitable, given the fact that education—unlike police, sanitation, public housing or fire protection—has historically carried most of the hopes of Americans for social stabilization and improvement of economic opportunity. In light of these high expectations, the schools have been most vulnerable to charges of incompetence.

The record of New York's schools in terms of the educational attainments of African American and Hispanic children was dismal by all accounts. The efforts of community groups and parent coalitions to integrate schools, at least at the intermediate and secondary levels, had produced no tangible results. As we shall see, the confrontation that took place between the city, the Board of Education, the teachers' union (the United Federation of Teachers—U.F.T.), and groups in ghetto areas demanding control over their district schools, grew directly out of the crisis in public education and municipal services in general. But it is important to appreciate the political context that worked to dislodge older, more all-encompassing approaches to city problems.

Voters were increasingly opting out of the city's political system—not surprising in light of the failure of the system to perform adequately, at least for some sectors. In the sixties, only some 45 percent of eligible voters turned out to vote for mayor; after 1969, that proportion dropped to 30 percent and continued to sink steadily thereafter.[8] In the face of such political alienation, urban planners and sociologists of the time promoted the value of reconstructing "communities" within the city, ostensibly to develop citizens' interest in and attachment to their own neighborhoods as well as to recreate a texture of "interest groups" that could compete in the political marketplace, and thus minimize the risk of civil insurrection. The solution to urban breakdown and anomie was said to lie in diffusing authority—not through existing political mechanisms (party-based patronage and local administration), but through new, participatory, grassroots committees. By 1969, according to a New York *Daily News* poll, 62 percent of New Yorkers favored "more control for local neighborhoods."[9]

Given this climate of opinion, as well as directives from state and federal poverty-program agencies, Mayor John Lindsay—whose first years in office were fraught with major power struggles with the police, transit, and sanitation workers as well as with municipal nurses and doctors—found it expedient to circumvent his own city administration. In his first term, Lindsay increased spending on contracts with outside consultants from $8 million to $70 million. Urban political analyst Martin Shefter noted that this strategy enabled the mayor to fund neighborhood-based groups to provide the services that city agencies failed to provide. (The approach has been compared to the role that Tammany Hall's Democratic machine once played for Irish and Italian immigrants: helping the poor "where the government would not.")[10]

Thus, for example, the federally mandated "Model Cities" program was used to hire sanitation "aides" who cleaned the streets in stricken neighborhoods in Brooklyn, Manhattan, and the South Bronx, bypassing the sanitation workers' union and the city's Sanitation Department, which had been slow to hire more black and Puerto Rican staff.[11]

At the time of his reelection in 1969, Lindsay declared, "We cannot plan for the citizenry unless we plan with them, unless we are willing to give to individuals, to neighborhoods, and to communities the power to be heard and the power to challenge, the power most of all to decide as much as possible what their communities will look like and how they will work."[12] Neighborhood "corporations" were set up through the Office of Economic Opportunity. By 1970, noted one observer, "more than 14,000 people were receiving salaries from 26 neighborhood organizations, ranging from the Lower East Side Community Corporation, the Downtown Brooklyn Development Corporation, and the Crown Heights Community Corporation (the latter receiving a $700,000 appropriation and 30 employees) to the . . . Hunts Point Multi-Service Center (the last with a $4,000,000 budget, an $18,000-a-year director, and a payroll approaching 300)."[13]

It may have been innovative on the part of the activist-liberal mayor, ever mindful of the need to keep the city from exploding, to outflank his own municipal subordinates with ad hoc solutions in order to accomplish pressing strategic goals for the city. But by the same token, it rendered city life more haphazard and it fragmented city politics. Services and budgets became more sectoral and tended to be allocated to those who made the most noise.[14]

In a process that fed upon itself, new leaders of inner-city constituencies built their reputations on community-service agency lobbying. They did not need to mobilize their already alienated constituents to work within the citywide political system, because they were effectively working outside it.[15] The logic of neighborhood networking was that people with a "stake" in their own immediate environment would be more committed to improving it, but this did not take into account the competition between different sectors within neighborhoods, the war over allocations that soon became thinly stretched, and the ways in which a neighborhood focus undermined citywide or even national policymaking. "Even at that time," it has been observed, "critics on the left contended that urban poverty resulted from the larger context of social inequality rather than the particular deficiencies of poor people and their neighborhoods."[16]

A parallel critique (that went largely unheeded), was articulated by Theodore Lowi in his analysis of democratic processes and the progressive aspects of political disorder. Lowi argued the case against "buying off" nascent groups mobilized by grievances against the system by vaguely delegating government funds and discretionary powers to local administrators. Such policy-by-delegation avoided making the tougher decisions that government ought to be making and merely added a layer of new groups (which inevitably represented the better-organized factions or lobbyists) forced to dicker with one another.[17]

Lowi readily admitted that negotiation among plural groups in the private sector normally helps government to maintain an equilibrium or to achieve slow, incremental change, while also preventing government from becoming "too big." By definition, however, this piecemeal process cannot bring about *fundamental changes* when these are required, for example, in response to severe social pathologies, such as racism and social inequality.[18]

Lowi presciently saw that the government's "war on poverty" program, with its community self-help mindset, was, at least in its effect, if not by design, most likely to "kill the civil rights movement and protect existing [social] relationships":

> The war on poverty left almost completely intact the national pattern of racism. It set up a program that expressed hope that relief for the poor would be coordinated at local levels. . . . The 1950s movement for social justice was lost during the 1960s; it was given over to a set of . . . administrative goals. All that seems to be left of the national movement now is a dead martyr [Dr. Martin Luther King, Jr.] and the rhetoric of black withdrawal.[19]

With city services, civil order, and the political process itself "up for grabs," rather than formally redrawn by force of law, raw conflict was unavoidable and negotiation deteriorated into a frustrating confrontationalism—most often, between vying groups or competing minorities within the neighborhood communities themselves (as was the case with the Maccabees in Crown Heights).

"But the doctrine of community control was by now a sacred rubric," wrote one observer, adding, "The white [supervisors of poverty programs] could do little but peer into the dark ghettos, vainly trying to distinguish indigenous leadership from mere demagoguery." A Lindsay administration consultant agreed that "street-fighting pluralism" was the characteristic form of urban politics.[20]

Something very much along these lines is what happened in New York when earlier plans for school integration—which had been feasible but never really implemented in the mid-fifties—were tacitly scrapped as unrealistic in the mid-sixties, and in their place, local school boards were proposed as a means of redistributing power to the black poor.

The Schools Crisis, 1966–68

New York's public school system, its relationship with the black and Hispanic communities, and the furor that erupted in the late sixties form a thicket or minefield so dense that it is difficult to steer a clear path through it. Feelings run high, even thirty years later, whenever the matter is discussed. Despite (or rather, because of) the lack of consensus, a great deal has been written about the schools crisis, and especially about the teachers' strike of 1968. So much, in fact, has been written that it would be redundant to rehearse once again the details of what transpired. The summary I offer follows closely the very lucid accounts written by Naomi Levine and by Diane Ravitch, supplemented by other studies.[21]

The roots of the schools crisis go back to the findings, published in the mid-fifties, that New York's public schools were racially segregated, de facto. Efforts on the part of pro-integration groups in the education profession and in the wider community were directed, from 1954 to 1966, primarily toward extracting from the Board of Education a realistic, specific plan to reduce the number of city schools where registration was wholly black or black and Hispanic. Integration was meant to ensure that equal educational opportunity was spread more evenly throughout the city, in line with the U.S. Supreme Court decision of 1954 and prevailing feeling in the black community, that racially segregated schools were, by definition, inimical to equal educational achievement.

Quite apart from the principle involved, ghetto-area schools were objectively inadequate: Dilapidated and poorly equipped facilities, high rates of staff turnover, rough classroom conditions, and self-fulfilling expectations of low achievement levels on the part of pupils, teachers, and supervisors, were among the factors cited to support the contention that de facto segregation was indeed discriminatory.[22]

The Board sought various means to meet state-mandated integration standards: voluntary transfers of minority students to schools that were primarily white; greater funding and professional backup for targeted schools; and "twinning" racially homogeneous white and minority schools in such a way that the students of one would spend several years studying at the other. Other plans included bringing largely minority-populated vocational high schools and white-dominated academic high schools under one roof; altering the zoning of elementary "feeder schools" to achieve a better racial balance at the junior high level; and reshuffling the existing system (6 years elementary, 3 years junior high, 3 years high school) in favor of a 4–4–4 plan that would keep the youngest children in their own neighborhoods till grade four, but would progressively mix school populations as students grew older.

But the Board's efforts were largely ineffectual. All of these plans ran into difficulty and interminable delay in implementation. School supervisors of inner-city schools objected to large-scale voluntary transfers on the grounds that this tended to deprive their schools of the most motivated children of aspiring middle-class black families, thus contributing to a further lowering of educational standards. Some black parents, too, were apparently not eager to transport their children over long distances every day. Perhaps most of all, strong protests on the part of white parent-groups, including school boycotts, led the Board to reject any plan that involved involuntary transfers of white students—something that, in any case, state education authorities also refused to mandate.[23]

Confrontations took place between black, Hispanic, and other pro-integration activists and the Board in the early 1960s. Integrationists were angry at what they saw as foot-dragging and intransigence on the part of the Board, which implemented only palliative measures and refused to commit itself to a timetable. At the same time, because of the overall loss of white population to the suburbs and the preference of a growing number of white families for private and parochial schools (such schools served some 400,000, mostly white students in the mid-sixties), the black and Hispanic population in the city's public schools rose steadily. By 1966, minority students represented fully half the total public school registration (75 percent in Manhattan), and this trend could not but continue, given New York's demographics. There were simply no longer enough white students in the system to spread around, even by hypothetically forcing white parents to accept large-scale bussing.[24]

Pro-integration activists nevertheless persisted in agitating against such partial remedies as greater spending on disadvantaged schools, construction of new school buildings in ghetto areas, and new proposals to bring more minority students to white neighborhoods, at least for junior high and high school. (This, despite the fact that some parents in inner-city neighborhoods were just as adamant in demands for new school facilities for their children in their own neighborhoods.)

At this stage, teachers were not perceived to be part of the problem, except insofar as inner-city schools tended to lose experienced teachers to other districts. The United Federation of Teachers, which only began to represent most New York teachers and achieve solid professional gains in the early sixties, had its own proposals to offer with regard to improving educational equality in the city: chiefly, to funnel extra funding into disadvantaged schools—a program that the U.F.T. dubbed More Effective Schools (M.E.S.). To the teachers, intensive pooling of staff, remedial and counseling services, enrichment programs, and other resources at trouble spots promised relief from difficult classroom conditions. In return, the U.F.T. was willing to agree to work to minimize teacher transfers out of disadvantaged school districts. With its pro-civil rights posture, the teachers' union was perceived as an active partner whose members were directly in touch with ghetto problems, rather than an adversary.[25]

Similarly, as long as the main issues revolved around white-black integration and as long as the chief obstacle appeared to be the Board of Education, there was no Jewish issue involved. Jews did represent a very large proportion of school personnel, but the ethnic factor as such only came into play when black and Hispanic ethnicity became the basis for political demands.

Ravitch's study makes clear that the Board of Education suffered a loss of credibility not just in the eyes of minority parents' and community groups, but also in the estimation of state education commissioners, special review panels, and the media—especially when New York's once-envied achievement levels began to falter and drop below national scores. To that list of critics we must add Mayor Lindsay, whose attitude to city agencies and bureaus was determined by a reformist's low regard for existing procedures and hierarchies.[26]

Moreover, the schools crisis was engendered, paradoxically, by the prevailing optimistic perceptions of the schools' inherent capacity to educate slum children out of poverty. These perceptions, Ravitch's study argued, were exaggerated and were based on a serious misreading of the historical record. All past waves of immigration to New York had resulted in downward trends in scholastic performance, an uneven record of educational achievement among different ethnic groups, tension between neighborhood communities and school authorities, and demands for a major overhaul of the system. The "legend" of the schools as an omnipotent tool of social reform now worked to frustrate school officials and to convince some activists in the black community that willful and transparent racism was the only explanation of the schools' otherwise unaccountable failure to educate all children alike.[27]

Beyond these immediate irritants, however, lay the fact that the schools crisis was only one feature of the more general context of urban poverty, unrest, and demographic change that determined the ways in which society related to the schools and objectively changed the options available to administrators. Thus, the growing exit of white families from the city and the concomitant higher proportion of nonwhite pupils in the school system meant that integration was bound to recede as a viable plan. Putting it simply: schools could not be integrated in a society that continued to adhere to racially patterned residential and socioeconomic nonintegration.

At the same time, certain black educators and community activists began to question the thesis that all-black schools must, by definition, be considered educationally inferior. The unintended implication behind older integration campaigns—that black children could only achieve in a white-dominated environment—now seemed likely to perpetuate problems of poor self-image and low expectations of success among ghetto children. If integration was being blocked by racism, on the one hand, and if, on the other, an implication of inherent black inferiority appeared to be embedded in the integrationist argument to begin with, an alternative approach lay in empowering the black community to offer its children a better educational experience in their own terms and on their own ground.

This new trend of thought, coupled to the apparent failure of the system to offer any realistic hope for racial integration, and combined with the proactive strategy in the administration of the city's poverty programs through neighborhood or "community" involvement, resulted in persistent calls from state authorities, city hall, and forces within the black community to implement long-discussed plans for decentralization of the school system and the creation of local school boards. Decentralization was intended to give district supervisors greater initiative and latitude in problem solving and correspondingly greater responsibility for achieving results, while making them more accountable to community and parents' groups.[28]

The confluence of these trends first took shape in a confrontation in East Harlem, where the city, in an effort to improve school facilities and to implement the state's proposal to create intermediate schools (grades 5 through 8) as a venue for integration, had built a state-of-the-art, windowless, air-conditioned school, designated I.S. (Intermediate School) 201, and staffed by an experienced inner-city principal (who was Jewish) and a hand-picked faculty.

While the school was certainly bound to improve the physical and even pedagogical quality of schools in the district, its location in the heart of the ghetto rather than at a more suitable spot for mixing white and minority students virtually assured an all-black and Hispanic registration—despite the Board's limp claim that the proximity of the school to the Triborough Bridge made it accessible to Bronx and Queens students. The collision between the Board's integrationist rhetoric and continued de facto segregation in practice prompted a strong response in the community in favor of local (black and Hispanic) control over the school. (It was not until June 1968, well after the crisis had reached its peak, that an alternative approach was implemented: namely, that of empowering the black community on a *citywide* basis by adding distinguished minority-group and sympathetic members to the Board of Education.)

Mobilized by a local committee, and with the initial cooperation of the school's teachers, a boycott was mounted against the opening of the school in September 1966. Demands of the neighborhood school committee included the delegation of supervisory authority to a local board and the replacement of the Board-appointed principal. Although the school eventually opened and a modus vivendi was established, with extra funding arranged on an M.E.S.-type model, the struggle served as a prelude to the drama that was to unfold in Brooklyn and engulf the entire city. The episode at I.S. 201 was also the occasion for the first articulation of feeling directed against white teachers and principals and of antisemitic rhetoric. Though the Board of Education was the primary target of ghetto rage and frustration, white society at large, which had proven itself unable and unwilling to educate black and Hispanic children, was represented by the teachers and principals who were, following this argument, the direct agents of racist cultural deprivation ("educational genocide").[29]

During 1967–68, with the backing of the Ford Foundation, teachers, and community groups, three experimental local school boards were formed in order to test the premise that community involvement, combined with administrative decentralization, might lead to improved educational achievement in disadvantaged neighborhoods. Apart from the East Harlem district that included I.S. 201, there was one such local board in lower Manhattan ("Two Bridges"), and one in Brooklyn, in a desperately impoverished area between Bedford-Stuyvesant and Brownsville, known as Ocean Hill. The group that formed in Ocean Hill-Brownsville, which enjoyed political support from the Brooklyn chapter of CORE and activist neighborhood clergy, quickly became the focal point of an aggressive campaign of minority self-assertiveness. During that year a local school board was elected (the somewhat irregular voting was later contested—to no avail—by other local residents), which hired Rhody McCoy, an assistant principal from Manhattan, as "unit administrator," and proceeded to draw up plans for a fully self-governing school district that would be under the nominal authority of the Board of Education.

It was also during the 1967–68 school year that teachers in the district and the union that represented them came to be seen as yet another adversarial group. Given the atmospherics of "black power" and the determination of the local board's leaders to use the schools as a base for political self-assertion, teachers were not informed of board planning meetings. Teachers objected to this and to the ad hoc procedures in the naming of new principals for the district. In particular, they strenuously opposed the nomination of one Herman Ferguson (a man who had been indicted for conspiracy to murder) for the post of principal for the district's I.S. 55. Teachers and supervisors began to filter out of the district.[30]

The Ocean Hill-Brownsville school district kept its schools open in September 1967 during a twelve-day strike by the U.F.T.—one more cause of contention with the teachers. And in the spring of 1968, the U.F.T., led by its president, Albert Shanker, put its political weight behind efforts to block a pending school decentralization bill in the New York State legislature.[31]

At that point, the local board had still not received proper authorization from the central Board and its actual powers were not spelled out. Such arrangements were due to be made in the wake of the school decentralization law then pending (to which the Ocean Hill group had its own objections).

Notwithstanding, the Board was prepared to work with the local group, even to the extent of quietly assisting McCoy to exchange a few of the teachers and supervisors with those of his own choosing.

The local board chose this moment, however—the beginning of May 1968—to force a confrontation and assert full local control. A group of nineteen (mostly Jewish) teachers and assistant principals were notified, without explanation, that their services were no longer required. Under existing rules, involuntary transfer with an "unsatisfactory" rating required a due-process hearing; if there was no such rating (and none was specified in this case), then transfer had to be voluntary—which this certainly was not. In any case, transfers were the prerogative of the central Board's superintendent of schools, who—despite his willingness to quietly help transfer individual teachers—was unwilling to countenance the public dismissal of a large group, in what amounted to a coup d'état.

When the local board refused to reinstate the teachers, as ordered, 350 U.F.T.-represented teachers in the Ocean Hill-Brownsville district walked out in protest. When they in turn ignored McCoy's order to return to work, the local board, sidestepping the existing citywide vetting system for hiring personnel, hired an equivalent number of replacement staff (which was not difficult: in those years young men just out of college were not subject to military draft if they worked as teachers). From this point on, the issue for the union was no longer the original nineteen dismissals, but the dismantling of local control and the reinstatement of all dismissed and/or protesting teachers.[32]

Over the summer of 1968 negotiations failed to resolve the issues. In the meantime, the original nineteen dismissals were invalidated by a distinguished (black) New York jurist, Judge Francis Rivers, who ruled conclusively that the ten teachers still willing to return to Ocean Hill-Brownsville be returned to their posts. Though the choice of Rivers had been acceptable to the local board, it refused to abide by his order.[33]

The events that began in May 1968 did not end until 17 November of that year. The New York City school system was struck by the U.F.T. three times (negotiated agreements broke down twice) to win the central Board's commitment to reinstate its members—some eighty teachers still wanted to return to their jobs—and to make sure that community boards were not empowered to hire and fire teaching and supervisory staff at will. The crisis killed the decentralization bill then pending in Albany, though a stop-gap, twelve-month measure was passed and, a year later, a modest decentralization plan went into effect.

The schools crisis, ostensibly one of politics and procedures, directly concerned those Jews and those black and Puerto Rican groups whose interaction took place chiefly in the public education system. Pupil segregation in the public schools and low scholastic achievement in ghetto areas were not "Jewish" issues per se: they were products of a powerful social hierarchy and racial tensions between blacks and whites in American society at large. Educational policy and minority self-assertion were or should have been citywide matters of concern. But school professionals and their inner-city clientele were constantly aware of the ethnoracial dimension of the situation because of the way the numbers were stacked. As in other New York matters, a numerical overrepresentation of Jews created a "Jewish presence"—in this case, in the teaching profession (the ethnic preponderance of Jews in the union and in the school system made "teacher" and "Jew" almost synonymous)—just as the reality of all-black or black-Hispanic school populations reflected racially determined neighborhood concentrations.

There were (and still are) those who saw the ensuing ethnic conflict as an irrelevant deflection from the real issues and who pointed out—truthfully but rather uselessly—that there were Jews and blacks on *both* sides of the issues. Both sides defended themselves against charges of ethnic or racial bigotry (the union pointing to its long and active record on behalf of civil rights and to its teachers' involvement in advocacy for ghetto schools and in working to foster students' positive interest in the African American heritage; the Ocean Hill-Brownsville leaders disavowing any antisemitism, arguing that the teachers they had dismissed were interfering with the district's experiment and that the replacement teachers who were hired included mostly whites, of whom many were Jews). Both the union and the community-control faction, however, accused the opposing side of engaging in hate-mongering.

In assessing the Brooklyn case, it is worth comparing it with events that took place simultaneously on Manhattan's Upper West Side (school district 5), an area where a reasonable white-minority balance was maintained in the mid-sixties, school integration remained the goal of local parents (including white liberals, many of whom were Jews), and rancor over educational politics between the local community and the schools administration—even militant action on the part of parents' groups—did not spill over into an interethnic confrontation. Parents and teachers at P.S. 84 in that district organized a "freedom school" during the teachers' union strike in the fall of 1967 and persisted in bringing pressure to bear for greater community participation in the school throughout the 1967–69 period. They won the removal of two successive principals and the district superintendent (all Jewish), conducted sit-ins, kept their school open during the U.F.T. strike of 1968 (with the help of parents and sympathetic nonstriking teachers), instituted innovative "open classroom" pedagogic approaches, and did away with the tracking of students in ways that had promoted segregated classes even within integrated schools. The transformation of P.S. 84 was won by a coalition—black, white, and Jewish, teachers, parents, and a sympathetic new (Jewish) district superintendent—that was in agreement on basic educational goals, without becoming involved in separatist racial politics.[34]

Nevertheless, in Ocean Hill-Brownsville, ethnoracial interests did lie at the core of the U.F.T.'s clash with militant black circles over the experimental school districts. Any attempt to screen out the ethnoracial dimension as something illegitimately introduced by one side or the other is an obfuscation of the underlying issues.

Ocean Hill's project administrator, Rhody McCoy, justified his appointment of new principals for four of his district's schools as follows: "The reason for my selections has been based on a number of criteria—people who have demonstrated particular abilities in programs and people who fit a situation. . . . For instance, the community around one of these particular schools is predominantly Puerto Rican. Hence the characteristics and qualifications of . . . Mr. Fuente fit the bill."[35] The entire thrust of the community-control campaign was ethnoracial in origin and intent, and amounted to treating ethnoracial subdivision of city services administration as normative.

In all fairness, the fragmentation of the city along ethnoracial lines was not something that black militants had started: It was a reality into which they had grown up and it was now being given de facto and even de jure confirmation by the city and federal governments (through community-run poverty agencies).

Opinion varies today as to whether or not Albert Shanker deliberately inflated incidents of antisemitism in the Ocean Hill-Brownsville confrontation, thus infusing the Jewish issue where it didn't belong.[36] But this point may not be crucial, given the fact that local control—as was already evident in the I.S. 201 case—was primarily an ethnoracial argument: namely, that teachers and the system that they served/controlled were (deliberately or otherwise) crippling the minds of black and Hispanic children. Antisemitism was not essential to this argument, but it was undeniably present as a corollary. Clearly, it had not originated with Shanker.

The antisemitic dimension of the schools affair was given further exposure and credence when, in December 1968, Julius Lester devoted air time to the topic during his call-in talk show on radio station WBAI. He had invited Leslie Campbell, one of the more outspoken of the black teachers, to come to the studio to talk about the scars left by the schools crisis. Campbell, who had brought along a number of poems written by his students, was somewhat surprised when Lester asked him to read aloud a piece of verse that was filled with crude antisemitic sentiment, "dedicated" to Albert Shanker. The broadcast drew sharp protests against Campbell, Lester, and the station, which was an important mouthpiece in New York for black culture and public affairs. Lester claimed that his own aim was simply to demonstrate to the public, and to Shanker personally, how much damage had already been done, in order to bring all sides to their senses. His claims were later upheld by the F.C.C.[37]

In any event, Shanker was not in the arena on his own. It has been argued, for example, that Mayor Lindsay and the Ford Foundation also needlessly polarized the situation by engaging in a policy that fostered confrontation along ethnoracial lines.[38] One of Lindsay's close advisors acknowledged that the mayor was convinced that the union was fighting a losing war and that confrontation was necessary. "What you see here," the mayor's aide explained, "and what you're going to see in other institutions in this city, is the beginning of a shift of power. It won't happen peacefully. It never has. There'll be more tensions, more arrests, just plain more trouble. . . . But in time the blacks and the Puerto Ricans will get their share of power, as others have before them."[39]

Lindsay himself was quoted publicly to the effect that radical change in the political status of "disadvantaged people" was necessary if violence was to be averted. He was disappointed to discover that resentment against radical change ran as deeply as it did in New York: "[E]verywhere else in the country, New York is supposed to be so liberal a city, even a cauldron of radicalism. The school battle showed us who we actually were."[40] Lindsay's delegitimation of racism was fully justified. Unfortunately, this also led him up a blind alley toward a delegitimation of the teachers' union, as if it were a hotbed of racist opposition—which it was not. All the while, he was prepared to countenance spoken and unspoken threats of impending violence, leaning on this argument to justify his policies.

◆ ◆ ◆

The teachers' strike and the ethnoracial fallout that pitted blacks against Jews involved real differences over civic culture and sectoral interests. This confrontation cut deeper and was far more significant than the more superficial (if hurtful) matter of mutual hate-speech and epithets that were so freely thrown about.

The union was playing by rules that had governed labor relations in the city since the Wagner administrations in the fifties and early sixties and, arguably, had characterized urban life in general in New York since the La Guardia era: namely, that everyone was entitled to fair play and that demands for procedural safeguards were a legitimate defense of sectoral interests. In the give-and-take of city life, the demands of each different constituency could be presented, then brokered, reconciled, and ratified "at the top." That is, sectors such as municipal unions or electoral constituencies did not have to rein in their own demands by prior self-censorship, but they did have to barter, through the agency of city government, with other constituencies.

Clearly, under these rules, sectoral and citywide interests could be articulated and could conflict; but there was an assumed level playing field. Groups that aspired to work within the city as a society of the whole, groups that historically included aspiring middle-class groups (immigrant and minority groups, organized labor, civil service employees), had internalized these assumptions. Certainly that was the way in which the U.F.T. viewed the decentralization question: an issue that could be legitimately opposed in the name of teachers' professional interests, even if this pitted them against "management" (the State Education Department, the Board of Education, the mayor) or against other community interests.

Even Reverend Milton Galamison, New York's veteran crusader for school integration, a militant leader in his own right, attempted to move the Ocean Hill-Brownsville dispute with the U.F.T. onto negotiable grounds. At one point in the crisis he brokered a possible deal with the union for a cosponsored parent-teacher-backed decentralization bill ("Al [Shanker]," he reportedly said, "is honestly dishonest—let's slice the pie and divide it between the union and the community"); but Galamison's efforts were rejected out of hand by the leadership in the local board.[41]

The community-control faction was saying that the rules were not functional. There was no level playing field in reality. Procedural safeguards based on stacked rules were bound to work against black people and, on those grounds, ought not to be honored. Violation of procedure was precisely the way to end a situation of unfairness, and home rule was the way to implement a new regime. The combined force of de facto segregation and municipal failure at the service-delivery level had turned a militant leadership away from further cooperation with the existing system. The "planning council" that preceded the Ocean Hill local school district project spoke frankly of the "last threads of the community's faith in the school system's purposes," and warned that these "last threads" were fragile indeed: "The ending of oppression and the beginning of a new day has often become a reality only after people have resorted to violent means."[42]

In pressing the case for minority empowerment, black militant leaders were attacking those urban values that Jews had identified with and internalized, and upon which Jews depended for their own self-regard. Indeed, it went against what New York "Jewishness" had become: Being a "New York Jew," for many, was identical to being a New York native, a citizen, a member of the public. Jews, in particular, were never willing to encode their own ethnicity in explicit political forms. They had shied away from acknowledging that the unions they led were ethnic per se, preferring to merge into a wider craft- and class-based, multiethnic labor movement. They had participated actively in Liberal and Democratic Party operations, but never as a party or faction in their own name. And they had used "defense" agencies (like the American Jewish Committee, the American Jewish Congress, and the ADL) to reconfigure their ethnic interests as civil or interdenominational interests. Ethnicity, they seemed to say, should be seen but not heard: objectively present, but sublimated. It was an ethnicity defined largely by the space that it occupied, more than by identifiable cultural or communal markers. In Ocean Hill-Brownsville it was contended that black (or Hispanic) ethnicity also occupied space, quite literally; but rather than a diffuse ethnicity, oppressed minority groups required self-administration. They were claiming that urban space, if not truly shared, must be subdivided.

The Jewish reaction—quite apart from the U.F.T.—was strong indeed: The New York Board of Rabbis called the plan for community control "a potential breeder of local apartheid." And even the American Jewish Congress, which called the school decentralization plan "imaginative," and expressed the hope that parents' desires for high-quality education for their children might serve to prevent abuses, prefaced its qualified approval with the warning, that, "It is possible that . . . we may open the door to personal and politically motivated appointments and increase racial and religious interference in the selection of staff."[43]

One of the ironic results of the schools crisis, however, was that in the defense of the civic culture they treasured, Jews were goaded into bringing their own ethnocentrism out into the open. Or, perhaps, one might say that as the cosmopolitan civic ideal lost its congruence with social reality, the "tribal" ideal and those sectors of New York Jewry that were its champions emerged with greater force than ever before. The urban crisis, as symbolized by the schools affair, was instrumental in the reinforcement of ethnic boundaries. It was doubly ironic, then, that ethnocentric defensiveness emerged among New York Jews precisely at the end of a decade that had been marked by a decline in Jewish religious and cultural vitality (as explored in chapters 3 and 4).

In the mayoralty election a year after the teachers' strike, Jewish voters split, as noted in the last chapter, and tilted closer to Lindsay's right-leaning opponents. Hecklers made it difficult for Lindsay to speak in some New York synagogues, and it has been alleged that only the endorsement that he received from Israeli prime minister Golda Meir (while on a visit to New York) salvaged for Lindsay some part of that Jewish constituency that was prepared to prioritize its own ethnic interest.[44]

That same year, the Crown Heights Lubavitcher community, some three-thousand-strong, was ordered by its leader, Rabbi Schneerson, to stand its ground in the neighborhood and maintain a viable Jewish turf, despite the flight of most other white residents. And in 1970–71, angry demonstrators in

Forest Hills, Queens, including many Jews, confronted the city administration over plans to build public housing in their neighborhood for low-income residents—in effect, black and Hispanic people.[45]

The end of the sixties, then, were the hinge on which the urban ethnic paradigm of the past—unselfconscious particularism wedded to a metropolitan outlook—gave way finally to a protective, self-conscious politics of confrontation. It was significant, in this regard, that the urban crisis coincided with two overseas crises that directly affected the tenor of Jewish life by raising Jewish group consciousness: the 1967 Arab-Israeli war and the problems involving Soviet Jewry, which we will discuss presently.

Some wider perspective on the Jewish-black confrontation in New York is required, however. One relevant factor is the radicalization of political discourse in America in 1968 and the concomitant personalization of virtually all public issues. (That was the year in which both Martin Luther King, Jr. and Robert F. Kennedy were murdered—and assassination is, among other things, an extreme form of the personalization of political conflict.)

Veteran liberal Arthur Schlesinger, Jr., addressing a City University commencement ceremony in June that year, just after the Kennedy assassination, complained sardonically that, "After all, our conventional liberalism is to a discouraging degree a liberalism of promises and excuses. After all, social renewal can only come from personal commitment."[46]

Schlesinger's complaint may help us to understand that, just as integration of the schools was a moot point if society at large was racially divided, so too would it be impossible to conduct a power struggle like the one in Ocean Hill-Brownsville without the personalism, extremism, and tendencies toward physical or verbal violence that characterized protest politics in urban America at large. To feel personally aggrieved or victimized implied a personal vendetta against the (personalized) victimizers. Political debate was removed from the impersonal realm to the realm of emotional engagement.

These tendencies prompted historian Walter Laqueur, two years after the teachers' strike, to publish an article in the Sunday *New York Times Magazine* on the lessons of Weimar Germany. The essay bore the subheadline, "The Cry Was, 'Down with *Das System.*' " The magazine's cover, featuring Laqueur's essay as the lead article, bore a lurid 1932 anti-Nazi poster ("The Third Reich? No!").[47] Laqueur was concerned about the way that Weimar's contentious and tragic history had become the object of avid interest—almost a fixation—in American discourse in the sixties. "Some writers have detected striking parallels with present-day America, but even those who deny this feel sufficiently troubled. . . . The debate itself is a manifestation of deep malaise."[48]

In a related vein, Nathan Glazer warned Jews who participated in the movement against the Vietnam War that they might raise the specter of the old "stab in the back" accusation that was leveled against Jews in Weimar Germany.[49] And we recall that Hannah Arendt was reminded of Weimar by the assassination of President Kennedy.

Such views—and the dark premonition that lay behind it—did not constitute a general consensus. In fact, it was angrily rejected by the New York head of the American Federation of Jews from Central Europe, Curt Silberman: "I think that we are doing a great injustice to America and to ourselves if we feel that there is such a parallel. . . . The Jewish situation in . . . America is not comparable to the Jewish situation in 1932 in Germany."[50]

Another figure in the American German-Jewish community, Herbert Strauss, a historian, did see some parallels between America at the end of the sixties and the German past; but he was struck more by some of the positive rather than the negative congruencies. It was undoubtedly true, he argued, that, along with the rest of American society, German-Jewish Americans faced the "social upheaval" of "urban problems, student impatience, [and] Black racialism"; and, he argued, German Jews in America were not, on average, terribly keen on "radical criticism or political action," given their history. Nonetheless, he thought that the "restless children" of the American middle class (and especially, he stressed, the children of the American Jewish middle class) had opened the door, through their revolt against the "great suburban wasteland of American affluence," to a cultivation of inwardness, authentic values on a human scale, and cultural integrity that Strauss identified as traits and aspirations worthy of the best of the old German Jewish *mentalité*. "For the German Jewish immigrant, his descendants and his organisations, this might present a last, final opportunity to recreate . . . the intellectual and emotional culture that was his, in a new language and a new environment."[51]

It was thus possible to be deeply disturbed by the turn of events in American political and social life and yet be aware that the activation of inner energies—while perhaps disorderly and divisive—were in some sense necessary. Nowhere was this more the case, in Strauss's words, than within American Jewish life, which was overdue for an internal challenge:

> Most observers agree that American Jewry's organisational and philanthropic excellence is not paralleled by its cultural achievements. The American Jewish middle class, like much of the rest of its peers in other religions, has not used its affluence and its ethical and political culture to create an aesthetically or intellectually satisfactory style of life, away from mass media, sports, small talk, or status-seeking consumerism.[52]

Internal challenge, in fact, was the order of the day in the Jewish community.

The Divisions Within

In the spring of 1964, even as Rabbi Schrage was contemplating the organization of his "Maccabees," a group styling themselves "Zealots" (this name, too, borrowed from a Jewish insurgent group of late antiquity) picketed the offices of the New York Board of Rabbis to protest housing conditions among the poor in areas like the Lower East Side.

Led by a Harvard-trained student of city planning, the protesters released the following statement:

> We petition the rabbis of New York to seek out the slum owners in their congregations and to threaten them with denunciation from the pulpit and even *herem* or excommunication. . . . The majority of buildings with 50 or more violations listed in the *New York Times,* January 24, 1963, have identifiably Jewish landlords. . . . We have submitted to the rabbis a list of 250 Jewish landlords who own 500 slum buildings in Manhattan. The House of Israel must be cleansed of those who exploit the poor.[53]

The Board of Rabbis, an interdenominational committee of Jewish clergy primarily concerned with smoothing intramural, interfaith, and community-relations issues, may have been selected for a public protest because American clergy (especially since the sixties) are expected to exert moral leadership in the public sphere, not just in the private realm of faith and worship. If so, the "Zealots" (probably not very familiar with the world of rabbis) had the wrong address: As we saw in chapter 4, major Jewish religious intellectuals did don the mantle of prophetic battle for human morality, but such an exalted role did not extend to rabbinical functionaries.

This particular misapprehension aside, it is more than likely that, rather than picket the homes of selected slumlords, the "Zealots" chose their target because of its publicity value: Jews picketing rabbis was deliberately provocative, a sort of grandstanding that was akin to the proverbial "man bites dog" news item.

Accordingly, the protest had little noticeable effect on New York's slumlords; but its very occurrence, its militant rhetoric, and the fact that a mainstream Jewish representative organization was targeted were all significant evidence of the devaluation of a fifties-style politics of consensus in the Jewish community.

First, in keeping with a pattern that was very American (indeed, almost universal), the demonstration was meant to showcase intergenerational tension. The demonstration certainly served the titillating function of *épater les bourgeois.*

Second, the "Zealots" emphasized the particular culpability of the Jewish community ("the House of Israel") in the matter of slum conditions—thus directly flouting a Jewish rule of thumb, according to which collective responsibility was invoked only when individuals were called upon to contribute to the group's welfare or else when individual achievement (like Nobel prizes) reflected credit on Jews at large, but never when individual Jews acted discreditably.

The "Zealots," however, claimed that there was guilt by association. Slumlords were members in good standing of their ethnic-religious community when they deserved in fact to be pilloried. Having set out to make a point about universal ethical principles, they wound up asserting a point about ethnic cohesiveness: Their *social conscience* prompted them to object to slumlords, but their *Jewishness* prompted them to turn the moral argument into an ethnic one: to wit, that slumlords were a disgrace to their community.

Third, and in direct consequence of this last point, the protesters sought to disparage the community elders (represented in this case by the Board of Rabbis) for having been derelict in carrying out their moral obligations and communal functions. That implied a doctrine of accountability and thus, in effect, an appeal to direct democracy—the "people" had spoken. This appeal to democracy and accountability was almost by definition misdirected in a community that was organized solely in voluntary associations, none of which encompassed mechanisms of representation or hierarchical authority. But by placing a greater burden upon the professional "leadership," notice was thus served that the "community" was bestirring itself to assert a new social awareness.

For New York Jewry this sort of intramural protest demonstration was a legacy of the receding past. Its precedents lay long ago, in the era of mass Jewish immigration that had come to an end in the 1920s, when it was unremarkable to make demands in the name of the Jewish people. It was, perhaps, not even terribly atypical for the Depression years, when Jewish neighborhoods were reputed to provide a venue for soapbox debates between Zionists, Stalinists, and Trotskyists. But the intervening years of family-mediated, middle-class ethnicity, followed by the suburbanization and congregationalism typical since the late fifties, meant that New York had seen little of intra-ethnic Jewish political factionalism for many years. Postwar Jews had seemingly banished the fervor of confrontational politics from their midst. Certainly they had routinely eschewed the sort of ethnic self-flagellation that the "Zealots" represented.

Nevertheless, this reappearance in New York Jewish life of factional politics was not an isolated incident but an augury of what was to come. Perhaps because "communities" and minorities had risen to new political importance in the city; perhaps because the flight of upper-middle-class families to the suburbs had left behind a more contentious collection of Jews, including college students, more recent immigrants, and the Orthodox, who were less apt to accept a quiescent role; perhaps because public virtue in the sixties was most clearly expressed in the culture of protest and confrontation—internal discord in New York Jewry was expressed publicly and sharply in that decade.

This may surprise those who remember the sixties—especially from about 1964–65—primarily as a time of resurgent Jewish solidarity and self-assertion. Indeed, there was much evidence of both. It was at that time that Jews in New York began to use the city's main public stage—its streets—to express collective pride (Israel Independence Day) or collective anger (against Soviet policies adversely affecting Jews). But group self-assertion led, almost by definition, to an internal version of what was happening outside the community: namely, competition over the right to speak in the community's name and to champion its values and interests.

Soviet Jewry and the Six-Day War

From the end of the 1950s, media reports and statements by Jewish public figures in the West, in Israel, and in America began to focus attention on the ill-favored status of Jews in the Soviet Union. By 1962 (the year of the Cuban Missile Crisis), concern began to turn into alarm as Western Jews discerned what appeared to be an anti-Jewish campaign in Russia. There were indications that Jews were being singled out by the Soviet authorities for their alleged role in "economic crimes" (black market, smuggling, and speculation). During 1962–63, dozens of Jews were reported to have been convicted and sentenced to death for such crimes, including the rabbi of Vilnius (Vilna), Lithuania, and a seventy-six-year-old Jew from Kazakhstan. Robert Kennedy, then the U.S. attorney general, put the figure at "over one hundred," most of them Jews. At the same time, it was reported that prayerbooks, Passover matzos, and other items related to the practice of Judaism were in drastically short supply, and that some sixty synagogues had been closed since 1959 in large Jewish centers, such as L'vov (L'viv) and Chernovtsy in the Ukraine—the implication being that Jewish culture as such was targeted for repression.[54]

Existing mechanisms for transmitting Jewish concern to the U.S. administration and to Congress—mechanisms that included all the major Jewish defense and community relations agencies as well as the willing cooperation of such public figures as Eleanor Roosevelt, Bishop Pike, or the two U.S. senators from New York State (Kenneth Keating and Jacob Javits)—were increasingly used during the period between 1962 and 1964. In response, the State Department agreed only to issue a general statement of "concern" over antisemitism in Russia at the beginning of January 1962. The following month, New York Congressman Charles Buckley introduced a resolution in the House of Representatives calling on President Kennedy to intervene personally in the Soviet Jewish situation. Meanwhile, New York Representative Leonard Farbstein, a member of the House Foreign Affairs Committee, issued his own statement, saying that, while Soviet Jews were not the targets of "government-sanctioned pogroms, organized mass-murder or wholesale deportation," it was clear that the object of the Kremlin campaign was "the extinction of Jewish life."[55]

Javits, Farbstein, and Keating all rapped the State Department for its inaction in the matter and once again called on the president to intervene. The policy of the State Department was to continue to raise the issue "from time to time" in the United Nations, while recommending that private religious groups in the United States continue to protest, "without reference to the U. S. Government."[56]

The New York State Senate passed a resolution in April 1962 calling upon the U.N. Commission on Human Rights to investigate antisemitism in the Soviet Union. In July, Connecticut Senator Thomas Dodd urged the recall of the American ambassador from Moscow—a step that the State Department declined to take. In its statement on the matter, on 8 August of that year, the department argued that reports of large-scale repressive actions against Jews "and other religious groups" in the Soviet Union were possibly exaggerated.[57]

On the one hand, it seemed, Jewish groups were succeeding in placing the Soviet Jewish issue on the American political agenda (at least on Capitol Hill and in the press), while on the other hand, there was little mobilization at the grass roots and few if any tangible results, apart from Soviet denials of antisemitism.[58] The issue within the Jewish community rapidly became one of strategy and tactics: Should the existing community organizations continue to lobby individually for public attention on the Soviet Jewish situation (a course of action that at least one group, the Rabbinical Assembly of the Conservative movement, called "chaotic, conflicting, and competitive"); or would it be wiser to set up a new, one-issue agency to coordinate such efforts—a step that some existing organizations questioned (who needed yet another Jewish organization in an already crowded field?)?[59]

The slow inroads of consciousness-raising efforts lay at the root of this debate; therefore, self-criticism within the Jewish community focused both on public apathy on an issue of conscience as well as on the political issues of leadership and methods. Insofar as the Jewish community had faced these same issues once before, in the 1940s—difficulties in crossing a threshold of political inhibition, political efficacy, and collective conscience—there was an air of *déjà vu* about the whole thing that was, indeed, regularly invoked. Abraham

Joshua Heschel, speaking in 1963 at the Jewish Theological Seminary, told his listeners: "There is a dreadful moral trauma that haunts many of us: the failure . . . to do our utmost . . . to save the Jews under Hitler. [The] nightmare that terrifies me today [is] the unawareness of our being involved in a new failure, in a tragic dereliction of duty [toward] Russian Jewry."[60]

It was at this stage, as the Soviet Jewry issue began to emerge as a divisive problem within American Jewry, that New York became a major focal point of more radical agitation. The line that divided the "establishment" from those demanding more direct action was not necessarily only a generational one, though that was one factor. Rather, the line seemed also to run between the old-line New York ethnic leadership—largely comprised of second-generation figures—and newcomers from outside. Among those most responsible for goading the community into more effective political action were moral spokespeople like Heschel and writer Elie Wiesel (both of them relatively recent arrivals on the New York scene); the Israeli government, acting through an office quietly set up in New York under Meir Rosenne to encourage the efforts on behalf of Soviet Jewry; and Jacob Birnbaum, recently arrived from England, who founded the Student Struggle for Soviet Jewry (SSSJ). Directed by one of Birnbaum's first recruits, Glenn Richter, the SSSJ quickly became the spearhead of the radicalized movement and drew most effectively on the Orthodox sector of the community. (Apart from being readily recruitable through their day schools and synagogues, Orthodox students, like their parents, were largely alienated from the formal and informal structures of New York Jewish secularized ethnic or intellectual leadership.)[61]

That being the case, the message was conveyed that the existing communal ethic of New York Jewry was woefully inadequate, insofar as its capacity to bear moral witness and to mobilize for action were concerned—a point that (as we have seen in the case of the "Zealots" of 1964) seemed to be common coin. The divisions between "outsiders" and "establishment," between older communal organization figures and restive young people, were heavily laced with implicit or explicit accusations of past and ongoing incompetence, pusillanimity, and moral failure on the part of the second-generation old guard. Echoing Heschel, Elie Wiesel's widely read 1966 report on Soviet Jewry, *The Jews of Silence,* concluded that the title more aptly referred to the American Jewish community: "That the Jews in the free world do not heed [the plight of Soviet Jewry] will never be forgiven them. . . . For the second time in a single generation, we are committing the error of silence. . . . What torments me most is not the Jews of silence I met in Russia, but the silence of the Jews I live among today."[62]

Other outside factors included the Israeli-Arab War of June 1967, so often cited as a turning point for Jewish ethnic consciousness and pro-Israel activity in all Diaspora communities. The war, in effect, problematized Diaspora Jewishness itself, and one result was a disaffection from the older, second-generational, communal ethos and from existing ethnic paradigms.[63] During the month before the war broke out, the Jewish world anticipated a serious blow to the very survival of the State of Israel—perhaps even a new danger of mass slaughter—but proved unable to do anything to avert disaster. Fully reliant on the United States, France, the interfaith movement, or the United Nations, Diaspora Jews in the West found (once again, as in the 1940s) that their own best strategies for survival counted for very little. On 2 June 1967 U.S. Secretary of State Dean Rusk rejected as pure speculation the reports then circulating that the American government might organize other maritime countries to break Egypt's blockade of the Gulf of Eilat. The United States, in the words of the State Department, would remain "neutral in thought, word, and deed"—a formula so insensitive that the White House thought it politic to retract it several days afterward.[64]

The rather bitter encounter with the role of passive spectator into which the Diaspora Jewish communities had been cast, despite critical danger to the Jewish people, was not dissipated entirely by the surprise and relief that attended Israel's unexpectedly swift victory over Egypt, Syria, and Jordan. Given the exposure of the Diaspora's meagerness of resources, the hypothetical "what if?" of an Israeli defeat relativized Jewish life outside Israel, just as Israel's victory dwarfed the Diaspora's erstwhile sense of security. [65]

Characteristically, Alfred Kazin reacted to the Six-Day War by projecting onto Israelis a crisis of Jewish identity—a crisis of "the Jewish idea" and of "religious experience"—that, while detectable on the Israeli scene in later years, was much more ubiquitous at the time in New York and among Diaspora Jews generally. Indeed, it was this crisis that the war accentuated.[66]

Harlem-bred sociologist Irving Louis Horowitz noted that, in the aftermath of the war, "the Israelis have come to behave as marginal members of the international Jewish community"—that is, intent upon their own independent agenda—"despite Israel's protestations of concern for [the Jewish] community," and that "the victory of the Israeli army . . . may be the great historical watershed separating the Jew and the Israeli." By showing that Israel's "need for sovereignty" (i.e., acting like a regional power, seeking rationalized borders, and demanding recognition by its neighbors) was greater than anything that philanthropic support could provide, the war, Horowitz concluded, "could drive a wedge between Israel and Judaism . . . deeper than any in the past."[67]

Saul Bellow's dispatches from Israel in the second week of June 1967, as correspondent for *Newsday*, similarly noted the disparity between the Israeli frame of reference and the normal attitudes and constraints that characterized world Jewry. Dressed in his blatantly American, white seersucker jacket, Bellow toured the front lines. On the West Bank, he watched Israeli army trucks rounding up tons of ammunition from captured Jordanian munitions dumps—all still bearing American or British labels ("They bear a proud sticker—stars, stripes, red, white, and blue—and come from the Anniston Army Depot in Alabama"):

> Apparently Israelis decided that they need not concern themselves with the great powers since the great powers had apparently decided to let the Arabs have their way. The great powers had allowed Nasser, Hussein, and the Syrians to mobilize and to threaten to run the Israelis into the sea. . . . Now, Nasser, one Israeli told me, is clearly a lunatic. Yet the Americans had given this lunatic wheat, and the Russians had given him arms and military advice. The French courted him; the Yugoslavs believed that he headed the progressive elements of the Middle East; the Indians sympathized with him. . . . [T]hese leaders who let him lead the world to the brink of a wider war shared his dementia.[68]

In Bellow's novel *Mr. Sammler's Planet*, where he reused some of his frontline dispatches, the eponymous hero is forced to turn to his Israeli son-in-law, Eisen (i.e., "iron"), for help in rescuing a fellow Jew from violence in a New York fight: "And there was only Eisen to break up the fight. . . . [Sammler] knew what to do, but had no power to execute it. He had to turn . . . to an Eisen! a man himself far out on another track, orbiting a very different foreign center."[69]

Judd Teller, the Yiddish poet and journalist, felt that the prelude to the Six-Day War was haunted, for American Jews in particular, by the charges of implied coresponsibility for the Holocaust that, five years after Arendt's *Eichmann,* were still percolating through the Jewish public. "The events of May-June 1967, therefore, seemed to present to every Jew another fateful test, which he must not fail for it might confirm the charge in the eyes of all." However, these same Jews were unsuccessful in improving Israel's odds: "In 1948, . . .there was the illusion of Big Powers' and United Nations concern for [Israel's] fate; in 1956 it had France and Britain . . . ; in 1967 Israel was terribly alone."[70]

Having aroused unprecedented angst about Jewish political or ethnic self-sufficiency, the events of May-June 1967 threw into relief the apparent gulf between Israelis (who could fend for themselves) and Jews (who could not). It is not far-fetched to suggest that the dissonance that affected Western Jewish communities in this regard and the recognition that Diaspora life had become existentially problematic fuelled what became, in the years (indeed, in the decades) ahead, a wide-ranging campaign to revitalize the inner life of Jewish communities. While Jews celebrated their solidarity with Israel, they also became more conscious of what their own lives as non-Israeli Jews lacked in cultural and political terms—and hence, what was required to make such lives more worthwhile and more capable of being sustained. In this paradoxical cultural dialectic, the confrontation with a victorious Israel became the basis for an enlivened Diasporism.

In that light, it is surely not coincidental that beginning in 1968 there was renewed interest in Yiddish studies at the college level; signs of a new sustained growth in academic Jewish studies generally; an escape from what Arthur Hertzberg called "the shame of powerlessness," and a turn to what political scholar Peter Medding has called "the new Jewish politics."[71]

This renewed quest for an active, mobilized ethnicity was considerably sharpened by what ensued in the Soviet Jewry movement. The war brought into the open a more extreme adversarial relationship between the Soviet Union and the Jewish people, stemming from the Soviet government's commitment to its Arab clients. Although the seeds of a Soviet Jewish counterculture had been planted before 1967, after the war, somewhat to the surprise of many outsiders who had all but written off Soviet Jewry as moribund and in any case unable to act in its own behalf, Soviet Jews mounted an emigration and cultural rights campaign that, in turn, quickly became the chief focus of a worldwide Jewish protest movement.[72]

What should be noted about the way this played out in the New York community, however, is that the Soviet Jewry campaign was driven not by factors of Jewish solidarity alone, but also by internal division and revolt against old, accepted standards of ethnic behavior. Heightened ethnic awareness necessitated, to borrow Schlesinger's text about activist politics, a "personal commitment" that eschewed conventional "promises and excuses" and almost by definition entailed a contest against competing rationales. A realignment was taking place within a shrinking New York Jewry—a realignment that was bringing to the fore a group of ethnic activists, many of whom (though not all) were Orthodox, many of whom were relatively young, and few of whom were committed members of the existing ethnocommunal apparatus. American Jewish Committee executive vice president Bertram Gold observed that, since 1967, Jews seemed to go through "a crisis of confidence in the United States generally and a crisis of confidence in the [organized] Jewish community, in particular . . . a questioning of the Jewish 'establishment,' the rich heterodoxy versus the poor orthodoxy. There has been a sharp differentiation."[73]

The style of intracommunal protest and direct action that advance scouts of the new Jewish ethnicity learned within the Soviet Jewry movement (and/or in the anti-Vietnam War protest movement) was soon deployed elsewhere in the Jewish communal field. Hillel Levine, a Columbia student who helped organize a sit-in of activists in 1968 at an "establishment" Jewish conference on Soviet Jewry, proceeded the following year to apply the same tactics at the Council of Jewish Federations and Welfare Funds, meeting that year in Boston, where he and several busloads of "young Turks" demanded budgets for Jewish education, youth activity, and Soviet Jewry-related programs.[74]

On into the 1970s, disaffection from the regnant institutions of second-generation Jewish ethnicity in America continued to reshape new constituencies with charismatic, activist, ethnocommunal agendas, spawning such varied offshoots as the Havurah movement, an energetic outreach program emanating from the headquarters of the Lubavitch Hasidic community in Brooklyn, and Jewish feminism.

What was being invented, in short, was a Jewishness that was quite different from the one in Nathan Glazer's and Deborah Dash Moore's portrayals of Jewish interwar ethnicity. Shorn of any common axis or social bond, such as existed in the civic-integrationist-oriented Jewish neighborhood in the twenties and thirties, which had symbolically linked all New York Jews to their city and, thus, to one another, Jewish public life in New York now saw the emergence of ideologically driven and generationally segregated subgroups. Indeed, one can say that, in this sense, the Jews mirrored the larger ethos of the city itself at that time, in terms of its disassociative tendencies.

Disaffection from second-generation Jewishness took other forms as well, however, including ethnocommunal and religious indifference and alienation. The interwar communality of ethnic intimacy did not travel well over time, or perhaps it had outworn its usefulness. In the popular humor of a Woody Allen, for example, it was reduced to vulgarity, or to a species of cultural, social, and sexual neurosis.

The Jewish Defense League

The extent of this deconstruction of the old, second-generation ethnicity was limned most clearly by a radical version that pushed these trends to their logical limit. In the summer of 1968, a new Jewish anticrime patrol group—superficially similar to Rabbi Schrage's Maccabees—formed under the name of the Jewish Defense League (JDL), led by an obscure thirty-six-year-old former rabbi, Meir Kahane.

A native of Brooklyn, and a graduate of both Brooklyn College and New York University (as well as the Mirrer Yeshiva), Kahane led a checkered career from the late fifties to the late sixties: Having failed to pass the New York bar exam, he worked for two years at a Jewish congregation in Howard Beach,

Queens, where he attracted quite a following, but lost that position owing to intractable conflicts with the synagogue leadership. He then worked briefly as a sports writer; left his wife and four children suddenly in 1962 for a brief, disastrous first attempt to settle in Israel, but returned to New York; and, according to at least one report (first published in the *New York Times* in 1971), also allegedly worked under a pseudonym as a U.S. government-paid informant against leftist and antiwar groups. He proved more successful, however, in the field of Jewish consciousness-raising. Among other things, he was instrumental in turning a local Brooklyn Orthodox Jewish English-language newspaper, the *Brooklyn Daily*, into a large-circulation (perhaps 200,000 copies), sensationalist tabloid, *The Jewish Press*, which he coedited with Sholom Klass.[75]

Kahane and his associates may have believed that the time for an organization such as theirs had come. Like the Maccabees in 1964–66, the JDL originally worked those "fringe" neighborhoods where black, Puerto Rican, and Jewish populations lived in uneasy proximity and where violent crimes had become an everyday occurrence (though the JDL also turned up on Fifth Avenue to "protect" Temple Emanu-El and to protest the Metropolitan Museum's "Harlem on My Mind" exhibit catalogue).[76] Like other radical groups, the JDL rejected civic integrationism in the name of identity politics. Like Heschel, Wiesel, and the SSSJ, the JDL accused the Jewish establishment of moral and political weakness. Like others in the Orthodox community, the JDL warned against assimilation as a threat to Jewish cultural and religious integrity. Like Albert Shanker, the JDL raged against black antisemitism.

On the surface, then, there appeared to be a gathering consensus in New York Jewry that validated the JDL position; yet nothing could have been further from the truth. Jewish ethnic consciousness of the late sixties was tuned to a different register, perhaps, than had been true a generation earlier, but, by virtually unanimous consent, New York Jews were appalled by Kahane's group. It is because they viewed the JDL as subversive that we thereby learn, indirectly, what those values were that New York Jews did *not* want to subvert.

The distinction between the rest of Jewish New York and the JDL is most easily drawn through the dimension of violence. Unlike any of the abovenamed groups and persons, the JDL openly advocated the use of violent methods in response to perceived threats. Its recruits were trained in the martial arts and the use of weaponry (including firearms), and they cultivated the image of "tough Jews," closely paralleling the way the Black Panther Party cultivated a posture of violence.

Unlike Rabbi Schrage's Crown Heights group, the JDL did not grow out of a coherent neighborhood community with local, personal, and civic commitments and a stake in stability (a stake that very quickly led Schrage to co-operate with non-Jewish and black clergy in his area, and subsequently to be co-opted by the city administration). Rather, Kahane, who was very much an outsider, attracted the most alienated and marginalized young people from lower- or lower-middle-class homes. They had an ax to grind when it came to the rest of the Jewish community, and especially its upper-class, liberal establishment. The JDL's first adversary (despite its rhetoric) was, therefore, the Jewish community itself.

In the 1970s, as the focus of the JDL's activities shifted away from black-Jewish tensions and anticrime patrols to protest activity directed against the Soviet Union, the group escalated its antiestablishment rhetoric. It publicized its support for extreme action and reveled in the role of "the flea which moved the elephant, Russia," though it routinely and with transparent disingenuousness disclaimed legal responsibility for the shootings, bombings, and intimidation that were employed against Soviet-related targets in the United States. (In one memorable atrocity, the office of Sol Hurok, a Jewish impressario involved in arranging performance tours for the Bolshoi Ballet in America, was bombed. The sole victim was a Jewish secretary who worked in the office.)[77]

The rest of the Jewish community recoiled from this approach precisely because, unlike the JDL, which was uninhibited by integrationist commitments, most Jews considered themselves, first and foremost, model citizens. Some of them might indeed have been attracted by an ethos of mobilized ethnic consciousness; however, this type of self-assertiveness, already evident in 1968, was concerned with working out the *distinction* between Israelis and Jews, a problem that had attained new urgency because of renewed Jewish *identification with* Israel. That meant embracing a division of labor: between those wielding the gun and the sword, on the one hand, and those wielding the book, the pen, the checkbook, and the protest demonstration, on the other. Civic integrationism of the old style may have drawn criticism for being too self-effacing, too hesitant, too "polite"; but in transcending such norms, most Jews still held themselves accountable to integrationist American values of civility.

As a second-generation writer, Saul Bellow may not be the best example to choose, but his voice carried cultural authority in the waning of the sixties. Just as he was drawn to rush to Israel even before the shooting stopped in June 1967, he was also revolted by the rotting corpses of Egyptian soldiers that he saw in the Sinai. Later he would use his own notes to depict his fictional Mr. Sammler as disgusted by the same sights and smells. Moreover, Bellow symbolically replayed Sammler's dismay a second time when, in the incident in which Sammler found it necessary to enlist Israeli muscle, he was aghast at his son-in-law's overenthusiastic eagerness to shed blood, even in a defensive operation that he himself had encouraged. Behavior that, however extreme,

Meir Kahane, 1971. The founder of the Jewish Defense League, as he and six other League members were being arrested on charges of conspiracy and the possession of illegal firearms and explosives. Photograph by UPI. Courtesy of the Jerusalem Post *photographic collection.*

could be sanctioned in war in the Middle East, could never be accepted in Manhattan. Here the Israeli and the Diaspora Jew parted company.[78]

The JDL's willing recourse to violence is not the only way in which it allows us to probe the boundaries of what constituted normative Jewish identity in the late sixties. A second avenue lies in Kahane's use of Holocaust imagery and terminology. Here, again, it is possible to see some continuity between what was being said by various other persons and groups in the Jewish community and what the JDL seemed to be saying. This was especially true with regard to the analogies that were being drawn between the Holocaust and the plight of Soviet Jewry. Yet here again, the similarity belies an underlying and fundamental difference.

"Never Again!" the JDL's slogan, was a direct Holocaust reference and this phrase encoded a further set of inferences: "Never again" would American Jews "sit still" while their relatives were in peril. Many Jewish ethnic mobilizers could agree with such a sentiment as a way to rally to a higher level of group consciousness the Jews in America, who were called upon to demonstrate and to vocally assert their political demands for world attention to issues of Jewish survival (be it in Israel or the Soviet Union).

The JDL, however, deployed the terminology of "Never Again!" not only to rally the troops, but also to overcome the shame of victimhood. "Never again" would Jews be weak, be slaughtered with impunity, and never would they have to suffer again the shame of thus having been violated. The shame, in short, was not just that of the American Jewish establishment, accused of failing to do its duty, but in a real sense, that of the six million. In creating a Jewish pseudo-underground, Kahane was acting out a Holocaust fantasy in which the dignity of the murdered could be retroactively and symbolically saved. The JDL thus embodied a kind of Jewish self-hatred, for its projection of Jewish "toughness" and violence was a claim to be acting as the victims "should" have acted.

In actual fact, of course, neither the dead nor their supposedly injured dignity could be restored, even by proxy, so that Kahane needed to assert a further claim: that the Holocaust was not over and, indeed, that the "next Holocaust" could be prevented *in real life*. That "next Holocaust" could be expected to occur in the United States in a paroxysm of social and racial revolution and backlash that would inevitably claim the Jews as its first victims—an eventuality that the JDL could see approaching but most American Jews, blinded by their assimilation-distorted liberalism, (as Kahane saw it), could not.[79]

Putting his case this way assured Kahane's complete rejection by all other elements in the Jewish community (apart from *The Jewish Press*), because he had so completely gone beyond recognizable reality. American Jews, even in a troubled time for world Jewry, even in New York in the wake of the teachers' strike, were able to make the distinction between the actual Holocaust and virtual or vicarious Holocaust-fantasy. Indeed, they were deeply troubled by the manipulation of genocide-terminology by others; they were even less willing to countenance it in their fellow Jews. Ethnic identity, even at its most self-aware or self-assertive, they seemed to affirm, could still be embraced within a Diasporist faith in America.

The Revolt of the Sons

The sixties marked one further division that affected the Jewish community, though it was not, strictly speaking, an internal communal matter: the emergence in America of a "youth rebellion" that posed an alternative to the conservative middle-class mores of the nation at large. As the political expression of this counterculture, there emerged a popular but amorphous "Movement" (of which the New Left was a leading or defining element) that challenged the American "system" as a whole.

What made this political challenge so personally relevant to the Jewish community was its perceived "oedipal" quality, for the rebellion of the young was not against the materialistic values of successful middle-class suburban families alone, but also against an existing urban leftist tradition in which Jews felt they had played an honorable role.

"When New Left students painted . . . 'Up against the wall, motherfuckers!' on campus buildings," Irving Howe complained, "they had in mind not just the corporate state or the Pentagon or the CIA; they had in mind the only 'enemy' they knew first hand, their liberal and socialist teachers; they had in mind parents of the New Deal generation."[80]

"The sons were out to get their fathers—especially if the fathers had been 'radicals' during a certain ancient Depression," Alfred Kazin concurred:

"They attacked our attachment to libraries; to books uselessly piled on more books; to our fondest belief that violence had nothing proper to do with sex and sex nothing to do with politics."[81] And indeed, young Jewish radicals of the sixties tended, more so than their non-Jewish peers, to have actual family ties with adults associated with the American Left between the wars and in the 1950s.[82]

The confrontation between Old and New Left is relevant to our particular discussion because Jews were quite prominent in both camps and because—as was the case with second-generation ethnicity—the cosmopolitan-leftist politics of second-generation intellectuals had played a formative role in the shaping of a New York Jewishness. And just as the old ethnicity underwent a critique during the mid- to late-sixties, so, too, the politics of the old radical guard did not go unchallenged. This, in turn, would affect Jewish public life as well as the tenor of New York Jewish intellectual activity, which came in time to include an assertive neoconservative element.

The conflict was not a political one in the proper sense of the term, but a family feud. Very little was at stake in the way of political influence brokering, competition over constituencies, or representation. Rather, while the Old Left charged the young radicals with antinomian and anarchic tendencies—with being, in short, children—the New Left charged the "Old" with feebleness, a charge that even prominent Old Leftists acknowledged was justified. "Although I was as much a target to my own son as my old friends were to *their* sons," Kazin admitted, "I had a secret sympathy with the sons in general." "The truth," Irving Howe later recalled, "is that the 'kids . . . got to me.' I might score in polemic, but they scored in life."[83]

Clearly there was a paternal quality to the way in which some second-generation New York socialists related to the upstart youngsters, who were themselves quite content to join in the discourse of family hierarchy and successionism: "From the 'child's' point of view," explained Todd Gitlin, "nothing was more important than its claim to be taken seriously; from the 'parent's' point of view, nothing was more important than the question of what to say and do about Communism and Communists. . . . The 'child flexed its muscles; the 'parent' clamped down, losing its chance of control."[84]

It is in light of the foregoing that we can understand what happened when relations between the "fathers" and the "sons" broke down at an early and defining encounter. The meeting, held in New York in 1963, involved leading members of SDS (Students for a Democratic Society, the standard-bearing political core of the New Left in the United States) and editors of *Dissent*.[85] Here, as perhaps never before or since, the representatives of the Old and the New Left sat together within the familial intimacy created by second-generation New York Jewish intellectuals.

The ethnic Jewish aspect of the encounter was by no means uppermost in the minds of those who attended the meeting, or even clear-cut in objective terms (some, but not all of the participants, were Jews). Ethnic ambivalence was in any case part and parcel of leftist self-understanding, regardless of generation. Nevertheless, the session took place in the "home" of a "family," connoting certain kinship qualities and quasi-sanctified cultural patterns. Irving Howe, then forty-two years old, presided over this ill-fated dialogue as symbolic "grandfather and father" (as Todd Gitlin put it).[86] Thus, if not necessarily an intracommunal ethnic event per se, it was nevertheless symbolic of the passing from leadership of a predominantly Jewish-ethnic leftist intellectual elite, and so it was perceived by participants and observers alike. With this passing, no coherent Jewish Left remained intact in New York—a fact that became evident, at the very latest, by the time of the New York teachers' strike.

Tom Hayden, who played the role of chief iconoclast at that meeting in 1963, spoke disparagingly about his interlocutors' shrill moral tone, deriving from what he euphemistically termed "the New York intellectual culture." Todd Gitlin was more explicit, using in-group Jewish code words to characterize the older group as "seasoned scrappers, trained in the Talmudic disputation characteristic of Trotskyism," who "could not sit there sagely while we, young and inexperienced *pishers,* apparently ducked the lessons of Stalinism."[87]

What truly upset the second-generation Jewish intellectual Left about the New Left was a sense of personal and historical betrayal, which was captured very aptly in a novel by New York writer Johanna Kaplan: "[E]very time it's brought home to me how profoundly cut off so many kids are from the *sense,* the *feel* of anything that came before them—well, my God, that is disturbing, *deeply* disturbing. First of all, it's dangerous. But aside from that, can you imagine . . . how *boring* that must be! . . . when [a sense of the past] doesn't *naturally* stand peering over the shoulders of the present for them."[88]

Howe's response was to undertake a single-handed crusade against the New Left that even he, in retrospect, agreed might have been extreme. In the process, he recovered the ethnic-Jewish dimension of his own cause. Of all the charges that he leveled at the New Left, its allegedly authoritarian proclivities were just the tip of the iceberg. (The young Hayden, he averred, had the makings of a "commissar.") Leading on from this accusation, Howe proceeded to portray the New Left—especially its hard core—as essentially *un-Jewish.* Though he did not use this term explicitly, he might as well have, since he labeled the New Left as Christian, "American," and religious-revivalist. Their moral absolutism seemed to him to reflect a Christian ethic of "ultimate ends" rather than of proximate responsibility (otherworldly Faith versus this-worldly Law?). Their "utterly American" quality (a damning epithet, that,

Irving Howe, writer and critic on the political left, 1982. Photograph courtesy of the Jerusalem Post *photographic collection.*

when wielded by someone bred on totems of marginality) led them naturally to the "arts of publicity," taking to them "like Tom Sawyer to games of deceit, offering the mass media the verbal, sometimes actual violence on which it dotes." Most of all, Howe agreed with Paul Goodman that "many of those drawn to New Left politics were really trying to satisfy formless religious hungers"—both pagan and Christian—in their pilgrimages (Woodstock), their "Quaker meetings," and their ecstasies.[89]

Although Howe still pulled his punches when it came to avowing his own specific ethnic point of view, little imagination is required to fill in the particular label that represented all that was at odds with "American," ecstatic, religious absolutism. Thus, in a backhanded way, it was the New Left's challenge to the second-generation, Depression-era leftism that brought Howe back to a consciousness of his ethnically rooted point of view. That, in turn, brought him back to the immigrant Jewish experience, as he made explicit in *World of Our Fathers,* which he wrote in the wake of the New Left debacle.

The New Left "sons" may, indeed, have betrayed that legacy (a charge that stuck, as the New Left began to pursue an anti-Israel tilt after 1967). But if we are to take at all seriously the metaphor of a familial relationship between the Old and New Left, then it was Howe's own generation of New York socialists, raised in the immigrant milieu of the city's gray neighborhoods, that had clearly failed to transmit a comprehension of the ethnocultural basis of its politics. Having eschewed that ethnic basis consistently up through the 1950s, that generation was behaving disingenuously at such a late date to reclaim the ethnic mantle so as to chastise the young for their infidelity, their ingratitude, and their lack of roots. The point seems to be that, as a conduit for ethnic awareness, second-generation leftism was never very convincing. Its latter-day rediscovery as a Jewish lifestyle, therefore, also lacked verisimilitude.

What is even more to the point, however, is that second-generation Jewish ethnicity, the product of the postimmigration neighborhoods of New York, was everywhere in disarray during the sixties. The dilemma posed by the New Left to the stalwarts of the Old was, therefore, something that was common throughout the New York Jewish community. Living in a culture of fragmentation and confrontation, in a city that was one of the flashpoints of that era, New York Jews' relations with one another were primed by the larger forces that defined their society.

7

City and Ethnicity

> This is how their repressed Jewishness has always manifested itself: in their desire to stay in New York without ever having to think about leaving it, about uprooting. There are enough Jews in the city to afford a kind of protection—safety in numbers—but not enough to require affiliation.
>
> —Martha Cooley,
> *The Archivist*

> It's a city where almost everyone has come from elsewhere—a market, a caravansary—bringing with them their different ways of dying and marrying, their kitchens and songs. A city of forsaken worlds; language a kind of farewell.
>
> —Anne Michaels,
> *Fugitive Pieces*[1]

In 1951, the Shulsinger Press (once a fixture in the world of Yiddish and Hebrew letters in New York) published a twelve-volume collection of the oeuvre of Yiddish poet Avrom Reisin, spanning the years from 1891 to 1951. One of Reisin's immigrant-era poems, dedicated to his "promised city," was a "Hymn" (as he subtitled it), called simply, "New York," in which he praised it as a "city of joy":

> All tongues are spoken, clamorous and in prayer.
> You wander through different quarters—
> nay, not quarters, countries—
> but are never lost, nowhere a stranger. . . .
> As you grow attached to these 'countries,'
> New York grows dear to you.
> You are nowhere a stranger,
> everywhere, a free man.[2]

Reisin may have identified empathetically with his Chinese or Italian or Irish neighbors as he walked through the "countries" of Lower Manhattan; but surely he was mostly projecting here his sense of inhabiting the city, as a citizen of the whole, all the while living in an urban Jewish-land in one corner of that city. The hymn he sang, after all, was addressed to his city, not to his fellow immigrant-ethnics.

In all of this, he prefigured Alfred Kazin as a Jewish "walker in the city." Both Kazin and Reisin transcended neighborhood turf, but Reisin recognized not just the permeability of the borders between "countries," but the requirement that there actually be such "countries."

As we have seen, the notion of distinct-yet-shared experience is basic to Jewish perspectives on New York, articulated as early as the era of mass Jewish immigration. Yet, Reisin's poem was already a historical document in 1951, and from our end-of-the-century perspective we realize that his poem could not have been written today. That, in essence, is the burden of this book's message.

The possibilities of urban ethnicity and, simultaneously, a free embrace of the city ("nowhere a stranger, everywhere a free man") envisioned in Reisin's poem are quite close, if not identical, to the concept of "metropolitan space" as articulated by New York historian Thomas Bender:

> At the heart of the metropolitan experience is a mechanism that connects, without destroying, mixed and homogeneous urban collectivities. Smaller *gemeinschaftlich* groups defined by various categories— . . . based on class relations, gender relations, ethnic identity, family and kinship networks, spatial distributions, and the like—come into contact in the public life of their city. Their coming together in fact constitutes the public culture of the city.[3]

But Bender, in asserting this paradigm as a positive urban ideal, is also acutely aware of the degree to which it may no longer be viable: "Is [this] a phenomenon of the past? Is the city still a place of multiple voices in public? Of *gemeinschaftlich* groups engaging one another?"[4]

In this he is not alone. Were Reisin writing today, he would not have described New York the way he did then, and he would not have done so in Yiddish. The conditions necessary for that kind of writing have not been in evidence since the sixties drew to a close. At the heart of the matter is the Jews' inability to maintain and transmit the urban ethnic lifestyle that their parents had invented. New York Jews' notion of themselves as an essential part of their city—and their parallel notion of the city as an essential part of themselves—were predicated on the integrative function of the city. That function has been cast into doubt, and with it, that form of Jewish urban ethnicity that was always more a by-product of city life than anything else.

When group self-awareness is strongly (and for some, solely) defined by the nexus with city and invested in the shifting sands of neighborhoods, it is inevitably bounded by the city's own limited possibilities. If we look at New

York in the fifties and sixties—a period of urban crisis, political upheaval, and far-reaching social change—it becomes clear that Jews lost their sense of home-groundedness, their tacit communal cohesion, and, perhaps, some fraction of their own self-regard. Half of the Jews, as we have seen, simply left.

It may come as a rude awakening to some, but not to those who would agree with my evaluation, to note that when the Sunday *New York Times Magazine* published a special issue on the city's diverse subcultures in October 1997 ("New York's Parallel Lives"), Jews were omitted. (This is in marked contrast, of course, with the 1960 special issue of *Fortune,* which had showcased the Jews as a unique element contributing their "élan" to the character of the city.) The only group covered in the *Times*'s 1997 *tour d'horizon* that might arguably have been intended as a stand-in for the Jews was the "Lingering Liberals" of Manhattan's Upper West Side (portrayed as a vanishing breed).[5] It is, of course, nonsense to argue that such dismissiveness reflects reality on the ground—New York Jews are *not* a vanishing breed—but the oversight is nevertheless indicative of the recent climate.

That being the case, it is worth asking, at least in a final retrospective glance at the Jews of New York, why their culture and ethnic pattern developed in the first half of the twentieth century in such a way that it depended so strongly on the ethos of metropolitan "New Yorkishness," only to remain hobbled by that very condition? Why, in short, did New York "make" the Jews what they became, more than the reverse?

Clarification of this question entails two factors: the overwhelming force of New York in imposing a mode of life, and the "soft" or partial quality of the ethnic Jewishness that the immigrants in New York (and their children) were capable of developing. Both themes are implied in Arthur Goren's *New York Jews and the Quest for Community,* but they deserve to be restated.

In New York, where millions live virtually anonymously, it should come as no surprise to find, as has been noted in various forms by numerous observers, that "The most notable aspect of the Jewish community [in New York] compared to other parts of the country, is that there is no real community here. There are many communities, but not a sense of one."[6] It would have been surprising had it been otherwise in a megacity where impersonal patterns are so dominating. Even—to go back to Bender's perspective—when small communities do create their own intimacies and bring these to bear on the public culture of the city, over time, as discussed, these pockets of personality may be eroded. Or, as novelist Martha Cooley (quoted in one of this chapter's epigraphs) put it, "If you don't want them to be, New York's intimacies aren't personal."[7] It may, finally, be stated that, insofar as Jews created community life in New York, their common attachment to their city is what gave them common focus and identity as "New York Jews." New York Jews took basic ethnic attributes (language, religion, family) and transformed these into a generic Jewish urban "character." It is, thus, New York that gave them their distinctiveness, not their distinctiveness that gave New York its *"élan."*

Further, I believe that it was not second-generation Jews in New York who were primarily responsible for establishing the guiding parameters of Jewish ethnicity—although they certainly added American components: it was the *first* generation, the immigrants themselves, whose ethnic capabilities were truncated and limited by the very act of uprooting that had brought them far from their families, their provincial communities, and their still only vaguely modernized religion, to a new and formidable urban landscape. The "forsaken worlds" (see the epigraph from Anne Michaels) and forsaken languages could never be completely forsaken by the immigrants, but neither could they be anything *but* forsaken. The elements contributed by the second generation were, in large measure, transitory. They served the second generation well, but were questioned or rejected as inadequate by the generation that followed.

The legacy that first-generation Jews in New York bequeathed to their children included, for one thing, a labor movement that de-emphasized ethnic issues generally in favor of progressive political and social issues, and then reinterpreted ethnicity as equivalent to progressive politics—a posture adopted by many in the second generation. Third-generation Jews who looked to the political Left, however, found the purportedly ethnic aspects unconvincing and rebelled against them.

At the other end of the Jewish social scale, first- and second-generation upper-class Jews interpreted ethnicity as philanthropy—at least in part because elite WASP society was their reference group. Again, this proved uncompelling as an ethnic model for the third generation.

In between the upper- and lower-class segments of New York Jewry was that broad middle class that came to typify the post-immigrant, second generation. These were: the small businesspeople, the civil service or white collar employees; the ones whose urban childhoods had been shaped by the New York neighborhoods where their immigrant parents had settled; the ones whose speech betrayed little of their parents' European accents but, instead, possessed the characteristic sounds of Brooklyn, the Bronx, or Queens; the ones to whom a clean-shaven, American-raised rabbi who gave English sermons was preferable, if one was to have one at all; the ones who served their country in World War II or Korea; the ones for whom American culture was the precious gift bequeathed by the public school and to whom a college diploma (whether they managed themselves to get one or pushed their children to do so) was the defining middle-class aspiration. They were also the ones who, by and large, would choose to raise their own children in suburban communities. Urban Jewishness, once the immigration period came to an end, was perhaps best represented by this class of people; yet the lifestyle that they constructed owed less to the ethnic component per se than to the class component and to the various ways that their lives were clustered together in the city. As the New York (white) middle class made its way up and out of the city's neighborhoods, inevitably the Jewish, second-generation cohort was less and less able to define (much less perpetuate) the group-mediated urban ethic that had shaped it.

The secularization of the second-generation Jewish family cleared the path for a growing phenomenon of third-generation intermarriage—and intermarriage, in turn, helped to erode the basis of secular Jewishness by displacing the primarily secular categories of kinship and common ancestry as pillars of group identity. In a not unrelated development, a religionist Judaism found new strength within younger cohorts of the second generation after the 1960s, but chiefly among those whose parents had immigrated after 1930 and who, by and large, were closer to immigrant culture than most other second-generation Jews.

Second-generation New York Jews found their assumptions about humanity in modern societies profoundly challenged by the implications of the Holocaust. With shaken confidence in the merits of mass social forms, they emerged into the turbulent sixties nursing a sense of grievance, even victimhood, and found themselves in a now more crowded field of claimants for political and cultural recognition. In recovering the rage of victimhood, Jews lost some of the confidence and ebullience of metropolitan optimism.

Perhaps most famously, a second-generation intellectual elite emerged that saw ethnicity (at best) as a springboard to cosmopolitanism, insofar as ethnicity provided a counterweight to American WASP parochialism. As literary scholar Emily Budick has recently noted, "Jewishness, for many Jewish intellectuals from the 1930s and 1940s on, was, as it had been among European Jewish intellectuals before them, a card they played to lose, in order to win the hand or perhaps the game itself. The game in America was not Jewish identity."[8]

Finally, even those leading minds of the second-generation intelligentsia were upstaged by newly arrived first-generation Jewish New Yorkers who, by and large, provided the community's most innovative and compelling examples of high scholarly, cultural, and social achievement, well into the postwar period—including (to recall but a few) Salo Baron, Hannah Arendt, Isaac Bashevis Singer, Abraham Joshua Heschel, and Elie Wiesel. To credit their achievements to the Jewish community around them would be to stretch any credible form of the truth. But to note that such a collection of talent did in fact fuel the cultural and ethnopolitical output of New York Jewry in recent decades is to acknowledge the ubiquitous, magnetic power of New York City—a force capable of continually drawing new and aspiring talents from around the country and around the world. That, indeed, is its function as a great city. Alfred Kazin, whose observations on Jewish issues are suspect but who was generally incisive in his readings of New York, recognized this when he remarked, "Even in its 'last days,' the secret of New York is raw power, mass and volume, money and power."[9]

In the end, then, New York's most significant function for Jews and for the construction of Jewish ethnicity has been less as a "home" than as a goal. New York (as Kazin, once again, perceived quite well) is not about staying—the second-generation's anomalous experience notwithstanding—but about discovering one's destination. *Coming* to the city, recognizing its magnetic force, submitting to its power in one's walks abroad or in the privacy of one's home, and seeking to ride the energy of the city by grappling with its social, intellectual, artistic, literary, and business worlds—these are goals that characterize New Yorkers of all varieties. They define, therefore, also what Jews have tried to find in New York.

Ezra Slavin, the rambunctious old New York Jewish rebel in Johanna Kaplan's novel, *O My America,* forsook the city for the rustic life in rural New England, but retained his deeply ingrained sense of it: "What this city *is*! The life that it has! I forget it, and I'm away from it, but God almighty, there is nothing like it! That smell—the grit and electricity of the subways? One breath and it's like the rush of euphoria mountain climbers are supposed to feel when they reach the top. It's the energy, and I love it. My God, I love it."[10]

Jews, individually and as a group, have reaped the windfall benefits that came from living at the epicenter of such great activity. They have, by the same token, risked great losses, as the tenor of life in the city and its human capacities have been challenged.

Looking more widely, we can see that the decline of the New York Jewish community expresses the changed expectations that Jews have as Americans and as city-dwellers. The New York Jewish story in the postwar period shows how people respond when society fails in its mission to mobilize its members for the general good. That failure, in turn, has fed a resurgent conservative politics in America as well as a conservative religion, both of which are based on an ideology of personal responsibility. This turn in American affairs—felt most sharply at the flashpoints of twentieth-century American life, America's cities—means that Jews must retool their social and cultural points of view. They can either reengage with other groups to recover an urban politics of cooperation, or they can further adapt themselves to the conservative politics of self-assertion and self-reliance. Knowing the Jews, they will probably do both.

That, however, is the subject of another book.

Notes
Works Cited
Index

Notes

Preface

1. Clifford Geertz, *The Interpretation of Cultures: Selected Essays* (New York: Basic Books, 1973), 22.

2. Deborah Dash Moore, *At Home in America: Second Generation New York Jews* (New York: Columbia Univ. Press, 1981).

3. Beth S. Wenger, *New York Jews and the Great Depression* (New Haven and London: Yale Univ. Press, 1996); Henry L. Feingold, *A Time for Searching: Entering the Mainstream, 1920–1945* (Baltimore and London: Johns Hopkins Univ. Press, 1992).

4. For further elaboration of this shift in perspective, see my essay, "New York City, the Jews, and 'The Urban Experience,' " in *Studies in Contemporary Jewry,* vol. 15, *People of the City: Jews and the Urban Challenge,* ed. Ezra Mendelsohn (New York: Oxford Univ. Press, 1999).

5. See her essay, "I'll Take Manhattan," *Judaism* 44, no. 4 (1995): 420–26.

6. Peter Novick, *The Holocaust in American Life* (Boston and New York: Houghton Mifflin Co., 1999).

7. *Paper Bridges: Selected Poems of Kadya Molodowsky/Papirene brikn: geklibene lider fun Kadye Molodovsky,* translated, introduced, and edited by Kathryn Hellerstein (Detroit: Wayne State Unviersity Press, 1999); Hasia Diner, *Lower East Side Memories: A Jewish Place in America* (Princeton and Oxford: Princeton Univ. Press, 2000).

1. Jews and the Great Urban Utopia

1. Data on Russian Jews arriving in the United States between 1899 and 1914 (including figures on return-migration) are cited in Simon Kuznets, "Immigration of Russian Jews to the United States: Background and Structure," *Perspectives in American History* 9 (1975): 35–124. On Jewish immigrants in Imperial Germany, including urbanization, see Jack Wertheimer, *Unwelcome Strangers* (New York: Oxford Univ. Press, 1987). Efforts by Jewish agencies in the United States to disperse incoming Jewish immigrants to communities in the Midwest, West, and South are described by Bernard Marinbach, *Galveston: Ellis Island of the West* (Albany: State University of New York Press, 1983). On the history of Jewish agricultural settlement in the United States in the period of mass immigration, see Joseph Brandes, *Immigrants to Freedom* (Philadelphia: Jewish Publication Society, 1971); cf. A. Menes, "The Am Oylom Movement," *YIVO Annual of Jewish Social Science* 4 (1949), pp. 9–33.

2. Marshall Sklare: "Jews, Ethnics, and the American City," *Commentary* 56, no. 3 (Apr.

1972): 70–77; repr. in Sklare, *Observing America's Jews* (Hanover and London: Brandeis Univ./Univ. Press of New England, 1993), 131–37.

3. See Todd M. Endelman, *The Jews of Georgian England: Tradition and Change in a Liberal Society* (Philadelphia: Jewish Publication Society, 1979; Michael Graetz, *Haperiferiyah haytah lamerkaz* (Jerusalem: Mossad Bialik, 1983).

4. On the refiguring of Jewish folk culture and its shtetl ambience in neoromantic, national terms, see, e.g., Mark W. Kiel, "A Twice Lost Legacy: Ideology, Culture, and the Pursuit of Jewish Folklore in Russia Until Stalinization" (Ph.D. diss., Jewish Theological Seminary of America, 1991); David G. Roskies, *A Bridge of Longing: The Lost Art of Yiddish Storytelling* (Cambridge and London: Harvard Univ. Press, 1995); S. Ansky, *The Dybbuk and Other Writings,* edited and with an Introduction by David G. Roskies, "Introduction" (New York: Schocken Books, 1992), xi-xxxvi; cf. Ismar Schorsch, *From Text to Context: The Turn to History in Modern Judaism* (Hanover and London: Brandeis University/University Press of New England: 1994), 93–117, on the related use of "ghetto" themes by German Jewish artist Moritz Oppenheim.

5. Jewish immigrant, from a letter to the editor of the *Forverts* (1915), as translated in *A Bintel Brief,* edited by Isaac Metzker (New York: Ballantine Books, 1972), 129; "New York" quote: Harry Golden, *The Greatest Jewish City in the World* (Garden City, N.Y.: Doubleday, 1972), 2.

6. Literary "myth" noted by Murray Baumgarten, *City Scriptures. Modern Jewish Writing* (Cambridge: Harvard Univ. Press, 1982), 1. This urban code was rooted in what another scholar has called "a well established convention of Yiddish fiction [in which] the city embodies the possibilities of enlightenment, assimilation, anonymity, and radical alienation": Anita Norich, *The Homeless Imagination in the Fiction of Israel Joshua Singer* (Bloomington and Indianapolis: Indiana Univ. Press, 1991), 50.

7. The classic 1940s study of African Americans in Chicago, *Black Metropolis: A Study of Negro Life in a Northern City,* by St. Clair Drake and Horace R. Cayton (New York: Harcourt, Brace, 1945), took a remarkably similar view of the potential of the city for the solution of minority marginality. On this, see the comment by Andrea Tuttle Kornbluh, "From Culture to Cuisine: Twentieth-Century Views of Race and Ethnicity in the City," in *American Urbanism: A Historiographical Review,* edited by Howard Gillette, Jr. and Zane L. Miller (New York, Westport, and London: Greenwood Press, 1987), 55.

8. William Isaac Thomas, preface to *Old World Traits Transplanted* (New York: Harper and Bros., 1921; reprint, Montclair, N.J.: Patterson Smith, 1971), 238; Moses Rischin, *The Promised City. New York's Jews, 1870–1914* (Cambridge: Harvard University, 1962; reprint, New York: Schocken, 1970); cf. Rischin, "The Jews and the Liberal Tradition in America," *American Jewish Historical Quarterly,* 51 (1961): 4–16; cf. Arthur A. Goren, "The Promises of *The Promised City*: Moses Rischin, American History, and the Jews," *American Jewish History* 73 (1983): 177.

9. Shimon Ginsburg, "Nyu york," in *Antologiah shel hashirah ha'ivrit beamerikah,* edited by Menahem Ribalow (New York: Ogen Press, 1938), 163–66. English translation by EL. On the symbolism of Brooklyn Bridge, see Alan Trachtenberg, *Brooklyn Bridge: Fact and Symbol* (New York: Oxford Univ. Press, 1965). In terms very reminiscent of Ginsburg, Trachtenberg argues that the bridge "embodied physically the forces, emotional as well as mechanical, which were shaping a new civilization" (137).

10. My thanks to my friend and colleague, Sidra Dekoven Ezrahi, for the "rivers of Babylon" parallelism—from a course we co-taught, "By the Rivers of Manhattan."

11. A. Leyeles (Aaron Glanz-Leyeles), *Amerike un ikh* (New York: Der Kval, I. London, Publisher, 1963); "Bay di taykhn fun nyu-york" ("By the Rivers of New York"), 25. English translation by EL.

12. Louis Wirth, *The Ghetto* (Chicago: Univ. of Chicago, 1928); cf. Fred Matthews, "Louis Wirth and American Ethnic Studies: The Worldview of Enlightened Assimilationism, 1925–1950," in *The Jews of North America,* edited by Moses Rischin (Detroit: Wayne State Univ. Press, 1987), 123–43.

13. Deborah Dash Moore, "The Construction of Community: Jewish Migration and Ethnicity in the United States," in *The Jews of North America,* edited by Moses Rischin, 112.

14. Ibid.

15. H. Leyvik, "Do voynt dos yidishe folk," in idem *Alle verk, band 1: lider* (New York: H. Leyvik Jubilee Committee, 1940), 138–39. English translation by Benjamin and Barbara Harshav, *Yiddish Poetry in America* (Berkeley, Los Angeles, London: Univ. of California Press, 1986), 697.

16. On the emergence of the vertical perspective and its relationship to such ideas as "skyline," see William R. Taylor, *In Pursuit of Gotham: Culture and Commerce in New York* (New York and Oxford: Oxford Univ. Press, 1992), chap. 2 and 4.

17. Lloyd P. Gartner, "Metropolis and Periphery in American Jewry," *Studies in Contemporary Jewry,* vol. 1. Edited by Jonathan Frankel (Bloomington: Indiana Univ. Press, 1984), 342.

18. Hyman B. Grinstein, *The Rise of the Jewish Community of New York, 1654–1860* (Philadelphia: Jewish Publication Society, 1945); Rischin, *Promised City*; Irving Howe, *World of Our Fathers: The Journey of the East European Jews to America and the Life They Found and Made* (New York: Harcourt, Brace, Jovanovich, 1976); Wenger, *New York Jews and the Great Depression*; Moore, *At Home in America.*

19. Arthur A. Goren, *New York Jews and the Quest for Community* (New York: Columbia Univ. Press, 1970).

20. Grinstein, *Rise of the Jewish Community of New York,* 20.

21. Ibid., 464.

22. Moore, *At Home in America,* 241. Commenting upon Moore's work on New York Jewry between the two world wars and upon Marsha Rozenblit's study of *fin-de-siècle* Viennese Jewry, historian Todd M. Endelman has made the same point: "A reading of [their works] would not suggest that these were communities whose health would one day be endangered by widespread disaffiliation and defection (in the [Viennese] case) and indifference and drift (in [New York])." Endelman's remarks appeared as his "Response," in *The State of Jewish Studies,* ed. Shaye J. D. Cohen and Edward Greenstein (Detroit/New York: Wayne State Univ. Press/ Jewish Theological Seminary of America, 1990), 161. In her subsequent work dealing with trends in internal migration by Jews in postwar America, however, and in her later book on Los Angeles and Miami, Moore documents the shift of Jewish population away from the New York metropolitan area and a note of moderate skepticism tempers her evaluation of Jewish cultural life in Los Angeles: Deborah Dash Moore, *To the Golden Cities: Pursuing the American Jewish Dream in Miami and L. A.* (New York: Free Press, 1994); see also Moore, "Jewish Migration in Postwar America," in *Studies in Contemporary Jewry,* vol. 8, *A New Jewry?* ed. Peter Y. Medding (New York: Oxford Univ. Press, 1992), 102–17.

23. Wenger, *New York Jews and the Great Depression,* esp. chaps. 1, 6, 8.

24. Bethamie Horowitz, *The 1991 New York Jewish Population Survey* (New York: New York UJA-Federation, 1993); Sidney Goldstein and Alice Goldstein, *Jews on the Move: Implications for Jewish Identity* (Albany: State Univ. of New York Press, 1996), 48; C. Morris Horowitz and Lawrence J. Kaplan, *The Jewish Population of the New York Area, 1900–1975* (New York: Federation of Jewish Philanthropies of New York, 1959), 14–16, 73–75.

25. Daniel Boorstin, *The Americans: The Democratic Experience* (New York: Random House, 1973), 246.

26. Max Lerner, *America as a Civilization* (New York: Simon and Schuster, 1957), 172, and cf. 170, 181.

27. Nathan Glazer, "The National Influence of Jewish New York," in *Capital of the American Century: The National and International Influence of New York,* edited by Martin Shefter (New York: Russell Sage Foundation, 1993), 172. On the Jewish concentration by borough, see Paul Ritterband, "Why Did the Brooklyn Jewish Community Survive? The Response of a Cliometrician" (paper presented at The Hebrew University of Jerusalem, November 1998) Table 5, Part C. Jews constituted 38 percent of the population of the Bronx in 1920, 47 percent in 1930, 37 percent in 1950, but only 12 percent in 1970. The parallel figures for Brooklyn are as follows: 30 percent (1920), 42 percent (1930), 34 percent (1950), 23 percent (1970). In Manhattan: 29 percent (1920), 16 percent (1930), 18 percent (1950), 13 percent (1970). For Queens there are no reliable figures for 1920, but thereafter the Jewish share of the population in the borough grew from 9 percent in 1930 to 18 percent in 1950, rising to 22 percent in 1970.

28. On the ubiquitous Yiddish presence in New York slang up until the recent past, see "Oy Gevalt! New Yawkese An Endangered Dialect?" *New York Times,* 14 Feb. 1993, pp. 1, 50.

29. Dan Wakefield, *New York in the Fifties* (Boston and New York: Houghton Mifflin, 1992), 197.

30. Jewish Telegraphic Agency (JTA) *Daily News Bulletin,* 27 (1960): 13 Jan., p. 4; 26 Apr., p. 3; 2 May, p. 4; cf. Nathan Glazer and Daniel Patrick Moynihan, *Beyond the Melting Pot: The Negroes, Puerto Ricans, Jews, Italians and Irish of New York City* (Cambridge, Mass.: M.I.T. Press, 1963), 146. Bayor's study of ethnic groups in interwar New York cites findings that 56 percent of those entering the teaching profession in the city in 1940 were Jewish: Ronald H. Bayor, *Neighbors in Conflict: The Irish, Germans, Jews, and Italians of New York City, 1929–1944* (Urbana and Chicago: Univ. of Illinois Press, 1988), 26.

31. On the "New York Jewish intellectuals" in the thirties and forties and the issues of American culture and identity, see, for example: Alexander Bloom, *Prodigal Sons: The New York Intellectuals and Their World* (New York and Oxford: Oxford Univ. Press, 1986), esp. chap. 1; Terry A. Cooney, *The Rise of the New York Intellectuals: "Partisan Review" and Its Circle* (Madison: Univ. of Wisconsin Press, 1986), chap. 1; Irving Howe, *A Margin of Hope: An Intellectual Autobiography* (San Diego, New York, and London: Harcourt Brace, Jovanovich, 1982); Norman Podhoretz, *Making It* (New York: Random House, 1967).

32. Isa Kapp, "By the Waters of the Grand Concourse," *Commentary* 8, no. 3 (Sept. 1949): 269, 272–73.

33. Leonard Wallock, ed., *New York, Culture Capital of the World 1940–1965,* (New York: Rizzoli, 1988), 9.

34. Willie Morris, *New York Days* (Boston and New York: Little, Brown, 1993), 3; Wakefield, *New York in the Fifties,* 7 and cf. 19–21.

35. Glazer and Moynihan, *Beyond the Melting Pot,* 173.

36. Podhoretz, *Making It,* 4.

37. "Under Forty: A Symposium on American Literature and the Younger Generation of American Jews," *Contemporary Jewish Record* 7, no. 1, (Feb. 1944): 10, 15–17, 33–34.

38. Norman Podhoretz, "Jewishness and the Younger Intellectuals," *Commentary* 31, no. 4 (Apr. 1961): 307.

39. Howe, *World of Our Fathers,* 599; idem, *A Margin of Hope,* 28, and cf. 251; cf. idem , "A Memoir of the Thirties," in *Steady Work: Essays in the Politics of Democratic Radicalism, 1953–1966* (New York: Harcourt, Brace, and World, 1966), 352–53.

40. Lionel Trilling, introduction to Robert Warshow, *The Immediate Experience* (New York: Atheneum, 1975), 14, cited in Alan M. Wald, *The New York Intellectuals: The Rise and Decline of the Anti-Stalinist Left from the 1930s to the 1980s* (Chapel Hill and London: Univ. of North Car-

olina Press, 1987), 34; Alfred Kazin in "Under Forty: A Symposium," 11; Sydney Hook, in a personal communication cited by Wald, ibid., 28.

41. Emily Miller Budick, *Blacks and Jews in Literary Conversation* (Cambridge: Cambridge Univ. Press, 1998), 122, 134.

42. Podhoretz, *Making It,* 122; Bloom, *Prodigal Sons,* p. 276; Schwartz and Rosenfeld in "Under Forty," 14, 35.

43. "Our Country and Our Culture" (editorial statement), *Partisan Review,* 19 (May-June 1952), 284.

44. Podhoretz, *Making It,* 88–92.

45. Howe, *World of Our Fathers,* 603.

46. Alfred Kazin, "In Puerto Rico" (1959), repr. in Kazin, *Contemporaries* (Boston: Little, Brown, 1962), 320.

47. Mark Zborowski and Elizabeth Herzog, *Life Is with People: The Culture of the Shtetl,* Foreword by Margaret Mead (1952; reprint, New York: Schocken, 1967), cf. back cover.

48. Podhoretz, "Jewishness and the Younger Intellectuals," 307–8; Judd L. Teller, *Strangers and Natives: The Evolution of the American Jew from 1921 to the Present* (New York: Delacorte Press, 1968), 262.

49. David G. Roskies, "Jazz and Jewspeech: The Anatomy of Yiddish in American Literature," in *Ideology and Jewish Identity in Israeli and American Literature,* ed. Emily Budick (Albany: SUNY Press, forthcoming, 2001); Steven J. Zipperstein, *Imagining Russian Jewry—Memory, History, Identity* (Seattle and London: Univ. of Washington Press, 1999), 19.

50. Sociologist Robert E. Park equated "the emancipated Jew" with the "marginal man, the first cosmopolite," and poet W. H. Auden equated the modern existential predicament with the Jews' historical homelessness. Robert E. Park, "Human Migration and the Marginal Man," *American Journal of Sociology* 33 (1928), repr. in *Classic Essays on the Culture of Cities,* ed. Richard Sennett (Englewood Cliffs, N.J.: Prentice-Hall, 1969), 141. On Auden, see Daniel Bell, "Reflections on Jewish Identity," in *The Winding Passage: Essays and Sociological Journeys, 1960–1980* (Cambridge: Abt Books, 1980), 319: "Auden once said of Kafka, 'It was fit and proper that [he] should have been a Jew, for the Jews have for a long time been placed in the position in which we are all now to be, of having no home.' "

51. Alfred Kazin, preface to *On Native Grounds: An Interpretation of Modern American Prose Literature* (New York: Reynal and Hitchcock, 1942), ix-x.

52. Kazin, "Sholem Aleichem," in idem, *Contemporaries,* 271–278 (originally published 1956).

53. Daniel Bell, "Reflections on Jewish Identity," 318 (originally published in 1961); Kazin, "In Puerto Rico," 320.

54. Cooney, *The Rise of the New York Intellectuals,* 268.

55. Lewis Mumford, *The Culture of Cities* (New York: Harcourt, Brace, 1938), 3.

56. Robert Warshow, "Poet of the Jewish Middle Class," *Commentary* 1, no. 7(May 1946): 17–18.

57. Social and demographic data on American Jews in the early postwar period: see Erich Rosenthal, "The Jewish Population of the United States: A Demographic and Sociological Analysis," in *Movements and Issues in American Judaism,* ed. Bernard Martin (Westport: Greenwood Press, 1978), 25–62; Marshall Sklare (ed.), *The Jews: Social Patterns of an American Group* (New York and London: The Free Press and Collier-Macmillan, 1958). See also the annual reports in the *American Jewish Year Book.*

58. *American Jewish Year Book,* vol. 56 (New York and Philadelphia: American Jewish Committee/Jewish Publication Society, 1955), 517–35.

59. Martin Shefter, "New York's National and International Influence," in idem, *Capital of the American Century,* 17.

60. Glazer and Moynihan, *Beyond the Melting Pot,* 142. The proportion of inhabitants to synagogues is based on the listing of 285 New York City synagogues in Bernard Postal and Lionel Koppman, *Jewish Landmarks of New York: An Informal History and Guide* (New York: Hill and Wang, 1964), 250–56, 275–77.

61. Lucy S. Dawidowicz, "Middle-Class Judaism: A Case Study," *Commentary* 29, no. 6 (June 1960): 493. On church-member ratios, see Barry A. Kosman and Seymour P. Lachman, *One Nation under God: Religion in Contemporary American Society* (New York: Harmony Books, 1993), 5. The general American ratio of churches to members has averaged about one for every one thousand members.

62. Daniel J. Elazar, *Community and Polity: The Organizational Dynamics of American Jewry,* rev. ed. (Philadelphia: Jewish Publication Society, 1995), 325. On the historical assessment of Jewish communal fragmentation, see Aryeh Goren, "Haherut umigbelotehah," in *Yehudei artsot habrit,* ed. Aryeh Gartner and Jonathan Sarna (Jerusalem: Shazar Center, 1992), 239–58.

63. Joshua A. Fishman, "U.S. Census Data on Mother Tongues: Review, Extrapolations and Predictions," in *For Max Weinreich on His Seventieth Birthday: Studies in Jewish Languages, Literature, and Society* (The Hague: Mouton, 1964), 53–54.

64. Ibid., 53, 55, 59, 61; cf. Fishman, *Yiddish: Turning to Life* (Amsterdam and Philadelphia: John Benjamin's Publishing, 1991), 130; cf. Ira Rosenwaike, *Population History of New York City* (Syracuse: Syracuse Univ. Press, 1972), 128.

65. Leonard Dinnerstein, *America and the Survivors of the Holocaust* (New York: Columbia Univ. Press, 1982), 287–88. Jewish immigration figures: volumes 42 through 51 (1940–1950) of the *American Jewish Year Book.* The Orthodox component of the refugee immigration is estimated by Joel Kortick, "Transformation and Rejuvenation: The Arrival in America of Habad and Other Orthodox Jewish Communities, 1940–1950" (M. A. thesis, The Hebrew University of Jerusalem, 1996), 9.

66. On secular Yiddish schools, see Joshua A. Fishman, "Yiddish in America," *International Journal of American Linguistics* 31, no. 2, pt. 2 (Apr. 1965), Publication no. 36 of the Indiana University Research Center in Anthropology, Folklore, and Linguistics (Bloomington: Indiana Univ./The Hague: Mouton, 1965), 21–25, 57–63; cf. Fishman, *Yiddish: Turning to Life,* 96–100.

Fishman cites figures for Yiddish secular school enrollment in New York City, which declined from 3,827 in 1949 to 3,198 in 1958. By 1960 enrollment for New York City and suburbs had dipped below the three-thousand mark. The number of such schools in America as a whole stood at 146 in 1945 and at only 98 by 1960. Cf. Sandra Parker, "An Educational Assessment of Yiddish Secular School Movements in the United States," in *Never Say Die: A Thousand Years of Yiddish in Jewish Life and Letters,* ed. Joshua A. Fishman (The Hague: Mouton, 1981), 495–511. On Orthodox day schools, see Solomon Poll, "The Role of Yiddish in American Ultra-Orthodox and Hassidic Communities," *YIVO Annual of Jewish Social Science* 13 (1955): 125–52, also reprinted in Fishman, *Never Say Die,* 197–218.

67. The *Forverts,* which soon remained the last New York Yiddish daily, became a weekly in 1982.

68. Fishman, *Yiddish in America,* 41; Fishman, *Yiddish: Turning to Life,* 104–5; B. Z. Goldberg, "The American Yiddish Press at Its Centennial," *Judaism* 20, no. 2 (1970): 224–28, reprinted in Fishman, *Never Say Die,* 513–28. On the change to more varied multilingual broadcasting on WEVD in the sixties, see William H. Honan, "The New Sound of Radio," *New York Times Magazine,* 3 Dec. 1967, reprinted in *Pop Culture in America,* edited by David Manning White (Chicago: Quadrangle Books, 1970), 113. More recent figures from the U.S. Bureau of

the Census show that in 1990, there were 213,000 Americans over the age of five who spoke Yiddish at home *(New York Times,* 28 Apr. 1993, p. A18). That figure represents about 4 percent of the total American Jewish population, a proportion that conforms very closely to the estimated share of the ultra-Orthodox communities in the overall Jewish population. In 1960, according to Fishman ("U.S. Census Data"), Yiddish stood in eighth place in the United States, in a field of twenty-three non-English languages. In 1990, Yiddish ranked only sixteenth among the top twenty-five ethnic languages (see *New York Times,* as cited above).

69. Fishman, *Yiddish: Turning to Life,* 111.

70. The phrase "ministry of Yiddish" is used by Lucy Dawidowicz in her memoir, *From That Place and Time: A Memoir, 1938–1947* (New York: Bantam, 1989), and by Fishman, "The Sociology of Yiddish," in idem, *Never Say Die: A Thousand Years of Yiddish in Jewish Life and Letters* (The Hague: Mouton, 1981); on YIVO, see also Fishman, *Yiddish in America,* 43–45. The Yiddish thesaurus is: Nahum Stutchkoff, *Der oytser fun der yidisher shprakh,* ed. Max Weinreich (New York: YIVO, 1950). The two journals are: *YIVO bletter* and the *YIVO Annual of Jewish Social Science.* The collection of studies appeared under the title, *The Field of Yiddish,* ed. Uriel Weinreich (New York: The Linguistic Circle of New York, Columbia Univ., 1954).

71. Wakefield, *New York in the Fifties,* 284; Shmuel Niger (Charney), *Fun mayn togbukh* (New York: Congress for Jewish Culture, 1973), 303: entry for 15 May 1950. On the available translations of Yiddish literary classics in English in the early fifties, see the catalogue in Weinreich, *The Field of Yiddish.*

72. Carole S. Kessner, ed., *The "Other" New York Jewish Intellectuals* (New York: New York Univ. Press, 1994).

73. Mira Katzburg-Yungman, " 'Hadassah'—'asiyah ve'ide'ologiah, 1948–1956" (Ph.D. diss., Hebrew University of Jerusalem, 1998).

74. Elazar, *Community and Polity,* 173–74, 323–24; and for further details, see the earlier edition of the same book (Philadelphia: Jewish Publication Society, 1980), 134–35, 230, 235.

75. Kate Simon, *New York Places and Pleasures: An Uncommon Guide Book* (New York: Meridian Books, 1959), 162–63.

76. Teller, *Strangers and Natives,* 251–53.

77. Harshav and Harshav, *Yiddish Poetry in America,* 53

78. Jacob Glatstein, *"Etlekhe shures"* (A few lines), translated by Benjamin and Barbara Harshav, *Yiddish Poetry in America,* 53 (also 363).

79. H. Leyvik, "To America," translated by Benjamin and Barbara Harshav, *Yiddish Poetry in America,* 767.

80. Fred J. Cook and Gene Gleason, "The Shame of New York," *The Nation,* Special Issue, 31 Oct. 1959, 261; cf. Leonard Wallock, "New York City: Capital of the Twentieth Century," in *New York: Culture Capital of the World,* 40–42; *New York Times,* 1 June 1959, pp. 1, 16, and 19 Oct. 1959, pp. 1, 24; *Newsweek,* 27 July 1959: 29–31.

81. Andrew Hacker, *The New Yorkers: A Profile of an American Metropolis* (New York: Twentieth Century Fund, Mason/ Charter, 1975), 2, 27; cf. Rosenwaike, *Population History of New York City,* 131–74; Horowitz and Kaplan, *The Jewish Population of the New York Area, 1900–1975,* 2–3. Large cities' populations peaked in 1970, when there were twenty-six cities with populations of over half a million. They comprised half the population contained in their immediate areas. Ten years later, the number of such cities had declined to twenty-two; their combined populations had fallen from 31.8 million to 28.4 million, and their share of metropolitan area inhabitants fell below 50 percent: Matthew P. Drennan, "The Decline and Rise of the New York Economy," in *Dual City: Restructuring New York,* ed. John H. Mollenkopf and Manuel Castells (New York: Russell Sage Foundation, 1991), 27.

82. Frederick M. Binder and David M. Riemers, *All the Nations under Heaven: An Ethnic and Racial History of New York City* (New York: Columbia Univ. Press, 1995), 205–6.

83. Sklare, "Jews, Ethnics, and the American City," 144.

2. Past and Premonition: Mass Society and Its Discontents

1. Sam Welles, "The Jewish *Élan*," *Fortune Magazine*, Feb. 1960, 134.

2. "Third Seders" were a neotradition initiated by secular Jewish organizations, designating the third evening of Passover as a gala annual cultural event.

3. Jewish Telegraphic Agency *Daily News Bulletin* (henceforth JTA), 27, no. 17, 26 Jan. 1960, 3; no. 55, 21 Mar. , 4; no. 74, 19 Apr. , 4; no. 75, 20 Apr. , 4; no. 97, 20 May, 3. The CBS documentary, written by Rod Serling, was called, "In the Presence of Mine Enemies."

4. Miller, *Timebends*, 497.

5. Burt Bernstein, "Leonard Bernstein's Separate Peace with Berlin," *Esquire*, Oct. 1961, 96.

6. Norma Rosen, *Green, A Novella and Eight Stories* (New York: Harcourt, Brace and World, 1959), 37.

7. JTA, 27, no. 34, 18 Feb. 1960, 4.

8. JTA, 27, no. 1, 3 Jan. 1960, 1; no. 13, 20 Jan. 1960, 4; no. 75, 20 April, 1; Sidney Liskofsky, "International Swastika Outbreak," *American Jewish Year Book*, 62 (1961): 209–13.

9. JTA, 27, 4 Jan., 5 Jan., 6 Jan., 7 Jan., 8 Jan., 13 Jan., 14 Jan., 20 Jan., 21 Jan. 1960; *New York Times*, 3 Jan. 1960, 3; 4 Jan., 1, 3; 5 Jan., 1, 2; 6 Jan., 3; 7 Jan., 3; 9 Jan., 2; 10 Jan., 26, 29; 11 Jan., 15; 13 Jan., 1–2 (Eisenhower); 15 Jan, 1, 5; 19 Jan., 7; 20 Jan., 15; 21 Jan., 12; *Why the Swastika: A Study of Young American Vandals* (New York: Institute of Human Relations Press [American Jewish Committee], 1962); Martin Deutsch, *The 1960 Swastika Smearings: Analysis of the Apprehended Youth* (New York: Anti-Defamation League of B'nai B'rith, 1962); reprinted from *Merrill-Palmer Quarterly of Behavior and Development* (April 1962); Liskofsky, "Swastika Outbreak," 211–13. On 1959–60 as a "particularly ugly period," see Leonard Dinnerstein, *Antisemitism in America* (New York: Oxford Univ. Press, 1994), 163. The UN Subcommission then submitted its resolution to its parent body, the Commission on Human Rights, which ratified the decision.

10. Boorstin, *The Americans*, 558.

11. JTA, 27, no. 76, 21 Apr. 1960, 3; no. 78, 25 Apr., 1–2.

12. Bruno Bettelheim and Morris Janowitz, *Social Change and Prejudice* (New York: Free Press, 1964), 3–4, 80–97, 276–90.

13. Erich Fromm, foreword to *Escape from Freedom* (1941; reprint, New York: Avon, 1969).

14. Ibid., 265–66.

15. Theodor W. Adorno, ed., *The Authoritarian Personality* (New York: Harper, 1950); David Riesman, *The Lonely Crowd: A Study of the Changing American Character* (New Haven: Yale Univ. Press, 1950); Bruno Bettelheim, *The Informed Heart: Autonomy in a Mass Age* (New York: Free Press, 1960).

16. Norman Podhoretz, *Breaking Ranks* (London: Weidenfeld and Nicolson, 1980), 33, 60, comments on Glazer's role as collaborator with Riesman on *The Lonely Crowd* and on Riesman's relationship with Fromm. Riesman's wide influence was such that it even became the subject of intellectual horseplay. According to Podhoretz (ibid., 36), Jason Epstein (who launched Anchor Books) once proposed writing a Gilbert and Sullivan-type operetta set at a party of Upper West Side Jewish intellectuals, in which a stranger enters and musically introduces himself as: "I am the man who wrote the piece / About the man who wrote the piece / On David Ries-man."

17. Stephen J. Whitfield, *Voices of Jacob, Hands of Esau: Jews in American Life and Thought* (Hamden: Archon Books, 1984), 40. In a subsequent interview, Mailer spoke of "the collective sense of pending violence which has hovered over the twentieth century [that] became so real at the time of the concentration camps." Norman Mailer, "Talking of Violence," as interviewed by W. J. Weatherby, *Twentieth Century,* 173 (1964–65): 109–14; also printed in Shalom Endleman, ed., *Violence in the Streets* (Chicago: Quadrangle Books, 1968), 90.

18. Bellow, *Mr. Sammler's Planet,* 133, 180.

19. Ibid., 70.

20. Richard Hofstadter, *American Violence* (New York: Knopf, 1970). At the same time, he also penned the first section of a projected three-volume work of historical interpretation. Published posthumously, *America at 1750* examined the social underpinnings of America's national character on the eve of independence, with particular emphasis on themes of divisiveness and oppression. Though incomplete when he died, the book opened up the issue of what it was that held American society together, if anything, a theme that suggested itself quite naturally to Hofstadter, given the polarized atmosphere of the 1960s. My thanks to my friend, Aaron Berman, for this insight. See: Richard Hofstadter, *America at 1750: A Social Portrait* (New York: Knopf, 1971).

21. Hofstadter, *American Violence,* 41–42; Kazin, *New York Jew* (New York: Vintage, 1979), 21, 397.

22. Jane Jacobs, *The Death and Life of Great American Cities: The Failure of Town Planning* (New York: Random House, 1961).

23. Paul and Percival Goodman, *Communitas: Means of Livelihood and Ways of Life,* rev. ed. (New York: Vintage Books/Random House, 1960). The phrase "utopian thinking" was used by sociologist Herbert Gans in his appreciative review of the book *(Dissent,* [summer 1961]: 327) as well as by his colleague, David Riesman (in the blurb printed on the back cover of the Vintage edition).

24. Hortense Calischer, *The New Yorkers* (London: Jonathan Cape, 1970 [1966]), 93.

25. Herbert J. Gans, *People and Plans. Essays on Urban Problems and Solutions* (New York: Basic Books, 1968), esp. 25–48. Cf. Sandra Perlman Schoenberg and Patricia L. Rosenbaum, *Neighborhoods That Work: Sources for Vitality in the Inner City* (New Brunswick: Rutgers Univ. Press, 1980), 8: "In the 1950s and early 1960s, Herbert Gans's studies of the cultures of different types of neighborhoods served as an antidote to gloomy generalizations about the death of cities and the sterility of suburbs. . . . Gans's community studies highlighted the importance of ethnic ties, stage in the life cycle, work, and social class as determinants of social origin within neighborhoods."

26. Daniel Bell, "The Theory of Mass Society: A Critique," *Commentary,* 22, no. 1 (July 1956): 75–83.

27. Daniel Bell, "The Three Faces of New York," *Dissent* (summer 1961): 223–24.

28. Ibid., 224–25.

29. Ibid., 225–26.

30. In 1957–58, comparisons of the occupations of heads of family, separated according to religious preference, showed that in New York City, where Jews formed 29.6 percent and Catholics 46.0 percent of the population, 23 percent of Jewish family heads were owners, managers, and officials, as compared with only 6 percent for Catholics; an additional 18 percent of Jewish family heads were engaged in clerical and sales occupations, compared to 10 percent among Catholics. See Bernard Lazerwitz, "Jews in and out of New York City," *Jewish Journal of Sociology* 3, no. 2 (1961): 257. At the end of the sixties one observer could still note that Jews owned roughly 80 percent of the small businesses in the city. In the garment district alone there were "more than ten

thousand firms . . . squashed into a few dozen buildings between Thirty-fifth Street to the south and Forty-second Street to the north": Golden, *Greatest Jewish City,* 38, 153.

31. Ibid., 226. Similarly, Harry Golden noted, "The New York theater is Jewish, or at least its milieu is Jewish. This is not because the Jews have superior genetic arrangements for donning mask and buskin or because they are smarter producers. It's because Jews buy the tickets. . . . Jews attend the theater. They attend with a fervor a reformed drunk attends an AA meeting"—in Golden, *Greatest Jewish City,* 39.

32. Glazer and Moynihan, *Beyond the Melting Pot,* 171–72.

33. Bell, "The Three Faces of New York," 227–28.

34. Deborah Dash Moore, "I'll Take Manhattan," 424, 426.

35. Bernard Rosenberg and Ernest Goldstein, *Creators and Disturbers: Reminiscences by Jewish Intellectuals of New York* (New York: Columbia Univ. Press, 1982), 110.

36. Jim Sleeper, "Boodling, Bigotry, and Cosmopolitanism: The Transformation of a Civic Culture," *Dissent,* Special Issue: *In Search of New York,* (fall 1987): 414; republished as Jim Sleeper, ed., *In Search of New York* (New Brunswick and Oxford: Transaction Books, 1989).

37. Kazin, *New York Jew,* 240.

38. Ibid., 280–82.

39. Irving Howe, "New York in the Thirties: Some Fragments of Memory," *Dissent* (summer 1961): 241–42.

40. Ken Auletta, *The Streets Were Paved with Gold* (New York: Random House, 1979 [1975]), xv.

41. Leonard Kriegel, "In the Country of the Other," *Dissent* Special Issue (fall 1987): 617–22.

42. Marshall Berman, "Ruins and Reforms: New York Yesterday and Today," *Dissent* Special Issue (fall, 1987): 423.

43. Ibid., 426.

44. Rischin, *Promised City* (1970 ed.), 267.

45. Hannah Arendt, *Eichmann in Jerusalem. A Report on the Banality of Evil,* rev. ed. (New York: Viking Press, 1964), 6–7, 244–45.

46. Ibid., 272–79, 286–98; cf. Elisabeth Young-Bruehl, *Hannah Arendt: For Love of the World* (New Haven and London: Yale Univ. Press, 1982), 330, 338.

47. Arendt, *Eichmann,* 273. At about the same time, Harold I. Lief published an article on "Contemporary Forms of Violence" in the journal *Science and Psychoanalysis* (6 [1963]: 56–63), in which he concurred: "If we were certain that the people who ran these chambers of death so efficiently were sadists, who in another society would have been placed in institutions, we would be able to discuss this sickening chapter of history as proving only that our most sadistic fantasies can be acted out. But, in fact, it is quite certain [*sic!*] that they were not sadists, but that they were efficient, dispassionate destroyers of personality and will. Given a combination of societal factors, especially those which promote automatic obedience, it 'could happen here' or anywhere. If the process of dehumanization continues unchecked, given man's inventiveness, it is only a matter of which type of mass violence he will decide to use. At this point in time, the odds are in favor of nuclear extermination." Reprinted in Endleman, *Violence in the Streets,* 60.

48. Arendt, *Eichmann,* 289; Daniel Bell, *The End of Ideology: On the Exhaustion of Political Ideas in the Fifties* (New York: Free Press, 1960), 393; Bellow, *Mr. Sammler's Planet,* 180–81; cf. Raul Hilberg, *The Politics of Memory: The Journal of a Holocaust Historian,* (Chicago: Ivan R. Dee, 1996), esp. 124–25: "I had asserted that the process of destruction was bureaucratic, that for its successful completion it fed upon the talents and contributions of all manner of specialists, that a bureaucrat became a perpetrator by virtue of his position and skills at the precise time when

the process had reached a stage that required his involvement, that he was a thinking individual, and that, above all, he was available, neither evading his duty nor obstructing the administrative operation. . . . I was braced for a protest: the resurrection of the old emphasis on the role of seducers, henchmen, and sadists in Nazi Germany, and the reaffirmation of the essential goodness of ordinary people the world over. Yet there was hardly any objection to my description of the machinery of destruction. Most commentators simply bypassed my analysis or considered it a matter of course."

49. See, for example, Deborah E. Lipstadt, "America and the Memory of the Holocaust, 1950–1965," *Modern Judaism,* 16 (1996): 193–214.

50. Richard I. Cohen, "Breaking the Code: Hannah Arendt's *Eichmann in Jerusalem* and the Public Polemic. Myth, Memory, and Historical Imagination," *Michael* 13 (1993): 62.

51. See, for example, the statement of 31 January 1960 by Dr. Miriam K. Freund, national president of Hadassah Women's Zionist Organization, that she was "pained" that President Eisenhower had implied that there was a "Jewish vote" in the United States "and that it is being used to influence the Administration's attitude toward Israel." JTA, 27, no. 21, 1 Feb. 1960, 5. Also pertinent is the Jewish preference for joining wide coalitions with non-Jewish groups, instead of taking positions in the name of Jewish groups alone: Thus, five Jewish women's organizations joined twelve other national women's groups in January 1960 to fight segregation in American public schools, calling the new group the "National Organization of Women for Equality." The Jewish women's organizations involved were the National Women's Division of the American Jewish Congress, Hadassah, National Women's League of the United Synagogue of America (Conservative), Pioneer Women (Labor Zionist), and the Women's Branch of the Union of Orthodox Jewish Congregations. JTA, 27, no. 12, 19 Jan. 1960, 4. The quoted phrase is from Judd Teller, *Strangers and Natives,* 278, who noted the shift in Jewish organizational nomenclature: former so-called Jewish defense organizations were now preferring to be known as "communal relations" groups.

52. Hannah Arendt, *The Origins of Totalitarianism,* new ed. (New York: Harcourt, Brace, 1973); idem, "The Moral of History," in, *Hannah Arendt, the Jew as Pariah: Jewish Identity and Politics in the Modern Age,* ed. Ron H. Feldman (New York: Grove Press, 1978), 109.

53. Arendt, *Eichmann,* 278–79, 286–98.

54. Stephen J. Whitfield, *Into the Dark: Hannah Arendt and Totalitarianism* (Philadelphia: Temple Univ. Press, 1980), 138–41.

55. Nathan Glazer, "City Problems and Jewish Responsibilities," *Commentary* 33, no. 1 (1962): 27 (the talk was delivered the previous June before the National Community Relations Advisory Council—a key Jewish community umbrella agency).

56. Young-Bruehl, *Hannah Arendt,* 355.

57. Held in New York in October 1963 under the auspices of *Dissent* magazine, the panel was made up of heavyweight intellectual speakers: Marie Syrkin, Lionel Abel, historian Raul Hilberg, and Daniel Bell. Arendt had declined an invitation, as had Bruno Bettelheim.

58. Norman Fruchter, "Arendt's Eichmann and Jewish Identity," *Studies on the Left* 5 (1965): 22–42, cited in Cohen, "Breaking the Code," 70, and in Young-Bruehl, *Hannah Arendt,* 360.

59. Gitlin, *The Sixties,* 26.

60. Henry L. Feingold, "The Jewish Radical in His American Habitat," *Judaism* 22, no. 1 (1973): 104.

61. See Norman Podhoretz, "Hannah Arendt on Eichmann," *Commentary* 36, no. 3 (Sept. 1963): 201–8 (cited by Young-Bruehl, *Hannah Arendt,* 347): "In the place of the monstrous Nazi, she gives us the 'banal' Nazi; in the place of the Jew as a virtuous martyr, she gives us the Jew as accomplice in evil; and in the place of the confrontation of guilt and innocence, she gives

us the 'collaboration' of criminal and victim." Cf. Irving Howe, "*The New Yorker* and Hannah Arendt," *Commentary* 36, no. 4 (Oct. 1963): 318–19.

62. Young-Bruehl, *Hannah Arendt,* 338; Morgenthau, in Rosenberg and Goldstein, *Creators and Disturbers,* 79.

63. Howe, *Margin of Hope,* 270, 273–74.

64. Young-Bruehl, *Hannah Arendt,* 349, 356, 358.

65. Lionel Abel, "The Aesthetics of Evil," *Partisan Review* (summer 1963): 219; Barbara Tuchman, "The Final Solution," *New York Times Book Review,* 29 May 1966, 3, 12.

66. Morgenstern, in Rosenberg and Goldstein, *Creators and Disturbers,* 108.

67. Nathan Glazer, *American Judaism* (Chicago and London: Univ. of Chicago Press, 1957), 114; Glazer and Moynihan, *Beyond the Melting Pot,* 293–94.

68. Rosenberg and Goldstein, *Creators and Disturbers,* 222–223.

69. Glazer and Moynihan, *Beyond the Melting Pot,* 294.

3. A Culture of Retrieval

1. Rosenberg and Goldstein, *Creators and Disturbers,* 82.

2. Ibid., 351, 359.

3. Marion K. Sanders, "The Several Worlds of American Jews: An Unauthorized Guide," *Harper's Magazine,* Apr. 1966, 53–54.

4. Paley, in Rosenberg and Goldstein, *Creators and Disturbers,* 297; Robert Alter, *After the Tradition: Essays on Modern Jewish Writing* (New York: E. P. Dutton, 1971), 117. Alter uses the felicitous phrase in reference to Bernard Malamud's metaphorical Jews. The essay in which the reference appears was originally published in *Commentary* 42, no. 3 (Sept. 1966).

5. Michael Wood, "What Did You Want from the Jews?" *New Society,* 12 May, 1966, 9.

6. Ibid., 10.

7. Ibid.

8. There is a very useful collection of reviews and other essays on *The Deputy* that was edited by Eric Bentley, *The Storm over the Deputy* (New York: Grove Press, 1964).

9. Bennett M. Berger, *Looking for America* (Englewood Cliffs, N.J.: Prentice-Hall, 1971), 83.

10. Irving Howe, "The Lower East Side, Symbol and Fact," in *The Lower East Side: Portal to American Life (1870–1924),* ed. Allon Schoener (New York: The Jewish Museum, 1966), 12–13.

11. Ibid.

12. Eisig Silberschlag, "The Jewishness of Jewish Writers," *Hadassah Magazine,* Mar. 1963, 3.

13. Howe, "The Lower East Side," 14.

14. Morris Dickstein, *Gates of Eden: American Culture in the Sixties* (New York: Basic Books, 1977), 4–5; Leon Wieseltier, "The Prince of Bummers," *New Yorker,* 26 July 1993, 43.

15. Howe, "The Lower East Side," 11.

16. Norich, *The Homeless Imagination,* 8–9.

17. Glatshteyn, "Mayn kinds-kinds fargangenhayt," translated by Harshav and Harshav, in Harshav and Harshav, *Yiddish Poetry in America,* 329–33. "Gemore-melodies" refers to the singsong cadence used by yeshiva students when reciting the talmudic text aloud.

18. Ibid.

19. Ruth R. Wisse, "Language as Fate: Reflections on Jewish Literature in America," *Studies in Contemporary Jewry,* vol. 12, *Literary Strategies: Jewish Texts and Contexts,* ed. Ezra Mendelsohn (New York and Oxford: Oxford Univ. Press, 1996), 140.

20. David G. Roskies, "Rabbis, Rebbes and Other Humanists: The Search for a Usable Past

in Modern Yiddish Literature," in *Studies in Contemporary Jewry,* vol. 12, *Literary Strategies: Jewish Texts and Contexts,* ed. Ezra Mendelsohn (New York and Oxford: Oxford Univ. Press, 1996), 70–71.

21. Irving Howe, "Jacob Glatstein," *Jewish Frontier,* 38, no. 11 (Dec. 1971): 8–9; cf. Budick, *Blacks and Jews in Literary Conversation,* 19–41, 59–60.

22. Isaac Bashevis Singer, "What's in It for Me," *Harper's Magazine,* Special Supplement ("The Writer's Life"), Oct. 1965, 172–73. On the cultural politics of translation from Yiddish to English and Bashevis's position, see Anita Norich, "Isaac Bashevis Singer in America: The Translation Problem," *Judaism* 44, no. 2, (spring 1995): 208–18. Norich notes (on 214): "The English clarifies the Yiddish but for a growing audience it also replaces the Yiddish as the definitive text. This is typical of the history of Yiddish literature in America, but Singer is remarkable among Yiddish writers in the extent to which he contributes to and validates this usurpation of Yiddish by English even as he suggests a different model. He can hardly be expected to celebrate the English triumph—and thus betrayal—of the Yiddish in which he always creates, but he is clearly willing to embrace it, to make it his own, and to give it equal standing."

23. Roskies, "Rabbis, Rebbes and Other Humanists," 70.

24. Rosenberg and Goldstein, *Creators and Disturbers,* 37, 44.

25. Passage from *Meshuga* (serialized in Yiddish in the *Forverts* in 1981–82, but written much earlier, probably in 1955); published posthumously (New York: Farrar, Straus, Giroux, 1994), 114. The passage is spoken by Bashevis's fictional representative, Aaron Graydinger.

26. Alter, *After the Tradition,* 75 (originally published as: "Sabbatai Zevi and the Jewish Imagination," *Commentary* 43, no. 6 (June 1967). On the relationship between Bashevis and I. J. Singer, see Norich, *Homeless Imagination,* chap. 6.

27. Singer, "Author's Note," *In My Father's Court* (Philadelphia: Jewish Publication Society, 1966), viii; cited by Roskies, "Rabbis, Rebbes and Other Humanists," 71.

28. Singer, "The Extreme Jews," *Harper's,* Apr. 1967, 56–62.

29. Cynthia Ozick, "Envy; or Yiddish in America, A Novella," *Commentary* 48, no. 5, (Nov. 1969): 33–53.

30. Ibid., 9.

31. *Lider fun khurbn, ta"sh-tash"ah: antologye (Poems of the Destruction, 1939–1945*), compiled by Kadia Molodovsky (Tel-Aviv: I. L. Peretz Farlag, 1962).

32. Molodovsky, *Likht fun dornboym* (Buenos Aires: Farlag "Kiyum," 1965), 5–6. The poem is dated 1954.

33. Ibid., 118–19; translated by EL.

34. Ibid., 122; translated by EL.

35. The Yiddish *omud* (Hebrew: *'amud*) has several connotations: a lectern, but also the reader's desk in the synagogue, thus implying a liturgical function; the word can thus also be rendered in English as "altar."

36. Ibid., 143–44, translated by EL. I have omitted a stanza in which Molodovsky challenged the other poets of her day (apparently Avrohom Sutzkever, perhaps Glatshteyn, too), with regard to their definition of the Yiddish canon and the writer's task as a commitment to the "golden chain" of literary tradition—a concept that implies a closure, which Molodovsky sought to prevent. The "golden chain" is a reference to the premier postwar Yiddish literary journal of that name, *Di goldene keyt,* based in Israel and edited by Sutzkever and also a metaphor for the imprisoned imagination, in Molodovsky's reply:

> And maybe there is no "last" generation.
> I am no goldsmith forging a chain at the smithy:

> See, there he's fashioned his very last link,
> He's ready to go home and call it a day—
> Eat his meal and drink his fill—
> And have done with it for ever and ever.

37. Fishman, "Di sotsiologye fun yidish in amerike: 1960–1970 un vayter," *Di goldene keyt,* no. 75 (1972), 111, 115–17.

38. Ibid., 118. Recall that student enrollment in Yiddish secular afternoon schools in New York City alone had been about three thousand in 1958.

39. Ibid., 115–16, 122.

40. Ibid., 123–25.

41. Ibid., 124.

42. Horowitz and Kaplan, *The Jewish Population of the New York Area,* 208–9, 226–27, 232–33.

43. Harry Gersh and Sam Miller, "Satmar in Brooklyn, A Zealot Community," *Commentary* 28, no. 5 (Nov. 1959): 389–90, 392.

44. Menachem Friedman, "Haredim Confront the Modern City," *Studies in Contemporary Jewry,* vol. 2, ed. Peter Y. Medding (Bloomington and Indianapolis: Indiana Univ. Press, 1986), 91.

45. William Helmreich, *Against All Odds: Holocaust Survivors and the Successful Lives They Made in America* (New York: Simon and Schuster, 1992), 171.

46. Gersh and Miller, "Satmar in Brooklyn," 398.

47. Ibid., 87, 91.

48. Such donations appear to serve a need on the part of less traditional Jews to do something positive to "preserve" an Old World form of Judaism.

49. Gersh and Miller, "Satmar in Brooklyn," 87–90.

50. Yossi Klein Halevi, *Memoirs of a Jewish Extremist: An American Story* (Boston and New York: Little, Brown, 1995), 30–32.

51. Ari L. Goldman, *The Search for God at Harvard* (New York: Ballentine Books/Random House, 1991), 71–74.

52. Charles S. Liebman, "Orthodoxy in American Jewish Life," *American Jewish Year Book* 66 (1965): 74–75.

53. Friedman, "Haredim," 88–89.

54. Gabriel Preil, "Van Gogh: Williamsburg," in *Sunset Possibilities and Other Poems,* trans. Robert Friend (Philadelphia: Jewish Publication Society, 1985), 103. The poem is from Preil's volume of poems, published in 1968, *Ha'esh vehadmamah (Fire and Silence).*

55. Joseph Heller, *Good as Gold* (New York: Simon and Schuster, 1976), 447. Heller was not alone in finding a special fascination in this sort of playground scene. In Gersh and Miller's report on Williamsburg in 1959, we find the following account:

"The exotic earlock is . . . no impediment to the familiar Brooklyn street play. A five-year-old boy with blue skullcap atop his brown *peyes* rides a tricycle in circles, chased by a younger playmate, with blond earlocks and yellow skullcap, who is trying to mount the back treads. . . . [A] fifteen-year-old, with the usual skullcap and *peyes,* sinks baskets with two non-Hasidic fellow players. . . . 'Okay, Pinchas, *tsu mir* [i.e., pass it to me, Pinchas].' " Gersh and Miller, "Satmar in Brooklyn, 390.

56. Robert Liberles, *Salo Wittmayer Baron, Architect of Jewish History* (New York and London: New York Univ. Press, 1995), 240.

57. Today the J.I.R. constitutes an integral part of the Reform movement's Hebrew Union College, and it was the basis of the College's New York campus.

58. Ibid., 1–3, 16, 21–36, 58–84.

59. Salo W. Baron, "The American Experience," in *Great Ages and Ideas of the Jewish People,* ed. Leo W. Schwarz (New York: Random House/Modern Library, 1956), 480–81; also "Can American Jewry Be Culturally Creative?" (versions of this essay were published in *Jewish Heritage* 1, no. 2 (1958); in *Bookmark* 9, no. 2 (1962); and in Salo W. Baron, *Steeled by Adversity: Essays and Addresses on American Jewish Life,* ed. Jeannette Meisel Baron (Philadelphia: Jewish Publication Society, 1971), 542–51.

60. Schorsch, *From Text to Context,* 385–86.

61. Liberles, *Salo Wittmayer Baron,* 345–46.

62. Hannah Arendt, "Creating a Cultural Atmosphere," in "Jewish Culture in This Time and Place, A Symposium," *Commentary* 4, no. 5 (Nov. 1947): 424.

63. Ibid., 425.

4. What's to Become of Man, Then?

1. See, for example, Martin E. Marty, *The New Shape of American Religion* (New York: Harper and Row, 1959); idem, *Modern American Religion,* vol. 3, *Under God, Indivisible, 1941–1960* (Chicago and London: Univ. of Chicago Press, 1996); Andrew M. Greeley, *The Denominational Society* (Glenview, Ill.: Scott, Foresman, 1972).

2. Marshall Sklare and Joseph Greenblum, *Jewish Identity on the Suburban Frontier* (New York: Basic Books, 1967); Wertheimer, *A People Divided*; Glazer, *American Judaism*; Charles S. Liebman, *The Ambivalent American Jew* (Philadelphia: Jewish Publication Society, 1973). Rabbinics scholar Jacob Neusner, writing in the 1960 *American Jewish Year Book* (61: 52), stated: "Indeed, sociologists have been quick to point out the element of conformity. Protestants 'go' to church and Roman Catholics 'go' to Mass, and Jews are expected to 'go' somewhere too."

Orthodox theologian Eliezer Berkovits put it similarly in 1959 in *Judaism,* the journal of Jewish religious thought: "The reawakened interest in Judaism is often a sign of assimilation. Within the climate of American culture, religion has become a sign of respectability. . . . Because the main function of religion has become to confirm us in our way of living, and since no interference with our life practices may be tolerated, Judaism has been relegated back to the precincts of the temple and limited to specific observances on specific occasions"—"From the Temple to Synagogue and Back," *Judaism* 8, no. 4 (fall 1959): 310–11.

3. Will Herberg, *Protestant, Catholic, Jew* (Garden City, N.Y.: Anchor/Doubleday, 1960 [1955]); cf. Gerhard Lenski, *The Religious Factor* (New York: Doubleday, 1955).

4. John Krumm, "College Students and Religious Belief," *Columbia College Today* 10, no. 3 (spring-summer 1963): 18; Frimer: in *The Condition of Jewish Belief: A Symposium Compiled by the Editors of* Commentary *Magazine,* introduced by Milton Himmelfarb (New York: Macmillan/The American Jewish Committee, 1966), 83; Alfred Jospe, "Religion in the University—A Terminal Case?" Inaugural Convocation, Interfaith Chapel, Univ. of Rochester, New York, 8 October 1970.

5. See, for example, Greeley, *The Denominational Society*; Phillip E. Hammond, ed., *The Sacred in a Secular Age* (Berkeley and Los Angeles: Univ. of California Press, 1985); Phillip E. Hammond and Benton Johnson, eds., *American Mosaic: Social Patterns of Religion in the United States* (New York: Random House, 1970).

6. See Thomas Luckmann, *The Invisible Religion* (New York: Macmillan, 1967).

7. Glazer, *American Judaism,* 116–17.

8. The Upper West Side (88th Street) Manhattan congregation B'nai Jeshurun dedicated its community center in 1928. At the ceremony, the rabbi, Israel Goldstein, stated: "A Jewish community . . . needs more than a house of worship. Children require adequate quarters where religious education may be imparted, spacious and well lighted classrooms, a commodious assembly hall. . . . Older boys and girls require facilities for social contacts as well as for cultural self-expression. [M]en and women . . . require a proper meeting place where friendship may be cultivated, where gatherings for social, recreational and educational purposes may be properly housed, and where the program of philanthropy which pertains to Congregations and Sisterhoods may be properly deliberated and fulfilled"—Israel Goldstein, *A Century of Judaism in New York* (New York: Congregation B'nai Jeshurun/Little and Ives, 1930), 320.

Isaac Berkson, prominent Jewish educator, wrote in the 1920s that, "[A]dolescents of the half baked second generation have become thoroughly 'Americanized.' .. They have lost whatever culture was inherent in the customs and institutions of their parents' traditional life." His solution: a heavy dose of cultural Zionism within a broader policy of ethnocultural pluralism. See Lloyd P. Gartner, ed., *Jewish Education in the United States: A Documentary History* (New York: 1969), 165–66.

9. Kaplan's diary (entry for 29 Dec. 1930) as quoted in Wenger, *New York Jews and the Great Depression,* 187.

10. Teller, *Strangers and Natives,* 62.

11. Figures from the 1920s and 1930s indicate that even outside Manhattan, and even in the more upscale suburban residential parts of Queens, Long Island, Brooklyn, and the Bronx, Orthodox synagogues were as prevalent as Conservative synagogues (11 Conservative synagogues to 19 Orthodox ones in Queens and Long Island; 11 for each denomination in the Bronx; 17 Conservative synagogues to 14 Orthodox ones in Brooklyn's newer Jewish neighborhoods—Flatbush, Bensonhurst, and Borough Park). See Jeffrey Gurock, *American Jewish Orthodoxy in Historical Perspective* (New York: Ktav, 1996), 308. Gurock argues that an upwardly mobile, modern, "American" Orthodoxy developed in New York from the turn of the twentieth century through the interwar period. Competing both with secular Jewishness and with the rising Conservative movement, it articulated a type of Judaism that both resisted accommodation to American culture and also tempered that resistance strategically. Cf. idem, *The Men and Women of Yeshiva: Higher Education, Orthodoxy, and American Judaism* (New York: Columbia Univ. Press, 1988); cf. Jenna Weissman Joselit, *New York's Jewish Jews: The Orthodox Community in the Interwar Years* (Bloomington: Indiana Univ. Press, 1990).

In 1959, on a national basis, the three national synagogue organizations claimed the following number of congregations: 660 Conservative, 575 Reform, and 1,500 Orthodox synagogues (*American Jewish Year Book,* 61 [1960]: 52). Assuming that at least 50 percent (perhaps more) of the Orthodox congregations were located in New York, they would have outnumbered the combined number of Reform and Conservative congregations in the city. Though the membership of each Orthodox congregation is likely to have been quite small, the presence of numerous such congregations throughout Jewish neighborhoods made them seem typical.

Charles Liebman, in *The Ambivalent American Jew* (60), points out the difficulty involved in assessing denominational affiliations in American Judaism and in New York specifically. He cites a study he conducted in the late 1960s for the United Synagogue of America (the lay organization of Conservative congregations) in which he found that 40 percent of the members of Orthodox congregations in the Washington Heights area of Upper Manhattan considered themselves to be "Conservative," (a code meaning 'less than totally observant') while in fact continuing to affiliate with an Orthodox synagogue—and this, it should be remembered, was thirty years after the Conservative synagogue began to make its first major inroads in the Jewish community. These data, while indicating the organizational weakness of the Conservative movement in the Washington Heights area, indicate as well the doctrinal weakness of Orthodoxy there. Washington Heights, it should be noted, was more heavily populated by first-generation immigrants with traditional backgrounds than some other New York neighborhoods at that time, so that the profile there might be taken to reflect immigrant-Jewish responses to some extent.

12. Howe, *World of Our Fathers,* 190.

13. Arthur Hertzberg, *The Jews in America: Four Centuries of an Uneasy Encounter* (New York: Simon and Schuster, 1989), 159–60; Liebman, *The Ambivalent American Jew,* 67. Clearly, not only factory workers were involved in this lifestyle. The shopkeeper parents of Jewish educator Isaac Berkson (Berkson was born in 1891 in Brooklyn) were members of an Orthodox synagogue and kept a kosher home, but opened their shop for business on Saturdays. For pertinent biographical details, see Henry Franc Skirball, "Isaac Baer Berkson and Jewish Education," (Ph.D. diss., New York, 1977).

14. There is something akin to the "chicken and the egg" about this argument: The new Orthodoxy of the late nineteenth century was itself a response to secularizing and modernizing trends in certain sectors of Jewish society—trends that, in turn, responded to the less functional aspects of traditional Jewish norms. On the dialectic between the institutional specialization of religion and the rise of a "secular" laity, see Luckmann, *The Invisible Religion,* 86, 90–91. Luckmann concludes that "institutional specialization of religion, along with the specialization of other institutional areas, starts a development that transforms religion into an increasingly 'subjective' and 'private' reality."

15. On the innovative Lithuanian yeshivot of the nineteenth century, see Shaul Stampfer, *Hayeshivah halita'it behithavutah* (Jerusalem: Merkaz Shazar, 1995); cf. Joseph B. Soloveitchik, *Halakhic Man,* trans. Lawrence Kaplan (Philadelphia: Jewish Publication Society, 1983), who notes that his illustrious forebear, Rabbi Hayyim, founder of the Volozhin yeshiva, had his students trained in a far more theoretical academic mode than was the previous norm.

16. *Musar* is translatable as "ethics" or "morality," as well as chastisement, but here connotes moral self-perfection in service to the inner spirit of the Torah.

17. On the elitist Orthodoxy in nineteenth-century eastern Europe, and especially the Musar movement, see Immanuel Etkes, *Rav yisrael salanter vereishitah shel tnu'at hamusar* (Jerusalem: Magnes Press, 1982); cf. Allan L. Nadler, *The Faith of the Mithnagdim* (Baltimore: Johns Hopkins Univ. Press, 1997); and Eli Lederhendler, *Jewish Responses to Modernity: New Voices in America and Eastern Europe* (New York: New York Univ. Press, 1994), 67–103.

18. On the *kheyder* as an issue in Jewish public debate in Russia at the turn of the twentieth century, see Zipperstein, "Reinventing Heders," in *Imagining Russian Jewry,* 41–62.

19. The one attempt (in the late 1880s) to confer upon a prominent rabbinical figure from Lithuania, Rabbi Jacob Joseph, the status of "chief rabbi" in New York ended in complete failure, and during Prohibition the enforcement of laws concerning the sale of sacramental wine was bedeviled by the underworld's use of so-called fake rabbis. On the Jacob Joseph fiasco, see Abraham J. Karp, "New York Chooses a Chief Rabbi," *Publications of the American Jewish Historical Society* 44, no. 3 (Mar. 1955): 129–98. On rabbis and bootlegging, see Jenna Weissman Joselit, *Our Gang* (Bloomington: Indiana Univ. Press, 1983), and Henry L. Feingold, *Lest Memory Cease. Finding Meaning in the American Jewish Past* (Syracuse: Syracuse Univ. Press, 1996), 153.

20. Exemplars of this neo-Orthodoxy were a cluster of Orthodox synagogues with American-led, middle-class-oriented, fairly youthful congregations; educational endeavors like the Ramaz school; and the modern Orthodox flagship school of higher learning, Yeshiva University.

21. Howe, *World of Our Fathers,* 191.

22. Liebman offers a sensitive reading of these issues: *Ambivalent American Jew,* esp. 3–7, 12–14, 20–22, 52ff; cf. Hertzberg, *The Jews in America: Four Centuries of an Uneasy Encounter,* esp. 156ff., 168, 171.

23. On the chaotic nature of New York Orthodox religious life—particularly in the realms of rabbinic leadership, religious education, and kashrut supervision see Goren, *New York Jews and the Quest for Community,* chaps. 4–6. On the conflicts and cultural politics of modernity and tradition in East European Jewish society and among Jewish immigrants in America, see Lederhendler, *Jewish Responses to Modernity.*

24. The Jewish affinity for learning is so ubiquitously referred to in popular as well as academic writing that it defies full bibliographical acknowledgment. For one typical study, see Thomas Kessner, *The Golden Door* (New York: Oxford Univ. Press, 1977). On the neglect of religious education even by Orthodox philanthropists, see Gurock, *American Jewish Orthodoxy,* 314. On Jewish religious education in New York City, see Goren, *New York Jews and the Quest for Community,* 88ff; Wenger, *New York Jews and the Great Depression,* 184.

25. On intermarriage involving immigrant Jews up to the World War I period, see Julius Drachsler, *Democracy and Assimilation: The Blending of Immigrant Heritages in America* (New York: Macmillan, 1920), pt. 2: Intermarriage among Ethnic Groups in the United States; on more contemporary developments, see Steven M. Cohen, *American Assimilation or Jewish Revival?* (Bloomington: Indiana Univ. Press, 1988), chap. 2; and see the discussion in our chapter, below.

26. Luckmann, *The Invisible Religion,* 88–89.

27. For example, in a study of attitudes toward intermarriage, conducted in the early sixties among 5,407 students in forty colleges, the respondents' answers were classified according to the type of college they attended (private, state university, Catholic, Negro), rather than their religion, although it was stated that Jews comprised 12 percent of the total sample: A. I. Gordon, *Inter-Marriage* (Boston: 1964).

28. W. Seward Salisbury, *Religion and the College Student* (Albany: State Univ. of New York, Research Foundation, 1957), 31, table 5.

29. Greeley, *The Denominational Society,* 137–39; cf. idem, *Religion in the Year 2000* (New York: Sheed and Ward, 1969); cf. Martin E. Marty, Stuart E. Rosenberg, Andrew M. Greeley, *What Do We Believe?* (New York: Meredith, 1968).

30. I. Steinbaum, "A Study of the Jewishness of Twenty New York Families," *YIVO Annual of Jewish Social Science* 5 (1950): 232–55 (originally published in Yiddish, in *Yivo bleter* 21/22 [1948], the study was based on a survey carried out in 1940).
See Liebman's comment, reflecting the state of research on Jewish religious identity at the end of the sixties *(The Ambivalent American Jew,* 60): "[W]e lack any reliable data for New York and its suburbs, where over 40 percent of the American Jews are located."

31. Cohen, *American Assimilation or Jewish Revival?* The study, known as the 1981 Greater New York Jewish Population Study, surveyed 4,505 Jewish households in the five boroughs and three suburban counties (Westchester, Suffolk, and Nassau).

32. Ibid., 28–30.

33. Ibid., 30, 41.

34. "Generation" refers to immigration, where those of the first generation are immigrants born abroad; second-generation connotes American-born children of foreign-born immigrant parents, and so on.

35. Cohen, *American Assimilation or Jewish Revival?* 49.

36. Ibid., 49, table 3–4.

37. Ibid.

38. Steinbaum, "Twenty New York Families," 245–55.

39. Cohen, *American Assimilation or Jewish Revival?,* 49, table 3–4. It should be noted that the second-generation Jews and the third-generation Jews involved in the study formed the great bulk of the entire sample of 4,500: There were 1,968 second-generation respondents and 1,265 third-generation respondents (see table 3–1 in Cohen, 44).

40. Ibid., 54, table 3–5.

41. About half of the Jewish immigrants arriving in the United States in the 1940s to 1960s settled in New York City. In 1950, out of an estimated New York Jewish population of 2.1 million, 679,520 (= 32.4 percent) were foreign-born. The majority were over 45 years of age, but 150,000 were under 44. Among heads of household (i.e., adults only), 50.8 percent were foreign-born. In communities elsewhere in the United States, the foreign-born comprised from 15 to 32 percent of the total Jewish population, with the average being around 20–25 percent. In Port Chester, Long Island (N.Y.), in 1949 the percentage of foreign-born Jews was 25 percent; in Passaic, New Jersey, 31 percent. In 1960, in Trenton, New Jersey, the proportion of foreign-born was 15 percent; in Los Angeles, 25 percent, and in San Francisco, 23 percent. In Boston, 20 percent of Jewish adults were foreign-born in 1965. Ben Seligman, "Some Aspects of Jewish Demography," in *The Jews: Social Patterns of an American Group,* ed. Marshall Sklare (New York: Free Press, 1958), 87, table 16; idem, "The Population of New York City: 1952," ibid., 104; *American Jewish Year Book* 62 (1961): 64, table 1; ibid., 63 (1962): 147–48; ibid., 64 (1963): 58, 64; ibid., 68 (1967): 234; ibid., 72 (1971): 46; cf. Rosenwaike, *Population History of New York City,* 155, table 80 and 159, table 84.

42. Glazer, *American Judaism,* 105.

43. Jewish Education Committee of New York, *JEC Bulletin* no. 126 (Sept. 1962): 5, 12; Horowitz and Kaplan, *The Jewish Population of the New York Area, 1900–1975,* 18–19, table 8; Rosenwaike, *Population History of New York City,* 155, table 80. The Jewish school-age population cited (410,000) is from 1957 data and the enrollment figures are from 1961–62; the percentages are therefore close approximations. Cf. JTA, 27, no. 23, 3 Feb. 1960, 5.

44. Ibid.; cf. Borowitz, *A New Jewish Theology in the Making,* 32: "In 1925 only 40 percent of American Jewish children enrolled in Jewish schools were being educated by congregations, with most of the remainder in communal schools whose tone was largely cultural and Zionist. By 1957, over 90 percent of children receiving a Jewish education were doing so under communal auspices."

45. The 1971 National Jewish Population Study found that, although New York stood second to last (just before Los Angeles) in the proportion of Jewish religious school enrollment, enrollment in Jewish religious schools in the city had reached 67 percent of the school-age population (age 6–17). The national average in 1971 stood at 73 percent and the range was between Los Angeles (64 percent) and Atlanta (98 percent). See Sergio DellaPergola and Nitza Genuth, *Jewish Education Attained in Diaspora Communities: Data for the 1970s.* Jewish Educational Statistics Research Paper 2 (Jerusalem: Hebrew Univ., Institute of Contemporary Jewry, 1983), 33, 35, table 6.

46. Haym Soloveitchik, "Rupture and Reconstruction: The Transformation of Contemporary Orthodoxy," *Tradition* 28, no. 4 (1994): 87–88.

47. Egon Mayer, *From Suburb to Shtetl: The Jews of Boro Park,* (Philadelphia: Temple Univ. Press, 1979), 86–88.

48. The term "gastronomic Judaism" is pejorative, in-group slang, referring to Jews who chiefly expressed their attachment to Jewish identity through eating Jewish foods; closely related is the term "cardiac Jews," i.e., with a Jewish "heart" or "feelings."

49. Irving Greenberg, in "Toward Jewish Religious Unity: A Symposium," *Judaism* 15, no.

2 (spring 1966): 133–50; repr. in *The Ghetto and Beyond: Essays on Jewish Life in America*, ed. Peter I. Rose (New York: Random House, 1969), 155–56.

50. Luckmann, *The Invisible Religion*, 84–85.

51. Liebman, *The Ambivalent American Jew*, 67.

52. Borowitz, *New Jewish Theology*, 33.

53. Saul Goodman, "Jewish Secularism in America—Permanence and Change," *Judaism* 9, no. 4 (fall, 1960): 330.

54. Kazin, *Partisan Review* Mar., 1950: 236.

55. Luckmann, *The Invisible Religion*, 90–103; cf. Greeley, *The Denominational Society*, 60–62.

56. A 1991 study of Jewish life in New York indicated that 43 percent of Jews living in a mixed-religion household personally fasted on Yom Kippur; 32 percent attended synagogue on the High Holidays; and 3 percent actually attended synagogue weekly (compared to 18 percent among Jews in Jewish-only households): Horowitz, *The 1991 New York Jewish Population Survey*, 106, table 4.6.

57. In a study undertaken among students at Columbia University (D. Caplowitz, H. Levy, "Inter-religious Dating among College Students," [Bureau of Applied Social Research, Columbia Univ., 1965]), social class emerged as a higher barrier to intermarriage than religion. See Israel Ellman, "Jewish Inter-marriage in the United States of America," *Dispersion and Unity* no. 9 (1964): 111–42. On individualization and its effect on the institution of marriage since the seventies, see Kosmin and Lachman, *One Nation under God*, 224–26.

58. Horowitz, *The 1991 New York Jewish Population Study*,. 57, tables 2.4 and 2.5, and 102, tables 4.2 and 4.3.

59. On the issue of church-state separation and the historical evolution of Jewish positions on the matter, see Jonathan D. Sarna and David G. Dalin, eds., *Religion and State in the American Jewish Experience* (Notre Dame: Notre Dame Univ. Press, 1997); cf. Naomi W. Cohen, *Jews in Christian America: The Pursuit of Religious Equality* (New York and Oxford: Oxford Univ. Press, 1992).

60. "Safeguarding Religious Liberty," statement by the Joint Advisory Committee of the Synagogue Council of America and the National Jewish Community Relations Council, 1957, revised 1971, as published in Sarna and Dalin, *Religion and State*, 238.

61. The Union of Orthodox Jewish Congregations of America, at its biennial convention in 1962, declined to take a definitive stand on federal aid to religious schools. It passed a resolution defending the U.S. Supreme Court's ban on prayer in public schools but saw "no problem" with silent meditation. Meanwhile, the Lubavicher Rebbe, Menachem Mendl Schneerson, urged the reversal of the Supreme Court's ban: see JTA, 29, no. 226 26 Nov. 1962, 2–3. Agudath Israel, representing the most traditionalist wing of Orthodox Jewry, told a House subcommittee in Washington in 1961 that "private schools had a right to benefit from government aid" (cited in Murray Friedman, *The Utopian Dilemma. American Judaism and Public Policy* [Washington, D.C.: Ethics and Public Policy Center, 1985], 32). For other dissident Jewish views on religion in the schools, see Sarna and Dalin, *Religion and State*, 215–16, 245–69; cf. Cohen, *Jews in Christian America*, 177–86.

62. See Naomi W. Cohen, *Not Free to Desist: The American Jewish Committee, 1906–1966* (Philadelphia: Jewish Publication Society, 1972), chap. 16; idem, *Jews in Christian America*; Marty, *Modern American Religion*, chaps. 14, 18; Stuart Svonkin, *Jews Against Prejudice* (New York: Columbia Univ. Press, 1997), 69–70, 77; Frank J. Sorauf, *The Wall of Separation: The Constitutional Politics of Church and State* (Princeton: Princeton Univ. Press, 1976); Donald E.

Boles, *The Bible, Religion, and the Public Schools* (Ames: Iowa State Univ. Press, 1965); Friedman, *The Utopian Dilemma*, 29–31.

In January 1960, the United States report to the U.N. Subcommittee on Prevention of Discrimination and Protection of Minorities included mention of the following as problems of "concern" to American Jews: Bible reading in public schools, "released time" for religious study, and Sunday closing laws for businesses: JTA, 27, no. 20, 29 Jan. 1960, 3.

63. Cohen, *Jews in Christian America*, 131–58; Marty, *Modern American Religion*, 228–29.

64. Cohen, *Jews in Christian America*, 166.

65. JTA, 27, no. 20, 29 Jan. 1960, 4.

66. Ibid., 167–71; 29, no. 26, 6 Feb. 1962, 4; Sarna and Dalin, *Religion and State*, 211–15; *American Jewish Year Book* 65 (1964): 42–44; ibid., 66 (1965): 218–26.

67. Luckmann, *The Invisible Religion*, 116.

68. Cohen, *Not Free to Desist*, 444–45; idem, *Jews in Christian America*, 171–86. In 1962, forty-nine (!) state governors voted at their annual conference to petition Congress to adopt a constitutional amendment to invalidate the Supreme Court ruling against official prayers in public schools. Only New York Governor Nelson Rockefeller abstained: JTA, 29, no. 127, 5 July 1962, 3.

69. Editorial in *Christianity and Crisis* by John C. Bennett (8 June 1964) quoted in Lucy Dawidowicz, "Church and State," *American Jewish Year Book* 66 (1965): 208; poll data cited ibid., 222.

70. Marty, *Modern American Religion*, chap. 14; Naomi Cohen, *Not Free to Desist*, chap. 16.

71. Norma Rosen, *Green, a Novella*, 74–78, 89–91.

72. Paul Goodman, *Growing Up Absurd. Problems of Youth in the Organized System* (1956; reprint, New York: Random House, 1960), 138–39, 143–44, 148, 154.

73. Luckmann, *The Invisible Religion*, 115–16.

74. Abraham Joshua Heschel, "The Religious Message," in *Religion in America: Original Essays on Religion in a Free Society*, ed. John Cogley (New York: Meridian, 1958), 256–57, 267–71.

75. Heschel, "No Religion Is an Island," *Union Seminary Quarterly Review* 21, no. 2, pt. 1 (Jan. 1966): 133.

76. Arthur A. Cohen, "The Myth of the Judeo-Christian Tradition," *Commentary* 48, no. 5 (Nov. 1969): 73–77.

77. Eugene B. Borowitz, *The Mask Jews Wear: The Self-Deceptions of American Jewry* (New York: Simon and Schuster, 1973), 139: "The New York Federation of Jewish Philanthropies . . . has long been considered by its critics a classic case of budgetary self-hate. Compared to the millions of dollars it channeled into settlement houses, clinics and welfare agencies to benefit an essentially non-Jewish clientele, the million-or-so dollars a year it gave to Jewish education, including America's largest community of impoverished Jews, seemed paltry."

78. Mordecai M. Kaplan, "Religious Imperatives of Jewish Peoplehood," address delivered at the convention of the Rabbinical Assembly, May 1959, published in *The Reconstructionist* 25, no. 9.

79. Soloveitchik, *Halakhic Man*, 42–43.

80. Eugene B. Borowitz, in *The Condition of Jewish Belief. A Symposium Compiled by the Editors of* Commentary *Magazine* (New York: Macmillan/ American Jewish Committee, 1966), 32.

81. Will Herberg, *Judaism and Modern Man: An Interpretation of Jewish Religion* (Philadelphia: Jewish Publication Society, 1951), 3; see generally 3–8.

82. Arthur A. Cohen, "The Natural and the Supernatural Jew: Two Views of the Church," in *American Catholics: A Protestant-Jewish View*, ed. Stringfellow Barr *et al.* (New York: Sheed and Ward, 1959), 131, 139.

83. Borowitz, *The Mask Jews Wear,* 200–203. Borowitz's point—that there could be no appeal against mass murder to a standard of absolute good if such a standard did not exist—is also stated in Saul Bellow's novel *Herzog*:

> But what is the philosophy of this generation? Not God is dead, that point was passed long ago. Perhaps it should be stated Death is God. This generation thinks . . . that nothing faithful, vulnerable, fragile can be durable or have any true power. . . . "You think history is the history of loving hearts? You fool! Look at these millions of dead. Can you pity them, feel for them? You can nothing! There were too many. We burned them to ashes, we buried them with bulldozers. History is the history of cruelty. . . . If the old God exists he must be a murderer." . . . Our own murdering imagination turns out to be the great power, our human imagination which starts by accusing God of murder. At the bottom of the whole disaster lies the human being's sense of a grievance, and with this I want nothing more to do. It's easier not to exist altogether than accuse God. (290)

84. Abraham Joshua Heschel, *The Prophets* (Philadelphia: Jewish Publication Society, 1962), xix.

85. Herberg, *Judaism and Modern Man,* 94.

86. The tenor of this discourse was finely captured by rabbinics scholar Jacob Neusner in 1966: "And who are these Jews, who cannot despite themselves achieve secularization? They are bearers of an unbroken myth, a this-worldly group affirming the world and joining in its activities with religious fervor. . . . They see their history as one history, though they are not everywhere involved in it. They reflect upon the apocalyptic events of the day as intimately and personally important to them. They died in Auschwitz. They arose again in Jerusalem and Galilee. They responded passionately, no matter how remote they are from Judaism, to the appeal of the flesh, of Israel after the flesh, and see themselves in a way that no one can call secular, no matter how secular they themselves would claim to be" (Jacob Neusner, "Judaism in the Secular Age," *Connecticut Jewish Ledger* [New Haven], Thursday, 14 July 1966, 5).

87. Soloveitchik, *Halakhic Man,* 91, 94.

88. In a public forum held at a prestigious Manhattan synagogue, B'nai Jeshurun, at the end of the sixties, Kaplan again emphasized his view that the "desegregation" of Jewish life in eighteenth- and nineteenth-century Europe was the root cause of the contemporary dilemmas of Jewish identity and survival, likening the emancipation of the Jews to an earthquake and a tidal wave. Consequently, he continued to view the issue as primarily sociological in nature and therefore, he retained his "sociological" view of American Judaism. See William Berkowitz, ed., *Let Us Reason Together* (New York: Crown Publishers, 1970), 73ff.

89. Ibid., 80–81. Kaplan restated his naturalist deism in the sixties ("Divinity is to be conceived as that aspect of nature which impels and helps man to transcend his animal nature") in his book, *The Purpose and Meaning of Jewish Existence* (Philadelphia: Jewish Publication Society, 1964), 58.

90. Kaplan, "Religious Imperatives"; cf. *The Condition of Jewish Belief,* 117–23.

91. See, for example, Borowitz, *The Mask Jews Wear,* 60, 62.

92. The phrase is originally that of Charles Péguy: *"être ailleurs"*—"Being elsewhere, the great vice of this race [the Jews], the great secret virtue, the great vocation of this people"—quoted by Gershom Scholem in his essay, "Jews and Germans," repr. in idem, *On Jews and Judaism in Crisis: Selected Essays* (New York: Schocken, 1976), 82.

93. Cynthia Ozick, "America: Toward Yavneh," *Judaism* 19, no. 3 (summer 1970): 278.

94. Ibid., 267–72.

95. The phrase is used by Ozick in her introduction to "Toward a New Yiddish" when the essay was republished in her collection of essays, *Art and Ardor* (New York: E. P. Dutton, 1983), 152.

96. "Toward Yavneh," 282.

97. Elie Wiesel, in his autobiography, *All Rivers Run to the Sea* (New York: Alfred A. Knopf, 1995), 292–93, relates that he began to avoid public prayer after he got to New York and that his crisis of faith manifested itself behaviorally when, in his first visit to Israel, he "forgot" for the very first time to put on his *tefillin* in the morning. "It was in Jerusalem, most sacred and spiritual of cities, that I first felt the need to protest against divine justice and injustice."

98. Elie Wiesel, *Night* (original French, *La Nuit,* 1958; English translation, © MacGibbon and Kee, 1960, published by arrangement with Hill and Wang, New York; quoted here from the Avon Books edition, New York, 1969), 76.

In his recent autobiography, Wiesel felt constrained to apologize for the death-of-God passage: "[That passage] has given rise to an interpretation bordering on blasphemy. Theorists of the idea that 'God is dead' have used my words unfairly as justification of their rejection of faith. . . . I have never renounced my faith in God. I have risen against His justice, protested His silence and sometimes His absence, but my anger rises up within faith and not outside it. . . . As I have said elsewhere, Auschwitz is conceivable neither with God nor without Him. Perhaps I may someday come to understand man's role in the mystery Auschwitz represents, but never God's." See idem, *All Rivers Run to the Sea,* 84.

99. Jean Ennis, "An Interview with Elie Wiesel," promotional blurb for *One Generation After* (New York: Random House, 1970).

5. Why Can't They Be Like Us? Race, Class, and Civic Culture

1. In September of that year, the Board of Education put into effect a program of school pairing and student busing in a new, but largely ineffective effort to meet integration goals, despite vocal white opposition and a two-day school boycott by white pupils' families. See Glazer and Moynihan, *Beyond the Melting Pot* (1963), 48; *American Jewish Year Book* 66 (1965): 180–81; Carl N. Degler, *Affluence and Anxiety: 1945-Present* (Glenview, Ill.: Scott, Foresman, 1968), 193: "Over half of the 700 public schools surveyed in New York City in the mid-1960s were either 90 percent Negro and Puerto Rican or 90 percent white."

2. Gary T. Marx, *Protest and Prejudice: A Study of Belief in the Black Community* (New York: Harper and Row, 1969 [1967]), 141.

3. The 1958 New York Jewish Federation survey predicted: "[T]he character of various neighborhoods is likely to be quite stable in the next decade and a half." It forecast wrongly that Jewish population in the area of West Harlem (west of Fifth, from 110th St. up to 155th) would *increase* from 5.5 to 8.3 thousand by 1975. The study also predicted that in 1975 African Americans, then some 11.6 percent of the population in New York City, would comprise only 14 percent. In fact, black New Yorkers were already 14 percent of the total by 1960; and by 1970, their share stood at about 20 percent. Horowitz and Kaplan, *The Jewish Population of the New York Area,* xi, 8; Nathan Kantrowitz, *Ethnic and Racial Segregation in the New York Metropolis. Residential Patterns among White Ethnic Groups, Blacks, and Puerto Ricans* (New York: Praeger, 1973), 22, 56.

4. Louis Harris and Bert E. Swanson, *Black-Jewish Relations in New York City* (New York: Praeger, 1970), 54–55, 60–63, 72–75.

Religion or ethnicity constituted only one set of factors that affected attitudes on race. College-educated Jews and (white) college-educated non-Jews supported integration by an almost identical margin (71–72 percent); age was clearly a factor as well: Jewish and white non-Jewish young adults under thirty-five years of age (70 and 69 percent respectively) supported integration.

5. Henry L. Feingold, "The American Component of American Jewish Identity," in *Jewish Identity in America,* ed. David M. Gordis and Yoav Ben-Horin (Los Angeles: Univ. of Judaism/Wilstein Institute, 1991), 76.

6. Arthur Hertzberg, "Changing Race Relations and Jewish Communal Service," presented at a symposium on "Jewish-Negro Relations," New York, Feb. 1964; published in *Journal of Jewish Communal Service* 41, no. 4 (summer, 1965): 324–33; cf. Ben Halpern, *Jews and Blacks, the Classic American Minorities* (New York: Herder and Herder, 1971).

7. In Graenum Berger, ed., *The Turbulent Decades: Jewish Communal Service in America, 1958–1978* (New York: Conference of Jewish Communal Service, 1981), 2: 888.

8. James Baldwin, "Negroes Are Anti-Semitic Because They're Anti-White," *New York Times Magazine,* 9 Apr. 1967 (repr. in *Blacks and Jews: Alliances and Arguments,* ed. Paul Berman [New York: Dell, 1994], 34, 38).
Compare this statement by Roger Wilkins: "It was a conversation I had had many times with white people who had grown up poor. They had known deprivation. They had been outsiders. They knew. It was all the same. . . . It was not the same. Being poor and white in my generation was not the same as being black and middle class. And it was surely not the same as being black and poor." Cited from Wilkins, *A Man's Life* in Jennifer L. Hochschild, *Facing Up to the American Dream: Race, Class, and the Soul of the Nation* (Princeton: Princeton Univ. Press, 1995), 122.

9. Baldwin, "Negroes Are Anti-Semitic Because They're Anti-White," in Berman, *Blacks and Jews,* 39.

10. James Baldwin, "The Harlem Ghetto: Winter 1948," *Commentary* 5, no. 2 (Feb. 1948): 169–70.

11. *New York Times,* 22 Feb. 1967, 34; 1 Mar., 29.

12. New York author Kate Simon claimed that New York had indeed achieved most (if not all) that the melting pot symbol entailed, although that "melting" was not an immediate result of the polyglot influx of immigrants early in the century. Rather, the various immigrant groups had, in the first generation, accommodated themselves to their new home by sectioning off their own home ground and observing invisible boundaries. Cross-cultural sharing and "swapping" occurred, she argued, only later—when the second generation, the youngsters emerging out of immigrant enclaves, laid claim to "the whole city": its night life, its baseball teams, its medley of Italian, Jewish, and Chinese foods. Only two groups, Simon admitted, had "not yet" won an assured place in this "free, restless flow, shift, and mixture. . . , these are the Negro and Puerto Rican populations, largely still restrained in too-enclosed areas"—Simon, *New York Places and Pleasures,* 17–20.

13. Harris and Swanson, *Black-Jewish Relations,* xviii-xix.

14. David T. Bazelon, "A Writer Between Generations," *Commentary* 47, no. 2 (Feb. 1969): 43–44; later published as the introduction to his collection of essays, *Nothing But a Fine Tooth Comb* (New York: Simon and Schuster, 1969).

15. David T. Bazelon, *Power in America. The Politics of the New Class* (New York: New American Library 1963), 142–43.

16. Horace M. Kallen, *Culture and Democracy in the United States* (1924; reprint, New York: Arno, 1970), 61.

17. On ethnic conflicts in New York in the 1930s and 1940s, see Ronald H. Bayor, *Neighbors in Conflict: The Irish, Germans, Jews, and Italians of New York City, 1929–1944* (Urbana and Chicago: Univ. of Illinois Press, 1988).

18. Paul Goodman, *The Empire City* (1942; reprint, Indianapolis and New York: Bobbs-Merrill, 1959), 25.

19. See Svonkin, *Jews Against Prejudice.*

20. Ibid., 192.

21. See Bettelheim and Janowitz, *Social Change and Prejudice,* 57.

22. Teller, *Strangers and Natives,* 259. Laura Hobson's autobiography, *Laura Z,* as Stephen Whitfield has pointed out, "revealed no interest in Judaic religion or values." See Whitfield, "The Paradoxes of Jewish Culture," *David W. Belin Lecture in American Jewish Affairs, 2* (Ann Arbor: Center for Judaic Studies, Univ. of Michigan, 1993), 17.

23. Svonkin, *Jews Against Prejudice,* 180, 191.

24. The belief that American Jews and blacks were comparable and, therefore, that blacks had "failed" in not following Jewish patterns, was not just a popular laymen's notion. "[S]ocial policy makers of the late 1950s and 1960s perceived education as the panacea for social problems [rather than] policies that responded directly to racist employment practices. . . . Given the conventional wisdom that children of uneducated Jewish immigrants were able, through hard work, to succeed once barriers were lifted, there were high expectations of black success. When supportive educational policies did not result in dramatic increases in black college graduates, many decided that internal inadequacies were responsible." Robert Cherry, *Discrimination: Its Economic Impact on Blacks, Women, and Jews* (Lexington, Mass.: Lexington Books, 1989), 192–93; Sherry Gorelick, "Jewish Success and the Great American Celebration," *Contemporary Jewry* 4 (1980): 40.

25. Baldwin, "Negroes Are Anti-Semitic Because They're Anti-White," in Berman, *Blacks and Jews,* 35.

26. Roy Innis, in *The Endless Crisis: America in the Seventies,* ed. François Duchene (New York: Simon and Schuster, 1970), 105.

27. Halpern, *Jews and Blacks,* 107.

28. Hochschild, *American Dream,* 150.

29. Chris McNickle, *To Be Mayor of New York: Ethnic Politics in the City* (New York: Columbia Univ. Press, 1993), 203, 205.

30. Charles Brecher and Raymond D. Horton, with Robert A. Cropf and Dean Michael Mead, *Power Failure: New York City Politics and Policy since 1960* (New York and Oxford: Oxford Univ. Press, 1993), 86. Cf. Halpern, *Jews and Blacks,* 117:

> It is striking that Jewish politicians have never had a recognized role among American Jews in any way comparable with their status in other groups. Not only the WASPs, with their established top leaders in national and local government, but the Irish, the Italians, and the Negroes, . . .accepted the ethnic politician, from ward-heeler to mayor and Congressman, as an essential instrument of their group adjustment. . . . [But] a Jewish politician is regarded as a Jew who is taking one of many available ways, and not a very noteworthy way, to advance himself in American society. If he gains the respect and recognition of Jews for his role, it is never at the ward-heeler's level or as an ethnic politician; it is only when he attains the stature of leadership in general American affairs."

31. Welles, "Jewish *Élan,*" 160.

32. JTA, 29 , 16 July 1962, 4.

33. Roger Waldinger, who has studied New York's ethnic and racial groups' economic development closely, noted that: "In World War II, desperate for workers, Jewish employers hired [first Italians, and then] blacks in great numbers. By 1950, there were 25,000 African American gar-

ment workers, 20,000 more than [in 1940]. . . . Blacks moved into less-skilled, poorer paying positions, from which mobility into better-remunerated positions proved difficult. Although the garment unions made explicit efforts to organize black workers and integrate them into union structures, few blacks moved up to elected offices. . . . To protect jobs from southern competitors, the unions adopted a policy of wage restraint, which inevitably meant a softened stance on union employers at home—much to the dismay of black New York garment workers." Roger Waldinger, "When the Melting Pot Boils Over: The Irish, Jews, Blacks, and Koreans of New York," in *The Bubbling Cauldron: Race, Ethnicity, and the Urban Crisis,* ed. Michael Peter Smith and Joe R. Feagin (Minneapolis: Univ. of Minnesota Press, 1995), 269–70.

34. Nancy L. Green, "Blacks, Jews, and the 'Natural Alliance': Labor Cohabitation and the ILGWU," *Jewish Social Studies,* n.s., 4, no. 1 (fall 1997): 79–104; Paul Jacobs, "David Dubinsky: Why His Throne Is Wobbling," *Harper's,* Dec. 1962: 75–84; idem, *Is Curly Jewish?* (New York: Atheneum, 1965), 311–13.
Gus Tyler, the union's assistant president (another New York Jew and a personal friend of both Hill and Jacobs), dismissed the entire affair as a red herring: Powell, he claimed, had cooked it all up to seek revenge against Dubinsky, who had refused to contribute to Powell's election campaign fund. Gus Tyler, in Rosenberg and Goldstein, *Creators and Disturbers,* 173–74.

35. Joel Schwartz, *The New York Approach: Robert Moses, Urban Liberals and Redevelopment of the Inner City* (Columbus: Ohio State Univ. Press, 1993); Jeanne R. Lowe, *Cities in a Race with Time: Progress and Poverty in America's Renewing Cities* (New York: Vintage/Random House, 1967), chap. 2; Joseph Epstein, "The Row over Urban Renewal," *Harper's,* Feb. 1965: 55–61; Fred J. Cook and Gene Gleason, "The Shame of New York," *The Nation,* special issue, 31 Oct. 1959: 284–300.

36. American Jewish Committee, *Group Life in America: A Task Force Report* (New York: Institute of Human Relations/American Jewish Committee, 1972). In 1968, in the wake of widespread rioting in American cities, the president appointed inquiry commissions. In its report on the roots of black poverty and disaffection, the Kerner Commission pointed to three options: a "present policies choice," an "enrichment choice" (greater federal outlays and programs for the ghettos), and an "integration choice"—and recommended the latter. The AJC task force's 1972 report, perhaps because of Jewish tendencies to favor economic, not race-oriented solutions, essentially opted for the middle choice.

37. Richard H. King, "Up from Radicalism," *American Jewish History* 75, no. 1 (1985): 67; (second quote:) Brecher, Horton, et al., *Power Failure,* 11.

38. Diana Trilling, *The Beginning of the Journey* (New York: Harcourt, Brace, 1993), 10. On the drift to particularism, see also Svonkin, *Jews Against Prejudice,* chap. 8.

39. Alfred Kazin, "The Writer and the City," *Harper's,* Dec. 1968, 116.

40. Kazin, in Rosenberg and Goldstein, *Creators and Disturbers,* 201, 207.

41. Phillip Lopate, *Portrait of My Body* (New York: Anchor Books, 1996), 274.

42. Malamud, *The Tenants,* 11, 22, 24–25, 173.

43. Nora Sayre, *Sixties Going on Seventies: New York for Natives* (New York: Arbor House, 1970), 313–14; Steven C. Dubin, "Harlem Still in Our Minds," *Commonquest/The Magazine of Black-Jewish Relations,* vol. 4, no. 2 (1999), 28–41.

44. Ibid., 315; Glazer and Moynihan, *Beyond the Melting Pot,* 77. Cf. Murray Friedman, *What Went Wrong? The Creation and Collapse of the Black-Jewish Alliance* (New York: Free Press, 1995); cf. Harris and Swanson, *Black-Jewish Relations,* 153–56.

45. Saul Bellow, "New York, the World-Famous Impossibility," repr. in idem, *It All Adds Up: From the Dim Past to the Uncertain Future* (New York: Penguin Books, 1994), 217–20.

46. Abraham Joshua Heschel, "The Spirit of Jewish Prayer," *Proceedings of the Rabbinical*

Assembly 17 (1953): 163. The phrase, "inescapable discrepancy [etc.]," is from Edward K. Kaplan, "The American Mission of Abraham Joshua Heschel," in *The Americanization of the Jews,* ed. Robert Seltzer and Norman Cohen (New York and London: New York Univ. Press, 1995), 366.

47. The religious moralism of the sixties was more self-consciously Jewish compared with the "social action" liberalism of turn-of-the-century Reform rabbis, according to historian Naomi Cohen, who notes the Reform movement's debt to the Protestant "social gospel" movement: "Liberal Protestants had fathered the new doctrines, and their adoption by Jews owed more to Christian influence than to any concerted Jewish interest in adapting the ethics of their heritage to the contemporary world." Naomi W. Cohen, *Encounter with Emancipation* (Philadelphia: Jewish Publication Society, 1984), 202

48. Bellow, *Mr. Sammler's Planet,* 278.

49. Ralph Ellison, "Harlem Is Nowhere," *Harper's,* Feb. 1964: 57.

50. Henry L. Feingold, "The Jewish Radical in His American Habitat," *Judaism* 22, no. 1 (winter 1973): 104.

51. Baldwin, "Negroes Are Anti-Semitic Because They're Anti-White," in Berman, *Blacks and Jews,* 37.

52. Nat Hentoff, *Black Anti-Semitism and Jewish Racism* (New York: Schocken, 1970), 232.

53. Stokely Carmichael quoted in the *New York Times,* 22 May 1967; Roy Innis, in Duchene, *Endless Crisis,* 107.

54. Ellen Willis, in "Pride, Prejudice, and Politics: Jews on the American Left," *Response* no. 43 (autumn 1982):. 17.

55. Jack Newfield, ibid., 12.

56. Malamud, *The Tenants,* 36. For a classic Jewish statement on this theme, see Earl Raab, "The Black Revolution and the Jewish Question," *Commentary* 47, no. 1 (Jan. 1969): 29.

57. Harris and Swanson, *Black-Jewish Relations,* 45, 80, 185–96.

58. Ibid., 4.

59. Ibid., 6–7.

60. Ibid., 108–13.

61. Ibid., 201–2.

62. Marx, *Protest and Prejudice,* 137.

63. Ibid., 21, 25. Thus, 60 percent of the Jews claimed that racial tensions were partly to blame for the lack of safety in the streets at night—as compared with only 40 percent among non-Jewish whites. Among Jews, 35 percent blamed racial tensions for their tax burden, though only 12 percent of non-Jewish whites did so. Similar gaps of 37 to 22 percent, and 33 to 18 percent, respectively, were found when Jews and non-Jews assessed the role of racial tension in the quality of schooling and in the moral atmosphere for children in the city.

64. Shlomo Katz interview, in Rosenberg and Goldstein, *Creators and Disturbers,* 59.

65. Harris and Swanson, *Black-Jewish Relations,* 27–40.

66. Ibid., 45; for data, see 44–54.

67. See Robert Huckfeldt and Carol Weitzel Kohfeld, *Race and the Decline of Class in American Politics* (Lexington, Mass.: Lexington Books, 1989); Hochschild, *American Dream.*

68. The pattern of rapid suburbanization was national. "Between 1950 and 1959," one major study pointed out, "over 99 percent of the 16.1 million population increase in the nation's metropolitan areas was reported outside of the central cities." In the single year of 1953, as many Americans moved to the suburbs as had entered the country as immigrants in 1907, the peak year for such entry: 1.2 million. By 1960, 32.8 percent of the U.S. population lived in cities and 30.9 percent in suburbs, and the suburbs took the lead in the next decade. See Raymond Vernon, *Me-*

tropolis 1985 (Cambridge: Harvard Univ. Press, 1960), 88ff, 135, and chap. 9 generally; Degler, *Affluence and Anxiety,* 186. For the detailed report of the research on which the Vernon book is based, see also Edgar M. Hoover and Raymond Vernon, *Anatomy of a Metropolis: The Changing Distribution of People and Jobs Within the New York Metropolitan Region* (Cambridge: Harvard Univ. Press, 1959).

69. Rosenwaike, *Population History of New York City,* 131–32; Vernon, *Metropolis 1985,* 158, 160–65; Hoover and Vernon, *Anatomy of a Metropolis,* 26–28; cf. Kantrowitz, *Ethnic and Racial Segregation*; Vernon, *Metropolis 1985,* 143ff., 152–53; Homer Hoyt, *The Structure and Growth of Residential Neighborhoods in American Cities* (Washington, D.C.: U.S. Government Printing Office, 1928); Vivian Klaff, "Models of Urban Ecology and Their Application to Jewish Settlement in Western Cities," in *Jewish Settlement and Community in the Modern Western World,* ed. Ronald Dotterer, Deborah Dash Moore, and Steven M. Cohen (Selinsgrove: Susquehanna Univ. Press/London and Toronto: Associated Univ. Presses, 1991), 140–41.

70. Kantrowitz, *Ethnic and Racial Segregation,* esp. chap. 1, chap. 5; data cited on 65ff.

71. Harold X. Connolly, *A Ghetto Grows in Brooklyn* (New York: New York Univ. Press, 1977), 129–30.

72. Degler, *Affluence and Anxiety,* 191. The view that segregation is normal is taken by Kantrowitz in the study cited above.

73. Kristol (1966), quoted in Peter K. Eisinger, *The Politics of Displacement: Racial and Ethnic Transition in Three American Cities* (New York: Academic Press/Harcourt, Brace, Jovanovich, 1980), 11.

74. Fred Massarik, "Basic Characteristics of the Greater New York Jewish Population," *American Jewish Year Book* 76 (1976): 238, 242; Horowitz and Kaplan, *The Jewish Population of the New York Area,* 17.

75. Historian Oscar Handlin wrote in 1957 that "Jews have been particularly susceptible" to the lure of the protection afforded by the suburbs against the "harshness of life" in the city. "For all groups, the move to the suburbs entails a reversal of the dynamic factors in the development of American culture in the past, factors which for at least a century emanated from the city. . . . That question is particularly significant for the Jews, for the cohesive elements in their past have been a complex of cultural traits derived from Europe but shaped in the matrix of American metropolitan life." See Oscar Handlin, "What Will U. S. Jewry Be Like in 2000? Two Views," *National Jewish Monthly,* May 1957, 5, 32.

76. Glazer and Moynihan, *Beyond the Melting Pot,* 57; Seymour Martin Lipset, in American Jewish Committee, *Group Life in America,* 52.

77. Sklare, "Jews, Ethnics, and the American City." 144.

78. Horowitz and Kaplan, *The Jewish Population of the New York Area, 1900–1975,* 108–9, 154–55, 184–85, 238–39.

79. Andrew M. Greeley and William C. McCready, *Ethnicity in the United States: A Preliminary Reconnaissance* (New York and London: John Wiley and Sons, 1974), 200: Among non-Jews, native Protestants showed the lowest percentage (6 percent) living in racially mixed census tracts; West European Catholics—8 percent; southern and eastern European Catholics—18 percent.

80. These findings bear out the observation, as restated by sociologist Vivan Klaff, that historically, "Jews tend to retain their affinity to the inner city more than non-Jews." In addition, it tends to fit with the results obtained for 1960 by Kantrowitz, who noted that the white foreign-stock population (immigrants, their children, and the third-generation under age fifteen) accounted for some three-quarters of New York City's population; outside the city, a much greater proportion of the inhabitants were native-born American adults with two native-born parents.

See: Klaff, "Models of Urban Ecology," 135, 141–43; Kantrowitz, *Ethnic and Racial Segregation,* 21–23.

Klaff cites a thirteen-city study of suburbanization patterns in the United States in the 1950s: "Negroes, other non-whites, Russians [i.e., predominantly composed of Jews], and Italians are distinctly more concentrated in the central city than is the total population." See P. H. Rees, *Residential Patterns in American Cities, 1960* (Research Paper no. 189, Univ. of Chicago, Department of Geography, 1979).

81. Hoover and Vernon, *Anatomy of a Metropolis,* 13, 84. In the fifties, over 80 percent of workers lived inside the same "zone" of the metropolitan area in which they worked (the five boroughs constitute one zone, followed by the "inner ring" of suburbs and finally an "outer ring."

82. Ibid., 70.

83. Ibid., 155.

84. Ibid., 164–67; Bernard Lazerwitz, "Jews in and out of New York City," *Jewish Journal of Sociology* 3, no. 2 (1961): 256.

85. More Jewish men and women were employed in the 1980s in the field of advanced corporate services, for example, than in wholesale trade (an older, but now depressed sector), and there were more Jews (both male and female) in corporate services than WASPs or whites from other groups. In finance and real estate, an area in which Jews were not generally prominent before the 1970s, there were still fewer Jews than WASPs, Italians, or Irish; but among Jews, this was a growing field in which almost as many of them found employment as in retail trade—a sector where Jews still formed a large presence. John Hull Mollenkopf, "The Postindustrial Transformation of the Political Order in New York City," in *Power, Culture, and Place: Essays on New York City,* ed. John Hull Mollenkopf (New York: Russell Sage Foundation, 1988), 228, 235–36, 255–56.

86. Edward Shils, *The Virtue of Civility: Selected Essays on Liberalism, Tradition, and Civil Society,* ed. Steven Grosby (Indianapolis: Liberty Fund, 1997), 4, 333–34, 340.

87. Edward C. Banfield and James Q. Wilson, *City Politics* (Cambridge: Harvard Univ. Press, 1963), 38–44, 229–231.

88. Edward C. Banfield and James Q. Wilson, "Public-Regardingness as a Value Premise in Voting Behavior," *American Political Science Review* 58, no. 4 (1964): 876–87.

89. See, e.g., Leonard Fein, *Where Are We?*; J. J. Goldberg, *Jewish Power: Inside the American Jewish Establishment* (Reading, Mass. and New York: Addison-Wesley, 1996); Milton Himmelfarb, *The Jews of Modernity* (New York: Basic Books, 1973); Stephen D. Isaacs, *Jews and American Politics* (New York: Doubleday, 1974); Irving Kristol, "The Liberal Tradition of the American Jews," in *American Pluralism and the Jewish Community,* ed. Seymour Martin Lipset (New Brunswick: Transaction Books, 1990); Halpern, *Jews and Blacks,* 93–141; William Spinrad, "Explaining American-Jewish Liberalism: Another Attempt," *Contemporary Jewry* 11, no. 1 (1990): 107–19; Michael Walzer, "Liberalism and the Jews: Historical Affinities, Contemporary Necessities," in *Studies in Contemporary Jewry,* vol. 11, *Values, Interests and Identity: Jews and Politics in a Changing World,* ed. Peter Y. Medding (New York: Oxford Univ. Press, 1995), 3–10. For a review and critique of approaches to Jewish liberalism, see Steven M. Cohen, *American Modernity and Jewish Identity* (New York and London: Tavistock, 1983), 135–39; Steven M. Cohen and Charles S. Liebman, *Two Worlds of Judaism: The Israeli and American Experiences* (New Haven and London: Yale Univ. Press, 1990), 96–99; Liebman, *The Ambivalent American Jew,* 135–59.

90. In actual practice, however, only 19 percent actually gave financial support to non-Jewish charities. Sklare and Greenblum asked whether this split between "universal humanitarianism" in ideology and parochialism in practice could long endure. Some three decades later, a study of

Jews in New York City found that Conservative, Reform, and secular Jews alike supported both Jewish and general charities, but that Orthodox Jews—who were the most intensively involved in giving money and volunteering time for charitable causes—tended to restrict their largesse to the Jewish community. Marshall Sklare and Joseph Greenblum, *Jewish Identity on the Suburban Frontier* (Chicago: University of Chicago Press, 1967), 329–30; Jerome S. Legge, Jr., "Understanding American Judaism: Revisiting the Concept of 'Social Justice,' " *Contemporary Jewry* 16 (1995): 97–109.

91. Cohen, *Encounter with Emancipation,* 117; on the ambivalent record of the New York Federation of Jewish Philanthropies regarding Jewish communal leadership, see Charles S. Liebman, "Leadership and Decision-Making in a Jewish Federation: The New York Federation of Jewish Philanthropies," *American Jewish Year Book* 79 (1979): 3–76.

92. Arthur Hertzberg, in *The Turbulent Decades,* ed. G. Berger, 2:853–54 (originally published in the *Journal of Jewish Communal Service* 41, no. 4 [summer 1965]: 324–33).

93. Edward I. Koch with William Rauch, *Politics* (New York: Simon and Schuster, 1985), 171.

94. Henry Feingold, *A Time for Searching,* 213: "So strong was Roosevelt's hold on Jewish voters that even Jewish socialists were drawn to vote for him. The American Labor Party was organized in New York State in 1936 . . . to give Jewish socialists an opportunity to cast their ballots for Roosevelt without compromising their principles." In 1944, Roosevelt headed the Labor Party ticket as well as the Liberal ticket (in addition, of course, to the Democratic ticket), and thus "retained his remarkable drawing power in all parts of the Jewish political spectrum."

95. Melvin Urofsky, *We Are One: American Jewry and Israel* (Garden City, N.Y.: Anchor/Doubleday, 1978), 333; cf. Arthur Hertzberg, *The Jews in America,* 347–48; Glazer and Moynihan, *Beyond the Melting Pot,* 168.
Kennedy brought two Jews into his cabinet: Arthur J. Goldberg—Labor Secretary; and Abraham Ribicoff—Health, Education, and Welfare; in 1962 Kennedy appointed Goldberg to the U.S. Supreme Court to fill the place of retiring Justice Felix Frankfurter.

96. Hertzberg, in *The Turbulent Decades,* ed. Berger, 2:861—originally appeared in *Journal of Jewish Communal Service* 41, no. 4 (summer 1965): 324–33.

97. Julie Miller and Richard I. Cohen, "A Collision of Cultures: The Jewish Museum and the Jewish Theological Seminary, 1904–1971," in *Tradition Renewed: A History of the Jewish Theological America,* vol. 2, *Beyond the Academy,* ed. Jack Wertheimer (New York: Jewish Theological Seminary of America, 1997), 311.

98. Ibid., 341ff.; Sam Hunter, "The Jewish Museum: What Is It, Why Is It, and What Next?" *New York Times,* 8 August 1965.

99. Himmelfarb, *The Jews of Modernity,* 80–81. Lindsay had campaigned strongly for the review board, which was meant to restrain police, whose crackdown on crowd control in ghetto neighborhoods had been portrayed as overly violent and possibly racist. The shooting by police of a black youth in Harlem in 1964 had touched off extensive rioting in the ghetto.

100. *American Jewish Year Book* 71 (1970): 217. In 1965, Lindsay's plurality citywide was 45.3 percent; in 1969: 41 percent. In 1965, an estimated 49 percent of Manhattan's Jewish voters backed Lindsay, while only 35 percent did so in Brooklyn and the Bronx. In 1969, with Lindsay pitted against Procaccino and Marchi, the heavily Jewish neighborhood of Forest Hills (Queens) went even more strongly for Lindsay than it had in 1965 (when candidate Abraham Beame did fairly well there). But Williamsburg (Brooklyn) went even more heavily for Lindsay's Democratic and Republican-Conservative opponents in 1969 than it had done in 1965. See Brecher, Horton, et al., *Power Failure,* 86, 90; cf. William F. Buckley, Jr., *The Unmaking of a Mayor* (New York: Viking, 1966), 333.

101. Brecher, Horton, et al., *Power Failure,* 93.

102. See McNickle, *To Be Mayor of New York,* 210–70; Brecher, Horton, et al., *Power Failure,* 83–94.

103. Glazer and Moynihan, *Beyond the Melting Pot* (1963), 315; ibid. (1970), viii.

104. Ibid. (1970), xiii, xxvii.

6. Fragment and Confront: The Politics of Division

1. Nora Sayre, *Sixties Going on Seventies,* 297–302.

2. *New York Times,* 22 Apr. 1964, 31 ("Negroes Attack Jewish Students"); 23 Apr., 41 ("Two Ghetto Worlds Meet in Brooklyn"); 26 Apr., 86 ("Rights Commission Studies Negro Attack at Yeshiva"); cf. 28 Apr., 38; 4 May, 20 ("Views Exchanged by Negroes, Jews"), 27 May, 1964, 1 ("Hasidic Jews Use Patrols to Balk Attacks"), and 27 May–28 July (passim); cf. *American Jewish Year Book* 65 (1965): 188–89; Abraham G. Duker, "On Negro-Jewish Relations—A Contribution to a Discussion," *Jewish Social Studies* 27, no. 1 (1965): 23–24; *Saturday Evening Post,* 27 June–4 July 1964, 32–36 ("The Maccabees Ride Again"); *U.S. News and World Report,* 13 July 1964, 62–64; cf. Hugh Davis Graham and Ted Robert Gurr, *Violence in America: Historical and Comparative Perspectives. A Report to the National Commission on the Causes and Prevention of Violence, June 1969* (New York: Signet Books, 1969), 187–88.

3. Graham and Gurr, *Violence in America,* 188–89, 192. *New York Times,* 11 Mar. 1966, 36, and 26 June 1966, 75.

4. On the 1964 riots in New York see Graham and Gurr, *Violence in America,* 381. The *New York Times* of 18 June 1964 reported on the activities of the Interracial Council for Business Opportunity, a group set up the previous October under the joint sponsorship of the American Jewish Committee and the Urban League of Greater New York. The Council, which was involved in extending technical advice and loans to black businesses in New York, found that only 18 percent of Harlem retail businesses were black-owned. Cf. "Remarks by Morris U. Schappes," *Jewish Social Studies* 27, no. 1 (1965): 61.

5. Graham and Gurr, *Violence in America,* 386.

6. Hentoff, *A Political Life,* 317–18; Sayre, *Sixties Going on Seventies,* 217–18; R. M. MacIver, ed., *The Assault on Poverty and Individual Responsibility* (New York: Institute for Religious and Social Studies/Harper and Row, 1965), 65, 68.

7. Bernard J. Frieden, *The Future of Old Neighborhoods: Rebuilding for a Changing Population* (Cambridge, Mass.: M.I.T. Press, 1964), 25, and for the data, see generally 20–26.

8. Brecher, Horton, et al., *Power Failure,* 72.

9. Hacker, *New Yorkers,* 83. On the rise of a school of social thought that promoted "community" perspectives on city life, see Schoenberg and Rosenbaum, *Neighborhoods That Work,* 1–12; Susan S. Fainstein, Ian Gordon, and Michael Harloe, eds., *Divided Cities: New York and London in the Contemporary World* (Oxford: Blackwell, 1992), 54; Roger S. Ahlbrandt, Jr., *Neighborhoods, People, Community* (New York: Plenum, 1984); Albert Hunter, *Symbolic Communities: The Persistence and Change of Chicago's Local Communities* (Chicago: Univ. of Chicago Press, 1974); Howard W. Hallman, *Neighborhoods: Their Place in Urban Life* (Beverly Hills: Sage Publications, 1984); William R. Williams, *Neighborhood Organizations: Seeds of a New Urban Life* (Westport, Conn.: Greenwood, 1985); Anthony Downs, *Neighborhoods and Urban Development* (Washington, D.C.: Brookings Institution, 1981); Diane Ravitch, *The Great School Wars: New York City, 1805–1973* (New York: Basic Books, 1974), 287–88. Cf. Nicholas Lemann, "The Myth of Community Development," *New York Times Magazine* 9 Jan. 1994, 27–31, 50, 54, 60.

10. Ravitch, *School Wars,* 288.

11. Martin Shefter, *Political Crisis, Fiscal Crisis: The Collapse and Revival of New York City*

(New York: Basic Books, 1985; New York: Columbia Univ. Press, 1992), 89. On the series of municipal union strikes in 1966, see Charles R. Morris, *The Cost of Good Intentions: New York City and the Liberal Experiment, 1960–1975* (New York: Norton, 1980), 83–99; cf. McNickle, *To Be Mayor of New York,* 210–14, and Sayre, *Sixties Going on Seventies,* 214. On the roles of the Johnson administration and of U.S. Senator Robert Kennedy (New York) in mandating community participation in the administration of poverty agencies, see Schoenberg and Rosenbaum, *Neighborhoods That Work,* 21–25; Fainstein, Gordon, and Harloe, *Divided Cities,* 52; P. Marris and M. Rein, *Dilemmas of Social Reform* (Chicago: Aldine, 1973); Norman Fainstein and Susan S. Fainstein, *Urban Political Movements: The Search for Power by Minority Groups in American Cities* (Englewood Cliffs, N.J.: Prentice Hall, 1974), chap. 2; Gans, *People and Plans,* 291; and cf. Frances Fox Piven and Richard A. Cloward, *Poor People's Movements: Why They Succeed, How They Fail* (New York: Pantheon-Random House, 1977), 271.

12. John V. Lindsay, *The City* (New York: Norton, 1970), 130 (also quoted in Hacker, *New Yorkers,* 83).

13. Hacker, *New Yorkers,* 87; cf. Morris, *Good Intentions,* 61–67. Morris notes that the drift toward empowering community activists was resisted by Mayor Wagner, Lindsay's predecessor. "Radical community organization was alien to Wagner's concept of government, and community control was antithetical to his instinct for controlling patronage. Although he was committed to better service programs for the poor, he expected them to be city programs run out of city agencies." Wagner set up an Antipoverty Operations Board and an oversight council (the Council Against Poverty); however pressures from New York Governor Rockefeller and the federal Office of Economic Opportunity derailed this effort. It was left up to Lindsay to "start completely over" (Morris, ibid., 62–63).

14. Morris, *Good Intentions,* 64–65: "Local community corporations, which would be completely independent of the city . . . [passed funding proposals to a supervisory council and] in turn, the community corporations would subcontract to a host of local organizations in the target areas, most of which were just being organized to operate programs since funds had become available." Cf. Sayre, *Sixties Going on Seventies,* 217, who writes that the chain of command in city welfare services almost ceased to exist, so that U.S. Secretary of Labor Willard Wirtz noted that New York had the worst administrative problems of any antipoverty program in any city.

15. Shefter, *Political Crisis, Fiscal Crisis,* xxi-xxii, 69–71, 94–95. Cf. Fainstein and Fainstein, *Urban Political Movements,* 55; cf. Brecher, Horton, et al., *Power Failure,* 33–37, 42–45.

16. Fainstein, Gordon, and Harloe, *Divided Cities,* 17.

17. Lowi, *Politics of Disorder,* 78–79.

18. Ibid., 54–59.

19. Ibid., 60.

20. Morris, *Good Intentions,* 65; Lindsay consultant: Douglas Yates, *The Ungovernable City* (Cambridge, Mass.: M.I.T. Press, 1977), 33–37 (cited also by Shefter, *Political Crisis, Fiscal Crisis,* xxv); cf. Nick Buck and Norman Fainstein, "A Comparative History, 1880–1973," in Fainstein, Gordon, and Harloe, *Divided Cities,* 50.

21. Naomi Levine, with Richard Cohen, *Ocean Hill-Brownsville: Schools in Crisis. A Case History* (New York: Popular Library, 1969); Diane Ravitch, *School Wars*; cf. Maurice R. Berube and Marilyn Gittell, eds., *Confrontation at Ocean Hill-Brownsville: The New York School Strikes of 1968* (New York and London: Praeger, 1969); Morris, *Good Intentions,* 108–16; Jim Sleeper, *The Closest of Strangers* (New York: W. W. Norton, 1990), 86–90, 98–103; Jonathan Kaufman, *Broken Alliance: The Turbulent Times Between Blacks and Jews in America* (New York: Simon and Schuster, 1988, 1995), 127–64; Hentoff, *A Political Life,* 244–61, 327–30; Maurice J. Goldbloom, "The New York School Crisis," *Commentary* 47, no. 1 (Jan. 1969): 43–58 (and see the

responses by Marilyn Gittell and Aryeh Neier, "The School Strike," *Commentary* 47, no. 4 [Apr. 1969]: 22–28, followed by Goldbloom's further response, 28–30.)

22. Ravitch, *School Wars,* 251–58.

23. Ibid., 258–86.

24. Ibid., 261, 270–79, 292; cf. Marjorie Murphy, *Blackboard Unions: The AFT and the NEA, 1900–1980* (Ithaca and London: Cornell Univ. Press, 1990), 234–39.

25. Murphy, *Blackboard Unions,* 209–37; Morris, *Good Intentions,* 101; Ravitch, *School Wars,* 285, 317. For a hostile account of the U.F.T.'s emergence as a powerful contender on the New York scene, see Robert J. Braun, *Teachers and Power, The Story of the American Federation of Teachers* (New York: Simon and Schuster, 1972).

26. Ravitch, *School Wars,* 251–86, 290, 309–10, 329–330; cf. Morris, *Good Intentions,* 27–33, 90–97; cf. Murphy, *Blackboard Unions,* 246–47.

27. Ravitch, *School Wars,* 268, 310–11.

28. Quite fortuitously, the Lindsay administration also discovered that by splitting the city's public school system into five separate administrative districts, it could substantially increase its education budget allotment from state funds. The state approved such a move, but mandated a comprehensive decentralization plan. Even the board of education apparently saw in the idea of local school boards some relief from the decade-long battle over school integration. See Ravitch, *School Wars,* 287, 293–94, 298, 305, 312; cf. Levine, *Schools in Crisis,* 11–28.

29. Levine, ibid., 12–14, 59; Ravitch, *School Wars,* 298–306, 313–14.

30. Ravitch, *School Wars,* 320–26; Levine, *Schools in Crisis,* 47–51; Kaufman, *Broken Alliance,* 146–50.

31. Ravitch, *School Wars,* 326–28; Levine, *Schools in Crisis,* 51–52; cf. Murphy, *Blackboard Unions,* 236–38; cf. Braun, *Teachers and Power,* 162–63, 214–31; Berube and Gittell, *Confrontation at Ocean Hill-Brownsville,* 176–87.

32. Ravitch, *School Wars,* 338–61, 368; Levine, *Schools in Crisis,* 52–58.

33. Ravitch, *School Wars,* p. 365; Levine, *Schools in Crisis,* 60–67.

34. Fainstein and Fainstein, *Urban Political Movements,* 90–123.

35. Rhody McCoy, speaking to an interviewer from WCBS-TV on 1 Oct. 1967, quoted in Levine, *Schools in Crisis,* 47–48.

36. Ravitch, *School Wars,* 369–70, 373; Levine, *Schools in Crisis,* 67–84; Berube and Gittell, *Confrontation at Ocean Hill-Brownsville,* 163–214; Morris, *Good Intentions,* 108–16; Murphy, *Blackboard Unions,* 241–46; Sleeper, *Closest of Strangers,* 101; Hentoff, *A Political Life,* 329–30.

37. Kaufman, *Broken Alliance,* 158–61; Julius Lester, *Lovesong, Becoming a Jew* (New York: Henry Holt, 1988), 50–65.

38. Sleeper, *Closest of Strangers,* 101; Morris, *Good Intentions,* 116; Kaufman, *Broken Alliance,* 154–55; Sayre, *Sixties Going on Seventies,* 215–16.

39. Hentoff, *A Political Life,* 245–46.

40. Ibid., 327.

41. Ravitch, *School Wars,* 348–49.

42. Levine, *Schools in Crisis,* 34–35.

43. Ravitch, *School Wars,* 335–36.

44. Sayre, *Sixties Going on Seventies,* 221.

45. Paul Cowan, *An Orphan in History* (Garden City, N.Y.: Doubleday, 1982), 52–53; *Jerusalem Post,* 21 May 1993 (magazine).

46. Arthur M. Schlesinger, Jr., "America, 1968: The Politics of Violence," *Harper's,* Aug. 1968: 22.

47. Walter Laqueur, "A Look Back at the Weimar Republic—The Cry Was, 'Down with *Das System*,' " *New York Times Magazine,* 16 Aug. 1970, sect. 6, pt. 1: 12–13, 25–34.

48. Ibid., 12.

49. *Commentary* 49, no. 2 (Feb. 1971).

50. Curt C. Silberman, "The American Jewish Community in Need of a Program," in *Conference on Intellectual Priorities in American Jewry* (New York: American Federation of Jews from Central Europe, 1972), 8.

51. Herbert A. Strauss, "The Immigration and Acculturation of the German Jew in the United States of America," *Leo Baeck Institute Year Book* 16 (1971): 93–94.

52. Ibid., 93.

53. Quoted by Schappes in his "Remarks," *Jewish Social Studies* 27, no. 1 (1965): 62.

54. JTA, 27, no. 15, 22 Jan. 1960, 2; 27, no. 19, 28 Jan. 1960, 3; 27, no. 26, 8 Feb. 1960, 3; 27, no. 88, 9 May 1960), 3; 27, no. 94, 17 May 1960), 3; 29, no. 15, 22 Jan. 1962, 1; 29, no. 37, 21 Feb. 1962, 1; 29, no. 54, 19 Mar. 1962, 2; 29, no. 61, 28 Mar. 1962, 1; 29, no. 155, 13 Aug. 1962, 3; 29, no. 226, 26 Nov. 1962, 1; 29, no. 230, 30 Nov. 1962, 2; 30, no. 1, 2 Jan. 1963), 2; 30, no. 5, 8 Jan 1963, 1; 30, no. 8, 11 Jan. 1963, 1; 30, no. 9, (4 Jan. 1963, 1; 30, no. 17, 24 Jan. 1963, 1; 30, no. 22, 31 Jan. 1963, 1; 30, no. 39, 26 Feb. 1963, 2.

55. JTA, 29, no. 5, 8 Jan. 1962, 2; 29, no. 40, 27 Feb. 1962, 1; 29, no. 48, 9 Mar. 1962, 2; 29, no. 51, 14 Mar. 1962, 3; 29, no. 53, 16 Mar. 1962, 1; 29, no. 139, 20 July 1962, press release from the office of Senator Kenneth B. Keating (special insert); 29, no. 235, 7 Dec. 1962, 3.

56. JTA, 29, no. 53, 16 Mar. 1962, 1; 29, no. 54, 19 Mar. 1962, 3.

57. While individual Jews had been prosecuted, the State Department said, it was "not clear from the available information . . . whether police action [of this type had] its actual basis in anti-Semitism or whether this arises from the presently intensified campaign of the Soviet authorities to stamp out . . . chronic abuses." It counseled against official U.S. intervention regarding the shipping of matzos to Moscow. In response, Jewish affairs activist Moshe Decter published a lengthy article in the prestigious journal *Foreign Affairs* that detailed what he called the official Soviet policy of "strangulation" of Jewish life in Russia, from the civic, political, and educational point of view in addition to linguistic, cultural, and religious deprivation. JTA, 29, no. 64, 2 Apr. 1962, 3; 29, no. 153, 9 Aug. 1962), 3; cf. 29, no. 61, 28 Mar. 1962, 3; cf. Moshe Decter, "The Status of the Jews in the Soviet Union," *Foreign Affairs* 41, no. 2 (Jan. 1963): 420–30.

58. JTA, 29, no. 94, 15 May 1962, 3; 30, no. 9, 14 Jan. 1963, 1.

59. JTA, 29, no. 45, 6 Mar. 1962, 3; William Orbach, *The American Movement to Aid Soviet Jews* (Amherst: Univ. of Massachusetts Press, 1979), 7–8, 18, 23.

60. Quoted in Orbach, *American Movement,* 5, from Abraham Joshua Heschel, "The Jews in the Soviet Union," 4 Sept. 1963 (paper presented at the Jewish Theological Seminary of America, New York), reprinted in Heschel, *The Insecurity of Freedom* (New York: Noonday, 1967), 273.

61. Orbach, *American Movement,* 5, 20–21, 27–31,38; Goldberg, *Jewish Power,* 165–66.

62. Elie Wiesel, *The Jews of Silence* (New York: Holt, Rinehart and Winston, 1966), 125, 127.

63. On the ways in which the 1967 war in the Middle East affected Diaspora Jewry, see Eli Lederhendler, ed., *The Six-Day War and World Jewry* (Bethesda: University Press of Maryland, 2001).

64. JTA, 34, no. 107, 2 June 1967, 1; no. 109, 6 June 1967, 1.

65. For a sample of how Israelis were portrayed to American Jewish audiences in the wake of the 1967 war, see: William Stevenson, *Strike Zion!* with a special section by Leon Uris (New York:

Bantam Books, 1967); cf. Ruth Bondy, Ohad Zmora, and Raphael Bashan, eds., *Mission Survival* (New York: Sabra Books, 1968).

66. Alfred Kazin, "In Israel: After the Triumph," *Harper's,* Nov. 1967, 72–85.

67. Irving Louis Horowitz, "Israeli Imperatives and Jewish Agonies," first published in *Judaism* 16, no. 4 (fall 1967) and reprinted in Horowitz, *Israeli Ecstasies/Jewish Agonies* (New York: Oxford Univ. Press, 1974), 4, 6.

68. Saul Bellow, "Report on Israel," *Newsday,* 12, 13, and 16 June 1967, republished as "Israel: The Six-Day War," in Bellow, *It All Adds Up,* 206–7, 211.

69. Bellow, *Mr. Sammler's Planet,* 263–64.

70. Teller, *Strangers and Natives,* 287.

71. Arthur Hertzberg, "The Tragedy of Victory," in Hertzberg, *Jewish Polemics* (New York: Columbia Univ. Press, 1992), 32 (originally published in the *New York Review of Books,* 28 May 1987); Peter Y. Medding, "Segmented Ethnicity and the New Jewish Politics," *Studies in Contemporary Jewry,* vol. 3, *Jews and Other Ethnic Groups in a Multi-ethnic World,* ed. Ezra Mendelsohn (New York: Oxford Univ. Press, 1987), 26–48.

72. Zvi Gitelman, "The Psychological and Political Consequences of the Six-Day War in the USSR," *Six-Day War,* ed. Eli Lederhendler, 251–69.

73. Quoted in Isaacs, *Jews and American Politics,* 161–62. On the rejection of earlier integrationist models and the turn to "survivalism," see also Steven M. Cohen and Leonard J. Fein, "From Integration to Survival: American Jewish Anxieties in Transition," *Annals of the American Academy of Political and Social Science* 480 (July 1985): 75–88. A similar point is made by Stuart Svonkin in assessing the end of Jewish communal agencies' fifties-style commitment to civic integrationism. See Svonkin, *Jews Against Prejudice,* chap. 8.

74. Yosef I. Abramowitz, "To 1969 and Back," 16–26; cf. Orbach, *American Movement,* 40, 46.

75. Stanley S. Clawar, "Neo-Vigilantism in America: An Analysis of the Jewish Defense League" (Ph.D. diss., Bryn Mawr College, 1976); Janet L. Dolgin, *Jewish Identity and the JDL* (Princeton: Princeton Univ. Press, 1977), 16, n.6; Robert I. Friedman, *The False Prophet: Rabbi Meir Kahane, from FBI Informant to Knesset Member* (Brooklyn: Lawrence Hill Books, 1990), 4–5, 46–57; *New York Times,* 24 Jan. 1971, 1 ("The Complex Past of Meir Kahane").

76. The JDL picketed the Metropolitan Museum of Art on 20 January 1969 (see *New York Times* for that date, 22), and blocked the entrance of Temple Emanu-El against the expected arrival of black activist James Forman to demand reparations from the white community (Forman never showed up) on 10 May 1969 *(New York Times,* 18 May, 81, and 19 May, 33).

77. See, for example, Dolgin, *Jewish Identity and the JDL,* 8; Halevi, *Memoirs of a Jewish Extremist,* 77–79.

78. Bellow, *It All Adds Up,* 208–10; idem, *Mr. Sammler's Planet,* 227–31, 264–66.

79. In Jerusalem, in the seventies, the JDL opened an exhibit about antisemitism in America in what it dubbed, "the Museum of the Potential Holocaust."

80. Irving Howe, *Margin of Hope,* 314–15.

81. Kazin, *New York Jew,* 396.

82. See, e.g., Arthur Liebman, *Jews and the Left* (New York: John Wiley and Sons, 1979), 440, 540–64; cf. Stanley Rothman and S. Robert Lichter, *Roots of Radicalism: Jews, Christians, and the New Left* (New York and Oxford: Oxford Univ. Press, 1982); cf. Nathan Glazer, "The Jewish Role in Student Activism," in Glazer, *Remembering the Answers: Essays on the American Student Revolt* (New York: Basic Books, 1970), 222–44.

83. Kazin, *New York Jew,* 396; Howe, *Margin of Hope,* 315, and cf. also 286–87, 300–304,

309, 311, 318, 320–21, 326; idem, "Torment and Therapy," *Harper's*, July 1968: 102–3; cf. Todd Gitlin, *The Sixties*, 54–66, 75–77, 110.

84. Gitlin, *The Sixties*, 110.

85. Gitlin records the meeting as occurring in October 1963; Howe says that it was in 1962. Gitlin, *The Sixties*, 171; Howe, *Margin of Hope*, 291.

86. Gitlin, *The Sixties*, 171, and cf. generally 171–77.

87. Ibid., 175. *Pisher*: Yiddish slang: "still in diapers," or literally, one who wets himself: a dismissive reference to the young and inexperienced, equivalent to the English, "wet behind the ears."

88. Johanna Kaplan, *O My America!* (Syracuse: Syracuse Univ. Press, 1980), 256–57.

89. Howe, *Margin of Hope*, 301, 309, 311, 320.

7. City and Ethnicity

1. Anne Michaels's *Fugitive Pieces* actually does not refer to New York City. My apologies for using a reference to Toronto in this context, but the remark is equally apt for New York.

2. Avrom Reisin, *Di lider fun Avrom Reisin in tsvelf teyln (1891–1951)* (New York: Shulsinger, 1951), 153. Translation by EL.

3. Thomas Bender, "Metropolitan Life and the Making of Public Culture," in *Power, Culture, and Place: Essays on New York City*, ed. John Hull Mollenkopf (New York: Russell Sage Foundation, 1988), 262–63.

4. Ibid., 264, 268–69.

5. *New York Times Magazine*, 19 Oct. 1997, sect. 6: "New York's Parallel Lives: A City of Subcultures, Side by Side."

6. Gary Rosenblatt, "A Walk on the Wild Side," *Jewish Week*, 6–12 Aug. 1993, 17.

7. Cooley, *The Archivist*, 123.

8. Budick, *Blacks and Jews in Literary Conversation*, 96.

9. Kazin, *New York Jew*, 450.

10. Kaplan, *O My America*, 140.

Works Cited

Abel, Lionel. "New York City: A Remembrance." *Dissent* (summer 1961): 251.

———. "The Aesthetics of Evil." *Partisan Review* 30 (1963): 219.

Abramowitz, Yosef I. "To 1969 and Back." *Response* 63 (1995): 16–26.

Adorno, Theodor W., ed. *The Authoritarian Personality.* New York: Harper, 1950.

Ahlbrandt, Roger S., Jr. *Neighborhoods, People, Community.* New York: Plenum, 1984.

Alter, Robert. *After the Tradition: Essays on Modern Jewish Writing.* New York: E. P. Dutton, 1971.

American Jewish Committee. *Group Life in America: A Task Force Report.* New York: Institute of Human Relations/American Jewish Committee, 1972.

Ansky, S. *The Dybbuk and Other Writings.* Edited and with an Introduction by David G. Roskies,

Arendt, Hannah. "Creating a Cultural Atmosphere." *Commentary* 4, no. 5 (1947): 424.

———. *The Origins of Totalitarianism.* New ed. New York: Harcourt, Brace, 1973.

———. *Eichmann in Jerusalem: A Report on the Banality of Evil.* Rev. ed. New York: The Viking Press, 1964.

Auletta, Ken. *The Streets Were Paved with Gold.* New York: Random House, 1979.

Baldwin, James. "The Harlem Ghetto: Winter 1948." *Commentary* 5, no. 2 (1948): 165–70.

———. "Negroes Are Anti-Semitic Because They're Anti-White." *New York Times Magazine,* 9 Apr. 1967: 26–27, 135–40. Reprint. In *Blacks and Jews: Alliances and Arguments,* edited by Paul Berman, 31–41. New York: Dell, 1994.

———. "On Being 'White' and Other Lies." *Essence,* Apr. 1984: 90–92.

Banfield, Edward C., and James Q. Wilson. *City Politics.* Cambridge: Harvard Univ. Press, 1963.

———. "Public-Regardingness as a Value Premise in Voting Behavior." *American Political Science Review* 58, no. 4 (1964): 876–87.

Baron, Salo W. "The American Experience." In *Great Ages and Ideas of the Jewish People,* edited by Leo W. Schwarz, 480–81. New York: Random House/Modern Library, 1956.

———. *Steeled by Adversity: Essays and Addresses on American Jewish Life.* Edited by Jeannette Meisel Baron. Philadelphia: Jewish Publication Society, 1971.

Baumgarten, Murray. *City Scriptures: Modern Jewish Writing.* Cambridge: Harvard Univ. Press, 1982.

Bayor, Ronald H. *Neighbors in Conflict: The Irish, Germans, Jews, and Italians of New York City, 1929–1944.* Urbana and Chicago: Univ. of Illinois Press, 1988.

Bazelon, David T. *Power in America: The Politics of the New Class.* New York: New American Library, 1963.

———. *Nothing But a Fine Tooth Comb.* New York: Simon and Schuster, 1969.

Bell, Daniel. "The Theory of Mass Society: A Critique." *Commentary* 22, no. 1 (1956): 75–83.

———. *The End of Ideology: On the Exhaustion of Political Ideas in the Fifties.* New York: Free Press, 1960.

———. "The Three Faces of New York." *Dissent* (summer 1961): 223–24.

———. "Reflections on Jewish Identity." In *The Winding Passage: Essays and Sociological Journeys, 1960–1980.* Cambridge: Abt Books, 1980.

———. *The Winding Passage: Essays and Sociological Journeys, 1960–1980.* Cambridge: Abt Books, 1980.

Bellow, Saul. *Herzog.* New York: Viking, 1964.

———. *Mr. Sammler's Planet.* Greenwich: Fawcett Crest, 1969.

———. *It All Adds Up: From the Dim Past to the Uncertain Future.* New York: Penguin Books, 1994.

Bender, Thomas. "Metropolitan Life and the Making of Public Culture." In *Power, Culture, and Place: Essays on New York City,* edited by John Hull Mollenkopf. New York: Russell Sage Foundation, 1988. 261–271.

Bentley, Eric. *The Storm over "The Deputy."* New York: Grove Press, 1964.

Berger, Bennett M. *Looking for America.* Englewood Cliffs: Prentice-Hall, 1971.

Berger, Graenum, ed. *The Turbulent Decades: Jewish Communal Service in America, 1958–1978,* 2 vols. New York: Conference of Jewish Communal Service, 1981.

Berkovits, Eliezer. "From the Temple to Synagogue and Back." *Judaism* 8, no. 4 (1959): 303–11.

Berkowitz, William, ed. *Let Us Reason Together.* New York: Crown Publishers, 1970.

Berman, Marshall. "Ruins and Reforms: New York Yesterday and Today." *Dissent* Special Issue (fall 1987): 421–28.

Bernstein, Burt. "Leonard Bernstein's Separate Peace with Berlin." *Esquire,* Oct. 1961: 93–96, 162–63.

Berube, Maurice R., and Marilyn Gittell, eds. *Confrontation at Ocean Hill-Brownsville: The New York School Strikes of 1968.* New York and London: Praeger, 1969.

Bettelheim, Bruno. *The Informed Heart: Autonomy in a Mass Age.* New York: Free Press, 1960.

Bettelheim, Bruno, and Morris Janowitz. *Social Change and Prejudice.* New York: Free Press, 1964.

Binder, Frederick M., and David M. Riemers. *All the Nations under Heaven: An Ethnic and Racial History of New York City.* New York: Columbia Univ. Press, 1995.

Bloom, Alexander. *Prodigal Sons: The New York Intellectuals and Their World.* New York and Oxford: Oxford Univ. Press, 1986.

Boles, Donald E. *The Bible, Religion, and the Public Schools.* Ames: Iowa State Univ. Press, 1965.

Bondy, Ruth, Ohad Zmora, and Raphael Bashan, eds. *Mission Survival.* New York: Sabra Books, 1968.

Boorstin, Daniel. *The Americans: The Democratic Experience.* New York: Random House, 1973.

Borowitz, Eugene B. *A New Jewish Theology in the Making.* Philadelphia: Westminster Press, 1968.

———. *The Mask Jews Wear: The Self-Deceptions of American Jewry.* New York: Simon and Schuster, 1973.

Brandes, Joseph. *Immigrants to Freedom.* Philadelphia: Jewish Publication Society, 1971.

Braun, Robert J. *Teachers and Power, The Story of the American Federation of Teachers.* New York: Simon and Schuster, 1972.

Brecher, Charles, and Raymond D. Horton, with Robert A. Cropf and Dean Michael Mead. *Power Failure: New York City Politics and Policy since 1960.* New York and Oxford: Oxford Univ. Press, 1993.

Buck, Nick, and Norman Fainstein. "A Comparative History, 1880–1973." In, *Divided Cities: New York and London in the Contemporary World.*, edited by Susan Fainstein, Ian Gordon, and Michael Harloe. Oxford: Blackwell, 1992.

Buckley, William F., Jr. *The Unmaking of a Mayor.* New York: Viking, 1966.

Budick, Emily Miller. *Blacks and Jews in Literary Conversation.* Cambridge: Cambridge Univ. Press, 1998.

Calischer, Hortense. *The New Yorkers.* London: Jonathan Cape, 1966.

Caplowitz, D., and H. Levy. *Inter-religious Dating among College Students.* Bureau of Applied Social Research, Columbia Univ., 1965.

Cherry, Robert. *Discrimination: Its Economic Impact on Blacks, Women, and Jews.* Lexington, Mass.: Lexington Books, 1989.

Clawar, Stanley S. "Neo-Vigilantism in America: An Analysis of the Jewish Defense League." Ph.D. diss., Bryn Mawr College, 1976.

Cohen, Arthur A. "The Natural and the Supernatural Jew: Two Views of the Church." In *American Catholics: A Protestant-Jewish View,* edited by Stringfellow Barr *et al.,* 127–57. New York: Sheed and Ward, 1959.

———. "The Myth of the Judeo-Christian Tradition." *Commentary* 48, no. 5 (1969): 73–77.

Cohen, Naomi W. *Not Free to Desist: The American Jewish Committee, 1906–1966.* Philadelphia: Jewish Publication Society, 1972.

———. *Encounter with Emancipation.* Philadelphia: Jewish Publication Society, 1984.

———. *Jews in Christian America: The Pursuit of Religious Equality.* New York and Oxford: Oxford Univ. Press, 1992.

Cohen, Shaye J. D., and Edward Greenstein, eds. *The State of Jewish Studies.* Detroit/New York: Wayne State Univ. Press/ Jewish Theological Seminary of America, 1990.

Cohen, Richard I. "Breaking the Code: Hannah Arendt's *Eichmann in Jerusalem* and the Public Polemic. Myth, Memory, and Historical Imagination." *Michael* 13 (1993): 29–85.

Cohen, Steven M. *American Modernity and Jewish Identity.* New York and London: Tavistock, 1983.

———. *American Assimilation or Jewish Revival?* Bloomington: Indiana Univ. Press, 1988.

Cohen, Steven M., and Leonard J. Fein. "From Integration to Survival: American Jewish Anxieties in Transition." *Annals of the American Academy of Political and Social Science* 480 (1985): 75–88.

Cohen, Steven M., and Charles S. Liebman. *Two Worlds of Judaism: The Israeli and American Experiences.* New Haven and London: Yale Univ. Press, 1990.

The Condition of Jewish Belief: A Symposium Compiled by the Editors of "Commentary" Magazine. Introduced by Milton Himmelfarb. New York: Macmillan/American Jewish Committee, 1966.

Conference on Intellectual Priorities in American Jewry. New York: American Federation of Jews From Central Europe, 1972.

Connolly, Harold X. *A Ghetto Grows in Brooklyn.* New York: New York Univ. Press, 1977.

Cook, Fred J., and Gene Gleason."The Shame of New York," *The Nation,* Special Issue, 31 Oct. 1959: 284–300.

Cooley, Martha. *The Archivist.* London: Abacus/ Boston: Little, Brown, 1998.

Cooney, Terry A. *The Rise of the New York Intellectuals: "Partisan Review" and Its Circle.* Madison: Univ. of Wisconsin Press, 1986.

Cowan, Paul *An Orphan in History.* Garden City: Doubleday, 1982.

Dawidowicz, Lucy S. "Middle-Class Judaism: A Case Study." *Commentary* 29, no. 6 (1960): 492–503.

———. "Church and State." *American Jewish Year Book* 66 (1965) 208–229.

———. *From That Place and Time: A Memoir, 1938–1947.* New York: Bantam, 1989.

Decter, Moshe. "The Status of the Jews in the Soviet Union." *Foreign Affairs* 41, no. 2 (1963): 420–30.

Degler, Carl N. *Affluence and Anxiety: 1945-Present.* Glenview, Ill.: Scott, Foresman, 1968.

DellaPergola, Sergio, and Nitza Genuth, *Jewish Education Attained in Diaspora Communities: Data for the 1970s. Jewish Educational Statistics Research Paper 2.* Jerusalem: Hebrew Univ., Institute of Contemporary Jewry, 1983.

Deutsch, Martin. *The 1960 Swastika Smearings: Analysis of the Apprehended Youth* (New York: Anti-Defamation League of B'nai B'rith; reprintes from *Merrill-Palmer Quarterly of Behavior and Development* (Apr.1962).

Dickstein, Morris. *Gates of Eden: American Culture in the Sixties.* New York: Basic Books, 1977.

Dinnerstein, Leonard. *America and the Survivors of the Holocaust.* New York: Columbia Univ. Press, 1982.

———. *Antisemitism in America.* New York and Oxford: Oxford Univ. Press, 1994.

Dissent 8 (summer, 1961).

Dolgin, Janet L. *Jewish Identity and the JDL.* Princeton: Princeton Univ. Press, 1977.

Dostoyevsky, Fyodor. *The Brothers Karamazov.* 2 vols. Translated by David Magarshack. London: Penguin, 1970 [1958].

Downs, Anthony. *Neighborhoods and Urban Development.* Washington, D.C.: Brookings Institution, 1981.

Drachsler, Julius. *Democracy and Assimilation: The Blending of Immigrant Heritages in America.* New York: Macmillan, 1920.

Drake, St. Clair, and Horace R. Cayton. *Black Metropolis: A Study of Negro Life in a Northern City.* New York: Harcourt, Brace, 1945.

Drennan, Matthew P. "The Decline and Rise of the New York Economy." In *Dual City: Restructuring New York,* edited by John H. Mollenkopf and Manuel Castells. New York: Russell Sage Foundation, 1991.

Dubin, Steven C. "Harlem Still on Our Minds." *Commonquest, the Magazine of Black/Jewish Relations* 4, no. 2 (1999): 28–41.

Duchene, Franáois, ed. *The Endless Crisis: America in the Seventies* New York: Simon and Schuster, 1970.

Duker, Abraham G. "On Negro-Jewish Relations—A Contribution to a Discussion." *Jewish Social Studies* [old series] 27, no. 1 (1965): 23–24.

Eisinger, Peter K. *The Politics of Displacement: Racial and Ethnic Transition in Three American Cities.* New York: Academic Press/Harcourt, Brace, Jovanovich, 1980.

Elazar, Daniel J. *Community and Polity: The Organizational Dynamics of American Jewry.* Rev. ed. Philadelphia: Jewish Publication Society, , 1995.

Ellison, Ralph. "Harlem Is Nowhere." *Harper's,* Feb. 1964, 53–57.

Ellman, Israel. "Jewish Inter-marriage in the United States of America." *Dispersion and Unity* 9 (1964): 111–42.

Endelman, Todd M. *The Jews of Georgian England: Tradition and Change in a Liberal Society.* Philadelphia: Jewish Publication Society, 1979.

Endleman, Shalom, ed. *Violence in the Streets.* Chicago: Quadrangle Books, 1968.

Epstein, Joseph. "The Row over Urban Renewal." *Harper's,* Feb. 1965, 55–61.

Etkes, Immanuel. *Rav yisrael salanter vereishitah shel tnu'at hamusar.* Jerusalem: Magnes Press, 1982.

Fainstein, Norman I., and Susan S. Fainstein. *Urban Political Movements: The Search for Power by Minority Groups in American Cities.* Englewood Cliffs: Prentice-Hall, 1974.

Fainstein, Susan S., Ian Gordon, and Michael Harloe, eds. *Divided Cities: New York and London in the Contemporary World.* Oxford: Blackwell, 1992.

Fein, Leonard. *Where Are We?* New York: Harper and Row, 1988.

Feingold, Henry L. "The Jewish Radical in His American Habitat." *Judaism* 22, no. 1 (1973): 92–105.

———. "The American Component of American Jewish Identity." In *Jewish Identity in America,* edited by David M. Gordis and Yoav Ben-Horin, 69–80. Los Angeles: Univ. of Judaism/Wilstein Institute, 1991.

———. *A Time for Searching: Entering the Mainstream, 1920–1945.* Baltimore and London: Johns Hopkins Univ. Press, 1992.

———. *Lest Memory Cease: Finding Meaning in the American Jewish Past.* Syracuse: Syracuse Univ. Press, 1996.

Feldman, Ron H., ed. *Hannah Arendt, the Jew as Pariah: Jewish Identity and Politics in the Modern Age.* New York: Grove Press, 1978.

Fishman, Joshua A. "U. S. Census Data on Mother Tongues: Review, Extrapolations and Predictions." In *For Max Weinreich on His Seventieth Birthday: Studies in Jewish Languages, Literature, and Society.* The Hague: Mouton, 1964.

———. "Yiddish in America." *International Journal of American Linguistics* 31, no. 2, Part II (1965), Publication # 36 of the Indiana University Research Center in Anthropology, Folklore and Linguistics. Bloomington: Indiana Univ. Press/The Hague: Mouton, 1965.

———. "Di sotsiologye fun yidish in amerike: 1960–1970 un vayter." *Di goldene keyt* 75 (1972): 111–17.

———. *Yiddish: Turning to Life.* Amsterdam and Philadelphia: John Benjamin's Publishing, 1991.

———, ed.. *For Max Weinreich on His Seventieth Birthday: Studies in Jewish Languages, Literature, and Society.* The Hague: Mouton, 1964.

———, ed. *Never Say Die: A Thousand Years of Yiddish in Jewish Life and Letters.* The Hague: Mouton, 1981.

Frieden, Bernard J. *The Future of Old Neighborhoods: Rebuilding for a Changing Population.* Cambridge, Mass.: M.I.T. Press, 1964.

Friedman, Menachem. "Haredim Confront the Modern City." *Studies in Contemporary Jewry.* Vol. 2. Edited by Peter Y. Medding, 74–96. Bloomington and Indianapolis: Indiana Univ. Press, 1986.

Friedman, Murray. *The Utopian Dilemma. American Judaism and Public Policy.* Washington, D.C.: Ethics and Public Policy Center, 1985.

———. *What Went Wrong? The Creation and Collapse of the Black-Jewish Alliance.* New York: Free Press, 1995.

Friedman, Robert I. *The False Prophet: Rabbi Meir Kahane, from FBI Informant to Knesset Member.* Brooklyn: Lawrence Hill Books, 1990.

Fromm, Erich. *Escape from Freedom.* 1941. Reprint, New York: Avon, 1969.

Fruchter, Norman "Arendt's Eichmann and Jewish Identity." *Studies on the Left* 5 (1965): 22–42.

Gans, Herbert J. *People and Plans: Essays on Urban Problems and Solutions.* New York: Basic Books, 1968.

Gartner, Aryeh, and Jonathan D. Sarna, eds. *Yehudei artsot habrit.* Jerusalem: Shazar Center, 1992.

Gartner, Lloyd P. "Metropolis and Periphery in American Jewry." *Studies in Contemporary Jewry.* Vol. 1. Edited by Jonathan Frankel, 341–46. Bloomington: Indiana Univ. Press, 1984.

———, ed. *Jewish Education in the United States: A Documentary History.* New York: Teachers College, Columbia University, 1969.

Geertz, Clifford. *The Interpretation of Cultures: Selected Essays.* New York: Basic Books, 1973.

Gersh, Harry, and Sam Miller. "Satmar in Brooklyn, A Zealot Community." *Commentary* 28, no. 5 (1959): 389–92.

Gillette, Howard, Jr., and Zane L. Miller, eds. *American Urbanism: A Historiographical Review.* New York, Westport, and London: Greenwood Press, 1987.

Ginsburg, Shimon. "Nyu york." In *Antologiah shel hashirah ha'ivrit beamerikah*, edited by Menahem Ribalow. New York: Ogen Press, 1938.

Gitlin, Todd. *The Sixties: Years of Hope, Days of Rage.* Toronto, New York, and London: Bantam Books, 1987.

Glanz-Leyeles, Aaron (A. Leyeles). *Amerike un ikh.* New York: Der Kval, I. London, Publisher, 1963.

Glazer, Nathan. *American Judaism.* Chicago and London: Univ. of Chicago Press, 1957.

———. "City Problems and Jewish Responsibilities." *Commentary* 33, no. 1 (1962): 24–30.

———. "The Jewish Role in Student Activism." In *Remembering the Answers: Essays on the American Student Revolt.* New York: Basic Books, 1970.

———. *Remembering the Answers: Essays on the American Student Revolt.* New York: Basic Books, 1970.

———, "The National Influence of Jewish New York." In *Capital of the American Century: The National and International Influence of New York*, edited by Martin Shefter. New York: Russell Sage Foundation, 1993.

Glazer, Nathan, and Daniel Patrick Moynihan. *Beyond the Melting Pot: The Negroes, Puerto Ricans, Jews, Italians and Irish of New York City.* Cambridge, Mass.: M.I.T. Press, 1963.

Goldberg, B. Z. "The American Yiddish Press at Its Centennial." *Judaism* 20, no. 2 (1970): 224–28.

Goldberg, J. J. *Jewish Power: Inside the American Jewish Establishment.* Reading and New York: Addison-Wesley, 1996.

Goldbloom, Maurice J. "The New York School Crisis." *Commentary* 47, no. 1 (1969): 43–58.

Golden, Harry. *The Greatest Jewish City in the World.* Garden City, N.Y.: Doubleday, 1972.

Goldman, Ari. *The Search for God at Harvard.* New York: Ballentine Books/Random House, 1991.

Goldstein, Israel. *A Century of Judaism in New York.* New York: Congregation B'nai Jeshurun/Little and Ives, 1930.

Goldstein, Sidney, and Alice Goldstein. *Jews on the Move: Implications for Jewish Identity* Albany: State Univ. of New York Press, 1996.

Goodman, Paul. *The Empire City.* 1942. Reprint, Indianapolis and New York: Bobbs Merrill, 1959.

Goodman, Paul. *Growing Up Absurd: Problems of Youth in the Organized System.* 1956. Reprint, New York: Random House, 1960.

Goodman, Paul, and Percival Goodman. *Communitas: Means of Livelihood and Ways of Life.* 1947. Reprint, New York: Vintage Books/Random House, 1960.

Goodman, Saul. "Jewish Secularism in America—Permanence and Change." *Judaism* 9, no. 4 (1960): 319–30.

Gorelick, Sherry. "Jewish Success and the Great American Celebration," *Contemporary Jewry* 5, no. 1 (1980): 39–55.

Goren, Arthur A. *New York Jews and the Quest for Community.* New York: Columbia Univ. Press, 1970.

———. "The Promises of *The Promised City*: Moses Rischin, American History, and the Jews." *American Jewish History* 73 (1983).

Goren, Aryeh. "Haherut umigbelotehah." In *Yehudei artsot habrit,* edited by Aryeh Gartner and Jonathan Sarna, 239–58. Jerusalem: Shazar Center, 1992.

Gordon, A. I. *Inter-Marriage.* Boston: Beacon Press, 1964.

Graetz, Michael. *Haperiferiyah haytah lamerkaz.* Jerusalem: Mossad Bialik, 1983.

Graham, Hugh Davis, and Ted Robert Gurr. *Violence in America: Historical and Comparative Perspectives. A Report to the National Commission on the Causes and Prevention of Violence, June 1969.* New York: Signet Books, 1969.

Greeley, Andrew M. *Religion in the Year 2000.* New York: Sheed and Ward, 1969.

———. *The Denominational Society.* Glenview: Scott, Foresman, 1972.

Greeley, Andrew M., and William C. McCready. *Ethnicity in the United States: A Preliminary Reconnaissance.* New York and London: John Wiley and Sons, 1974.

Green, Nancy L. "Blacks, Jews, and the 'Natural Alliance': Labor Cohabitation and the ILGWU." *Jewish Social Studies,* n.s., 4, no. 1 (1997): 79–104.

Grinstein, Hyman B. *The Rise of the Jewish Community of New York, 1654–1860.* Philadelphia: Jewish Publication Society, 1945.

Gurock, Jeffrey. *The Men and Women of Yeshiva: Higher Education, Orthodoxy, and American Judaism.* New York: Columbia Univ. Press, 1988.

———. *American Jewish Orthodoxy in Historical Perspective.* New York: Ktav, 1996.

Hacker, Andrew. *The New Yorkers: Profile of an American Metropolis.* New York: Twentieth Century Fund, Mason/Charter, 1975.

Halevi, Yossi Klein. *Memoirs of a Jewish Extremist: An American Story.* Boston: Little, Brown, 1995.

Halkin, Shimon. *Ad mashber.* Tel-Aviv: Am Oved, 1945.

Hallman, Howard W. *Neighborhoods: Their Place in Urban Life.* Beverly Hills: Sage Publications, 1984.

Halpern, Ben. *Jews and Blacks, the Classic American Minorities.* New York: Herder and Herder, 1971.

Hammond, Phillip E., ed. *The Sacred in a Secular Age.* Berkeley, Los Angeles, and London: Univ. of California Press, 1985.

Hammond, Phillip E., and Benton Johnson, eds. *American Mosaic: Social Patterns of Religion in the United States.* New York: Random House, 1970.

Handlin, Oscar. "What Will U.S. Jewry Be Like in 2000? Two Views." *National Jewish Monthly* May 1957: 5, 32.

Harris, Louis, and Bert E. Swanson. *Black-Jewish Relations in New York City.* New York: Praeger, 1970.

Harshav, Benjamin, and Barbara Harshav. *Yiddish Poetry in America.* Berkeley, Los Angeles, and London: Univ. of California Press, 1986.

Heller, Joseph. *Good as Gold.* New York: Simon and Schuster, 1976.

———. *Now and Then, A Memoir: From Coney Island to Here.* New York and London: Simon and Schuster, 1998.

Helmreich, William. *Against All Odds: Holocaust Survivors and the Successful Lives They Made in America.* New York: Simon and Schuster, 1992.

Hentoff, Nat. *A Political Life, The Education of John V. Lindsay.* New York: Knopf, 1969.

———, ed. *Black Anti-Semitism and Jewish Racism.* New York: Schocken, 1970.

Herberg, Will. *Protestant, Catholic, Jew.* Garden City: Anchor/Doubleday, 1955.

———. *Judaism and Modern Man: An Interpretation of Jewish Religion.* Philadelphia: Jewish Publication Society, 1951.

Hertzberg, Arthur. "Changing Race Relations and Jewish Communal Service." *Journal of Jewish Communal Service* 41, no. 4 (1965): 324–33.

———. *The Jews in America: Four Centuries of an Uneasy Encounter.* New York: Simon and Schuster, 1989.

———. *Jewish Polemics.* New York: Columbia Univ. Press, 1992.

Heschel, Abraham Joshua. "The Spirit of Jewish Prayer." *Proceedings of the Rabbinical Assembly* 17 (1953): 163.

———. "The Religious Message." In *Religion in America: Original Essays on Religion in a Free Society,* edited by John Cogley, 256–71. New York: Meridian, 1958.

———. *The Prophets.* Philadelphia: Jewish Publication Society, 1962.

———. "No Religion is an Island." *Union Seminary Quarterly Review* 21, no. 2, pt. 1 (Jan. 1966).

———. *The Insecurity of Freedom.* New York: Noonday, 1967.

Hilberg, Raul. *The Politics of Memory: The Journal of a Holocaust Historian.* Chicago: Ivan R. Dee, 1996.

Himmelfarb, Milton. *The Jews of Modernity.* New York: Basic Books, 1973.

Hochschild, Jennifer L. *Facing Up to the American Dream: Race, Class, and the Soul of the Nation.* Princeton: Princeton Univ. Press, 1995.

Hofstadter, Richard. *American Violence.* New York: Alfred A. Knopf, 1970.

———. *America at 1750: A Social Portrait.* New York: Alfred A. Knopf, 1971.

Honan, William H. "The New Sound of Radio." *New York Times Magazine* 3 Dec. 1967. Reprint. In *Pop Culture in America,* edited by David Manning White, 105–19. Chicago: Quadrangle Books, 1970.

Hoover, Edgar M., and Raymond Vernon. *Anatomy of a Metropolis: The Changing Distribution of People and Jobs Within the New York Metropolitan Region.* Cambridge: Harvard Univ. Press, 1959.

Horowitz, Bethamie. *The 1991 New York Jewish Population Survey.* New York: New York UJA-Federation, 1993.

Horowitz, C. Morris, and Lawrence J. Kaplan. *The Jewish Population of the New York Area, 1900–1975.* New York: Federation of Jewish Philanthropies of New York, 1959.

Horowitz, Irving Louis. *Israeli Ecstasies/Jewish Agonies.* New York and Oxford: Oxford Univ. Press, 1974.

Howe, Irving. "New York in the Thirties: Some Fragments of Memory." *Dissent* (summer 1961): 241–42.

———. "*The New Yorker* and Hannah Arendt." *Commentary* 36, no. 4 (1963): 318–19.

———. "The Lower East Side, Symbol and Fact." In *The Lower East Side: Portal to American Life (1870–1924),* edited by Allon Schoener. New York: The Jewish Museum, 1966, 11–14.

———. "Torment and Therapy." *Harper's,* July 1968: 9.

———. *Steady Work: Essays in the Politics of Democratic Radicalism, 1953–1966.* New York: Harcourt, Brace, and World, 1966.

———. "Jacob Glatstein." *Jewish Frontier* 38, no. 11 (1971): 8–9.

———. *World of Our Fathers: The Journey of the East European Jews to America and the Life They Found and Made.* New York: Harcourt, Brace, Jovanovich, 1976.

———. *A Margin of Hope: An Intellectual Autobiography.* San Diego, New York, and London: Harcourt Brace, Jovanovich, 1982.

Hoyt, Homer. *The Structure and Growth of Residential Neighborhoods in American Cities.* Washington, D.C.: U.S. Government Printing Office, 1928.

Huckfeldt, Robert, and Carol Weitzel Kohfeld. *Race and the Decline of Class in American Politics.* Lexington, Mass.: Lexington Books, 1989.

Hunter, Albert. *Symbolic Communities: The Persistence and Change of Chicago's Local Communities.* Chicago: Univ. of Chicago Press, 1974.

Isaacs, Stephen D. *Jews and American Politics.* New York: Doubleday, 1974.

Jacobs, Jane. *The Death and Life of Great American Cities: The Failure of Town Planning.* New York: Random House, 1961.

Jacobs, Paul. "David Dubinsky: Why His Throne Is Wobbling." *Harper's,* Dec. 1962, 75–84.

———. *Is Curly Jewish?* New York: Atheneum, 1965.

———. *Prelude to Riot. A View of Urban America from the Bottom.* New York: Vintage, 1966.

Joselit, Jenna Weissman. *Our Gang.* Bloomington: Indiana Univ. Press, 1983.

———. *New York's Jewish Jews: The Orthodox Community in the Interwar Years.* Bloomington: Indiana Univ. Press, 1990.

Jospe, Alfred. "Religion in the University—A Terminal Case?" Inaugural Convocation, Interfaith Chapel, Univ. of Rochester, New York, 8 October 1970.

Kallen, Horace M. *Culture and Democracy in the United States.* 1924. Reprint, New York: Arno, 1970.

Kantrowitz, Nathan. *Ethnic and Racial Segregation in the New York Metropolis. Resi-*

dential Patterns among White Ethnic Groups, Blacks, and Puerto Ricans. New York: Praeger, 1973.

Kaplan, Edward K. "The American Mission of Abraham Joshua Heschel." In *The Americanization of the Jews,* edited by Robert Seltzer and Norman Cohen, 355–74. New York and London: New York Univ. Press, 1995.

Kaplan, Johanna. *O My America!* Syracuse: Syracuse Univ. Press, 1980.

Kaplan, Mordecai M. *The Purpose and Meaning of Jewish Existence.* Philadelphia: Jewish Publication Society, 1964.

———. "The Religious Imperatives of Jewish Peoplehood." *The Reconstructionist* 25, no. 9 (1959): 3–9.

Kapp, Isa. "By the Waters of the Grand Concourse." *Commentary* 8, no. 3 (1949): 269–73.

Karp, Abraham J. "New York Chooses a Chief Rabbi." *Publications of the American Jewish Historical Society* 44, no. 3 (1955): 129–98.

Katzburg-Yungman, Mira. " 'Hadassah'—'asiyah ve'ide'ologiah, 1948–1956." Ph.D. diss., Hebrew Univ. of Jerusalem, 1998.

Kaufman, Jonathan. *Broken Alliance: The Turbulent Times Between Blacks and Jews in America.* New York: Simon and Schuster, 1988.

Kazin, Alfred. *On Native Grounds: An Interpretation of Modern American Prose Literature.* New York: Reynal and Hitchcock, 1942.

———. *Contemporaries.* Boston: Little, Brown, 1962.

———. "In Israel: After the Triumph." *Harper's,* Nov. 1967, 72–85.

———. "The Writer and the City." *Harper's,* Dec. 1968, 110–19.

———. *New York Jew.* New York: Vintage, 1979.

Kessner, Carole S., ed. *The "Other" New York Jewish Intellectuals.* New York: New York Univ. Press, 1994.

Kessner, Thomas. *The Golden Door.* New York and Oxford: Oxford Univ. Press, 1977.

Kiel, Mark W. "A Twice Lost Legacy: Ideology, Culture, and the Pursuit of Jewish Folklore in Russia Until Stalinization." Ph.D. diss., Jewish Theological Seminary of America 1991.

King, Richard H. "Up from Radicalism." *American Jewish History* 75, no. 1 (1985): 61–85.

Klaff, Vivian. "Models of Urban Ecology and Their Application to Jewish Settlement in Western Cities." In *Jewish Settlement and Community in the Modern Western World,* edited by Ronald Dotterer, Deborah Dash Moore, and Steven M. Cohen, 132–53. Selinsgrove: Susquehanna Univ. Press/London and Toronto: Associated Univ. Presses, 1991.

Koch, Edward I., with William Rauch. *Politics.* New York: Simon and Schuster, 1985.

Koppman, Lionel. *Jewish Landmarks of New York: An Informal History and Guide.* New York: Hill and Wang, 1964.

Kornbluh, Andrea Tuttle. "From Culture to Cuisine: Twentieth-Century Views of Race and Ethnicity in the City." In *American Urbanism: A Historiographical Review,* edited by Howard Gillette, Jr. and Zane L. Miller. New York, Westport, and London: Greenwood Press, 1987.

Kortick, Joel. "Transformation and Rejuvenation: The Arrival in America of Habad and Other Orthodox Jewish Communities, 1940–1950." M.A. thesis, Hebrew Univ. of Jerusalem, 1996.

Kosman, Barry A., and Seymour P. Lachman. *One Nation under God: Religion in Contemporary American Society.* New York: Harmony Books, 1993.

Kriegel, Leonard. "In the Country of the Other." *Dissent,* Special Issue (fall 1987): 617–22.

Kristol, Irving. "The Liberal Tradition of the American Jews." In *American Pluralism and the Jewish Community,* edited by Seymour Martin Lipset, 109–16. New Brunswick: Transaction Books, 1990.

Krumm, John. "College Students and Religious Belief." *Columbia College Today* 10, no. 3 (1963): 18.

Kuznets, Simon. "Immigration of Russian Jews to the United States: Background and Structure." *Perspectives in American History* 9 (1975): 35–124.

Laqueur, Walter. "A Look Back at the Weimar Republic—The Cry Was, 'Down with *Das System.*' " *New York Times Magazine,* 16 Aug. 1970, sect. 6, pt. 1: 12–13, 25–34.

Lazerwitz, Bernard. "Jews in and out of New York City." *Jewish Journal of Sociology* 3, no. 2 (1961): 254–60.

Lederhendler, Eli. *Jewish Responses to Modernity: New Voices in America and Eastern Europe.* New York: New York Univ. Press, 1994.

———. "New York City, the Jews, and 'The Urban Experience.' " *Studies in Contemporary Jewry* Vol. 15, *People of the City: Jews and the Urban Challenge,* edited Ezra Mendelsohn, 49–67. New York and Oxford: Oxford Univ. Press, 1999.

———, ed. *The Six-Day War and the Jewish People in the Diaspora.* Lanham: Univ. of Maryland Press, 2001.

Legge, Jerome S., Jr. "Understanding American Judaism: Revisiting the Concept of 'Social Justice.' " *Contemporary Jewry* 16 (1995): 97–109.

Lemann, Nicholas. "The Myth of Community Development." *New York Times Magazine,* 9 Jan. 1994, 27–31, 50, 54, 60.

Lenski, Gerhard. *The Religious Factor.* New York: Doubleday, 1955.

Lerner, Max. *America as a Civilization.* New York: Simon and Schuster, 1957.

Lester, Julius. *Lovesong, Becoming a Jew.* New York: Henry Holt, 1988.

Levine, Naomi, with Richard Cohen. *Ocean Hill-Brownsville: Schools in Crisis. A Case History.* New York: Popular Library, 1969.

Leyvick, H. *Alle verk, band 1: Lider.* New York: H. Leyvick Jubilee Committee, 1940.

Liberles, Robert. *Salo Wittmayer Baron, Architect of Jewish History.* New York and London: New York Univ. Press, 1995.

Liebman, Arthur. *Jews and the Left.* New York: John Wiley and Sons, 1979.

Liebman, Charles S. "Orthodoxy in American Jewish Life." *American Jewish Year Book* 66 (1965): 21–97.

———. *The Ambivalent American Jew.* Philadelphia: Jewish Publication Society, 1973.

———. "Leadership and Decision Making in a Jewish Federation: The New York Federation of Jewish Philanthropies." *American Jewish Year Book* 79 (1979): 3–76.

Lief, Harold I. "Contemporary Forms of Violence." *Science and Psychoanalysis* 6 (1963): 56–63.

Lindsay, John V. *The City.* New York: Norton, 1970.

Lipstadt, Deborah E. "America and the Memory of the Holocaust, 1950–1965," *Modern Judaism* 16 (1996): 193–214.

Liskofsky, Sidney. "International Swastika Outbreak." *American Jewish Year Book,* 62 (1961): 209–13.

Lopate, Phillip. *Portrait of My Body.* New York: Anchor Books, 1996.

Lowe, Jeanne R. *Cities in a Race with Time: Progress and Poverty in America's Renewing Cities.* New York: Vintage/Random House, 1967.

Lowi, Theodore J. *The Politics of Disorder.* New York: Basic Books, 1971.

Luckmann, Thomas. *The Invisible Religion.* New York: Macmillan, 1967.

MacIver R. M., ed. *The Assault on Poverty and Individual Responsibility,* New York: Institute for Religious and Social Studies/Harper and Row, 1965.

Malamud, Bernard. *The Tenants.* New York and London: Penguin, 1972.

Marinbach, Bernard. *Galveston: Ellis Island of the West.* Albany: State Univ.of New York Press, 1983.

Marris, P., and M. Rein. *Dilemmas of Social Reform.* Chicago: Aldine, 1973.

Marty, Martin E. *The New Shape of American Religion.* New York: Harper and Row, 1959.

———. *Modern American Religion.* Vol. 3, *Under God, Indivisible, 1941–1960.* Chicago and London: Univ. of Chicago Press, 1996.

Marty, Martin E., Stuart E. Rosenberg, and Andrew M. Greeley. *What Do We Believe?* New York: Meredith, 1968.

Marx, Gary T. *Protest and Prejudice: A Study of Belief in the Black Community.* New York: Harper and Row, 1967.

Massarik, Fred. "Basic Characteristics of the Greater New York Jewish Population." *American Jewish Year Book* 76 (1976): 239–48.

Matthews, Fred. "Louis Wirth and American Ethnic Studies: The Worldview of Enlightened Assimilationism, 1925–1950." In *The Jews of North America,* edited by Moses Rischin, 123–43. Detroit: Wayne State Univ. Press, 1987.

Mayer, Egon. *From Suburb to Shtetl: The Jews of Boro Park.* Philadelphia: Temple Univ. Press, 1979.

McNickle, Chris. *To Be Mayor of New York: Ethnic Politics in the City.* New York: Columbia Univ. Press, 1993.

Medding, Peter Y. "Segmented Ethnicity and the New Jewish Politics." *Studies in Contemporary Jewry.* Vol. 3, *Jews and Other Ethnic Groups in a Multi-ethnic World,* edited by Ezra Mendelsohn, 26–48. New York: Oxford Univ. Press, 1987.

Menes, A. "The Am Oylom Movement." *YIVO Annual of Jewish Social Science* 4 (1949): 9–33.

Metzker, Isaac, ed. *A Bintel Brief.* New York: Ballantine Books, 1972.

Michaels, Anne. *Fugitive Pieces.* London: Bloomsbury, 1996.

Miller, Arthur. *Timebends: A Life*. London: Methuen-Minerva, 1987.

Miller, Julie, and Richard I. Cohen. "A Collision of Cultures: The Jewish Museum and the Jewish Theological Seminary, 1904–1971." In *Tradition Renewed: A History of the Jewish Theological America*. Vol. 2, *Beyond the Academy*, edited by Jack Wertheimer, 311–61. New York: Jewish Theological Seminary of America, 1997.

Mollenkopf, John Hull. "The Postindustrial Transformation of the Political Order in New York City." In *Power, Culture, and Place: Essays on New York City*, edited by John Hull Mollenkopf New York: Russell Sage Foundation, 1988.

———, ed. *Power, Culture, and Place: Essays on New York City*. New York: Russell Sage Foundation, 1988.

Mollenkopf, John H., and Manuel Castells, eds. *Dual City: Restructuring New York*. New York: Russell Sage Foundation, 1991.

Molodovsky, Kadia. *Lider fun khurbn, ta"sh-tash"ah: antologye*. Tel-Aviv: I. L. Peretz Farlag, 1962.

———. *Likht fun dornboym*. Buenos Aires: Farlag "Kiyum," 1965.

Moore, Deborah Dash. *At Home in America: Second Generation New York Jews*. New York: Columbia Univ. Press, 1981.

———. "The Construction of Community: Jewish Migration and Ethnicity in the United States." In *The Jews of North America*, edited by Moses Rischin, 105–22. Detroit: Wayne State Univ. Press, 1987.

———. "Jewish Migration in Postwar America," *Studies in Contemporary Jewry*. Vol. 8, *A New Jewry?* edited by Peter Y. Medding, 102–17. New York: Oxford Univ. Press, 1992.

———. "New York City." In *Jewish-American History and Culture: An Encyclopedia*; edited by Jack Fischel and Sanford Pinsker, 464. New York and London: Garland, 1992.

———. *To the Golden Cities: Pursuing the American Jewish Dream in Miami and L. A.* New York: Free Press, 1994.

———. "I'll Take Manhattan," *Judaism* 44, no. 4 (1995): 420–26.

Morris, Charles R. *The Cost of Good Intentions: New York City and the Liberal Experiment, 1960–1975*. New York: Norton, 1980.

Morris, Willie. *New York Days*. Boston and New York: Little, Brown, 1993.

Mumford, Lewis. *The Culture of Cities*. New York: Harcourt, Brace, 1938.

Murphy, Marjorie. *Blackboard Unions: The AFT and the NEA, 1900–1980*. Ithaca and London: Cornell Univ. Press, 1990.

Nadler, Allan L. *The Faith of the Mithnagdim*. Baltimore: Johns Hopkins Univ. Press, 1997.

Niger (Charney), Shmuel. *Fun mayn togbukh*. New York: Congress for Jewish Culture, 1973.

Norich, Anita. *The Homeless Imagination in the Fiction of Israel Joshua Singer*. Bloomington and Indianapolis: Indiana Univ. Press, 1991.

———. "Isaac Bashevis Singer in America: The Translation Problem." *Judaism* 44, no. 2 (1995): 208–18.

Orbach, William. *The American Movement to Aid Soviet Jews.* Amherst: Univ. of Massachusetts Press, 1979.

Ozick, Cynthia. "Envy; or Yiddish in America, A Novella." *Commentary* 48, no. 5 (1969): 33–53.

———. "America: Toward Yavneh." *Judaism* 19, no. 3 (1970): 264–82.

———. *Art and Ardor.* New York: E. P. Dutton, 1983.

Park, Robert E. "Human Migration and the Marginal Man." *American Journal of Sociology* 33 (1928). Reprint. In *Classic Essays on the Culture of Cities,* edited by Richard Sennett, 131–42. Englewood Cliffs: Prentice-Hall, 1969.

Parker, Sandra. "An Educational Assessment of Yiddish Secular School Movements in the United States." In *Never Say Die: A Thousand Years of Yiddish in Jewish Life and Letters,* edited by Joshua A. Fishman. The Hague: Mouton, 1981.

Piven, Frances Fox, and Richard A. Cloward. *Poor People's Movements: Why They Succeed, How They Fail.* New York: Pantheon-Random House, 1977.

Podhoretz, Norman. "Jewishness and the Younger Intellectuals." *Commentary* 31, no. 4 (1961): 307.

———. "Hannah Arendt on Eichmann." *Commentary* 36, no. 3 (1963): 201–8.

———. *Making It.* New York: Random House, 1967.

———. *Breaking Ranks.* London: Weidenfeld and Nicolson, 1980.

Poll, Solomon. "The Role of Yiddish in American Ultra-Orthodox and Hassidic Communities." *YIVO Annual of Jewish Social Science* 13 (1955): 125–52.

Postal, Bernard, and Lionel Koppman. *Jewish Landmarks of New York: An Informal History and Guide.* New York: Hill and Wang, 1964.

Preil, Gabriel. *Sunset Possibilities and Other Poems.* Translated by Robert Friend. Philadelphia: Jewish Publication Society, 1985.

Raab, Earl. "The Black Revolution and the Jewish Question." *Commentary* 47, no. 1 (1969): 29.

Ravitch, Diane. *The Great School Wars: New York City, 1805–1973.* New York: Basic Books, 1974.

Rees, P. H. "Residential Patterns in American Cities, 1960." Research Paper no. 189, Univ. of Chicago, Department of Geography, 1979.

Reisin, Avrom. *Di lider fun Avrom Reisin in tsvelf teyln (1891–1951).* New York: Shulsinger, 1951.

Ribalow, Menahem, ed. *Antologiah shel hashirah ha'ivrit beamerikah.* New York: Ha-'Ogen Press, 1938.

Riesman, David. *The Lonely Crowd: A Study of the Changing American Character.* New Haven: Yale Univ. Press, 1950.

Rischin, Moses. "The Jews and the Liberal Tradition in America." *American Jewish Historical Quarterly* 51 (1961): 4–16.

———. *The Promised City, New York's Jews, 1870–1914.* 1962. Reprint. New York: Schocken, 1970.

Ritterband, Paul. "Why Did the Brooklyn Jewish Community Survive? The Response of a Cliometrician." Paper presented at The Hebrew University of Jerusalem, November 1998.

Rose, Peter I., ed. *The Ghetto and Beyond: Essays on Jewish Life in America.* New York: Random House, 1969.

Rosen, Norma. *Green, a Novella and Eight Stories.* New York, Harcourt Brace and World, 1959.

Rosenberg, Bernard, and Ernest Goldstein. *Creators and Disturbers: Reminiscences by Jewish Intellectuals of New York.* New York: Columbia Univ. Press, 1982.

Rosenwaike, Ira. *Population History of New York City.* Syracuse: Syracuse Univ. Press, 1972.

Roskies, David G. *A Bridge of Longing: The Lost Art of Yiddish Storytelling.* Cambridge and London: Harvard Univ. Press, 1995

———. "Rabbis, Rebbes and Other Humanists: The Search for a Usable Past in Modern Yiddish Literature." *Studies in Contemporary Jewry.* Vol. 12, *Literary Strategies: Jewish Texts and Contexts,* edited by Ezra Mendelsohn, 55–77. New York and Oxford: Oxford Univ. Press, 1996.

Rothman, Stanley, and S. Robert Lichter. *Roots of Radicalism: Jews, Christians, and the New Left.* New York and Oxford: Oxford Univ. Press, 1982.

Salisbury, W. Seward. *Religion and the College Student.* Albany: State Univ. of New York, Research Foundation, 1957.

Sanders, Marion K. "The Several Worlds of American Jews: An Unauthorized Guide." *Harper's,* Apr. 1966, 53–54.

Sarna, Jonathan D., and David G. Dalin, eds. *Religion and State in the American Jewish Experience.* Notre Dame: Notre Dame Univ. Press, 1997.

Sayre, Nora. *Sixties Going on Seventies.* New York: Arbor House, 1970.

Schlesinger, Arthur M., Jr. "America, 1968: The Politics of Violence." *Harper's,* Aug. 1968. 19–24.

Schoenberg, Sandra Perlman, and Patricia L. Rosenbaum. *Neighborhoods That Work: Sources for Viability in the Inner City.* New Brunswick: Rutgers Univ. Press, 1980.

Schoener, Allon, ed. *The Lower East Side: Portal to American Life (1870–1924).* New York: The Jewish Museum, 1966.

Scholem, Gershom. "Jews and Germans." Reprinted in *On Jews and Judaism in Crisis: Selected Essays.* New York: Schocken, 1976.

Schorsch, Ismar. *From Text to Context: The Turn to History in Modern Judaism.* Hanover and London: Brandeis Univ./Univ. Press of New England, 1994.

Schwartz, Joel. *The New York Approach: Robert Moses, Urban Liberals and Redevelopment of the Inner City.* Columbus: Ohio State Univ. Press, 1993.

Seligman, Ben. "The Population of New York City: 1952." In *The Jews: Social Patterns of an American Group,* edited by Marshall Sklare. New York: Free Press, 1958.

———. "Some Aspects of Jewish Demography." In *The Jews: Social Patterns of an American Group,* edited by Marshall Sklare. New York: Free Press, 1958.

Sennett, Richard, ed. *Classic Essays on the Culture of Cities.* Englewood Cliffs: Prentice Hall, 1969.

Shefter, Martin, *Political Crisis, Fiscal Crisis: The Collapse and Revival of New York City.* New York: Basic Books, 1985; New York: Columbia Univ. Press, 1992.

Shefter, Martin, ed. *Capital of the American Century: The National and International Influence of New York*. New York: Russell Sage Foundation, 1993.

Shils, Edward. *The Virtue of Civility: Selected Essays on Liberalism, Tradition, and Civil Society*. Edited by Steven Grosby. Indianapolis: Liberty Fund, 1997.

Silberman, Curt C. "The American Jewish Community in Need of a Program." In *Conference on Intellectual Priorities in American Jewry*. New York: American Federation of Jews from Central Europe, 1972.

Silberschlag, Eisig. "The Jewishness of Jewish Writers." *Hadassah Magazine*, Mar. 1963, 3.

Simon, Kate. *New York Places and Pleasures: An Uncommon Guide Book*. New York: Meridian Books, 1959.

Singer, Isaac Bashevis. "What's in It for Me?" *Harper's*, Special Supplement ("The Writer's Life"), Oct. 1965, 172–73.

———. *In My Father's Court*. Philadelphia: Jewish Publication Society, 1966.

———. "The Extreme Jews," *Harper's*, Apr. 1967, 56–62.

———. *Meshuga*. New York: Farrar, Straus, Giroux, 1994.

Skirball, Henry Franc. "Isaac Baer Berkson and Jewish Education." Ph.D. diss., New York, Columbia Teachers College, 1977.

Sklare, Marshall. "Jews, Ethnics, and the American City." *Commentary* 56, no. 3 (1972): 70–77. Reprint. In *Observing America's Jews*, by Marshall Sklare, 131–37. Hanover and London: Brandeis Univ./Univ. Press of New England, 1993.

———, ed. *The Jews: Social Patterns of an American Group*. New York: Free Press, 1958.

Sklare, Marshall, and Joseph Greenblum. *Jewish Identity on the Suburban Frontier*. New York: Basic Books, 1967.

Sleeper, Jim. *The Closest of Strangers*. New York: W. W. Norton, 1990.

———, ed. *In Search of New York*. New Brunswick and Oxford: Transaction Books, 1989.

Soloveitchik, Haym. "Rupture and Reconstruction: The Transformation of Contemporary Orthodoxy." *Tradition* 28, no. 4 (1994): 64–130.

Soloveitchik, Joseph B. *Halakhic Man*. Translated by Lawrence Kaplan. Philadelphia: Jewish Publication Society, 1983.

Sorauf, Frank J. *The Wall of Separation: The Constitutional Politics of Church and State*. Princeton: Princeton Univ. Press, 1976.

Spinrad, William. "Explaining American-Jewish Liberalism: Another Attempt." *Contemporary Jewry* 11, no. 1 (1990): 107–19.

Stampfer, Shaul. *Hayeshivah halita'it behithavutah*. Jerusalem: Merkaz Shazar, 1995.

Steinbaum, I. "A Study of the Jewishness of Twenty New York Families." *YIVO Annual of Jewish Social Science* 5 (1950): 232–55.

Stevenson, William. *Strike Zion!* With a special section by Leon Uris. New York: Bantam Books, 1967.

Strauss, Herbert A. "The Immigration and Acculturation of the German Jew in the United States of America." *Leo Baeck Institute Year Book* 16 (1971): 63–94.

Svonkin, Stuart. *Jews Against Prejudice.* New York: Columbia Univ. Press, 1997.

Taylor, William R. *In Pursuit of Gotham: Culture and Commerce in New York.* New York and Oxford: Oxford Univ. Press, 1992.

Teller, Judd L. *Strangers and Natives. The Evolution of the American Jew from 1921 to the Present.* New York: Delacorte Press, 1968.

Thomas, William Isaac. *Old World Traits Transplanted.* 1921. Reprint, Montclair: Patterson Smith, 1971.

Trachtenberg, Alan. *Brooklyn Bridge: Fact and Symbol.* New York and Oxford: Oxford Univ. Press, 1965.

Trilling, Diana. *The Beginning of the Journey.* New York: Harcourt, Brace, 1993.

"Under Forty: A Symposium on American Literature and the Younger Generation of American Jews." *Contemporary Jewish Record* 7, no. 1 (1944): 10–17, 33–34.

Urofsky, Melvin. *We Are One: American Jewry and Israel.* Garden City: Anchor/Doubleday, 1978.

Vernon, Raymond. *Metropolis 1985.* Cambridge: Harvard Univ. Press, 1960.

Wakefield, Dan. *New York in the Fifties.* Boston and New York: Houghton Mifflin, 1992.

Wald, Alan M. *The New York Intellectuals: The Rise and Decline of the Anti-Stalinist Left from the 1930s to the 1980s.* Chapel Hill and London: Univ. of North Carolina Press, 1987.

Waldinger, Roger. "When the Melting Pot Boils Over: The Irish, Jews, Blacks, and Koreans of New York." In *The Bubbling Cauldron: Race, Ethnicity, and the Urban Crisis,* edited by Michael Peter Smith and Joe R. Feagin, 265–81. Minneapolis: Univ. of Minnesota Press, 1995.

Wallock, Leonard, ed. *New York, Culture Capital of the World 1940–1965.* New York: Rizzoli, 1988.

Walzer, Michael. "Liberalism and the Jews: Historical Affinities, Contemporary Necessities." *Studies in Contemporary Jewry.* Vol. 11, *Values, Interests and Identity: Jews and Politics in a Changing World,* edited by Peter Y. Medding, 3–10. New York and Oxford: Oxford Univ. Press, 1995.

Warshow, Robert. "Poet of the Jewish Middle Class." *Commentary* 1, no. 7 (1946): 17–18.

———. *The Immediate Experience.* New York: Atheneum, 1975.

Weinreich, Uriel, ed. *The Field of Yiddish.* New York: The Linguistic Circle of New York, Columbia Univ., 1954.

Welles, Sam. "The Jewish *Elan,*" *Fortune Magazine,* Feb. 1960: 134–39, 160, 164, 166.

Wenger, Beth S. *New York Jews and the Great Depression.* New Haven and London: Yale Univ. Press, 1996.

Wertheimer, Jack. *Unwelcome Strangers.* New York: Oxford Univ. Press, 1987.

———. *A People Divided.* New York: Basic Books, 1993.

Whitfield, Stephen J. *Into the Dark: Hannah Arendt and Totalitarianism.* Philadelphia: Temple Univ. Press, 1980.

———. *Voices of Jacob, Hands of Esau: Jews in American Life and Thought.* Hamden: Archon Books, 1984.

———. "The Paradoxes of Jewish Culture." *David W. Belin Lecture in American Jewish Affairs* 2. Ann Arbor: Center for Judaic Studies, University of Michigan, 1993.

———. *In Search of American Jewish Culture.* Hanover and London: Brandeis Univ. Press/Univ. Press of New England, 1999.

———. *Why the Swastika? A Study of Young American Vandals.* New York: Institute of Human Relations Press (American Jewish Committee), 1962.

Wiesel, Elie. *Night. (La Nuit,* 1958). Translated by Stella Rodway. New York: Avon Books, 1970, by arrangement with Hill and Wang.

———. *The Jews of Silence.* New York: Holt, Rinehart and Winston, 1966.

———. *Legends of Our Time.* 1968. Reprint, New York: Avon Books, 1970.

———. *All Rivers Run to the Sea.* New York: Alfred A. Knopf, 1995.

Wieseltier, Leon. "The Prince of Bummers." *New Yorker,* 26 July 1993, 40–45.

Wilkins, Roger. *A Man's Life.* New York: Simon and Schuster, 1982.

Williams, William R. *Neighborhood Organizations: Seeds of a New Urban Life.* Westport, Conn.: Greenwood Press, 1985.

Wirth, Louis. *The Ghetto.* Chicago: Univ. of Chicago Press, 1928.

Wisse, Ruth R. "Language as Fate: Reflections on Jewish Literature in America." *Studies in Contemporary Jewry,* Vol. 12, *Literary Strategies: Jewish Texts and Contexts,* edited by Ezra Mendelsohn, 129–47. New York and Oxford: Oxford Univ. Press, 1996.

Wood, Michael. "What Did You Want from the Jews?" *New Society,* 12 May 1966, 9.

Yates, Douglas. *The Ungovernable City.* Cambridge, Mass.: M.I.T. Press, 1977.

Young-Bruehl, Elisabeth. *Hannah Arendt: For Love of the World.* New Haven and London: Yale Univ. Press, 1982.

Zborowski Mark, and Elizabeth Herzog. *Life Is with People: The Culture of the Shtetl.* Foreword by Margaret Mead. 1952. Reprint, New York: Schocken, 1967.

Zipperstein, Steven J. *Imagining Russian Jewry—Memory, History, Identity.* Seattle and London: Univ. of Washington Press, 1999.

Index

Page numbers in italics denote illustrations.